D1408613

COMPLETE SCHOOL COMMUNICATIONS MANUAL

With Sample Letters, Forms Bulletins, Policies, and Memos

Also by the Mamchaks:

Educator's Lifetime Library of Stories, Quotes, Anecdotes, Wit and Humor

Encyclopedia of School Letters

The New Psychology of Classroom Discipline and Control

101 Pupil/Parent/Teacher Situations and How to Handle Them

School Administrator's Encyclopedia

School Administrator's Public Speaking Portfolio: With Model Speeches and Anecdotes

COMPLETE SCHOOL COMMUNICATIONS MANUAL
With Sample Letters, Forms Bulletins, Policies, and Memos

P. Susan Mamchak
Steven R. Mamchak

Prentice-Hall, Inc.
Englewood Cliffs, NJ

Prentice-Hall International, Inc., *London*
Prentice-Hall of Australia, Pty. Ltd., *Sydney*
Prentice-Hall Canada Inc., *Toronto*
Prentice-Hall of India Private Ltd., *New Delhi*
Prentice-Hall of Japan, Inc., *Tokyo*
Prentice-Hall of Southeast Asia Pte. Ltd., *Singapore*
Whitehall Books, Ltd., *Wellington, New Zealand*
Editora Prentice-Hall do Brasil, Ltda., *Rio de Janeiro*

Library of Congress Cataloging in Publication Data

Mamchak, P. Susan.
Complete school communications manual.

1. School management and organization—United States—Handbooks, manuals, etc. I. Mamchak, Steven R. II. Title.
LB2801.A2M34 1984 371.2'00973 83-21298
ISBN 0-13-162850-X

Printed in the United States of America

How the School Administrator Can Use This Book

Let's start with a basic fact of which we are all aware: the school administrator's foremost duty is to be an educational leader. School administrators are in the forefront of education. They are there to function as inspiration, guides, trend-setters, if you will. They help shape the curriculum, provide a safe environment conducive to learning, and ensure the quality of education for the youth of our nation. They forge the pathways that education will take in our viable and ever-changing society. We know this, because we live it each and every day of our professional lives.

It is, however, a duty that can be overwhelming, and which may not be taken lightly.

And, if we have an antagonist in this process, an ever-present entity which keeps us from our goals, that enemy is time.

There are just so many demands upon us. As administrators, we face a daily barrage of meetings, phone calls, conferences, and, most intimidating of all, paperwork. Indeed, the paperwork we face each day can leave little time for other, more productive activities. There are reports to file, letters to write, memos to dictate, budgets to prepare, and a host of other communications to be developed and composed, all of which usurp our precious time.

We all become very quickly aware that if we do not find a way to efficiently manage our paperwork, our paperwork will very quickly end up managing us.

Nor is this an isolated instance. School administrators throughout the nation have felt this need to "tame the paper tiger" who nibbles away at their time and energies. Yes, we are all a part of the problem, and, thankfully, we are all a part of the solution as well.

Across the nation, innovative school administrators, meeting a pressing need, have worked hard to come up with forms, memos, bulletins, letters, and other written materials that address needs common to all administrators in all schools and school systems; materials that bespeak education now, today; materials on a plethora of educational topics that lie at the heart of the modern school system and are so intrinsically a part of today's administrative duties.

Thankfully, these dedicated administrators are willing to share these materials with others in their profession. From the Eastern seaboard to Hawaii, from the Texas border to Alaska, they have been most generous in sending us those written forms, memos, letters, and bulletins that have served so well in solving their administrative problems and which will help all of us in the performance of our written work as well.

Because we all share common problems in public education, the materials in this book wait to serve our needs. With the change of a name or date, they can be adapted to meet our direct needs. Or, they can be used exactly as they are to help facilitate budget preparation, disciplinary procedures, classroom observations, and a host of other school-related activities, ones that can be made easier for us through the sharing of knowledge. This is, after all, the most outstanding hallmark of our profession.

Within the pages of this book, you will find highly effective letters, memos, bulletins, and forms for handling such topics as ABSENTEEISM, BIDS, BUDGETS, CUSTODIAL SERVICES, DISMISSAL PROCEDURES, LEAVE OF ABSENCE, and much, much more.

Here is material that strikes at the very heart of our day-to-day functioning as administrators. Here are topics such as ACADEMIC FREEDOM, DISCRIMINATION, EVALUATION, FAILURE, LEASE OF SCHOOL PROPERTY, MEDICAL FORMS, PROFESSIONAL IMPROVEMENT, REDUCTION IN FORCE, TRUANCY, and UNDERACHIEVEMENT.

This is also material that allows for the effective and quick handling of our troubling situations, such as ACCIDENTS, BEHAVIOR, CHILD ABUSE, DETENTION, DRINKING OF ALCOHOLIC BEVERAGES, DUE PROCESS, EXPULSION, FIGHTING, NON-RENEWAL OF CONTRACTS, RETENTION, SUSPENSION, USE OF FACILITIES, and ZONING.

Given the encompassing nature of the materials gathered from front-line administrators across the country, and the ease of access provided by the encyclopedic nature of this volume, we cannot help but feel this is a book that will serve the needs of the busy and involved administrator by providing practical and useable models of written materials which may be easily adapted to fill pressing, individual needs.

We think you will agree that *Complete School Communications Manual* is a book you will want to use in order to save time, to make the day-to-day operation of the school easier and more efficient, and to manage that load of paperwork—which will, in turn, leave you free to be the educational leader our profession needs. We hope it will find a favored place on your desk, ready for your use now and throughout the school year.

P. Susan Mamchak

Steven R. Mamchak

Acknowledgments

Throughout the writing of this book, it has been our privilege to come into contact with educators of the highest personal and professional caliber. If American education is alive and well and flourishing, it is due, in large part, to the efforts of fine people such as these. We humbly and gratefully acknowledge the contributions of the following administrators and school systems throughout the United States who have so unselfishly contributed materials, edited, or reviewed the contents of this book.

Harmon Baldwin, Vigo County Public Schools, Terre Haute, Indiana

Donovan Benzie and Gordon Paulsen, Dickinson Public Schools, Dickinson, North Dakota

George Dalgleish and Gordon Paulsen, School District #51, Grand Junction, Colorado

Harry Dickson, Carson City High School District, Carson City, Nevada

Teri L. MacGill, Anchorage School District, Anchorage, Alaska

Ronald McLeod and Ross Snyder, El Paso Public Schools, El Paso, Texas

William Milligan, School District #1, Butte, Montana

Kiyoto Mizuba, Hawaii School District, Hilo, Hawaii

Edward Mundy, Minot Public School System, Minot, North Dakota

Jack Sasser, Dothan City Schools, Dothan, Alabama

Bernhard W. Schneider, Middletown Township Public Schools, Middletown, New Jersey

CONTENTS

I

J

K

L

O

P

Q

V

W

X

Y

Z

COMPLETE SCHOOL COMMUNICATIONS MANUAL

With Sample Letters, Forms Bulletins, Policies, and Memos

ABILITY

memo on...

TO: Faculty

FROM: J. Benson, Principal

Welcome back! Here we are, facing another school year. If we can be certain of anything in this changeable world, it is that we will be facing many challenges during this coming year as we have faced them in the past. And, as in the past, I have no doubts about your ability to meet and conquer each and every challenge.

Over the years, I have seen you deal with challenges and obstacles with intelligence, tact, efficiency, and a deep concern for the good of our students. With abilities such as these, there is literally nothing we cannot handle.

Have a very good year!

message in student handbook...

As a student in Rock Township High School, all anyone will ask of you is that you perform your role as a student to the best of your ability. In a school the size of ours, we are bound to have individuals of varying levels of ability and capabilities of performance, but if each and every person does his or her best to live up to the finest of which he or she is capable—to utilize his or her abilities to the utmost—then we shall have a very fine year indeed.

(See Also: ACHIEVEMENT; AIDES; APPRECIATION; AWARDS; EVALUATION; FAILURE; HONOR ROLE; NATIONAL HONOR SOCIETY; PROGRESS REPORT; QUALIFICATIONS; RECOMMENDATION; UNDERACHIEVERS)

ABSENCE

employee absence record . . .

NAME ______________________________ SCHOOL ______________
last first middle

DATE OF HIRE ______________ SICK DAYS DUE ______________ VACATION TIME DUE ______________

19 ______

EMPLOYEE ABSENCE RECORD

																																ABSENCE SUMMARY											
	1	2	3	4	5	6	7	8	9	10	11	12	13	14	15	16	17	18	19	20	21	22	23	24	25	26	27	28	29	30	31	DA	DD	DF	J	SF	SS	V	TE	TS	TV	BS	BV
JAN																																											
FEB																																											
MAR																																											
APR																																											
MAY																																											
JUN																																											
JUL																																											
AUG																																											
SEP																																											
OCT																																											
NOV																																											
DEC																																											

DA – Doctor Appt.
DD – Days Deduct
DF – Death in Family
J – Jury

SF – Sickness in Family
SS – Sickness Self
V – Vacation (personal leave)
TE – Total Emergency

TS – Total Sickness
TV – Total Vacation (personal leave)
BS – Balance Sickness
BV – Balance Vacation (personal leave)

YEARLY TOTALS

of non-certified personnel...

Name of employee: ______________________________

Reason for absence: ______________________________

____

Date of absence: ______________________, 19____

Sick leave allowance: __________ days Vacation days: __________

Total sick leave days used to date: ______________________ days

Total vacation days used to date: ______________________ days

---

Deduct from pay: ______________ days ______________ rate of pay

______________ hours ______________ rate of pay

Total amount to be deducted: ______________________________

Explanation: ______________________________

____

Signed: ______________________ Date: ____________, 19____

Approved: ______________________ Date: ____________, 19____

(Supervisor)

(Remit one copy of this form to the business office only if there is to be a deduction from this person's pay.)

of students...

A pupil is absent if he or she is not in attendance at school or is away from school on school business. His or her absence may be "excused," that is, he or she may be permitted to make up class assignments without penalty because of the absence. The pupil's absence is unexcused if he or she is truant, absent in spite of admonition to be present, or for other reasons not deemed by the principal to rate "excused."

Parents are asked to call the principal's office when a student is absent or late for school. Upon returning to school, the student must bring a note signed by his or her parents/ guardians to be admitted to class.

* * *

ABSENCE FROM SCHOOL is defined as non-attendance in regular classes and assigned locations for the entire school day. Absence from school is either acceptable or non-acceptable.

Acceptable Reasons for Absence from Classes and/or School Include:

a. school-sponsored educational opportunities or externally sponsored activities sanctioned or approved by the principal

b. suspension from school or assignment to Alternate School Program

c. other special reasons approved by the principal, such as medical appointments, family emergencies, court appearances, etc.

d. illness, supported by a written statement from the parent, adult pupil (except when adult pupil is financially dependent upon his or her parents), or physician

e. death in the immediate family

f. religious holiday as prescribed by the State Department of Education

g. early release—The Board recognizes that the following situations may occur which would require an early release from school:

   1. illness that manifested itself after having reported to school
   2. verified appointment with a physician/dentist
   3. driver's test or court appearance with verification of appointment

   NOTE: Any class absences resulting from early release will become part of the student's attendance record.

h. the administration reserves the right to determine other acceptable causes for absence, such as college visits with verification, military interviews with verification, Scout trips, swim meets. Unacceptable absence is defined as any reason not listed in this section. It includes truancy, cutting and tardiness, and such categories as shopping, vacations, working, oversleeping, faulty private transportation, hairdresser appointments, personal grooming preparations, etc.

of teachers...

1. Operational Procedure for Reporting Absence
   a. Short-term Sick Leave
      (1) Call the secretarial service at 555-9876 by midnight, or in cases of emergencies by 6:00 a.m. and give the following information in sequence:
         (a) This is (first name) (last name).
         (b) I teach (subject and department) at (school).
         (c) I will be absent on (day) (date).
         (d) My substitute should report to (school) by (time).
         (e) My parking stall number is (stall number).
      (2) Notify the school if absence goes beyond one day and for each additional consecutive day. Please call the school office before 2:00 p.m. the day before the absence.
      (3) Do not call the secretarial service operator other than to report the need for a substitute. All other communications should be directed to your personnel officer.
      (4) DO NOT CALL SUBSTITUTE TEACHERS DIRECTLY.
   b. Long-term Sick Leave
      1. Must be approved by administration through normal channels.
2. Lesson Plans and Keys
   a. The teacher should make arrangements to see that the plans and keys are left with the main office.

   SUGGESTION: It may be wise to plan specific supplementary units to be used in case of emergency. Your effort to avoid giving verbal plans to the office will be greatly appreciated.

staff absence report...

STAFF ABSENCE REPORT

For Period from ________ 19___ thru ________ 19___
(Month, Day) (Year) (Month, Day) (Year)

____
Name of School or Department

Due date–10th of each month

	Payroll Use Only		Month 19																						MONTH 19								
Soc. Sec. & Name	Sick	Vac	10	11	12	13	14	15	16	17	18	19	20	21	22	23	24	25	26	27	28	29	30	31	1	2	3	4	5	6	7	8	9
SS #																																	
SS #																																	
SS #																																	
SS #																																	
SS #																																	
SS #																																	
SS #																																	
SS #																																	
SS #																																	
SS #																																	
SS #																																	
SS #																																	
SS #																																	

(Please type social security numbers and names. Use every line.)

CODE

E Educational
P Personal Leave
S Sick Leave
F Family Illness
B Bereavement

X Deduction
J Jury Duty
C Community Service
EM Emergency Leave
U Officiating & Judging

PR Professional Leave
SB School Business
V Vacation
W Witness

Date ________ By ________

Routing: White – Personnel
Canary – School

. . . teacher absence record

TEACHER ABSENCE RECORD

School ______________ School Year. . . . . 19____19____

1. Accumulated sick leave . . . . ________Days

Employee ______________

2. Less absence due to illness or bereavement. ________Days
3. Accumulated sick leave . . . . ________Days

Absence Month Day	Days	Periods	Cause for Absence	Cum. Sick Leave	Name of Substitute

(See Also: ABSENTEEISM; ADDRESS; CLASS; CUTTING; LEAVE OF ABSENCE; RECORDS; TARDINESS and TRUANCY)

ABSENTEEISM

message on...

ABSENTEEISM may be defined as the continued absence or repeated absences, over a period of time, by an individual or group of individuals.

It is important to note that we do not speak here of continued absence due to acceptable reasons or caused by the necessity of extended medical leave. Rather, we speak of continued absences for non-verifiable reasons. It should be understood that a student continually absent without cause can be held accountable by the administration and may face disciplinary action, either within the school or even from juvenile authorities. Continued absenteeism on the part of a staff member can constitute grounds for punitive action, possibly including dismissal.

We recognize that a high degree of absenteeism on the part of an individual or group is generally reflective of a problem or difficulty which inspires the action. In light of this, the administration stands ready to aid in whatever way possible toward the remediation of the group's or individual's difficulty, but it should be understood that the administration will, at no time, allow for the disruption of a beneficial school routine.

(See Also: ABSENCE; CUTTING; TARDINESS and TRUANCY)

ACADEMIC FREEDOM

controversial issues...

All teachers are required to follow Board policy when teaching controversial issues. This code, which does not infringe upon academic freedom, is available in every school office and library.

In addition, be sure that:

1. All issues are worked through the particular department that normally handles such subject areas.
2. Ample time be given to planning and these plans be submitted to the administration.

In short, the main objective should be to help students critically examine the facts under such conditions that will help them reach a rational decision.

Working it within the departments will also help ensure a constructive follow-through of the issue at hand. Teachers planning controversial curriculum should alert department heads and have plans available for review by the administration.

statement on...

ACADEMIC FREEDOM is a philosophy that teachers have the right to teach and students have the right to learn without being impeded or experiencing restriction or censorship of what is being taught. Both teachers and students have the right to exercise free thought without arbitrary restraint.

(See Also: **AMERICAN EDUCATION WEEK; CONTROVERSIAL TOPICS; DEMONSTRATIONS; EDUCATION; PHILOSOPHY)**

ACCEPTANCE

acceptance receipt...

Date: ____________

I have read the material in the Rock Township High School Handbook and understand that I will be expected to abide by its contents.

Signature of Student: ______________________________

Signature of Parent/Guardian: ______________________________

Please detach this form and return it to your child's teacher.

of a donation...

Dear Mr. Adams,

It gives me great pleasure to acknowledge your gift of a new set of the *Encyclopedia Brittanica* for use in our school library. It is in use at this very moment and will continue to serve our students for many years to come.

It is within our power to do little more than thank you for your generosity as we accept your donation. However, the knowledge that our students will gain through the continued use of your gift will stand as a constant tribute to your attention to our needs.

On behalf of the students and staff of Rock Township High School, I gratefully accept your donation and thank you again for your care and concern.

Sincerely,

of volunteer services...

Dear Mrs. Scott,

I am in possession of your letter in which you indicate a willingness to volunteer your time to help in the functioning of our school. I want to thank you for that kind offer and tell you that I gratefully accept your offer.

When the home and the school work together, every child benefits. Your presence in our school and the help you will provide will, in a very real way, help us to provide our students with the best education we can.

I admire your selflessness and accept your services as a valuable contribution to our school. Please contact me as soon as possible and we will arrange a schedule for you.

Yours sincerely,

(See Also: **ADVISORS AND ADVISORY COMMITTEES; APPLICATION; APPRECIATION; AWARDS; BIDS; DISTRIBUTION OF MATERIALS; EVALUATION; HONOR ROLL; NATIONAL HONOR SOCIETY)**

ACCIDENTS

accident/incident report form...

INJURED PERSON	Name of Injured Person: ______ Address: ______ Telephone–Home: ______ Work: ______ Nature of Injury: ______ Location of Incident: ______ Date: ______ Time: ______ ______ ______
PROPERTY DAMAGE	Owner of Property: ______ If Auto, Driver's License Number: ______ Address: ______ Telephone–Home: ______ Work: ______ Describe Property–If Auto, Make ______ Model ______ Year ______ Plate Number ______ ______ Describe Damage: ______ ______ If Auto, Owner's Insurance Company ______ Location of Incident: ______ Date: ______ Time: ______ ______ ______
WITNESS	Witness to Incident: ______ Address: ______ Telephone–Home: ______ Work: ______ ______ ______
	Person Reporting Incident: ______ Date: ______ Time: ______ School/Department: ______

automobile/equipment accident report . . .

TIME & PLACE OF ACCIDENT	DATE OF ACCIDENT	LOCATION: STREET OR HIGHWAY		
	TIME OF ACCIDENT HOUR: A.M. P.M.			
ABOUT SCHOOL DISTRICT AUTO	NAME OF DRIVER	DEPARTMENT & DIVISION	VEHICLE NO.	
	DRIVER'S AGE	DRIVER'S LICENSE NO.	DATE LICENSE EXPIRES	
	IS THIS A TAKE HOME VEHICLE?	YOUR DUTY HOURS		
	ARE YOU AUTHORIZED 24 HOUR USE?	BY WHOM?		
	DESCRIBE DAMAGE TO SCHOOL DISTRICT VEHICLE:			
OTHER AUTO INVOLVED	MAKE OF AUTO	YEAR	LICENSE NO.	ESTIMATED COST DAMAGE
	PARTS DAMAGED AND EXTENT OF DAMAGE			
	NAME OF DRIVER	ADDRESS	PHONE NO.	
	NAME OF OWNER	ADDRESS	PHONE NO.	
	IS AUTO INSURED?	NAME OF INSURANCE COMPANY		
PASSENGERS	NAMES OF PASSENGERS IN YOUR AUTO	ADDRESSES		
	NAMES OF PASSENGERS IN OTHER AUTO	ADDRESSES		
INJURIES (NO MATTER HOW MINOR)	NAMES OF PERSONS INJURED	ADDRESSES INJURIES AGE		
	IN WHICH AUTO WERE INJURED RIDING:			
	NAME OF DOCTOR OR HOSPITAL	ADDRESS		
PROPERTY DAMAGE OTHER THAN AUTO	NAME OF OWNER	ADDRESS		
	KIND OF PROPERTY			
	ESTIMATED COST OF REPAIR	WHERE MAY PROPERTY BE SEEN?		
WITNESSES	NAMES	ADDRESS: STREET CITY STATE ZIP CODE	PHONE NO.	

(Form continued)

automobile/equipment accident report (cont'd)

DESCRIPTION OF ACCIDENT

ON WHAT STREET OR ROAD WERE YOU DRIVING?	DIRECTION	SPEED	STREET OR ROAD OTHER AUTO WAS DRIVING ON?	DIRECTION	SPEED

WERE YOUR LIGHTS ON? ☐ Yes ☐ No ☐ Bright ☐ Dim	WERE OTHER AUTO'S LIGHTS ON? ☐ Yes ☐ No ☐ Bright ☐ Dim	WHAT TRAFFIC CONTROLS?	FOR WHOM?	SPEED LIMIT

DID EITHER DRIVER GIVE SIGNAL OF ANY KIND? ☐ Yes ☐ No If, Yes, who?	IF INTERSECTION, WHO ENTERED FIRST?	WHO HAD RIGHT OF WAY?

DID POLICE INVESTIGATE ACCIDENT? ☐ Yes ☐ No	LOCAL OR STATE	WHICH DRIVER CITED?

DESCRIBE IN YOUR OWN WORDS HOW ACCIDENT HAPPENED

SHOW ON THE DIAGRAM THE POSITIONS OF ALL AUTOS, PERSONS, STOP LIGHTS, STOP SIGNS, AND OTHER OBJECTS. SHOW STREET NAMES

MY AUTO
OTHER AUTO
THIRD AUTO
PEDESTRIAN
STOP SIGN
YIELD SIGN
STOP LIGHT

DATE OF REPORT	SIGNATURE

***NOTE* TO BE COMPLETED BY VEHICLE MAINTENANCE**

MAKE OF AUTO	YEAR	LICENSE NO.	WHERE MAY VEHICLE BE SEEN?

DESCRIBE PARTS DAMAGED AND EXTENT OF DAMAGE

VEH. MAINT. SIGNATURE

DISTRIBUTION LEGEND

White	Insurance/Safety
Yellow	Insurance/Safety
Pink	Vehicle Maintenance
Goldenrod	Employee Dept/Div

INSTRUCTIONS

1. To be completed by Vehicle Maintenance.
2. Vehicle Maintenance forward first 2 copies to Insurance Dept.

(Form continued)

student accident report...

Send To: Insurance/Safety Office-Administration

1. Name		2. Address	
3. School 4. Sex Male ☐ Female ☐ Coding Info Not Provided ☐		5. Age	6. Grade/Special Program
7. Date of Accident	8. Time		
9. Location of Accident (be specific)		10. Activity of person (be specific)	

CATEGORY "C"–NATURE OF INJURY: 11. ☐

1. WOUND
2. SPRAIN/ STRAIN
3. CONCUSSION
4. EYES
5. FRACTURE
6. AMPUTATION
7. BURNS
8. IRRITATION
9. ASPHYXIATION
10. ABRASION
11. NO APPARENT INJURY
12. BUMP/BRUISE
13. DAMAGED TEETH
99. CODING INFO NOT PROVIDED

CATEGORY "E"–ACCIDENT JURISDICTION: 13. ☐

1. SCHOOL GROUNDS
2. SCHOOL BUILDING
3. TO AND FROM SCHOOL
4. OTHER ACTIVITIES NOT ON SCHOOL PROPERTY
5. HOME (NON-SCHOOL)
6. OTHER (NON-SCHOOL)
99. CODING INFO NOT PROVIDED

CATEGORY "D"–TYPE OF ACCIDENT: 12. ☐

1. SLIP/FALL
2. PLAYGROUND EQUIPMENT
3. GYM EQUIPMENT
4. LABORATORY/ SHOP EQUIPMENT
5. HORSEPLAY
6. SWIMMING POOL
7. P.E. ACTIVITY
8. INTER-SCHOLASTIC SPORTS
9. INTRAMURAL COMPETITION
10. RECESS
11. FIGHTING
12. BITE
13. SLEDDING/ SLIDING
14. SKATING
15. FROSTBITE/ FREEZING
99. CODING INFO NOT PROVIDED

CATEGORY "F"–BODY AREA AFFECTED: 14. ☐

1. HEAD
2. EARS
3. EYE
4. NOSE
5. MOUTH
6. ARM
7. HANDS
8. FINGERS
9. SHOULDER
10. CHEST
11. LEG
12. FOOT
13. TOES
14. BACK
15. INTERNAL INJURIES
16. UPPER BODY–MULTIPLE INJURIES
17. LOWER BODY–MULTIPLE INJURIES
18. HEAD–MULTIPLE INJURIES
19. ABDOMINAL
99. CODING INFO NOT PROVIDED

DESCRIBE ACCIDENT, INCLUDE MACHINE, OBJECT, OR SUBSTANCE INVOLVED. GIVE FULL DETAILS AND EXTENT OF INJURY IF ANY. 15.	
16. Unsafe Mechanical/Physical Condition or Act	17. Supervision (if yes, give title & name of supervisor) Yes ☐ No ☐
18. Corrective Action Taken or Recommended	
19. Date of Report	20. Report Prepared by (signature & title)
21. Principal's Signature	Distribution–Original and Copy to Insurance/Safety Office, Retain copy for file

(See Also: DOCTORS; EARTHQUAKE; EMERGENCY; FIGHTING; HEALTH; NURSE; SAFETY**)**

ACHIEVEMENT

letter on...

Dear Mr. & Mrs. Kalczak,

A principal writes many letters during a school year. Many of them are difficult and sad, informing parents of difficulties between their child and the school. That is why it is such a pleasure to be writing you to congratulate you on the achievements of your son, Bob.

When Bob graduates later this month, he will do so with the honor of carrying the highest academic average in his class. With a graduating class of almost 700 students, this is no small achievement but is reflective of the diligence, hard work, and application on the part of your son. He is to be congratulated for his efforts.

In a very real sense, however, his achievement also stands as a living tribute to you, his parents. It is obvious that a nurturing, supportive base for Bob's achievement had to be present, and for this alone you deserve our compliments.

I look forward to meeting you at the graduation.

Yours sincerely,

memo on...

TO: Faculty

FROM: John Benson, Principal

RE: Achievement on Standardized Tests

The results of those standardized tests our students took last month have finally come in. I'll be giving you exact figures at our faculty meeting later this week, but I will tell you that the scores reflect the highest student achievement record in the history of our school.

This comes, of course, as no surprise to me. I have, for the longest time, been aware of the achievements of our faculty, and I could not doubt that this quality and excellence would be reflected in the test score achievement of our students as well.

I will be congratulating our students at the next assembly, but, in the meantime, let me congratulate you on an achievement that is not scored but which carries with it the admiration and thanks of the entire administrative staff.

(See Also: ADULT EDUCATION; AMERICAN EDUCATION WEEK; AWARDS; NATIONAL HONOR SOCIETY; RECORDS; REPORT CARDS; WARNING NOTICES**)**

ADDRESS

change-of-address form...

Name: ____________________ Date: ________
Effective Date of Change of Address: ______________, 19 ______

Old Address:
Street: ____________________
Town and State: ____________________
Zip: __________ Telephone: __________

New Address:
Street: ____________________
Town and State: ____________________
Zip: __________ Telephone: __________

Additional Information (include mailing address IF different from above):

general address information card...

Name ____________________
Last First Initial

Address ____________________

____
City State Zip

Permanent Address ____________________

____
City State Zip

Phone ( ) __________ Alternate ( ) __________

summer address form...

SUMMER ADDRESS

Name ______________________________

Summer Address ______________________________

Summer Plans*______________________________

____

Mailing Address for June Checks ______________________________

____

(Teachers taking payments in 12 months will receive total amount due in June check.)

Mailing address for Teacher Contracts ______________________________

____

Teachers not returning next year please give permanent address for mailing of W2's, etc.

____

____

*If attending school, please give inclusive dates.

(See Also: ENROLLMENT; PERMANENT RECORDS; RECORDS; STUDENT RECORDS)

ADMINISTRATOR

administrative application form...

ADMINISTRATIVE APPLICATION

Date of Application ______________ Position Applied for ______________

PERSONAL INFORMATION

Name: ______________________________ ______________
(Last) (First) (Initial) (Social Security Number)

Name on transcripts and placement papers: ______________

Present address: ______________________________ ______________
(Street, City, State, Zip) (Area Code-Telephone)

Permanent address: ______________________________ ______________
(Street, City, State, Zip) (Area Code-Telephone)

Date available for employment: ______________

Condition of health: Do you have any condition that may limit your ability to perform the position applied for? Yes ( ) No ( )

Have you ever been convicted of a felony? Yes ( ) No ( )

POSITION PREFERENCE

Please indicate the level(s) you are certified to administer:

Senior ( ) *Junior High ( )* *Elementary ( )* *Central Admin. ( )*

Which level do you prefer?______________

Do you hold the State's Administrator's Certificate? Yes ( ) No ( )

What endorsement(s)? ______________

Do you hold a valid State Vocational or Special Education Administrator's Credential? Yes ( ) No ( )

In what area(s)?______________

Your Administrative Practicum was done/or will be done at what level?______________

REFERENCES:

Include any administrator under whom you have taught, or a college instructor if you have not yet graduated. Do *not* include relatives or persons who have furnished references for your placement office credentials. You may include persons not connected with education who are qualified to answer regarding your fitness for the position you seek.

Name	Occupation	Address	Phone Number

(Form continued)

administrative application form (cont'd)

ACADEMIC PREPARATION

College/University Attended *(Names and Locations)*	Dates Inclusive	Degree	Major	Semester Hours	Minor	Semester Hours

TEACHING EXPERIENCE:
List most recent experience first

Date From–To	Name and Location of School	Number of Years	Assignment	Name of Supervisor

ADMINISTRATIVE EXPERIENCE:
List most recent experience first

Date From–To	Name and location of school	Number of Years	Assignment	Name of Supervisor

OTHER WORK EXPERIENCE:
Including Military Service

Date From–To	Date From–To	Job Title	Duties and Assignments

(Form continued)

DIRECTIONS: Please answer each of the following questions as best you can. If more space is needed, please attach additional pages. *Please complete in your own handwriting*.

1. As an Education Administrator, what is your mission?

2. What are the three most important functions of an administrator?

3. How do you build rapport with teachers?

4. What is the key factor in good delegation?

5. What do you believe is the best way to get people in your building to work together?

6. How will you get teachers excited about trying new ideas?

7. How do you know what parents and patrons are thinking?

(Form continued)

administrative application form (cont'd)

8. How do you improve and maintain staff morale?

9. Upon what basis do you believe school priorities should be established?

10. Upon what basis do you assess the performance of a teacher?

11. When you have an important decision to make, how do you make it?

12. Why is organization important for an administrator?

An application is considered active when the Personnel Office has received (1) this employment application (completed and signed) along with the applicant information card, (2) placement office credentials (or letters of reference), and (3) all official transcripts.

A medical examination (at the applicant's expense) and a valid Teaching Certificate will be required when employed.

Applications are placed in the active file from January 1 to December 31 of each year. Each applicant must notify the Personnel Office *in writing* by December 31 if he or she wants to have the application remain active during the next calendar year.

An on-site interview (at the applicant's expense) is required before hiring, unless specifically waived by the District.

PLEASE READ CAREFULLY BEFORE SIGNING

I certify that the information given by me on this application and any supplement is true and correct to the best of my knowledge. I understand that false statements on this application may result in termination of employment.

Date

Signature of Applicant

(Form continued)

(See Also: Those topics throughout the book in which an administrator is involved, such as DISCIPLINE; BUDGET)

ADULT EDUCATION

general information sheet...

REGISTRATION: Register by one of the following ways:

- Fill out and mail registration blank. Please include check.
- Telephone the Adult Education Office (555-9876).
- Stop by in person at the office, 123 Hilltop Drive.

A minimum of 12 people must be registered in order to start each class. All registrants will be notified if the class is cancelled and an immediate refund made. The Adult Education Director reserves the right to cancel any class if enrollment is not sufficient to warrant its continuation.

ADMISSION: Courses will be open to all residents or non-residents, 16 years of age or over.

COURSE FEES: Course fees are listed at the end of each course description and are payable in advance or not later than the first night of class. Checks should be made payable to Rock Township Public Schools and addressed c/o Adult Education Classes, Board of Education, 123 Hilltop Drive.

REFUNDS: Money will be refunded ONLY if the class is cancelled by the Director or if notified of your wish to withdraw *prior* to the starting date of each class term. NO REFUNDS can be made after these dates as the classes are started on the basis of enrollment and accompanying fees.

POSTPONING OF CLASSES: Adult Education Classes follow the public school calendar in regard to vacations. In the case of very inclement weather, classes are occasionally cancelled. If in doubt, call the Adult Education Center at 555-9876 or listen for local radio station announcements.

BOOKS/SUPPLIES: Students will be expected to furnish paper, textbooks, and supplies where needed. Many of the textbooks are on loan to the student by the school district at no extra cost.

FACILITIES: Most classes are held in the local schools. Parking is available at ALL school sites. The code for the buildings is as follows:

RTHS—Rock Township High School

WJH —Wilson Junior High School

TJH —Thomas Junior High School

WE —Waverly Elementary School

ADDITIONAL INFORMATION: Call the Adult Education Office at 555-9876. Information on other adult programs, such as G.E.D., Basic Education, etc., can be obtained by contacting Mr. Patrick Dancey, Rock Township Public Schools.

sample of adult course listings...

18 AEROBIC DANCING (6 weeks) — This class combines dance movements with aerobic exercise. Aerobics is a system of exercises based on oxygen consumption and physical fitness. Various dance/exercise routines are learned and put to music.

Tues. & Thurs. 7-7:45 p.m.

RTHS: Girl's Gym

Fee: $15.00

36 PAINTING FOR PLEASURE — This course is offered by a prominent local artist and should be of great interest to many people. It's an introduction to painting where students concentrate on oil media. Instruction includes painting methods, composition, and color technique.

Thursdays 7-10:00 p.m.

WJH: Room 206

Fee: $22.00 + supplies

42 BOOKKEEPING I — The beginning cycle of bookkeeping and accounting, debits, credits, journalizing, posting, work sheets, and financial statements are introduced. A course for everyone in business, for office workers, or for records at home.

Tuesdays 7:30-10:00 p.m.

TJH: Room 110

Fee: $18.00 + workbook

ADVERTISING

memo to students on...

TO: All Students

FROM: J. Benson, Principal

RE: Posters

On my last trip down the halls of our school, it became apparent that posters are blossoming on every wall. While this is to be expected considering the number of extracurricular activities, perhaps it would be wise to remind everyone of our responsibilities concerning these types of advertisements.

1. All posters are to be checked by a faculty advisor prior to posting.
2. Posters are to be attached using masking tape only. Any other type of tape damages the wall surfaces.
3. Posters advertising an event are to be removed and disposed of properly within three days after the event. (After all, we have to make room for new posters!)
4. Anyone caught defacing an advertising poster will be subject to disciplinary action.

If we all understand these rules and cooperate, our school will continue to be the lively and exciting place we all know.

policy statement on...

The only materials of an advertising nature that will be allowed in Rock Township Public Schools are those directly related to school-sponsored or school-approved activities. All extracurricular activities of a school are considered school-sponsored activities. School-approved activities are those listed as approved by the Board of Education. These may include community activities, civic association activities, etc. Any non-school-sponsored activity wanting Board approval must contact the Board Secretary in writing, and approval must be voted at a Board meeting.

No advertising poster or device shall be attached to school property in such a manner as to damage the school property. Content of the advertising device should be consonant with good taste and public morality. Each school will establish rules regarding the posting of such materials within the individual school and will be responsible for the implementation of these rules.

(See Also: ADULT EDUCATION; ANIMALS; BACK-TO-SCHOOL NIGHT; BOARD OF EDUCATION; INTRODUCTION; MEDIA; NEWSLETTER; NEWS RELEASES; OPEN HOUSE**)**

ADVISORS AND ADVISORY COMMITTEES

class advisor's duties...

JUNIOR CLASS ADVISOR'S DUTIES

1. Duties and Responsibilities
   a. Arrange for the organization of advisors and executive committee.
   b. Consult with Junior Class President before meetings.
   c. Attend all executive meetings.
   d. Assist president in initiating and organizing all activities.
   e. Check with advisors and co-chairperson on progress and needs.
   f. Attend all class functions.

g. Check and sign "Request to Hold" forms.
h. Sign all purchase orders *after* checking requests countersigned by advisor for that event.

2. Policies

a. Properly execute purchase orders from finance office *before* anything is purchased.
b. Have chairperson of advisors sign all purchase orders.
c. Complete "Request to Hold" forms and return to office two weeks before the event.
d. Execute contracts for orchestra—one copy for office file.
e. Sign "Orders Received" and "Permission to Pay" at request of finance office.
f. See that proper arrangements for functions are made with the following:
(1) Vice-Principal
(2) Custodian
(3) Police
(4) Student Body Advisor for Stereo
(5) Gym Teachers for Use of Gym

3. Procedure

a. Call a meeting of all Junior Class advisors for the purpose of dividing the year's responsibilities. (This can be done in the pre-class period at the beginning of the school year.)
b. Meet with the Junior Class President to discuss the calling of meetings, procedures, preparation of agendas, etc.
c. See that the class budget is one of the first items of business. Check on balance (if any) in treasury from sophomore year. Approximate what you hope to add to this for the junior year. (Most juniors don't realize the importance of building up a surplus to help with senior expenses.)
d. Assist the president in getting each function underway in ample time to ensure success.
e. Follow up on progress by checking with co-chairpersons and/or advisors.
f. Assume responsibilities for necessary announcements, signing of purchase orders, as liaison between administration and finance office and student chairpersons.
g. A very complete and helpful file of Committee reports and junior activity may be found in the junior class file which is located in the room of the chairperson of the junior class advisors.

NOTE: Chairperson of class advisors should brief the members of the committee concerning their duties far enough in advance so as to be effective. The chairperson should be prepared to assist if the need arises.

letter to advisory committee...

Dear Mrs. Harrington,

I am writing to you as Chairperson of the Student Activities Advisory Committee to formally express my thanks for the formation of the committee and to voice my positive expectations for the year to come.

The most positive sign of the health of our society is the fact that we find people like yourself and the members of your committee who are willing to give of themselves in terms of time and effort to help our students. The task ahead of us during this coming school year will be a difficult one, and it will be demanding. You are fully aware of this, yet you have volunteered your time with no other thought than to help. That is deeply appreciated by me, personally, and by our entire student body who will be the ultimate beneficiaries of your efforts.

With an attitude such as yours, we cannot help but have a productive and exciting year, and I look forward to working with you and your committee for the good of our students.

I look forward to the first meeting of our committee.

(See Also: ACCEPTANCE; APPRECIATION; CHAPERONE; COUNSELING; DUE PROCESS; STUDENT COUNCIL (GOVERNMENT); VOLUNTEERS)

AFFIRMATIVE ACTION

complete guidelines for a program of...

In accordance with the policy of the Board of Education to ensure that no student is excluded from participation in, denied the benefits of, or is subjected to discrimination under any education program or activity of this district on the basis of race, color, creed, religion, sex, ancestry, national origin, place of residence, or social or economic background, the Affirmative Action Officer has been delegated responsibility for planning, implementing and monitoring an affirmative action program with respect to School and Classroom Practices. All employees having responsibility for developing and implementing educational programs shall cooperate with and support the Affirmative Action Officer in the performance of his or her responsibilities.

A. Program Commencement

The affirmative action program shall commence in the following manner:

1. Meetings shall be held with staff and students to explain the objectives of the program and to solicit suggestions and concerns.
2. The community shall be made aware of the program and requested to participate in its development.
3. A council of staff, students and public participants shall be convened to ascertain the areas of study.
4. Committee assignments shall be made and schedules set. Each committee shall be specifically charged, assured district resource aid and given a schedule against which to work. Each committee should include representation from those with various interests.

B. Program Design

Committee assignments shall include but need not be limited to the following:

1. *Curricula Content*–Review current and proposed curriculum guides and textbooks to detect any bias based upon race, sex, religion, national origin, ancestry, or culture.

Ascertain supplemental materials singly or taken as a whole, fairly depict the contribution of both sexes and the various races, ethnic groups and the like towards the development of human society.

2. *Staff Training*–Devise a program of inservice training for school personnel designed to identify and solve problems of racial, sexual, religious, national, or cultural bias in all aspects of the school program.
3. *Student Access*–Review all programs, activities and practices to ensure that all students have equal access thereto and are not segregated on the basis of race, color, creed, sex, or national origin in any duty, work, play, classroom, or school practice except as may be permitted under State regulations.
4. *District Support*–Ensure that like aspects of the school program receive like support as to staff size and compensation, purchase and maintenance of facilities and equipment, access to such facilities and equipment, and related matters.
5. *Student Evaluation*–Ensure that tests, procedures or guidance and counseling materials which are designed to evaluate student progress or rate aptitudes or analyze personality or in any manner establish or tend to establish a category by which a student may be judged are not differentiated or stereotyped on the basis of race, color, creed, sex, or national origin.

C. Program Implementation

The Affirmative Action officer shall prepare the recommendations of all committees in the form of a report for review by the Board of Education. Said report shall include in addition to the salient findings, an affirmative action plan to correct existing deficiencies, a schedule of dates for the implementation of the plan, and the estimated cost of implementation.

Said plan shall include a standing committee of staff, students and community representatives to review on a continuing basis new curricula, inservice training programs, teaching practices, support practices and evaluative methods for evidence of bias. In addition a grievance procedure shall be devised to ensure staff and students a means for equitable administrative review of any matter that would appear to be in violation of these regulations.

(See Also: ACADEMIC FREEDOM; AMERICAN EDUCATION WEEK; ASSEMBLIES; CHANGE; CURRICULUM; DUE PROCESS; INSERVICE; LIBRARY; NEW POLICY OR PROGRAM; PHILOSPHY; TEXTBOOKS)

AIDES

guidelines for student aides...

STUDENT OFFICE AIDES—GUIDELINES

1. CONFIDENTIALITY: Any conversation(s) or observations encountered while in the office are STRICTLY confidential and are not to be discussed outside the office.
2. DISCIPLINE REFERRALS: Any student referred to the office should be directed to sit on the chairs outside the counter. A referral slip from the teacher must accompany the student. Place the referral slip in the appropriate grade level basket. DO NOT discuss the referral slip with the student or another aide. DO NOT carry on a conversation with ANY student on the chair.
3. MAIL: Office aides may sort and deliver (to teacher mailboxes) U.S. mail. However, mail is NEVER to be opened by an aide. If a question arises concerning a letter, consult one of the secretaries at once.
4. TELEPHONE: Student aides are expected to answer incoming calls by saying, "Good morning (afternoon), Rock Township High School. May I help you?"

   a. Ask the name of the person calling.
   b. If the call is for the Principal, give the call to the principal's secretary.
   c. If the call is for one of the vice-principals, ask the person if he or she would like to receive the call.
   d. Teacher phone calls: 1) Check teacher schedule and see if the teacher has a class or a professional period. 2) If the teacher has no class, locate the teacher. If the teacher has a class, take a message and have an aide deliver it to the teacher's room.
   e. Guidance calls: Put on hold, dial "0" and wait for someone in the guidance office to take the call.
   f. Parents reporting student absence: Take name of student and grade and give this information to the attendance secretary.

   Office aides are not allowed to make or receive personal calls. Calls to home for emergency purposes are allowed with the permission of the head secretary. Students may use the office telephone to make calls to their homes ONLY with permission. Check with authorized office personnel before giving a student permission to use the phone.
5. INTERCOM: All aides will be using the intercom at one time or another. Please be polite at all times. The intercom is never to be treated as anything other than a very important piece of office equipment.
6. TARDINESS: Aides are to leave promptly when the bell rings. Tardiness to class will not be excused unless the office was directly responsible for the tardiness. A pass will be issued by the secretary if that is the case.

7. MIMEO ROOM: The mimeo room is to be kept neat at all times. Unfinished work is to be brought to the attention of the secretary before leaving the office.
8. LEAVING OFFICE: Aides are not to leave the office unless they are directed to do so and have been given permission by authorized office personnel.
9. APPEARANCE: All aides should come to the office dressed neatly with hair combed (no coats, please). Many visitors come into our office every day; you will be dealing with some of them directly. Therefore, your appearance is important to us as well. Aides are requested not to chew gum (for obvious reasons).
10. MISCELLANEOUS: Any visitor who comes into the office should be acknowledged immediately. If a parent brings in a lunch, locker key, books, etc., find out the name of the student and the grade and deliver the item to the student in the proper class. The box of student schedules is located beside the intercom.

    Always bring some work to do in the event there is nothing for you to do. Some days are busier than others, so being prepared before time will save a trip to your locker.

    Aides are NOT to sit and talk at the counter.

    Other students are not allowed to visit you while you are serving as an aide in the office. If, at any time, you have a question (of any kind), please do not hesitate to ask. Many times a question (and answer) can make the difference between a job well done or unnecessary extra work.
11. These guidelines are a means for all aides to help run our office and our school in a pleasant and smooth manner. Abuse of these guidelines by any aide will result in dismissal from the program. Remember, you will be receiving a grade for being an office aide.

NOTE: *Period 1 and 2 aides*—If a student comes into the office who is tardy, and the attendance secretary is not at her desk, write the student's name, grade and reason for lateness on a sheet of paper and place it on the attendance secretary's desk. Fill out a pass with the name of the student, time, and have it signed by one of the secretaries.

message to teacher aides...

Welcome to Rock Township High School. The staff and I appreciate your presence and your generosity in volunteering as a teacher aide. We hope that you will enjoy the time you spend with us.

In order to facilitate your stay with us, there are a few guidelines of which you should be aware. These are intended to make your experience with us profitable for everyone.

1. Anything you see or hear related to the progress of an individual student is to be considered CONFIDENTIAL and is not to leave the school.
2. Check with the teacher in charge for your assignments. Any difficulties or exceptions should be reported to that teacher at once.
3. You are here to help; you need not take abuse from anyone. Any abusive or disruptive student should be reported to the teacher or this office at once.

4. All reports of progress should be submitted to the teacher in charge.

We hope that you enjoy your stay with us, and we look forward to having you with us for many years to come.

(See Also: ATTENDANCE; CHAPERONE; CLERICAL SERVICES; STUDENT COUNCIL (GOVERNMENT); VOLUNTEERS)

ALUMNI

administrator's message in alumni bulletin...

Dear Alumni,

The years have a way of moving on, whether or not we wish them to do so. Can you remember back to your very first day of school? Did it seem that it would take forever for you to become like those "big guys" in eighth grade? And, when you had become an eighth grader, didn't it seem as if it would be forever before you graduated from high school?

If you are like the rest of us, that's exactly the way it was. Yet, somehow, those days passed (all too quickly according to some) and here you are, graduated from our school, busy with your adult life, and reading this alumni bulletin.

It is my sincere hope that what you will read here will allow you to pause for a moment and reflect on the days you spent in our school. I hope that in those reflections you will smile a bit as you recall those days of youth. I hope you will return to your school for a while and savor the time you spent there.

This will always be YOUR school, just as it was then.

May this alumni bulletin bring you happy memories.

Sincerely,

fund-raising message...

Dear Alumnus,

When you saw this envelope, did you think, "Oh, no, not another request for money!"? If you did, you are not unique. Nowadays it seems that every time we turn around, somebody else needs money for something. Oh, certainly, the causes are worthy, but with the economy the way it is, it becomes more and more difficult to give.

We thoroughly realize this, so we have only one question to ask: do you feel that you owe anything to your high school? If your answer is NO, then there is nothing more we can say. If, however, you feel that during your stay at our school, you grew in knowledge and personality; if you think back to afternoons spent happily in extracurricular activities; if you remember those dances and field trips and sports games with affection; if this is the case, then we think you know what has to be done.

Our high school needs many things to help its students now, just as we were helped when we traveled its hallways. We can help our school as it helped us. Our contributions, however much they may be, will go towards making our school a special place for the students of today just as it was and continues to be a special place for us, its alumni.

Won't you help out? Any contribution placed in the enclosed envelope and mailed to us will be used to help YOUR school. Let's make our school the fine and wonderful place we all remember.

Sincerely,

(See Also: ADULT EDUCATION; ADVERTISING; AMERICAN EDUCATION WEEK; BACK-TO-SCHOOL NIGHT; OPEN HOUSE)

AMERICAN EDUCATION WEEK

message to administrators on...

TO: All Administrators
FROM: Office of the Superintendent
RE: American Education Week

American Education Week was started in 1921 under the joint sponsorship of the American Legion and the National Education Association. The National Congress of Parents and Teachers and the U.S. Office of Education later lent their support and sponsorship as well.

American Education Week is an excellent opportunity to build favorable community relations. Quite often, joint committees of educators and community members may be formed in order to establish programs and procedures for the week. These may include programs outside the school as well as such procedures as Open House and special programs for community members.

Administrators are urged to take advantage of this time by scheduling worthwhile programs, including those with community participation, some time during this week. Please let this office know of the plans for your specific school at least two weeks in advance in order that we may arrange for press coverage.

message to teachers on...

TO: Faculty
FROM: J. Benson, Principal
RE: American Education Week

As you may be aware, we shall shortly be celebrating American Education Week. As you may also be aware, during that week we will be having our annual "Open House" for parents and community members. This is nothing new to us, and if past Open House days are any example, our parents and the surrounding community cannot help but be impressed by the fine job we are doing.

I will remind you, however, that the day is traditionally well attended by the community. A number of people will be visiting your classroom for the specific purpose of seeing for themselves what goes on there. We are proud of our school, our staff, and our students, and we are most anxious to acquaint the community with the work we do. I would suggest, therefore, that we leave such aids as movies, filmstrips and tests for other, more quiet days, and prepare classes centered around student activity and student-teacher interaction.

The theme of this year's American Education Week is: SCHOOLS—INVESTMENT IN AMERICA'S FUTURE. Anything you can do to incorporate this theme into the day's lessons would only have beneficial effects.

(See Also: BACK-TO-SCHOOL NIGHT; EDUCATION; OPEN HOUSE; PHILOSOPHY)

ANIMALS

advertising for school "Pet Fair"...

PETS! PETS! PETS! PETS! PETS! PETS! PETS! PETS! PETS! PETS!

WAVERLY ELEMENTARY SCHOOL

presents

the 3rd annual

ALL-SCHOOL PET FAIR

Saturday, May 17 | Waverly School Gymnasium | 9:00 a.m.-4:00 p.m.

Prizes Awarded For

- Most Unusual
- Friendliest
- Most Waggy Tail
- Wettest Nose
- Best Groomed
- Most Loveable
- Fuzziest
- Laziest
- Best Trained
- Most Cuddly
- Fattest
- Noisiest
- Most Colorful
- Ugliest
- Best Overall

COME EARLY—STAY LATE | REFRESHMENTS AVAILABLE

ADMISSION 50¢

proceeds to school improvement fund

PETS! PETS! PETS! PETS! PETS! PETS! PETS! PETS! PETS! PETS!

school policy on...

It seems to be that time of year again when our students are bringing various pets to school for any number of reasons, some of them quite legitimate. I thought, therefore, that it might be well to remind everyone of our school's policy regarding the bringing of animals to school.

1. Students may bring animals to school only for legitimate reasons (show-and-tell; science project; etc.) and only with the permission of their teacher and the main office.
2. The office is to be advised of the impending visit of the animal at least two days prior to the event and is also to be advised of the type of animal to be brought in.
3. An adult must bring in the animal, checking first with the office and then conveying the animal directly to the classroom or area where it is required. Upon completion of the activity, the adult is responsible for removing the animal from school grounds.
4. It is to be understood that the adult bears full responsibility and liability for the behavior of the animal on school grounds.
5. Any cleaning chores necessitated by the animal's presence on school grounds becomes the responsibility of the adult in charge of the animal.

If this policy is understood and followed, the bringing of animals to school will become an orderly activity that will benefit everyone.

(See Also: ADVERTISING; MEDIA; NEWSLETTER; NEWS RELEASE)

APPLICATION

information and procedures for...

A. APPLICATION PROCEDURES AND REQUIREMENTS

1. The completed application document will consist of the completed application form, references, and a college transcript. (Please note that it is the responsibility of the applicant to see that all written references are filled with the Rock Township Public Schools.) The application form will be considered incomplete until it contains a copy of a valid state teaching certificate and all other information called for in the application. The attachment of a photograph is optional, but such photographs may be beneficial to the applicant in the event that interviewers have difficulty recalling a particular applicant.

   The application becomes the property of the Rock Township Public Schools upon its submission, and the applicant releases all rights to retrieve it or any portion of its contents.

   The application will be kept on active status until December 31 of the year in which it was filed. At that time, it will be placed in an inactive file unless a written request has been received to extend the time for another calendar year.

B. PROCEDURES AND REQUIREMENTS

1. Following the receipt of the completed application and its constituent parts, the applicant will be asked to respond in writing to some specific classroom situations in order to assess the applicant's written communication skills and general knowledge of education. The written responses are to be made on-site in the Superintendent's office. Such responses will be subjectively evaluated in terms of the following criteria:

   a. Sentence Structure
   b. Punctuation, Capitalization, Spelling
   c. Perceptiveness
   d. Organizational Skills
   e. Planning Skills
   f. Clarity
   g. Feeling/Awareness of Situation
   h. Self Objectivity
   i. Decision Making
   j. Learner Awareness
   k. Knowledge of Curriculum

2. Based on the above criteria, applicants will be selected and contacted for a formal interview.

C. RECOMMENDATION FOR EMPLOYMENT

On the basis of the factors outlined above, applicants will be selected by the Superintendent to be recommended to the Board of Education for employment. The Board of Education will accept or reject the recommendation. If accepted by the Board of Education, the applicant will be notified in writing, and a written response of acceptance or rejection must be received within ten days from the applicant.

NOTE: All steps in the process outlined above must be completed in the order listed. No applicant may proceed to a given step until after the completion of all previous steps except in emergency conditions as may be determined by the Superintendent or Director of Instruction.

A SPECIAL NOTE...

There are many examples of application forms throughout this book, to find the one you require, look under the topic for which you desire the application. For example, should you desire an application form for a clerical position, you would look under CLERICAL SERVICES for such an application.

APPRECIATION

open letter to parents...

Dear Parents,

During the recent budget crunch, one of the items eliminated in order to save money was funds for buses for after-school and special activities. At the time this happened, I contacted you in order to explain what this would mean to our students in terms of the loss of field trips and participation in extracurricular activities. I asked you, at that time, if you had any suggestions for overcoming this difficulty.

Your response has been overwhelming. I received call after call volunteering time, services and transportation for our students in order to maintain the extracurricular and special activities that have always been a part of our students' lives.

Thanks to you, our clubs and activities still flourish, our teams still practice and play, and our special events still take place, made all the more special by your participation in them.

Therefore, I want to thank you and express the deep and abiding appreciation of the entire faculty and staff of our school for your unselfishness, concern and dedication to the welfare of our students.

Thank you for being there.

Sincerely,

memo to teachers...

TO: Faculty
FROM: J. Benson, Principal
RE: Reflections on the "Open House"

Have I told you lately how much I appreciate your professionalism and your teaching expertise? Well, if I haven't, let me do so now.

As you know, several days ago we held our annual Open House for the community. It was the success I expected, and I have been literally deluged with phone calls from parents and community members telling me how impressed they were with what they saw and praising you, the faculty, for the fine job you are doing. Many of the callers wanted me to express to you their appreciation for a job well done.

This I do with all my heart, and I add my own appreciation for the support, the cooperation, and the dedication that has made my job all the easier and made this school the fine educational institution it is.

Thank you.

(See Also: ACCEPTANCE; AIDES; NATIONAL HONOR SOCIETY; RECOMMENDATION; VOLUNTEERS)

ART

description in public relations publication...

FINE ARTS

Creativity, a characteristic of children, needs to be challenged, encouraged, and guided. The fine arts curriculum strives to encourage a student's appreciation of literature, art, drama, and music by providing a wide range of activities in these areas. This happens through opportunities for group and individual performance.

outline of an Arts Block program...

6th and 7th Grade Related Arts Block

Characteristics

1. Physical Education is required.
2. All 6th Grade students are required to take the humanities wheel consisting of four nine-week sessions:

   9 weeks–Exploratory Music
   9 weeks–Industrial Art
   9 weeks–Interior Management
   9 weeks–Arts and Crafts

7th and 8th Grade Related Arts Block

Characteristics

1. Physical Education is required.
2. Students select from the following: year or semester courses (may elect band or choral music)
3. Semester courses (may take two):

   Interior Management–cooking and sewing
   Arts and Crafts
   Industrial Art
   Band (year)
   Choral Music (year)

(See Also: ADVERTISING; ELECTIVES; XEROXING)

ASP (ALTERNATE SCHOOL PROGRAM)

description of...

ALTERNATE SCHOOL PLAN

The Alternate School Plan was established for the purpose of referring students who ordinarily would be suspended from school.

Daily records are kept on each student who is referred. These records include steps taken to modify the student's behavior, counseling and instruction given, attendance in program, and a record of all conferences, including outcomes. This information will be made available to the principal upon the student's return to regular school.

Attendance in the program is mandatory for students who are referred from their regular school. Students who fail to report as assigned will be referred to the attendance officer to look into, and make, if necessary, recommendations involving juvenile or other authorities.

Transportation: Parents are responsible for transporting their child to and from the Alternate School.

Exam Exemptions: Students sent to the Alternate School lose the privilege of exam exemption for any reason.

Extracurricular Activities: Students sent to the Alternate School are not allowed to participate in any extracurricular activities or practices during the period of their referral.

referral to alternate school form...

ALTERNATE SCHOOL REFERRAL

School Name ______________________ Date ______________________

Name ______________________ Address ______________________ M or F ______

Birthday ______________________ No. of Days Referred ______________________ Parents ______________________

Telephone ______________________

Dear Mr. and Mrs. ______________________,

Your son/daughter has been referred to the student Alternate School Plan for a period of __________ days. This referral is a result of ______________________

____

____

He/she may return on ______________ at ______________ provided his/her behavior is satisfactory. In order for ______________________ to be reinstated, it will be necessary for one of the parents to accompany his/her return.

Respectfully,

____

DESCRIPTION OF OFFENSE(S):

NAME OF PERSON(S) REPORTING THE OFFENSE(S):

NAME OF PERSON IMPOSING THE ACTION:

ALTERNATIVES TO THE DISCIPLINARY ACTION THAT WERE CONSIDERED PRIOR TO THE REFERRAL:

PARENTS CONTACTED: ______________ SIGNATURE OF STUDENT: ______________

(See Also: ABSENTEEISM; BEHAVIOR; DISCIPLINE; REFERRAL; SUSPENSION)

ASSEMBLIES

assembly and petition—student rights and responsibilities...

ASSEMBLY AND PETITION

Students' rights to assemble and to circulate petitions carry with them the equal responsibility to respect the orderly operation of the school. School authorities have a right to restrict the times and places of such activities, and may require advance notice when necessary to avoid conflicts and to ensure proper protection of the school community.

rules for assembly behavior...

The number of assemblies and the privilege of students to attend is contingent upon the ability of students to conduct themselves properly at all times regardless of the type of assembly being viewed. The following points are emphasized:

a. Please remain quiet and attentive during all programs.

b. A courteous reception should be extended to everyone, regardless of the type of program.

c. Students are to remain in their places until they have been dismissed by the person in charge of the assembly.

d. Whistling, booing, talking, or other acts of discourtesy show lack of maturity, respect, and consideration. They also reflect upon the good name and reputation of the entire student body. Violators will be kept from attending all future programs and will also be subject to suspension.

e. Class yells are prohibited except during special pep rally assemblies.

f. At pep rally assemblies, all students are urged to enter into and help with school spirit by participation in school yells, etc. Again, however, whistling, booing or any other acts of ill manners have no place in the program.

(See Also: AIDES; BUILDING; DEMONSTRATIONS; NEWS RELEASES; USE OF FACILITIES**)**

ASSIGNMENTS

administrative duty assignments...

I. Administrative Duty Assignments (7:45–8:15 a.m.)

A. Departmental Conferences

1. English in Room 201 with Ms. Hansen
2. Mathematics in Room 207 with Mr. Smollett

3. Science in Biology Lab with Mrs. Roth
4. Social Studies in Room 111 with Miss Stanley
5. Physical Education in Boys' Gym Office with Mr. Bell
6. Fine and Industrial Arts in Room 98 with Mrs. Green
7. Special Ed and Special Services in Library with Mr. Graham
8. All others (Reading, Careers, AVA, etc.) in Room 96 with Mr. Hays

B. Safety Assignments
   1. September–January
      a. Outside Front—Mr. Harris and Mr. Gibbs
      b. Side Parking Lot—Mr. Curren
      c. Second Floor—Mrs. Godge
      d. First Floor—Mrs. Solee and Mrs. Gandreau
   2. February–June
      a. Outside Front—Miss Grewd, Mr. Downs and Mr. Leon
      b. Side Parking Lot—Mrs. Biro and Miss Oslow
      c. Second Floor—Ms. Galini
      d. First Floor—Mr. Webber and Mrs. Shaley

II. Administrative Duty Assignments (2:12–2:27 p.m.)

A. Bus Supervision (See Bus Charts for Locations)
   1. September–January

Bus 1–Mrs. Breen	5–Mr. Leon
2–Mr. Curren	6–Ms. Galini
3–Mr. Webber	7–Mrs. Solee
4–Mrs. Godge	8–Mrs. Biro

   1. February–June

Bus 1–Mr. Gibbs	5–Mr. Harris
2–Mrs. Gandreau	6–Mr. Downs
3–Miss Oslow	7–Miss Grewd
4–Mrs. Shaley	8–Mr. Drew

B. Back of Building
   1. September–January—Ms. Hasley
   2. February–June—Mr. Parsons

C. Side Parking Lot
   1. September–January—Miss Nathan
   2. February–June—Mr. Richards

D. Inside Assignments (year-long; * indicates locker keys)
   1. Second Floor—Mrs. Newman*
   2. Near Exit

1–Mrs. Bender*	6–Mr. Kyle*
3–Mr. Jones*	8–Miss Bloome*
4–Mr. Pyne	9–Mrs. Higgins
5–Mrs. Keene	11–Mr. Brewster

III. Late Schedule Duty (September–June)
   A. Halls—Mrs. Shatt and Mr. Greely
   B. Central Detention—Mr. McCleod

(See Also: CLOSE OF SCHOOL; COURSES; DUTIES; HALLS AND HALL DUTY; LUNCH AND LUNCH DUTY; SCHEDULE; TRANSFER)

ATTENDANCE

class attendance and school functions...

1. In all off-campus trips that occur during the school day, the request should state the educational reason for the trip, the students who are to go, the leaving time and the time they should return to school. Names, time to leave and time to return should be included on the bulletin the day before the trip for advance notification and the day of the trip.
2. Students who are going to miss school because of a school trip usually know this in advance. The school policy is that students make advance arrangements before the trip with each teacher.
3. Events that are not scheduled in advance and placed on the weekly bulletin will not occur. Names should accompany events on all occasions. Events once scheduled will occur unless the Principal has personally approved the cancellation.
4. A policy manual covering off-campus trips, club sponsorship, etc., will be developed. A special meeting will be held with all sponsors, coaches, etc., to ensure a full understanding of this procedure and the guidelines.
5. Rolls should be checked every period by every teacher. Students should not be excused from any class for any reason without the Principal's written approval. Teachers are not to accept students from other classes unless there is a note approved by the Principal assigning the students. If they come, send them to the office.
6. Board approval is necessary for all overnight trips sponsored by the school involving students.
7. Parking decals for faculty members and students who have permission to leave during the school day (COOP) will be provided.
8. Any request sent to the Principal's office for approval of students to be out of class must state the educational reason for this request.

full policy statement on attendance...

Being on time so that classes may begin or continue uninterrupted is essential to the well being of each student in class. Cuts and unexcused absences have many negative consequences, such as missing an assignment, failure in participating where that is an essential part of the learning process, and in increasing the workload of the teacher.

OBJECTIVE

The basic objective is to minimize or eliminate cuts, tardies and unexcused absences.

GUIDELINES

The following steps will be taken to achieve the above objective:

A. Student Responsibilities

1. To make a personal effort to understand and exercise a self-imposed discipline to meet this objective.
2. To make an effort to bring a note from his or her parent, doctor, or teacher if the reason for tardiness or absence was legitimate.
3. To be considerate of others and the teacher's increased workload.
4. To leave the campus during off-campus period. This includes those who are participating in sports.

B. Teacher Responsibilities

1. To make an effort to immediately discuss the matter with the student to see if an understanding can be reached. (Date and time should be documented.) To have a written agreement stating topics discussed and agreements reached.
2. To make the initial home contact if the student has three or more unexcused absences or cuts in any two-week period, or if a pattern of unexcused absences occurs. The teacher will also initiate home calls if the student has a continuous pattern of tardies after the first period of the day.
3. To mark the student absent if he or she is not in class when the tardy bell rings. During the first period of the day, do not admit students without a green slip from the administration. Attendance cards will be sent to the attendance office at 8:15 a.m. There will be no admittance to class after the tardy bell without an excuse from the previous teacher or a green slip from the attendance office.
4. To refer to the counselor for follow through if student behavior does not improve or if unable to contact the home. Previous action(s) taken by teacher should be written on referral form.
5. If unexcused absences continue, refer to the administration for disciplinary action. The student who is suspended will not be able to make up the work for credit in other classes while he or she is on suspension. However, the student may be penalized if he or she doesn't do the work. Final decision on whether the student can make up the work with credit will be left to the discretion of the teacher.
6. To make clear the grading policies and standards in the event that the teacher feels that the continued absences and/or cuts will result in failure.
7. To keep the student in class unless he or she has legitimate reasons to leave. A pass should then be issued to the student. Other students should not be released before the end of the period.

C. Counselor Responsibilities

1. To confer with the student and arrange for a parent conference. Agreements and discussion should be documented.
2. To make necessary referrals if warranted.
3. To provide the teacher immediate feedback.
4. To refer for administrative follow-through.

D. Administrator Responsibilities

1. To take a disciplinary action and call for parental conference.
2. To set conditions in written agreements.
3. To warn the student and parent of future consequences*, such as:
   a. referral to district committee
   b. more than ten absences in a quarter may result in failure
   c. student who is removed for that period becomes a parental responsibility
   d. failure in more than half of his or her courses in a quarter can result in dismissal for that semester

   *These consequences include absences due to suspensions.
4. To provide counselor and teacher feedback.
5. To supervise the campus during period 1, in particular during the first month and a half.
6. To determine what constitutes an excused or unexcused tardy and to take corrective measures in dealing with unexcused tardies during period 1. After period 1 classes, tardy is left up to the discretion of the teacher to make individual referrals.

DEPARTMENT OF EDUCATION, POLICY–SEC. 298-11. EXCLUSION FROM SCHOOL

If for any reason a child becomes a detriment to the morals or discipline of any school, the child may be precluded from attending school by the principal with the approval of the district superintendent. The Department of Education shall seek the active participation of other public and private agencies in providing help to such children before and after they have left school. An appeal may be taken on behalf of the child to the superintendent of education within ten days from the date of such action.

No child who is seventeen years of age or over shall be admitted to the ninth grade of a public four-year high school, and no child who is eighteen years of age or over shall be admitted to the tenth grade of a public senior high school, except upon the written permission of the superintendent when in his opinion the facts warrant such admission.

Any high school student whose work is below passing in half or more of his subjects shall be placed on probation and, if his work does not improve to the satisfaction of the superintendent during the subsequent semester, he shall be precluded from attending school. Such student may be reinstated by the superintendent, if, in his opinion, the facts warrant such reinstatement.

SCHOOL CONDITIONS

Parent conferences will be called from the third offense. This is for tardies, cuts, or absences. Written agreements will be called for by the fourth offense.

Students should realize that ten or more absences within a quarter may result in failure. In the event that the student is failing beyond the point where he can reinstate himself, he may be removed from that class and be under the direct responsibility of his parents.

STUDENTS PARTICIPATING IN OFFICIAL STUDENT ACTIVITIES

Students who participate in official student activities, such as school student council meetings and district and state student council meetings and conferences, are considered to be present.

out-of-area attendance form...

OUT-OF-AREA ATTENDANCE FORM
Rock Township Public Schools

NAME OF PUPIL ____
(last name) (first name) (middle initial)

NAME OF PARENT ____________________ TELEPHONE NUMBER ______________

ADDRESS OF PARENT ____

GRADE OF PUPIL ____________________ DATE OF ENROLLMENT ______________

SCHOOL OF ATTENDANCE ______________________________________

SCHOOL OF RESIDENCE ____

Reason for attendance change: ________________________________

____

____

____

SIGNED ____
Principal of School of Attendance

SUBMIT TO: Superintendent of Schools (to be filed with Assistant Superintendent)

procedures for attendance recording...

Students Report to School After an Absence

a. When a student is absent, he must, upon his return to school, present the teachers of classes he missed a note from his parent explaining the absence.

b. All teachers of classes missed must sign this note after which the note must be turned in to the attendance office.

Cards sent to the Attendance Office

a. Immediately after announcements, each teacher, period 1 or 3, will send one monitor to the attendance window with the card for each of the absent students. If there are no absentees, the teacher must send one monitor with the "NONE" card. The same student should be assigned to take the cards each day.

Absentee Lists

a. As soon as the list of absentees for the day has been typed and duplicated, the attendance office monitors will post a copy in the attendance office. Cards will be returned in the teacher's mailbox.

Absentees–Periods 2, 4, 5, and 6

a. Teachers are to keep attendance for each class.

Tardiness to School

a. Students who are tardy to school report to the attendance office for a tardy slip.

b. They MUST put their counselor's number in the upper right hand corner of the slip.

c. Students who report for a tardy slip after the absentee cards have been sent down must present the tardy slip to each of his teachers for classes missed that day.

d. TEACHERS put the tardy slips into the counselors' mailboxes at the end of that day.

Tardiness to Class

a. If a student is detained by a teacher, he should obtain an excuse from that teacher for the next class.

Cards Used for Reporting Absentees

a. Each teacher will receive two sets of cards; one for period 1; one for period 3.

b. There should be a card for each student in each of these two periods. Please check to be sure you have the correct cards.

1. White cards .... Sophomores
2. Yellow cards............. Juniors
3. Blue cards .... Seniors
4. "NONE" cards .... For no absentees

If you find some cards are missing, please fill in blank cards using the correct color for each grade.

c. New students enrolling—cards will be typed for their periods 1 and 3 and put into the respective teachers' mailboxes.

(See Also: ABSENCE; ABSENTEEISM; ENROLLMENT; PERMANENT RECORDS; RECORDS; ZONES AND ZONING)

AUTOMOBILES

letter to parents and students...

Dear Students and Parents,

Lately, we have been having some difficulties at the school due to the large number of automobiles that are driven onto and parked on school property daily. A number of times during the past weeks, we have had to search for the owners of certain cars in order to facilitate their movement to let important daily services, such as cafeteria deliveries and school buses, continue in an orderly fashion.

Therefore, I would like to remind our students and their parents of the established rules for bringing automobiles onto school grounds.

1. All student and faculty cars must have a permit slip for parking and must be in their assigned parking stall.
2. Under no conditions must any car be parked along the curb area painted yellow.
3. Visitors to the school should use the parking stalls with signs indicating "Visitors."
4. If a parking stall is used by an unauthorized vehicle, the office should be notified at once.
5. Parking in an unauthorized stall or area will result in disciplinary action from the school.

I hope that you will understand that our primary concern is the smooth and orderly functioning of the school. Toward that goal, we must make rules which will allow for the running of the daily routine of our school. If everyone cooperates and obeys the rules for the use of automobiles on school property, I am certain that we will avoid all further difficulties.

Sincerely,

school policy...

1. Any vehicle driven onto school grounds by a student or a member of the faculty and staff must be insured with liability coverage consonant with acceptable state standards.
2. Any parking on school grounds other than temporary visitor parking is by permit only. A parking sticker will be issued and is to be displayed in the left rear window of the vehicle.

3. Members of the faculty and staff are asked to sign a card attesting to proper liability insurance coverage and are automatically issued parking permits and stickers during the professional days prior to the start of the regular school year.
4. Students must apply for parking permits during June of the proceeding school year. Students must supply proof of driving eligibility and proof of insurance coverage at the time of application. When the application has been processed, eligible students will receive parking permits and stickers. An annual fee of one dollar is charged to help cover handling costs.
5. Each parking sticker has the number of the assigned parking stall printed on it. An assigned vehicle is to use that stall only.
6. Each school will set aside a certain number of parking stalls as they may determine sufficient to handle the vehicles of visitors to the school. These stalls are not to be assigned, and will be marked prominently as "Visitor Parking."

(See Also: BUILDING; BUS; DRIVING; INSURANCE; TRAVEL)

AWARDS

letter of congratulations to parents...

Dear Mr. and Mrs. Harrison,

Congratulations on the outstanding academic achievement of your son, Edward. He has placed among the top five students of his class and has earned an academic award as directed by the Rock Township School Board.

This award carries great significance in our district. Of our total 7,543 high school students this year, only 23 received this honor. Thus, his performance ranks him near the top one percent academically of all high school students in the entire school district. I know you are proud of him, and I want you to know that his teachers and other school officials are equally proud.

Please pass along to Edward our congratulations and gratitude for his accomplishments this past year. We are confident that he will maintain this record in the years ahead.

Sincerely,

news release...

FOR IMMEDIATE RELEASE:

ROCK TOWNSHIP—The Rock Township Board of Education has announced the names of the five top academic students in the junior class of Rock Township High School. These students have achieved a cumulative average of 98.5 or better during their junior year.

The juniors at Rock Township High School are Martin Abelyar, Edward Harrison, Judith Keeler, Marie Lambersini, and Emily Yarosh. They will receive a special award during class night ceremonies to be held on June 3 at the high school.

The award consists of a $500 scholarship to be held in trust until the students enter college. Superintendent of schools J. Patrick Ferril will present the awards during the ceremony.

(See Also: ABILITY; ACHIEVEMENT; NATIONAL HONOR SOCIETY; NEWS RELEASES)

BABY-SITTING

application for...

NAME ______________________________________ DATE ____________

CLASS ____________ HOMEROOM ____________ COUNSELOR ______________

HOME ADDRESS ____

____

HOME TELEPHONE NUMBER ______________________________________

WHEN ARE YOU AVAILABLE? Days ______________________________

Hours ______________________________

TRANSPORTATION (own car, parents', etc.) ______________________

In order to be recommended for baby-sitting jobs, you must have taken the Home Management course. Please fill in the date and teacher of the course in the space below.

______________________	______________________
Date you took course	Teacher of course

message in student handbook...

Rock Township High School often has baby-sitting jobs available for qualified students. As they come in, these jobs are offered to qualified students who apply for them in the guidance office. In order to qualify, the student must make a written application and file it with his or her guidance counselor. The student must have taken and passed the Home Management class offered as part of the curriculum in order to be considered. Personal transportation is not necessary.

(See Also: ADVERTISING; COUNSELING; INFORMATION; JOBS)

BACK-TO-SCHOOL NIGHT

logo for use on parent flyer...

message to faculty on...

TO: Faculty
FROM: J. Benson, Principal
RE: Procedure for Back-to-School Night

1. There will be a brief homeroom period Thursday, September 23, for the students to copy their schedule. The necessary forms will be in the teacher's mailbox on Tuesday. Please remind students to list their homeroom first and then their periods 1, 2, 3, etc.
2. Each period will be seven minutes in length. I will remind the parents that they are not to speak with teachers regarding the individual growth of their child at that time. Each teacher should inform parents that if they want a conference, they should call the Guidance Office for the necessary arrangements.
3. Department Coordinators: Please brief new staff members in your department.
4. Discuss: Goals, objectives of course, special procedures, homework, purpose of cluster for cluster teachers.

schedule for...

8:00-8:30 Welcome by
John Benson, Principal
Hank Barstowe and Helen Pope
PTA Co-Presidents
Introduction of Executive Board
Membership and items for sale, etc.

8:30-8:35	Parents move to Homeroom
8:35-8:42	Homeroom Period—Schedules given to parents
8:42-8:46	Parents move to Period 1
8:46-8:53	Period 1
8:53-8:57	Parents move to Period 2
8:57-9:04	Period 2
9:04-9:08	Parents move to Period 3
9:08-9:15	Period 3
9:15-9:19	Parents move to Period 4
9:19-9:26	Period 4
9:26-9:30	Parents move to Period 5
9:30-9:37	Period 5
9:37-9:41	Parents move to Period 6
9:41-9:48	Period 6
9:48-9:52	Parents move to Period 7
9:52-9:59	Period 7
9:59	Refreshments served in the cafeteria by the P.T.A.
NOTE:	ALL PHYSICAL EDUCATION AND HEALTH CLASSES WILL GO TO THE GYMNASIUM.

(See Also: ADVERTISING; AMERICAN EDUCATION WEEK; MEDIA; NEWS RELEASES; OPEN HOUSE)

BEHAVIOR

chart of behavior and consequences...

Type of Student Behavior	1st Offense	2nd Offense	3rd Offense	4th Offense	5th Offense
Destroying or Defacing Property	* Possible suspension; notify police				
Endangering Safety of Others (Unintentional)	* Parent conference and 3-5 day suspension				
Extortion/Shakedown	5-day suspension	9-day suspension Notify parent next offense referred to Child Study Team	9-day Suspension; Refer to Child Study Team		
False Alarms	* 9-day suspension; refer to Child Study Team. Notify police. Notify parent				
Fighting	* Parent conference and 2-9 day suspension				
Forgery	Parent conference	3-day suspension			
In hall or building without Authorization	Implement school procedures				
Malicious Damage to School Personnel's Property	* 9-day suspension				
Possession of Alcoholic Beverage	9-day suspension Notify police	9-day suspension; notify parent; refer to Child Study Team; notify police			
Possession of Dangerous and/or Offensive Weapons(s)	2-9 day suspension with option to refer to Child Study Team; confiscate and determine whether police should be notified				
Possession of Drugs	9-day suspension notify police	9-day suspension; refer to Child Study Team; notify police			
Smoking on School Property during Regular School Hours and other Indoor School Activities	3-day suspension Parent Conference Possible referral to Board of Health	5-day suspension	9-day suspension		
Starting or causing Fires	9-day suspension notify parent next offense begins referral to Child Study Team	9-day suspension; notify police; refer to Child Study Team			

chart of behavior and consequences (cont'd)

Type of Student Behavior	1st Offense	2nd Offense	3rd Offense	4th Offense	5th Offense
Stealing/Theft	2-9 day suspension	2-9 day suspension notify parent next offense begins referral to Child Study Team	9-day suspension; refer to Child Study Team		
Threatening or Attacking Another Student or School Personnel	* Parent conference with immediate suspension. Notify police where appropriate				
Trafficking Drugs	* Immediate suspension; referral to Child Study Team				
Unauthorized Inter-School Pupil Visitation/Trespassing	* Home School to charge truancy; school visited will charge trespassing; refer to juvenile authorities				
Unauthorized Occupancy of School Facilities by Pupils	2-9 day suspension; notify parent next offense begins referral to Child Study Team	Refer to police			
Unauthorized Possession of Non-School-Related Paraphernalia (1)	Pupil Warning; confiscate items temporarily	Parent conference; confiscate items temporarily	2-day suspension		
Under the Influence of Drugs or Alcohol	* Refer to Policy No. 522. Student not to be readmitted without parent conference and proof that child has had medical consultation concerning problem.				
Cheating	3-day suspension teacher/parent conference	5-day suspension principal/parent conference	9-day suspension		
Chewing Gum; Disrupting Class; Loud & Boisterous Talk	* Use local procedure; action will be based on teacher and administrative judgment at local school level				
Habitual Use of Profanity or Obscene Language (Cursing)	Pupil Warning	Parent Conference	3-day suspension		
Inappropriate Public Display of Affection	Pupil Warning notify parent	Parent Conference	3-day suspension		
Loitering in Auto during School Time	Pupil warning	Parent Conference	2-day suspension	5-day suspension	
Open Defiance of Authority	* Recommend parent conference with possible suspension				
Wanton, Willful and Gross Disrespectfulness	* Recommend parent conference with possible suspension				

school behavior policy...

SCHOOL BEHAVIOR

In order to function properly, public school education must provide equal learning opportunity for all students. In order for an individual to exercise his individual rights as afforded by our Federal and State Constitution he must be able to exercise self-discipline which will allow all individuals to exist in a changing world. The entire foundation and success of public school education depend on the basic concept of self-discipline.

In addition to the regular curriculum, principles and practices of good citizenship must be taught and demonstrated. This includes an appreciation for the rights of others. However, no school or school system can discharge these responsibilities if it permits students to act in an objectionable manner or to disregard rules and regulations adopted for the benefit of all persons.

A portion of the responsibility for the development and enforcement of regulations for the protection of the rights of individuals is delegated by the Board of School Trustees to responsible officials within the School Corporation. The purpose of discipline controls is to help create an atmosphere that promotes the best possible learning environment for all those involved in the educational process.

I. ESTABLISHMENT OF POLICIES, RULES AND REGULATIONS

The Board of School Trustees and the Superintendent of Schools may establish written policies, rules and regulations of general application, governing student conduct in all schools. In addition, each principal, within his or her school, may establish certain written rules and regulations not inconsistent with those established by the Board and the Superintendent.

II. AREAS OF PROHIBITED STUDENT CONDUCT

Any conduct that causes or creates a reasonable likelihood that it will cause a substantial disruption in or material interference with any school function, activity, or purpose, or that interferes or creates a reasonable likelihood that it will interfere with the health, safety or well-being, or the rights of other students, is prohibited.

Nothing herein is intended to restrict the exercise of legitimate First Amendment rights.

The preceding standard is a general standard that should be used as a guide by all students. Not all acts of misconduct can be itemized in this section. The following is an enumeration of some of the main areas of conduct which may lead to disciplinary action, including possible expulsion for a period in excess of five (5) school days or for the balance of the semester or school year:

A. Stealing, causing damage to, or destroying school property if done on school grounds or during a school function or event.

B. Causing or attempting to cause physical injury or harm to any student, teacher or other school employee, or visitor on school grounds or during a school function or event.

C. Threatening or intimidating any student, teacher or other school employee or visitor.

D. Interfering with school purposes or with the orderly operation of the school by using, threatening to use, or counseling other persons to use violence, force, coercion, threats, intimidation, fear, or disruptive means.

E. Possessing, using or transmitting any object that in fact or under the circumstances can reasonably be considered to constitute a weapon.

F. Possessing, using, selling, buying, transmitting, or secreting any alcoholic beverage, narcotic or hallucinogenic drug, marijuana, barbiturate, amphetamine, or intoxicant.

G. Involvement in any conduct on school premises or during a school function or event that violates local, state, or federal law, where such conduct or the likelihood of engaging in such conduct poses a clear and present danger to the health, welfare or safety of other students, teachers, or other employees, or visitors.

H. Refusal or failure to comply with state and local attendance laws, including, but not limited to, truancy from specific classes and tardiness to school in general or to specific classes.

I. Gambling on school premises or at school events.

J. Failure to comply with the smoking restrictions for school buildings as established by local and state government agencies.

K. Willful failure to comply with the directions of teachers, student teachers, school aides, bus drivers, principals, or other authorized school personnel. This shall include, but shall not be limited to, the refusal to show a student identification card when asked to do so.

L. Repeated violation of any rules or regulations governing student conduct.

M. Subject to the lawful exercise of First Amendment rights, participating in any activity which substantially disrupts or materially interferes with, or is likely to so disrupt or interfere with, any school function, activity or purpose.

N. Dressing or grooming in a manner which presents a clear and present danger to the student's health and safety, or in a manner which causes an interference with school work or which creates a classroom or school disruption.

III. OTHER COURSES OF ACTION

The superintendent, principal, administrative personnel, any teacher, or any other person authorized to be in charge of a school function or event, including but not limited to, bus drivers in the course of conveying students to and from school or school functions, are authorized to take such action in connection with student behavior as is reasonably desirable or necessary. Such action shall be taken to help any student, to further school purposes or to prevent an interference therewith, including, but not limited to counseling, parent conferences, assignment of additional work, rearrangement of class schedules, requiring the student to remain in school after regular school hours, or restriction of extracurricular activity.

(See Also: ABSENTEEISM; CITIZENSHIP; CORPORAL PUNISHMENT; CUTTING; DISCIPLINE; DUE PROCESS; EXPULSION; FIGHTING; REFERRAL; SUSPENSION)

BIDS

instructions to bidders (a sample)...

"5% BIDDER" PREFERENCE

1. Section 725, Paragraph 725.161, subparagraph (11) of the School District Purchasing–Contracting Policy states: "If two or more bids are substantially equal, preference may be given up to five percent (5%) not to exceed $5,000 preferential difference to bidders' maintaining offices within the school's area. For consideration for preference a bidder must include his State Business License Number with his bid."
2. Bidder shall check the box on the front of this form that indicates his eligibility for the "5% bidder" preference. Bidder shall also state his current State Business License Number in the space provided and the street address of his business location.

NONDISCRIMINATION

1. Bidders, in submitting bids, certify that if awarded a contract under this Invitation, they will not discriminate against any employee or applicant for employment because of race, color, religion, national origin, ancestry, age, or sex. The contractor will take affirmative action to ensure such nondiscrimination. Such action shall include, but not be limited to the following: employment, upgrading, demotion or transfer, recruitment or recruitment advertising, layoff or termination rates of pay or other forms of compensation, and selection for training, including apprenticeship. The contractor agrees to post in conspicuous places available to employees and applicants for employment, notices setting forth the provision of this nondiscrimination clause.

OCCUPATIONAL SAFETY AND HEALTH WARRANTY

1. Bidder, if awarded a contract, warrants that the product sold or service rendered to the buyer shall conform to the standards and/or regulations promulgated by the U.S. Department of Labor under the Occupational Safety and Health Act of 1970 (29 U.S.C. 651, PL 91-596). In the event the product sold does not conform to the OSHA standards and/or regulations, the buyer may return the product for correction or replacement at seller's option and at seller's expense. Services performed by the seller that do not conform to the OSHA standards and/or regulations must be corrected by seller at seller's expense or by buyer at seller's expense in the event seller fails to make the appropriate correction within a reasonable time.

FEDERAL EXCISE TAXES

1. The School District is exempt from Federal Excise Taxes. An Exemption Certificate will be furnished when required.

PROTECTION OF EQUIPMENT

1. The contractor assumes full responsibility for and shall indemnify the School District for any loss or damage to any School District property, including any equipment, supplies, accessories, or parts furnished while in his custody and care for storage, repairs, or services to be performed under the terms of the contract, resulting in whole or in part from the negligent acts or omissions of the contractors, or any employee, agent or representative of the contractor.

INSURANCE

1. The contractor shall obtain all insurance required under this section and shall file copies of the insurance policies and/or Certificates of Insurance in the office of the Rock Township District Purchasing Department prior to the start of the project.
2. WORKMEN'S COMPENSATION AND EMPLOYER'S LIABILITY including Federal Longshoremen and Harborworkers Compensation Act and Federal Maritime Employer's Liability Law (Jones Act).

3. COMPREHENSIVE GENERAL LIABILITY

	LIMITS MEET OR EXCEED
Bodily Injury	$100,000 Each Occurrence
Premises Operations	$300,000 Aggregate
Independent Contractors	
Products–Completed Operations	
Blanket Contractual	
Property Damage–Broad Form	$ 50,000 Each Occurrence
Premises Operations	$ 50,000 Aggregate
Independent Contractors	
Products–Completed Operations	
Blanket Contractual	
Personal Injury Liability	$300,000 Aggregate
Explosion, Collapse & Underground	$ 50,000 Each Occurrence

4. COMPREHENSIVE GENERAL AUTOMOBILE

	LIMITS MEET OR EXCEED
Bodily Injury	$100,000 Each Person
	$300,000 Each Occurrence
Property Damage	$ 50,000 Each Occurrence

5. CERTIFICATES OF INSURANCE shall be in the name of The Township of Rock operating as the Rock Township School District.
6. The successful contractor agrees to pay for the insurance specified and agrees to provide the Director of Purchasing, Rock Township School District, with a thirty (30) day written notice of cancellation of nonrenewal of such insurance, if such cancellation or nonrenewal occurs during the contract period.

INDEMNIFICATION

1. Any and all employees of the contractor and other persons, while engaged in the performance of any work or services required by the contractor under this agreement shall not be considered employees of the Rock Township School District or the State.
2. Any and all claims that might arise under the Workman's Compensation Act on behalf of the contractor or other persons while engaged in the performance of the duties or services contemplated and any and all claims that might be made by any third person as a result of any act or failure to act shall be the contractor's sole obligation and the contractor shall indemnify the Rock Township School District and hold it harmless from any liability for any act or failure to act on the part of the contractor.

PRICING AND PAYMENT

1. Pricing for annual maintenance agreement shall be on a per unit basis for each type of typewriter listed on the Bid Form and for the period July 1, 1985 through June 30, 1986.

2. Payment for annual maintenance agreement shall be made on a prorated monthly or quarterly basis upon receipt of invoices. Invoices shall be signed by the building principal or his designee and shall specify the serial numbers of the typewriters serviced. Payment will be made at the end of each month or each quarter.
3. Separate purchase order(s) will be issued for typewriters at each location.
4. In the event of termination, the contract price will be prorated for the period of service rendered.

CANCELLATION

1. The School District may cancel the contract at any time during the contract period should the contractor fail to provide the service specified on a timely basis or for unsatisfactory performance.

PREBID CONFERENCE

1. A prebid conference will be held at 2:00 p.m., Local Time, April 24, 1985 in CONFERENCE ROOM #301, third floor of the School District Administration Building, 4600 DeBarr Avenue, Rock Township, to discuss any matter concerned with this Invitation.

BIDS

1. All bids shall follow the format on the BID FORMS.
2. Award will be made to the overall low bidder based on the approximate quantity of typewriters for annual maintenance agreement as shown on Exhibit 'A.'
3. Signed bids *must* be in the Office of the Purchasing Director, Rock Township School District, on or before 2:00 p.m., Local Time, May 6, 1985 at which time they will be opened and publicly read in CONFERENCE ROOM #301, third floor of the School District Administration Building, 4600 DeBarr Avenue, Rock Township.
4. Bids shall be delivered by the bidder in person or by a representative of the bidder.
5. Bid shall be addressed as follows:

   Purchasing Section
   Rock Township School District
   4600 DeBarr Avenue
   Rock Township

6. Bids *must* be in SEALED envelopes with the outside of the envelope clearly marked as follows:

   BID: MAINTENANCE AGREEMENT for IBM TYPEWRITERS
   Due 2:00 p.m., Local Time
   May 6, 1985

7. Late bids will not be considered and will be returned to the bidder unopened after the award of the Invitation.
8. All bids shall be submitted on the attached Bid Forms in the spaces indicated and must comply with these instructions.

9. The School District reserves the right to accept or reject any or all bids, consider alternates and further reserves the right to waive informalities in bidding procedures.

FORMAL AWARD

1. Formal award of bids may be made by the School Board at their regular meeting to be held at 4:30 p.m., Local Time, May 19, 1985, in the School District Administration Building Board Room, 4600 DeBarr Avenue, Rock Township.

invitation to bid...

Sealed Bids Will Be Received Until TIME: 2:00 p.m., Local Time DATE: May 6, 1985	INVITATION TO BID THIS IS NOT AN ORDER Rock Township School District PURCHASING SECTION ROCK TOWNSHIP DATE ISSUED: April 10, 1985	Show the following on outside of Bid Envelope: INVITATION: MAINTENANCE AGREEMENT for IBM TYPEWRITERS DATE: May 6, 1985 DUE: 2:00 p.m., Local Time May 6, 1985

MAINTENANCE AGREEMENT for IBM TYPEWRITERS as per the attached Instructions to Bidders (5 pages), the Specifications (4 pages), Exhibit 'A' (3 pages), and the Bid Form (2 pages).

RESPONSE REQUIRED: Your response, whether you are bidding or not, is our only indication of interest in School District business. To assure continued receipt of invitations when not bidding, return only the "Bid Form" with the statement "No Bid All items" or "No Bid This Invitation" on its face and the name of your firm. Continued failure to do so will result in automatic removal of your firm from the commodity or service listing selected for this Invitation.

PREBID CONFERENCE: A prebid conference will be held at 2:00 p.m., Local Time, April 24, 1985, in CONFERENCE ROOM #301, third floor of the School District Administration Building, 4600 DeBarr Avenue, Rock Township, to discuss any matter concerned with this Invitation.

legal advertisement...

INVITATION TO BID

NOTICE IS HEREBY GIVEN that the Rock Township School District will consider bids for:

MAINTENANCE AGREEMENT for IBM TYPEWRITERS

A prebid conference will be held at 2:00 p.m., Local Time, April 24, 1985, in CONFERENCE ROOM #301, third floor of the School Administration Building, 4600 DeBarr Avenue, Rock Township, to discuss any matter concerned with this Invitation.

Bids must be submitted in single copy on the Bid Form provided no later than 2:00 p.m., Local Time, May 6, 1985, at which time they will be opened and publicly read in CONFERENCE ROOM #301, third floor of the School District Administration Building, 4600 DeBarr Avenue, Rock Township.

Bids must be in accordance with the specifications and general conditions available at the office of the Purchasing Director, telephone 555-9561, extension 341, or by addressing the Rock Township School District, Attention: Purchasing Department, 4600 DeBarr Avenue, Rock Township.

The School District reserves the right to accept or reject any or all bids and to waive informalities in bidding procedures.

Harold G. Cruthers,
Director of Purchasing

letter to unsuccessful bidders...

Subject: INVITATION TO BID

This is to inform you that the School Board, at their regular meeting held on May 19, 1985, awarded the item on subject Invitation to Bid to Mountainview Corporation.

Attached herewith is your bid security for this Invitation to Bid and also a copy of the Tabulation of Bids received for your information and file.

Thank you for participating in this Invitation and we shall look forward to your future participation as our needs exist.

Very truly yours,

Rock Township School District

Harold G. Cruthers,
Director of Purchasing

(See Also: BOARD OF EDUCATION; BUDGET: BUSINESS; EQUIPMENT; MONEY; PURCHASING; REQUISITIONS, REPAIRS, AND REPLACEMENTS; VENDORS)

BILINGUAL EDUCATION

letter to parents...

Dear Parent:

We are very pleased to announce that the Rock Township School District is beginning one of the most modern and extensive English to Speakers of Other Languages (ESOL) programs in the United States. Through its intensive curriculum, the student learns all of the communication skills and courses of study necessary to become a successful student.

Classes are very specialized since students are grouped according to language proficiency level and academic background. Beginning non-English speaking students receive four ESOL classes per day, plus regular content courses at one of our ten High Intensity Language Training (HILT) centers located on junior and senior high school campuses throughout the district. As the ESOL student progresses, he or she gains English skills and begins to earn higher grades. The student actually enjoys being in class.

ESOL teachers are specialized in their craft using the most effective up-to-date methods, materials, books, and equipment. Students are prepared for communication in everyday life along with the specialized language they will need for math, science, and social studies.

Successfully tested this past year in one of our high schools, the ESOL program produced remarkable results. In high school all credit accrued is applied toward graduation requirements.

We are very optimistic that this total curriculum program will help non-English speaking students meet their academic aspirations. Though students have very high standards to maintain, classes remain enjoyable and teachers and counselors make every effort to help. We hope you will visit one of our HILT centers.

Your son/daughter would attend the HILT center on this campus. We would like your permission to enroll your son/daughter in this excellent program. Would you please give us your permission by signing the enclosed, self-addressed, stamped postcard. Please return by mail at your earliest possible convenience.

Sincerely,

____

Principal

____

School

____

Telephone

translation of letter to parents into Spanish...

Estimados Padres:

Al fin hemos realizado nuestro sueño de poder ofrecerles a sus hijos uno de los programas más modernos y extensos de inglés (ESOL: ENGLISH FOR SPEAKERS OF OTHER LANGUAGES). El Distrito Escolar de Rock Township tiene mucho gusto en comunicarles esta muy grata noticia. Como Ud. comprende, el dominio del idioma es indispensable para que el alumno pueda cursar sus estudios con éxito. A través de esta serie de cursos intesivos, los alumnos adquieren los elementos de comunicación que los capacita para comprender cualquier materia.

Las classes son altamente especializadas ya que a los alumnos se les agrupa de acuerdo con sus conocimientos del idioma y su aprovechamiento académico. A los alumnos principiantes en inglés se les imparte hasta 4 clases de ESOL al día, además de otros cursos (matemáticas, ciencia, etc.). Estos cursos se impartirán en centros denominados "Centros de Capacitación Intensiva en el Idioma" (HILT: HIGH INTENSITY LANGUAGE TRAINING CENTERS). Los 10 centros están distribuídos entre las escuelas junior y high school del distrito escolar.

Naturalmente, al aumentar su competencia en el inglés, el alumno de ESOL se sentirá feliz al comprobar su progreso en todas las materias y la mejoría en sus calificaciones. Igualmente, verá como se le capacita para comunicarse en la vida diaria además de aprender el inglés especializado que necesita para las matemáticas, las ciencias y las ciencias sociales. En high school todos los créditos acumulados en estos cursos se aplicarán a los requeridos para graduarse.

Un programa tan efectivo como éste cuenta con maestros de ESOL especializados en su materia y que usan únicamente los métodos, materiales, libros, y equipo más modernos y eficientes. Las pruebas del programa que se llevaron a cabo el año pasado en de nuestras secundarias tuvieron resultados extraordinariamente positivos.

Tenemos plena confianza de que este programa total ayudará a los alumnos que no hablan actualmente el inglés a realizar sus aspiraciones académicas. Principalmente, nos hemos esforzado en que las clases sean amenas a pesar de lo que se le exige al alumno. Los maestros y los consejeros siempre estarán prestos a brindar su ayuda. Los invitamos a que visiten uno de nuestros centros HILT.

Su hijo(a) podrá asistir al centro HILT ubicado en esta escuela. Con su permiso su hijo(a) podrá beneficiarse de este programa extraordinario. Haga Ud. el favor de dar su permiso firmando la tarjeta postal aunada. Regrésela por correo lo más pronto posible. No es necesario ponerle estampilla.

Atentamente,

____

Director(a)

____

Escuela/Tel.

(See Also: COUNSELING; EDUCATION; NEW POLICY OR PROGRAM; PHILOSOPHY)

BOARD OF EDUCATION

citizen's request for audience with board of education...

CITIZEN'S REQUEST
For Audience with the Board of Education

Request initiated by ______________________________
Address ______________________________ Telephone ______________
Date to appear on agenda ______________________________

1. Petitioner represents _____ Self only
   _____ Organization (Name of Organization) ______________
   _____ Other group (Identify group) ______________
2. Name of spokesperson ______________________________
3. If more than one person is to speak, please list persons other than spokesperson.
   ____
4. Nature of concern ____ Board Policy No. ________ ____ General Input
   ____ Administrative Procedure ____ Other (Specify)
   ____ Personnel Complaint
5. State the nature of your concern.
   ____
   ____
   ____
   ____
6. Is this an individual concern? _____ Yes _____ No
7. Is this a district-wide concern? _____ Yes _____ No
8. What school personnel have you contacted in an attempt to resolve the concern?
   _____ Board member(s) _____ Building Principal(s)
   _____ Superintendent _____ Teacher(s)
   _____ Central Office Administrator(s) _____ Other (Specify) ______________
9. Have you exhausted appropriate administrative channels? _____Yes _____ No
10. Board Policy specifies a maximum of a 10-minute presentation. Do you anticipate your presentation will take more than 10 minutes? _____ Yes _____ No
11. If yes, how much total time do you anticipate? ______________
12. Do you have additional written documentation to present to the Board?
    _____Yes _____ No
13. What is your expectation of the Board of Education at the conclusion of your presentation?
    ____
    ____
    ____

______________________ ______________________

Date Signature of Petitioner

explanation of board functions for community brochure...

The purpose of this brochure is to acquaint you with how the Board of School Trustees of the Rock Township Schoools is structured and how it operates.

Public control of education is one of the cornerstones of a free society. The people exercise that control through their Board of School Trustees. So that you can take a more active part in its deliberations and operations, this brochure will explain how you can bring matters of concern to the attention of the board. We hope that this introduction will be just the starting point for your understanding and support of school affairs.

BOARD MEMBERS

Your Board of School Trustees is composed of seven citizens elected to serve overlapping terms of four years each. At the end of his/her terms, a board member wishing to continue service to the community must be reelected to an additional four-year term. State law does not limit the number of terms a member may serve.

Current board members and their terms of office are:

Office	Member	Term
President		
Vice Pres.		
Secretary		
Dep. Secy.		
Member		
Member		
Member		

BOARD MEETINGS

The Board of School Trustees meets regularly on the second and fourth Wednesdays of each month in the School Administration Building. All meetings start at 7:30 p.m. Occasionally a holiday occurs on Wednesday and will alter the schedule. In such case, a public notice is made well in advance of the change of date. Special Board meetings are rarely called. However, when a need does arise public notice is given. All official business of the Board is transacted in open session and minutes are recorded.

BOARD ACTIONS

No one person or group of persons acts in the name of the board. When an item of business comes before them in the form of a motion, it is necessary that a majority of the board members present vote in favor of the motion before it becomes official. No less than four Board members must be present to conduct an official Board meeting.

The Board has complete and final control over local school matters subject only to limitation imposed by State Law, Rules and Regulations of the State Department of Public Instruction, or common law. Primarily, the board has the responsibility to establish policies by which the Green County Schools are operated. To carry out these policies, the board employs administrators, teachers and classified personnel.

SUPERINTENDENT OF SCHOOLS

The Superintendent of Schools is appointed by the board and acts as its executive officer in administering its policies in the operation of the schools. He also acts as advisor in keeping the Board informed of the needs and progress of the schools.

A BOARD MEETING

Meetings of the Board follow a standard agenda. You may secure a copy of tonight's agenda from the table at the rear of the Board room.

Normally, at the beginning and at the conclusion of the agenda, there is recognition of visitors. During this portion of the meeting any resident of Rock Township is permitted to make a brief statement, express his viewpoint, or ask a question regarding matters related to the school system. It is the desire of the board to make this time available to residents, but if the pressure of business or circumstances dictate, the Board president may decide to limit the amount of time for this portion of the agenda.

(Note: The Board's function is decision making. It wants to hear the sentiments of the public to assist in making those decisions, but time spent

answering routine questions or criticisms must be taken from important Board business. If a resident has a question about the operation of the schools, he is encouraged to contact the teacher or administrator closest to the situation. Experience has shown that this is the best procedure. The questioner gets a response immediately and directly.)

BOARD MEETING DATES

January 13 - 27	July 14 - 28
February 10 - 24	August 11 - 18 - 26
March 10 - 24	September 8 - 22
April 14 - 28	October 13 - 27
May 12 - 26	November 10 - 22
June 9 - 23	December 8 - 22

(See also all those topics in which the Board of Education is involved such as BIDS, PURCHASING, etc., as well as those over which the Board holds control such as EXPULSION, SUSPENSION, etc. There are over 150 such headings in this book.)

BOMB THREATS

procedures for (1)...

BOMB THREAT (within the school)

A. A threat to bomb a school can never be taken lightly, for it is impossible to determine in advance whether the threat is serious or the work of a prankster.

B. The following procedures will be initiated:

1. Notify the Policy Department. The telephone number is 555-6676.
2. Execute action LEAVE BUILDING.
3. Notify the Fire Department. The telephone number is 555-5431.
4. Notify the School District Office Civil Defense Coordinator, or other appropriate school official.
5. Take roll. Teachers to develop procedure for quick roll taking. Initiate a search for any student found to be missing.
6. Caution *all* personnel against picking up or touching strange objects. IT COULD BE A BOMB.
7. *Students and staff should not return to the school until the Police Department or Fire Department officials declare the school safe.*

procedures for (2)...

In the event that the school should receive a bomb threat, the following actions will be implemented:

A. The individual taking the incoming call will be immediately questioned by the principal or person in charge. If the person taking the call felt that the caller was serious (or even if there is the *suspicion* that it *might* be serious), initiate the following:

   1. Clear the school using normal Fire Drill procedures.
   2. Call the police and fire departments.
   3. Notify the Central Administration Office of your action, then clear the building yourself and await further notice from police or an administrator from Central Administration.

B. If the person taking the call indicates that it is most likely a prank (giggling caller, young child's voice, etc.), you may, at your discretion, initiate the following:

   1. Get on the public address system and announce, "ATTENTION TEACHERS, WE NEED YOUR ROOM INVENTORY AT THIS TIME."
   2. Teachers will immediately and *personally* initiate a search of their classrooms.
      a. If nothing suspicious is found, they will send a note to the office stating "Room number – inventory O.K."
      b. If *anything* suspicious is found, the teacher will LEAVE IT ALONE, immediately send a note to the office stating, "Room number – object," and will immediately evacuate the class using Fire Drill procedures for that room.
   3. Upon receiving no notes from teachers indicating a foreign object in the rooms, the office may or may not initiate procedures under A above, upon discretion of the administrator involved.
   4. Should a note be received indicating a foreign object, the administrator will immediately initiate procedures under A above.

C. The administrator in each school will familiarize the faculty and staff of the school with the above procedures and hold at least one drill of these procedures within the first month of each school year.

D. REMEMBER: IF YOU ARE IN DOUBT, CONSIDER THE SAFETY OF THE STUDENTS TO BE OF OVERRIDING IMPORTANCE. WHEN IN DOUBT—EVACUATE THE SCHOOL.

(See Also: EMERGENCY; FIRE DRILLS)

BOOKS

book fine information...

Textbooks are loaned to students free of charge. However, students are responsible for lost or damaged books and will be expected to pay for them. The amount charged for lost or damaged textbooks, library books and resource books will be determined by the administration according to the original value of the book. The following schedule will be used as a guideline for most books:

a. Undue wear of book	$2.00
b. Unreasonable damage or loss of books	
One year old	8.00
Two years old	6.00
Three years old	4.00
c. Loss of book over three years old	3.00

book fine notice...

Date: ______________ Student: ______________________________
Grade: ______________ Teacher: ______________________________

The student named above has incurred the following book fine(s):

BOOK	REASON FOR FINE	AMOUNT OF FINE	TEACHER'S INITIALS

ordering books, instructions...

TO: Principals
FROM: District Superintendent
SUBJECT: Library Book Order Through CPC—1984–1985

Each school desiring to order library books through the State's Centralized Processing Center (CPC) shall complete the attached Form E-6, "Funds for School Library Books and Encyclopedias to be Processed Through CPC."

The amount to be committed to CPC shall be reflected in your school's Expenditure Plan (Form E-1) for the SECOND QUARTER. Be sure to record the amount committed to CPC in your Control Ledger and Sub-Ledger.

Books to be purchased with school-issued purchase orders may be purchased during any fiscal quarter.

DUE DATE: Submit two copies (original and first copy) of your CPC Commitment List to the District Business Office no later than April 30.

ordering books, form for...

FUNDS FOR SCHOOL LIBRARY BOOKS AND
ENCYCLOPEDIAS TO BE PROCESSED THROUGH CPC

Fiscal Year ________

School ______________________________ Date ____________
By ______________________________

Description	Amount
Hardback Books	$ ________
Paperbacks	________
Encyclopedias	________
*Sub-total to be transferred to CPC	________
**Purchase orders to be issued by school	________
TOTAL AVAILABLE FOR SCHOOL LIBRARY BOOKS	$ ________

*This amount should be reflected in the SECOND QUARTER of the expenditure plan of the school for transfer to CPC. Schools will follow the Book Order Schedule during the year up to this amount.

**This amount is the 10% or 20% schools normally use to purchase directly from vendors through the school's own purchase orders. This amount should be reflected in the expenditure plan in the quarter or quarters in which the purchase orders are expected to be issued by the school.

For opening-day collection for new schools where independent contracts are executed, the amount need not be reported.

(See Also: ASSIGNMENTS; BOARD OF EDUCATION; BUDGET; ELECTIVES; FEES, FINES, FUNDS AND CHARGES; HANDBOOK; HOMEWORK; LIBRARY; OBJECTIVES; REQUISITIONS, REPAIRS, AND REPLACEMENTS; TEXTBOOKS)

BUDGET

a special note...

The following is a complete budget "package" for current services operating budgets sent to principals of all schools within a district. It contains not only instructions but all forms necessary for filling out a thorough and effective budget. As such, it is indicative of all good budget procedures, whatever the classification and whatever forms may be peculiar to a specific school system.

instructions...

TO: All Principals
SUBJECT: Instructions for Preparation of School Level Operating Budgets for 1984–1985 and 1985–1986 — CURRENT SERVICES

Prepare and submit your *current services* operating budgets for the 1984–86 biennium according to the following guidelines:

I. BUDGET PROCEDURE

Adhere to the guidelines outlined and involve teachers, other staff members, and consult with school level Advisory Council in the budget development.

II. BUDGET BY PROGRAM

Prepare the budget to reflect resource requirements for the following programs:

A. Regular Instruction — EDN 105
B. Instructional Media — EDN 204
C. School Level Administration — EDN 203

A. REGULAR INSTRUCTION

1. Regular instruction includes all K-12 programs for regular students. Exclude all special education students.
2. Budget Items Under Regular Instruction
   a. Under regular instruction, budget for the following:
      (1) Supplies, Instructional
      This includes all workbooks, general classroom and special supplies including audio-visual supplies.
      (2) Equipment, Instructional
      This includes all classroom, instructional equipment, as well as audio-visual equipment.
      (3) Textbooks
      This includes all textbooks—soft and hard cover, and all reference books used specifically for instruction and *not* kept in the library.

   Note: DO NOT BUDGET FOR EXCURSIONS AND FIELD TRIPS.

B. INSTRUCTIONAL MEDIA

Budget for Instructional Media shall include:

a. Library Supplies (includes newspapers and magazines)............. Supplies Category
b. Library Equipment.. Equipment Category
c. Library Books .... Books Category

C. SCHOOL ADMINISTRATION

Budget all non-classroom supplies and equipment within this program including requirements for first aid, mileage, postage, etc.

The recommended budget for school administration is about 10% of the total ceiling.

III. BUDGET PREPARATION

A. CEILING

1. Prepare your budgets within the dollar budget ceiling allotted for each fiscal year in the biennium.
2. The budget ceiling allotted to each school is lump sum for current services and includes regular instruction, instructional media, and school administration.
3. While the budget ceiling allotted is lump sum, the school's budget submittal (on Form BPS-2) for current services must reflect budget requirements by programs—regular instruction, instructional media and school administration—and by objects within each program (supplies, equipment, textbooks, etc.)
   The principal determines the amounts for each program. The aggregate of the programs shall not exceed the lump sum ceiling.

B. EXCLUSIONS

Schools are not to budget for the following programs:

1. "A" requirements for personal services, inclusive of teachers, custodians, clerical personnel, cafeteria personnel and others.
2. Counseling services
3. Vo-Tech programs
4. Driver Education
5. English Program (HEP)
6. Secondary English Program (SEP)
7. Compensatory Education (CSAP)
8. PPB Math
9. PPB Vo-Tech
10. PPB Practical Arts
11. SLEP
12. All Federal projects—Title I, ESAA, etc.

C. BUDGET REQUEST

1. Current Services
   Current Services refers to the resources required to provide the same kind and amount of goods and services authorized for the current fiscal biennium (1984–1986) which are deemed appropriate and essential for continuance during the ensuing fiscal biennium (1987–1989).
   a. The school's budget request for current services for the biennium 1984–1986 shall be presented on Form BPS-2 for Regular Instruction, Instructional Media and School Administration.

   NOTE: The current services budget ceiling for regular education, instructional media, and school administration takes into account each school's projected enrollment for each fiscal year in the 1984–1986 biennium. Budget for workload increase will not be required.
2. Budget for Equipment Replacement Beyond Ceiling
   a. Schools that have equipment replacement needs that cannot be budgeted within the allotted budget ceiling will prepare a separate budget for replacement needs.
   b. Instructions and procedures will be issued separately (Budget Procedure B-1A).

D. BUDGET FORMS AND FORMAT

1. To enable teacher involvement and participation in the budget process, prepared budget forms are issued for your use.
2. Unless indicated otherwise, the following general instructions shall apply to all forms:
   a. Prepare separately for 1984–1985 and 1985–1986 in duplicate. Show estimated cost for all items.
   b. Reflect and include freight, postage and applicable estimated tax in the cost.
   c. Budget request forms—Teachers prepare budget request forms; Department head and/or grade-level chairpersons review budget forms.
   d. Principal reviews items and approves or deletes as necessary.
   e. Reflect the aggregate cost of all approved items on Budget Form BPS-2.
   f. The aggregate of all items approved by the principal shall not exceed the allotted budget ceiling.
   g. Name of Vendor—If vendor is known, indicate. If not known, leave blank.
   h. Textbooks—titles
   It may be too early to list titles as new books may come on the market later. Instead of titles, list Category and Subject. For example, Basal math textbooks, math reference books, etc. Textbook needs must correspond with the school's multi-year textbook plan—Form SO-0201.
   i. Library Books—Titles
   If titles known, list. If exact titles not known, list by Subject or Category.
   j. Prices—Allow for inflation. Figure 8% above 1983 for 1984–1985; 8% more over 1984–1985 for 1985–1986.
3. The following budget forms have been prepared for use by the school staff in the preparation of your budgets. Except for Form BPS-2, schools may duplicate the forms or call the District Business Office for additional forms. Type, print, or write information legibly on all forms. Form BPS-2 must be typed.
   a. Regular Instruction
      (1) Form BR-CT—REQUEST FOR TEXTBOOKS
         (a) Use to reflect new and additional textbooks required, inclusive of hard and soft cover books, and subject matter reference books not kept in the library.
         (b) Textbook needs must correspond with school's multi-year textbook plan. The textbook plan may be updated so that budget requests and plans correspond. Update must be made for all future years.
      (2) Form BR-CI—REQUEST FOR INSTRUCTIONAL EQUIPMENT
         (a) Use to indicate all instructional equipment used in the classroom or for the various subject elements, OTHER THAN audio-visual equipment.
         (b) Equipment needs must correspond to school's multi-year plan for equipment, Form SO-0202.
      (3) Form BR-BI—REQUEST FOR INSTRUCTIONAL MATERIALS AND SUPPLIES
         (a) Reflect all instructional materials and supplies used in the classroom or for the various subject elements OTHER THAN audio-visual supplies.
      (4) Form BR-BRM—REQUEST FOR A.V. SUPPLIES AND R&M OF A.V. EQUIPMENT
      Reflect all audio-visual instructional materials and supplies and *repairs and maintenance* of audio-visual equipment (to be part of regular instruction). Note: R&M of A.V. equipment must be separated on form.

(5) Form BR-CM—REQUEST FOR AUDIO-VISUAL EQUIPMENT
   (a) Prepared by the audio-visual coordinator and classroom teachers.
   (b) List all audio-visual equipment for use in the instructional process.

b. Instructional Media
Type, print, or write legibly on these forms.
(1) Form BR-BL—REQUEST FOR LIBRARY SUPPLIES
   (a) This form is used by the librarian or instructional media personnel only.
   (b) Reflect only library supplies and materials.
(2) Form BR-CL—REQUEST FOR LIBRARY EQUIPMENT
   (a) Used by the librarian or media personnel.
   (b) Indicate only library equipment. DO NOT indicate library furniture or audio-visual equipment.
(3) Form BR-CR—REQUEST FOR LIBRARY BOOKS
   (a) Used by all teachers and library staff.
   (b) Reflect all library books and reference books kept in the library. Subject area reference books kept in the classrooms should be budgeted on Form BR-CI.

c. School Level Administration
Type, print, or write legibly on these forms.
(1) Prepare a separate set for each fiscal year of the biennium.
(2) Form BR-BSA—REQUEST FOR SUPPLIES—SCHOOL ADMINISTRATION
   (a) On this form, indicate requirements for all non-classroom supplies, inclusive of mileage funds for staff, postage, R&M of office equipment, etc. Do not include librarian's mileage.
   (b) List requirements by object of expenditure.
   (c) Use your current level of expenditure as a guide.
(3) Form BR-CSA—REQUEST FOR EQUIPMENT—SCHOOL ADMINISTRATION
   (a) List all non-classroom equipment required.
   (b) Do not include any instructional or audio-visual equipment.
   (c) Items listed may include replacements as well as additional items.

IV. BUDGET SUMMARY AND SUBMITTAL

A. BUDGET SUMMARY

1. The principal shall review budget requests from all school level programs and subprograms. He/she may include school level parent advisory council in the review.
2. The aggregate of all requests for current services shall not exceed the allotted budget ceilings.
3. Budget requests for all programs shall be summarized for each of the two fiscal years in the biennium: 1984–1985 and 1985–1986.
4. Round off to nearest dollar.
5. Form
   a. Form BPS-2 (white)—(Mandatory for Submittal)
      (1) The school's operating budget request shall be summarized on budget request Form BPS-2. This form is for current services only. Note: Adjustment for enrollment already considered in establishing school's budget ceiling.
      (2) The summaries of both fiscal years are to be reflected on a single form.
      (3) Total horizontally (biennium total for each category) and vertically (fiscal year and biennium grand total).

(4) Prepare three copies of Form BPS-2.
(5) Form must be typed.
(6) Do not use your own form. Submit forms issued by the District.

B. TRANSMITTAL

Please transmit budget documents as follows:

Form BPS-2 (white)—two copies

Note: ALL BUDGET FORMS prepared for current services by the school staff shall be kept in complete sets by fiscal year (1984–1985 and 1985–1986) and sent in to the District Superintendent upon request. DO NOT DESTROY.

V. DUE DATE: Please submit your operating budget to the District Office by March 15, 1983.

summary of school budget request...

EDN 105 - Regular Instruction
EDN 204 - Instructional Media
EDN 203 - School Administration
School Levels B & C

BPS-2

SCHOOL LEVEL OPERATION BUDGET
SUMMARY OF SCHOOL REQUEST

BUDGET CEILING **19 -19**
19 - ____________
19 - ____________
Type all information.
Round off to nearest dollar.

School ____________
Grade Levels: ____________
Submitted by:

____
Principal's Signature

PROGRAMS	Total Fiscal Year 19 -	Total Fiscal Year 19 -	Total Biennium 19 -
A. REGULAR EDUCATION (EDN 105) Textbooks			
Equipment–Include A.V. Equipment			
Supplies–Include A.V., R&M and Supplies			
Regular Instruction Total			
B. INSTRUCTIONAL MEDIA (EDN 204) Library Supplies			
Library Equipment			
Library Books			
Instructional Media Total			
C. SCHOOL ADMINISTRATION (EDN 203) School Administration Supplies			
School Administration Equipment			
School Administration Total			
GRAND TOTAL			

budget request worksheet...

BR-CT

Prepare in Duplicate

For: (Check appropriate)
______ Regular Education
______ Special Education

SCHOOL LEVEL
BUDGET REQUEST WORKSHEET

TEXTBOOKS

19 -19

School ______________________

Prepared by: ______________________

Reviewed by: ______________________

TEXTBOOKS (List Titles)	VENDOR/PUBLISHER	QUANTITY			Unit Cost	Total Cost	JUSTIFICATION
		No. on Hand	Date Acquired	Replacement/ Addt'l Needs			
TOTAL COST							

APPROVED BY:

____
(for) District Superintendent

instructional equipment budget worksheet...

BR-CI

Prepare in Duplicate

For (Check appropriate):
______ Regular Education
______ Special Education

Note: Do not list:
A.V. Equipment
Library Equipment
Non-Classroom Equipment

SCHOOL LEVEL
BUDGET REQUEST WORKSHEET

INSTRUCTIONAL EQUIPMENT

19 -19

School: ________________

Prepared by: ________________

Reviewed by: ________________
Principal

EQUIPMENT ITEM	VENDOR	No. on Hand	Date Acquired	Replacement/ Addt'l Needs	Unit Cost	Total Cost	JUSTIFICATION
TOTAL COST							

APPROVED BY:

____
(for) District Superintendent

instructional materials and supplies budget worksheet...

BR-BI

Prepare in Duplicate

For: (Check appropriate)
______ Regular Education
______ Special Education

Note: Do not list any A.V. materials or supplies on this form.

SCHOOL LEVEL
BUDGET REQUEST WORKSHEET

INSTRUCTIONAL MATERIALS & SUPPLIES

19 -19

School: ______________________
Prepared by: ______________________
Reviewed by: ______________________
Principal

DESCRIPTION	Quantity Needed	Unit Cost	Total Cost	JUSTIFICATION
1. Workbooks–Student				
2. Magazines–Student				
3. Pamphlets				
4. Test Materials				
5. General Supplies				
6. Other Special Supplies (List)				
TOTAL COST				

APPROVED BY:

____
District Office

audio-visual supplies, repairs, and maintenance budget worksheet

Prepare in Duplicate

BR-BRM

SCHOOL LEVEL
BUDGET REQUEST WORKSHEET

AUDIO-VISUAL SUPPLIES
and
REPAIRS & MAINTENANCE-A.V. EQPT.
19 -19

School: ______________
Prepared by: ______________
Reviewed by: ______________
Principal

DESCRIPTION	Quantity Needed	Unit Cost	Total Cost	JUSTIFICATION
Filmstrips and slides				
Microfilms				
Transparencies				
Phonograph Records				
Tapes–Audio				
Tapes–Video				
Other–A.V. Supplies				
TOTAL COST AUDIO-VISUAL SUPPLIES				◀ TO BE REPORTED SEPARATELY ON SUMMARY OF REQUEST

REPAIRS & MAINTENANCE TO AUDIO-VISUAL EQUIPMENT

REPAIRS & MAINTENANCE TO A.V. EQUIPMENT ▶		TO BE REPORTED SEPARATELY ON SUMMARY OF REQUEST

APPROVED BY:

____
District Office

audio-visual equipment budget worksheet...

BR-CM

Prepare in Duplicate

For: (Check appropriate)
_____ Regular Education
_____ Special Education

SCHOOL LEVEL
BUDGET REQUEST WORKSHEET

AUDIO-VISUAL EQUIPMENT

19 -19

School: __________
Prepared by: __________
Reviewed by: __________
Principal

A.V. EQUIPMENT	VENDOR	QUANTITY			Unit Cost	Total Cost	JUSTIFICATION
		No. on Hand	Date Acquired	Additional Needed			
TOTAL COST							

Justification Key: a – increase in enrollment
b – replacement
c – program needs

APPROVED BY:

____
District Office

library supplies budget worksheet...

BR-BL

Prepare in Duplicate
Note: Do not list any audio-visual supplies on this form.

SCHOOL LEVEL
BUDGET REQUEST WORKSHEET

LIBRARY SUPPLIES

19 -19

School: ______
Prepared by: ______
Reviewed by: ______
Principal

DESCRIPTION	Quantity Needed	Unit Cost	Total Cost	JUSTIFICATION
Magazines				
Professional Magazines				
Newspapers				
Other Library Supplies				
Librarian's Mileage				
Library Administration				
TOTAL COST				

APPROVED BY:

______
District Office

library equipment budget worksheet...

BR-CL

Prepare in Duplicate

Note: Do not list A.V. equipment on this form.

SCHOOL LEVEL
BUDGET REQUEST WORKSHEET

LIBRARY EQUIPMENT

19 -19

School: __________
Prepared by: __________
Reviewed by: __________
Principal

DESCRIPTION OF LIBRARY EQUIPMENT	Vendor	Quantity	Unit Cost	Total Cost	JUSTIFICATION
TOTAL COST–LIBRARY EQUIPMENT					

APPROVED BY:

____
District Office

library books budget worksheet...

BR-CR

Prepare in Duplicate

Note: All library books, including reference and paperback books, are to be listed.

SCHOOL LEVEL
BUDGET REQUEST WORKSHEET

LIBRARY BOOKS

19 -19

School: ____________________
Prepared by: ____________________
Reviewed by: ____________________
Principal

LIBRARY BOOKS	Vendor	Quantity	Unit Cost	Total Cost	JUSTIFICATION
TOTAL COST–LIBRARY BOOKS					

APPROVED BY:

____
(for) District Superintendent

school administration equipment budget request...

BR-CSA

Prepare in Duplicate.
Prepare separately for each fiscal year.

SCHOOL LEVEL
BUDGET REQUEST

SCHOOL ADMINISTRATION EQUIPMENT

19 -19

Division: INSTITUTIONAL SUPPORT
Program: SCHOOL ADMINISTRATION
School: ______
Prepared by: ______

EQUIPMENT DESCRIPTION	Number of Units	Unit Cost	Total Cost	JUSTIFICATION
TOTAL				

school administration supplies budget request...

Prepare in Duplicate.
Prepare separately for
each fiscal year.

BR-BSA

Division: INSTITUTIONAL SUPPORT
Program: SCHOOL ADMINISTRATION
School: ____________
Prepared by: ____________

SCHOOL LEVEL
BUDGET REQUEST

SCHOOL ADMINISTRATION SUPPLIES

19 -19

DESCRIPTION	Object Code	19 -19	19 -19
Stationery & Office Supplies	3201		
Postage	3701		
Private Car Mileage—Employee	4111		
Other Freight & Delivery Charges	3602		
Other Advert. & Publication Notices	4001		
Rental of Office Equipment	5601		
Other Rental of Equipment	5701		
R & M Office Furn. Equip.	5806		
Dues	3501		
Subscriptions	3502		
Other Misc. Current Expenditures	7207		

BUILDING

application for use of school auditorium...

____________________ USING ORGANIZATION ________ BUP NO. ________ DATE OF EVENT

Auditorium Manager or Assistant will be present for all activities scheduled in West High Auditorium. When staffing charges are assessed for the facility, two District people will be on duty in the theater and are included in the base fee. When staffing charges are not assessed, the additional person may be supplied upon request at a rate consistent with District cost.

West High Auditorium is capable of supplying 100-3 ph. amps of power. A limited amount of additional power may sometimes be brought into the facility by special hook-up when advance arrangements have been made. The hook-up must be made by a School District electrician or under his/her direct supervision. An additional charge will be made for this service.

EQUIPMENT: (When using District equipment, all technicians employed by the user must be qualified and approved by the District.)

1. Are follow spots required? If yes, how many? (circle number) 1 2
2. Are light controls and dimmer panel required? Yes ______ No ______
3. Is sound control required? Yes ______ No ______
4. Is acoustical shell needed? Yes ______ No ______
   If yes, number of sections required ______
5. Is large stage projection screen required? Yes ______ No ______
6. Is projector required? (16 mm movie projector available) Yes ______ No ______
7. Is grand piano requested? Yes ______ No ______
8. Are risers requested? Yes ______ No ______
   Band (size and quantity) ____________ Choral (quantity) ____________

PERSONNEL: (District)

1. Is additional auditorium personnel required (for activities where staffing fees are not assessed)?
   Yes ______ No______ If yes, Date ____________ Time ____________
2. Is District electrician required for special hook-up? Yes ______ No______
   Date ______ Time ____________ Amount of power needed ____________

PERSONNEL: (User supplies)

1. Are there stage scene changes? Yes ______ No ______
   If yes, how many stage hands will be employed?______
2. Will there be concessions? (If yes, six (6) door attendants for auditorium lobby entrance doors are needed.) Yes ______ No ______
3. Follow spot operator(s)
4. Sound control operator
5. Light control operator
6. Number of security people/Name of security company: ____________
7. Parking lot attendants are required.
8. Showtimes: (1st) ________ (2nd) ________

Names of persons employed by the user to perform the above services and their assignments must be furnished to the School District Rental Office. (Please list on reverse side.)

____

SIGNATURE OF AGENT

building use permit (front and back)...

BUILDING USE PERMIT

SCHOOL ROOM NO. HOURS DATE OR DATES

THE USE OF SCHOOL FACILITIES IS AUTHORIZED AS SHOWN ABOVE

THE PREMISES WILL BE USED FOR
(SPECIFY TYPE AND PURPOSE OF ACTIVITY FULLY)

No. 22095

ORGANIZATION

DATE

MAILING
ADDRESS
ZIP CODE

PHONE NO.

BUILDING USE
REQUEST
SIGNED BY X

TITLE OF
OFFICER

SHOW PERMIT TO CUSTODIAN IN CHARGE OF BUILDING

ADDITIONAL INFORMATION

PURSUANT TO STATE LAW #18.35 ARTICLE IV, SMOKING WILL NOT BE PERMITTED IN ANY PORTION OF THE BUILDING COVERED BY THIS AGREEMENT.

COLLECTOR'S COPY

FOR ASSISTANCE ON WEEKENDS OR EVENINGS CALL 555-2417

DATE
APPROVED

RENTAL
OFFICER

SEE REVERSE SIDE FOR RULES AND REGULATIONS

RULES AND REGULATIONS

1. No person or group shall be entitled to the use of school facilities unless a permit for such use has been issued and signed by the Rental Officer.
2. Any financial or other commitment given by an applicant to another person, group or other concern, prior to the receipt in hand by such applicant of a Use Permit shall be at the applicant's own risk and shall have no bearing on the Rental Officer's issuance or denial of such a permit or his imposition of conditions on such a permit.
3. Any other permits required from police, fire, health or other governmental agencies must be obtained and copies presented to the Rental Officer prior to his issuance of any Use Permit.
4. Permit holders must comply with all applicable State and Federal laws, City ordinances, School District regulations, by-laws and policies, and permit conditions. All measures necessary to ensure the safe, healthy and lawful conduct of permit activities, including but not limited to crowd control measures and fire and police protection, shall be undertaken and financed by the permit holder.
5. Use Permits are limited to the specified room or rooms, during the hours and days specified. The permit holder shall insure that the remainder of the building used is not entered or molested. Facilities will be opened at the time scheduled for the activity to begin and closed at the time scheduled for its conclusion. The scheduled times must be adhered to strictly.
6. Use Permits include use of normal furniture and large equipment which is usually assigned to that particular area of the building (e.g., a piano in an auditorium). The permit holder will be expected to furnish his or her own expendable supplies (e.g., basketballs, ping pong balls, etc.).
7. Use of tobacco except in approved areas, possession or use of intoxicating liquor or illegal drugs, and fighting, betting or other forms of illegal gambling will not be allowed on the School District premises or within any facilities used.
8. Any damage to the building or equipment (other than normal wear and tear) will be charged to the permit holder. A cash bond in the amount of $5,000 will be required from sponsors who have previously sponsored activities which resulted in damage or when damage has previously occurred in connection with the type of activity for which a permit is sought.
9. The Rental Officer shall have authority to impose reasonable conditions, in addition to those specified in this section, when necessary.
10. The primary and priority use of school facilities shall be for the District's student educational program, including (but not limited to) programs sponsored by the school. A building use permit may be cancelled if facility is required for school use. A permit may also be cancelled due to fires, floods, earthquakes, labor disputes, epidemics, abnormal weather conditions, or acts of God.
11. If school kitchens are used, a School District Food Service employee must be present and have the general supervision of the kitchen and kitchen equipment. Additional labor fees are payable for this service.
12. Extra costs, including labor costs for special services performed by School District employees, will be charged to the using organization when such services are requested by the using organization.
13. If facility is not used in accordance with hours shown or additional personnel are required, a revised billing will be made.
14. Where an organization is being charged for the use of the facility, set-ups will be made by District Personnel and a custodian will be available to the organization during the time of use.
15. The Rental Officer may revoke a Use Permit for violations of this section which occur or come to the Rental Officer's attention after issuance of a Use Permit.

____

Signature of Organizational Representative

____

Title of Organizational Representative

building use request...

PLEASE PRINT BUILDING USE REQUEST

SCHOOL	ROOM NO.	HOURS	DATE OR DATES

THE UNDERSIGNED REQUEST THE USE OF SCHOOL FACILITIES ON THE DATE AND HOURS SHOWN ABOVE.

THE PREMISES WILL BE USED FOR:

ORGANIZATION DATE

MAILING ADDRESS PHONE NO.

ZIP CODE

Please sign reverse side and see rules and regulations.

CONFIRMATION TO USER WILL BE MAILED TO ADDRESSES GIVEN ABOVE.

ADDITIONAL INFORMATION:

follow-up report...

Building use permit #__________ Activity name ____________________

Activity date __________ Report date __________ Approx. attendance __________

Did hours of use in the auditorium coincide with hours requested on the permit? Yes_____ No_____

(If overtime was required, not in accordance with BUP, indicate time) __________

Reasons user requested overtime ____________________

Condition of carpet at conclusion of event:

Good _____ Fair _____ (explain) ____________________

Condition of seats at conclusion of event:

Good _____ Fair _____ (explain) ____________________

Condition of outside grounds & parking lot:

Good _____ Fair _____ (explain) ____________________

Were fire lanes, exits and entrances kept free of parked vehicles?	Yes_____	No_____
Were there enough qualified technicians provided by the user?	Yes_____	No_____
Did the user provide a refreshment concession in the lobby for this activity?	Yes_____	No_____
Was there adequate personnel provided to monitor theater entrances and lobby during intermission?	Yes_____	No_____
How many security personnel were provided for this activity?	__________	
Did user make any efforts to inform the public of State Law #18.35 Article IV, regarding smoking?	Yes_____	No_____
Did it appear that the user made a good faith effort to comply with District rules and regulations?	Yes_____	No_____

Additional comments:____________________

____

Signature of Auditorium Manager

licensing and safety confirmation...

PROMOTER'S LICENSING AND SURETY CONFIRMATION

Permit No. ____________ has been approved for ______________________________
(name of organization)

____ to use ______________
(facility)

____ for the purpose of presenting

____

(type of event – list of performing group)
pending receipt of the following by the School District Rental Office:

1. Balance of fee: ____
(Signature Rental Office)

2. Copy of insurance binder ($1,000,000 combined single limits property damage and public liability) naming the School District as additional insured.

____
(Signature Rental Office)

3. Cash damage deposit received: ______________________________________
(Signature Rental Office)

4. Proof of compliance with State requirements:

____
(Signature State Occupational Licensing Division Representative)

5. Proof of compliance with Municipal requirements:

a. ____
(Signature Municipal Risk Management Office)

b. ____
(Signature of Municipal Clerk's Office)

This document must be completed and returned to the Rental Office not less than 20 days prior to the event. The above permit becomes effective upon the District's receipt of the completed form.

____________ ____
Date (Signature of Rental Manager)

(See Also: AMERICAN EDUCATION WEEK; CUSTODIAL SERVICES; OPEN HOUSE; REQUISITIONS, REPAIRS, AND REPLACEMENTS; USE OF FACILITIES**)**

BULLETIN

example of daily school bulletin...

DAILY BULLETIN   FRIDAY   OCTOBER 4, 1985

DAILY BULLETINS ARE TO BE READ TO STUDENTS DURING PERIOD 2 EVERY SCHOOL DAY!

SOCCER NIGHT II:
SOCCER NIGHT II WILL BE THIS SATURDAY, OCTOBER 5, AT THE HIGH SCHOOL FIELD UNDER THE LIGHTS. THE GAME FEATURES ARCH-RIVALS ROCK TOWNSHIP AND CREST CITY. THE JV GAME IS AT 6:00 P.M. AND VARSITY IS AT 8:00 P.M. COME AND SEE SOCCER AT ITS BEST!

FOOTBALL OPENER: TODAY OUR FOOTBALL TEAM IS OPENING AGAINST HART AT 3:30 THIS AFTERNOON AT HOME. TONIGHT HARRIS PLAYS ROCK TOWNSHIP AT 7:30 P.M. UNDER THE LIGHTS AT HOME. LET'S GET OUT AND SUPPORT OUR SCHOOL TEAMS!!

PEP RALLY THIS AFTERNOON: ALL STUDENTS WILL BE CALLED DOWN ON THE PA SYSTEM AT APPROXIMATELY 1:15 P.M. ATHLETES WILL BE EXCUSED AT 1:10. TEACHERS ARE TO SUPERVISE THEIR CLASSES COMING TO AND DURING THE PEP RALLY.

THE FOLLOWING STUDENTS ARE TO ASSEMBLE IN THE LIBRARY ON MONDAY, OCTOBER 7, AT 8:45, TO MEET WITH MR. HIGGINS OF ROCK TOWNSHIP COMMUNITY COLLEGE.

KIKI LONG	MARY BETH FERRIS	CYNTHIA WALTERS
KIM O'DELL	GREG KAPLES	RAY CARLTON
JOHN MARSH	JEFF MILLARD	DAVID SALTEN
JEFF STRONG	DAVE MILTON	

TO ALL COACHES OF FALL SPORTS:
PLEASE TURN IN ALL DOCTORS' NOTES AND PARENT PERMISSION SLIPS TO THE HEALTH OFFICE.

YEARBOOK PICTURES: YEARBOOK PICTURES WILL BE TAKEN DURING ENGLISH CLASSES ON MONDAY, OCTOBER 7, AND TUESDAY, OCTOBER 8. ALL ENGLISH TEACHERS SHOULD HAVE DISTRIBUTED "PICTURE INFORMATION" ENVELOPES TO ALL OF THEIR CLASSES. ALL STUDENTS WILL BE PHOTOGRAPHED FOR THE YEARBOOK. IF STUDENTS WANT TO ORDER PICTURES, THE ENVELOPE CONTAINING MONEY IS TO BE GIVEN TO THE PHOTOGRAPHER AT THE TIME THE PICTURE IS TAKEN. ENGLISH TEACHERS ... PLEASE ADVISE EACH CLASS WHICH DAY THEY ARE SCHEDULED TO BE PHOTOGRAPHED.

JUNIOR VOLUNTEER PROGRAM: EIGHTH AND NINTH GRADE STUDENTS:
ROCK TOWNSHIP MEDICAL CENTER IS LOOKING FOR VOLUNTEERS IN THEIR JUNIOR VOLUNTEER PROGRAM. BOYS AND GIRLS FOURTEEN YEARS OLD OR OLDER ARE ELIGIBLE. IF INTERESTED, PLEASE CONTACT MRS. RITA HERZ, DIRECTOR OF VOLUNTEER SERVICES, 555-7778, EXT 133.

TEACHERS: PLEASE READ PAGE 2 FOR INFORMATION PERTAINING TO THE TESTING OF CERTAIN STUDENTS ON MONDAY, OCTOBER 7.

form for placing message in bulletin...

Today's Date: ______________________

I request that the following message be reproduced in the Daily Bulletin on the following date(s):

Date(s): ________ ________ ________ ________ ________

Message:

Signature of Teacher Making Request: ______________________________

school policy on placing notes in bulletin...

Morning Bulletin

a. All announcements to be put in the morning bulletin must be in the box in the general office by noon of the previous day.
b. The advisor or teacher in charge of the group entering the announcement must check the grammar, etc., and sign it.
c. An announcement will be printed for no more than two days.

(See Also: BACK-TO-SCHOOL NIGHT; CLERICAL SERVICES; NEWSLETTER; NEWS RELEASES)

BUS

bus request form...

School	Department		Requested By		Date of Application
Date(s) of Use	No. of Pass.	No. of Bus(es)	Time Leaving School		Scheduled Arrival Time
Estimated Time of Return to School	Destination		Purpose of Trip		
Check One:	Field Trip	Athletic	Pep Club	Other (Identify)	

Signature of Principal: ____________ Signature of Supervisor: ____________

TO BE FILLED IN ONLY FOR SPECIALLY FUNDED TRIPS

INCOME

No. of Passengers ________
X Rate ________

GROSS INCOME ________

EXPENSE

Drivers' hrs. ________ **X Rate** ________
Gas & Oil ________
Others ________
Check to Business Office ________
TOTAL ________
Signature ________

TO BE FILLED IN BY DIRECTOR OF TRANSPORTATION

Ending Miles ____________ Driver ____________

Beginning Miles ____________ Vehicles(s) Assigned ____________

Total Miles ____________ Driver's Hours ____________

Cost per Mile ____________ Comments ____________

APPROVAL

Date ________ **BUS SUPERVISOR** ____________

confirmation from parents and students of bus rules...

TO: Parents of Pupils Riding School Buses
FROM: Rock Township Board of Education, Transportation Department

Dear Parent:

In order for you to understand the regulations covering the conduct of your child riding a Rock Township school bus, we are sending you a copy of REGULATIONS FOR PUPILS RIDING SCHOOL BUSES. It is requested that YOU and YOUR CHILD read these regulations.

This will be used as a permanent record throughout your child's enrollment in the Rock Township Schools. Your cooperation with us will make it possible to provide a SAFER and MORE EFFICIENT Transportation Program.

PLEASE SIGN AND RETURN TO THE PRINCIPAL IN ORDER FOR YOUR CHILD TO CONTINUE RIDING THE SCHOOL BUS.

ALL STUDENTS

I have read and understand the REGULATIONS FOR PUPILS RIDING SCHOOL BUSES and agree, as a passenger, to abide by said regulations:

____

Student Signature

____

Grade Section

FOR PARENT OR GUARDIAN

I have read and understand the REGULATIONS FOR PUPILS RIDING SCHOOL BUSES and agree to assume full responsibility for my child's conduct on said buses:

____

Parent or Guardian Signature

regulations for students riding school buses...

REGULATIONS FOR PUPILS RIDING SCHOOL BUSES

THE RIGHT OF ALL PUPILS TO RIDE IN THE CONVEYANCE IS CONDITIONAL ON THEIR GOOD BEHAVIOR AND OBSERVANCE OF THE FOLLOWING RULES AND REGULATIONS. ANY PUPIL WHO VIOLATES ANY OF THESE WILL BE REPORTED TO THE SCHOOL PRINCIPAL.

1. The driver is in full charge of the bus and the pupils. Pupils shall obey the driver cheerfully and promptly.
2. Pupils shall obey and respect the orders of monitors or patrols on duty. (If Applicable)
3. Pupils shall be on time; the bus cannot wait for those who are not on time.
4. Pupils shall occupy the space designated for them by the driver.
5. Pupils shall observe the following:
   a. Stand on the sidewalk or side of the road, out of the roadway, while waiting for the bus.
   b. Clean footwear before entering the bus.
   c. Spitting on the bus is against health and safety rules. Such conduct will be reported to the school principal.

d. Papers or other rubbish should not be thrown on the bus floor.

e. No one should damage or deface the bus in any way.

f. Students should not start for school when ill, or when any member of the family has a contagious disease.

g. Students should avoid any unnecessary conversation with the driver of the bus.

h. Smoking is forbidden on all buses, at all times.

i. Safety requires that students do not lean their heads out of windows or extend their hands out of windows.

j. When the bus is in motion, students must not change seats or try to get on or off the bus.

k. Students may not leave the bus without the driver's consent except at their assigned bus stop or at school.

l. Courtesy and respect must be shown to fellow passengers, persons along the route, and the bus driver. Profanity on the bus will not be tolerated.

m. Damage or vandalism to the bus will be reported by the bus driver to the school principal.

n. Walk on the left side of the road, facing traffic, when walking to and from the bus stop.

6. Pupils who must cross the road after alighting from the bus should pass in front of the bus and not behind it. The driver should see that the way is clear before the child is permitted to cross the road.

7. SHOULD ANY PUPIL PERSIST IN VIOLATING ANY OF THESE REGULATIONS, IT SHALL BE THE DUTY OF THE DRIVER TO NOTIFY THE PRINCIPAL AND AFTER THE WARNING HAS BEEN GIVEN TO THE PUPIL, THE PRINCIPAL SHALL THEN DENY THE DISOBEDIENT PUPIL THE PRIVILEGE OF RIDING THE BUS UNTIL PERMISSION TO RIDE AGAIN HAS BEEN GIVEN IN ACCORDANCE WITH THE BOARD OF EDUCATION POLICY. (Written notice of the action of the principal shall be furnished the parent.)

8. Any complaints of drivers, pupils, or parents, not specified in the above regulations, shall be reported promptly to the principal.

9. Should the conduct of a pupil on the bus endanger the lives or morals of other people and the offending pupil fails to cease such conduct when requested by the bus driver to do so, with the permission of the principal, the offender may be removed from the bus. This will be done only in extreme cases and as a last resort to protect the safety of other pupils.

THESE REGULATIONS SHOULD BE KEPT BY THE PARENT OR GUARDIAN FOR REFERENCE DURING THE ENTIRE TIME THE STUDENT IS IN SCHOOL

(See Also: AUTOMOBILES; BUSINESS; FIELD TRIPS; INSURANCE; SAFETY; TRAVEL; TRIPS)

BUSINESS

business and distributive education description in handbook...

Distributive Education is a vocational training program operating through state and local systems to provide specialized education for those persons who are preparing to enter or who are already employed in a retail, wholesale or service occupation. Distributive Education provides training through a combination of classroom instruction and supervised on-the-job training in a marketing occupation.

Areas of instruction include advertising, communications, display, human relations, math, merchandising, product and service technology, management, selling, and operations. Leadership development, social awareness, civic consciousness and vocational understanding are integrated into the program through DECA (Distributive Education Clubs of America). On-the-job training and competency-based instruction in the model/school store are also provided.

business education description in handbook...

Business Education is a program that provides business skills applicable to business employment, personal use and college preparatory.

The Vocational Office Education Program is a three-fold one. The students participate in classroom instruction, on-the-job office work experience and club work. The FBLA (Future Business Leaders of America) club provides the students with leadership training. Student participation in club work is encouraged.

0300 Exploratory Business—½ Credit

Open to Grades 9, 10

This course is designed to introduce students to distributive, clerical, accounting, data processing and stenographic business fields. Student activities include stimulating on-the-job experience.

district business and facilities operations chart...

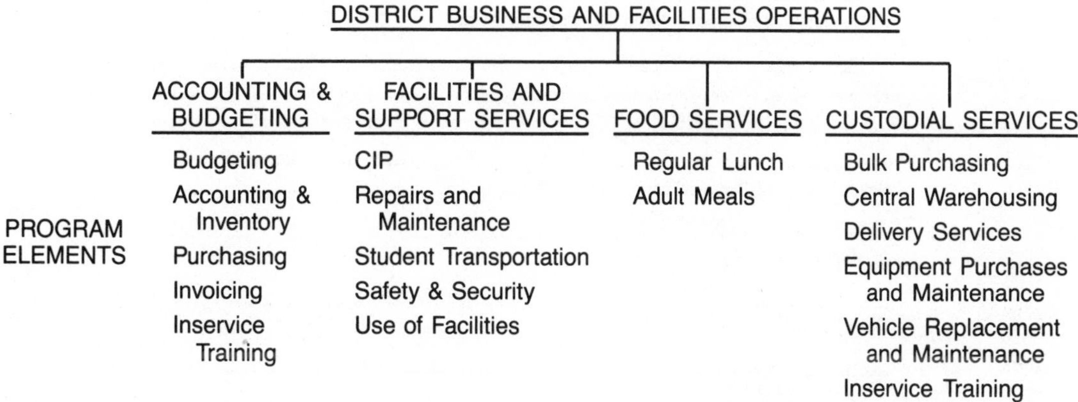

(See Also: BIDS; BOARD OF EDUCATION; BUDGET; BUILDING; CONTRACT; EQUIPMENT; FEES, FINES, FUNDS AND CHARGES; INVENTORY; PURCHASING; VENDORS; VOUCHERS)

CAFETERIA

application form for cafeteria employee...

Name:____

Address:____

Social Security No. _____/____/_____ Phone No: ____________________

In case of emergency, name and phone number of person to contact:

____

PERSONAL DATA

1. Do you know of any disability or communicable disease which would prevent your passing a physical examination and receiving a healthcard?

   ____

2. Previous work experience: (List type of experience, dates of employment, etc.)

Employer	Location	Dates From	To

3. Last place of employment and date of employment:

   ____

4. Have you ever been discharged from a position? ______ If answered "YES", please explain. (Include job title and date.)____________________

   ____

Would you be willing to substitute in Food Service?____________________

When could you begin work?______________________________

In what area would you prefer to work?

____

REFERENCES: (Name) (Present Address)

____

OTHER COMMENTS:

____

INTERVIEWED FOR:______ DATE/TIME:________________ INITIALS:__________

DATE:____________________ SIGNATURE OF APPLICANT________________

WE ARE AN EQUAL OPPORTUNITY EMPLOYER & FOLLOW FAIR EMPLOYMENT PRACTICES

daily lunch accounting form...

______________________ Daily Lunch Accounting for ________ ________ ________
Month Day Year

TO BE ACCOUNTED FOR:			No. of Tickets	Price	Dollar Amount Collected
1. Paid tickets (weekly)	Nos.______	thru______			
Paid tickets (daily)	Nos.______	thru______			
2. Reduced tickets (weekly)	Nos.______	thru______			
Reduced tickets (daily)	Nos.______	thru______			
3. Free tickets (weekly)	Nos.______	thru______		N/C	************
4. Special milk tickets	Nos.______	thru______			
5. Daily adult tickets	Nos.______	thru______			
6. Add: Extra milk (no ticket) Students and Adults					

$______

Subtotal $______

7. Add: Cash carried over from previous day $______

TOTAL CASH TO BE ACCOUNTED FOR: ***$______

ACCOUNTED FOR AS FOLLOWS:

8. Deposit (Must agree with bank deposit slip) $______

9. Less: Paid Daily Strip #______ sold completely
(Partially sold day before) $______

10. Add: Paid Daily Strip #______ partially sold $______

11. Less: Reduced Daily Strip #______ sold completely
(Partially sold day before) $______

12. Add: Reduced Daily Strip #______ partially sold $______

13. Add: Cash on hand—forward to next daily report $______

14. Add: Cash short OR $______

15. Less: Cash over $______

16. Add: Refunds made for unused portion of tickets
(tickets attached to Food Service Copy) $______

TOTAL ACCOUNTED FOR: ***$______

***These two lines must be the same

17. No. of Foster Grandparent tickets issued today ______
(to be billed by Food Service office)

Food Service is not authorized to maintain charge accounts for meals. It is also recognized that at given times a principal must have the authority to use his/her discretion of allowing charges where students would be deprived of a meal. Extra Petty Cash funds may be obtained from district office if extra cash is found to be necessary.

rules for student use of cafeteria...

CAFETERIA INSTRUCTIONS

1. Put books in locker before going to the cafeteria.
2. Walk through the halls to your place in line. **Do not run** at any time.
3. Take your place in line without shoving or cutting in.
4. Places for friends are not saved in the lines.
5. Have change ready and keep lines moving as rapidly as possible.
6. Sit at the table assigned to you.
7. You will be permitted to talk and leave your table for additional purchases. You are not permitted to shout, wander about the cafeteria, or behave in such a way as to disturb others.
8. Be courteous and use your best table manners.
9. Keep the cafeteria clean and orderly by taking trays and dishes to designated places and leave tables in proper condition for those who follow.
10. All food must be eaten in the cafeteria.
11. Respect cafeteria duty teacher's authority.
12. Each student in rotation is assigned as a table monitor.
13. During the last fifteen minutes of each lunch period, weather permitting, students will be allowed to go outside the school building. Use the rear entrance and proceed immediately out to the basketball court or the track area. THIS IS A MUST. Students found or seen in an area where they shouldn't be, or taking lunches outside the cafeteria, will immediately have this privilege revoked.

sample cafeteria menu...

LUNCHEONS FOR THE WEEK OF MARCH 12, 1984
(may contain ½ pint of whole or skim milk)

MONDAY

Luncheon #1 – Frankfurter on Roll
Luncheon #2 – Italian Sausage Patty on Bun
Luncheon #3 – Tuna Salad Sandwich

EACH OF THE ABOVE LUNCHEONS WILL CONTAIN YOUR CHOICE OF TWO:

Potatoes–Vegetable–Chilled Juice

* * * * * * * * * * *

TUESDAY

Luncheon #1 – Cheeseburger on Bun
Luncheon #2 – Oven-Baked Fish Filet with Tartar Sauce on Bun
Luncheon #3 – Bologna Sandwich

EACH OF THE ABOVE LUNCHEONS WILL CONTAIN YOUR CHOICE OF TWO:

Potatoes–Vegetable–Fruit

* * * * * * * * * *

WEDNESDAY

Luncheon #1 – Spaghetti with Meat Sauce–Bread and Butter–Tossed Salad with Dressing–Fruit
Luncheon #2 – Grilled Cheese Sandwich
Choice of Two: Whole Kernel Corn–Tossed Salad with Dressing–Fruit
Luncheon #3 – Egg Salad Sandwich
Choice of Two: Whole Kernel Corn–Tossed Salad with Dressing–Fruit

* * * * * * * * * *

THURSDAY

Luncheon #1 – Oven-Baked Chicken with Dinner Roll–Buttered Rice–Tossed Salad with Dressing–Fruit
Luncheon #2 – Tacos with Shredded Lettuce–Buttered Rice–Fruit
Luncheon #3 – Cold Submarine Sandwich with Lettuce–Fruit

* * * * * * * * * *

FRIDAY

Luncheon #1 – Pizza
Luncheon #2 – Hot Southern Baked Pork Roll on Bun
Luncheon #3 – Cold Sliced Meatloaf Sandwich

EACH OF THE ABOVE LUNCHEONS WILL CONTAIN YOUR CHOICE OF TWO:

Carrot and Celery Sticks–Fruit–Chilled Juice

* * * * * * * * * *

(See Also: CERTIFICATION; FREE LUNCHES; LUNCH AND LUNCH DUTY; TIME)

CALENDAR

example of school calendar...

SCHOOL CALENDAR
1985–86

August 25, 1985	Institute
August 26, 1985	In-School Professional Development
August 27, 1985	First Day of School (Buses will run)
September 1, 1985	Labor Day (School Closed)
September 11, 1985	Jewish Holiday (School Closed)
October 6–7, 1985	Professional Development (School Closed)
October 21, 1985	Schools Dismiss at 2:00 p.m.–Fair Day
November 3, 1985	End of First Grading Period
November 11, 1985	Veterans Day (School Closed)
November 25, 1985	Begin Thanksgiving Holdays at end of day
December 1, 1985	Return from Thanksgiving Holidays
December 19, 1985	Begin Christmas Holidays at end of day
January 5, 1986	Return from Christmas Holidays
January 23, 1986	End of First Semester
February 10, 1986	County Career Day
March 6, 1986	Begin Spring Holidays at end of day
March 16, 1986	Return from Spring Holidays
April 3, 1986	End of Third Grading Period
May 29, 1986	End of School

example of student school calendar...

STUDENT CALENDAR FOR 19XX-19XX

Friday	September 3, 19XX	Kindergarten Orientation
Tuesday	September 7, 19XX	First Day of School for Students
Monday	September 27, 19XX	School Closed
Friday	October 8, 19XX	Schools Closed for Students–Professional Workshop Day for Teachers
Monday	October 11, 19XX	School Closed–Columbus Day
Tuesday	November 2, 19XX	School Closed–Election Day
Thursday	November 11, 19XX	Schools Closed–Veterans Day, Teachers' Convention
Friday	November 12, 19XX	Schools Closed–Teachers' Convention
Thursday	November 25, 19XX	Schools Closed–Thanksgiving

Friday	November 26, 19XX	Schools Closed–Thanksgiving Recess
Thursday	December 23, 19XX	Schools Closed at End of Day–Winter Recess
Monday	January 3, 19XX	Schools Open at Regular Time
Monday	February 21, 19XX	Schools Closed–Washington's Birthday
Friday	March 25, 19XX	Schools Closed at End of Day–Spring Recess
Tuesday	April 5, 19XX	All Schools Open at Regular Time
Monday	May 30, 19XX	Schools Closed–Memorial Day
Monday	June 20, 19XX	Schools Close for Students at End of Day

weekly planning calendar...

Name: ______________________________

Homebase: ______________________________

Week Beginning: ______________________________

DAY	SCHEDULE	ENGLISH	SCIENCE	SOCIAL STUDIES	MATH
MONDAY					
TUESDAY					
WEDNESDAY					
THURSDAY					
FRIDAY					
NOTES					

(See Also: COURSES; DEPARTMENTAL MEETINGS; HANDBOOK; SCHEDULE; TIME**)**

CAREERS

description of career courses...

0400 Career Education Plus—2 hrs/day—1 Semester—1 Credit

Open to Grades 9, 10, 11, 12.

This course (Planning, Learning, Understanding, Succeeding) is designed as an alternative to traditional education. Instead of learning only in the classroom, each student learns at both the CE+ Learning Center and at job sites around Rock Township. The students have the chance to explore many different careers and their "learning plans" are centered directly around their interests and abilities. Students are not paid for their work, but do receive academic credit. While in the Learning Center, students work on projects, competencies and basic skills. All 9th through 12th grade students who have not taken the class in the past are eligible to enroll in CE+ for one semester. Student selection is based on: (1) Student willingness to enter the program; (2) Agreement of student's parents, and (3) Availability of program openings. Students in the program participate for a two-hour time block.

description of career program...

NINTH GRADE PROGRAM DESCRIPTION

COMPONENTS:

1. At least 30 hours of instructional time
2. Overview of careers in all areas
3. Three briefs in each area, differentiated by level of training or education required for the career (an alternate activity may be substituted at the discretion of the teacher)

DOCUMENTATION:

1. Responsibility for goals undertaken by various subject areas
2. Teacher lesson plans
3. Student folders containing work that is done throughout the year

The items above will combine to indicate that the required number of hours has been spent by the student in career-related activities. The folders will be kept in a central location or in one of the students' classes. The student will have the responsibility for placing all career-related materials in the folder.

EVALUATION:

Evaluation of the ninth grade program is only one part of the total evaluation of the career education program.

For the ninth grade year, there are two specific goals:

1. That at least 30 hours of career education be infused into the curriculum
2. That the student folder system be developed and implemented

Student compliance will not be graded, but implementation of the program must include a process by which a student's fulfillment of the career education requirement is documented and recorded.

Ultimately, evaluation must address the entire K-12 program and must include students' ability to make career decisions and to find satisfaction in those choices after leaving school.

(See Also: ADULT EDUCATION; AMERICAN EDUCATION WEEK; CITIZENSHIP; DUTIES; EDUCATION; GUIDANCE; INTERVIEW; PIP; WORK; WORKING PAPERS)

certified staff application form...

CERTIFIED STAFF APPLICATION

Date of Application ______________________

Position Applied For ______________________

PERSONAL INFORMATION

Name: ______________________ ______________
Last First Middle Social Security #

Name on Transcripts and Placement Papers ______________________

Present Address: ______________________ ______________
Street, City, State, Zip Area Code-Telephone

Permanent Address: ______________________ ______________
Street, City, State, Zip Area Code-Telephone

Condition of Health: Do you have any condition that may limit your ability to perform the position applied for? YES (____) NO(____)

Have you ever been convicted of a felony? YES (____) NO (____)

JOB REFERENCE

Indicate the levels and/or subjects in which you are certified to teach, and give preference by ranking 1, 2 and 3.

SENIOR HIGH (____) JUNIOR HIGH (____) INTERMEDIATE (____) PRIMARY (____)

Indicate your choice of GRADES if elementary or SUBJECTS if secondary:

____

ELEMENTARY

1st choice ______________

2nd choice ______________

3rd choice ______________

SPECIAL AREAS:

Music ______________

Art ______________

Special Ed. ______________

Phys Ed. ______________

Other ______________

SECONDARY:

Specify: ______________

EXTRACURRICULAR ACTIVITIES YOU ARE QUALIFIED BY PREPARATION TO INSTRUCT:

Specify: ______________________

____

____

SPORTS YOU ARE QUALIFIED BY PREPARATION TO COACH:

Specify: ______________________

____

____

(Form continued)

PROFESSIONAL PREPARATION

Do you hold a State Teaching Certificate? (____) YES (____) NO What type?____________

What endorsement(s)?____

Do you hold a valid State Vocational Education Credential? (____)YES(____) NO

In what area(s)?____

Date of graduation ________________ Date available for employment ________________

Your student teaching was done/or will be done at what level/subject?________________

College/University Attended *(Names and location)*	Dates Inclusive	Degree	Major	Semester Hours	Minor	Semester Hours

TEACHING EXPERIENCE: *List most recent experience first.*

Dates From–To	Name and location of school	No. of Years	Grade level and/or subjects taught	Name of Principal or Supervisor

WORK EXPERIENCE OTHER THAN TEACHING: *(Including Military Service)*

From Mo. Yr.	To Mo. Yr.	Job Title	Duties and Assignments

REFERENCES

Include any administrator under whom you have taught, or college instructor if you have not yet graduated. Do *not* include relatives or persons who have furnished references for your placement office credentials. You may also include persons not connected with education who are qualified to answer regarding your fitness for the position you seek.

Name	Occupation	Address	Phone Number

(Form continued)

certified staff application form (cont'd)

DIRECTIONS: Please answer each of the questions given below as best you can. The space provided should be adequate, but if more space is needed, please attach additional pages. Please complete in your own handwriting.

1. What do you want to accomplish as a teacher?

____

____

____

2. How will/do you go about finding out students' attitudes and feelings about your class?

____

____

____

3. An experienced teacher offers you the following advice: "When you are teaching, be sure to command the respect of your students immediately, and all will go well." How do you feel about this?

____

____

____

4. How do you go about deciding what should be taught in your class?

____

____

____

5. A parent comes to you and complains that what you are teaching his/her child is irrelevant to the child's needs. How would you respond?

____

____

____

6. What do you think will/does provide you the greatest pleasure in teaching?

____

____

____

7. When you have some free time, what do you enjoy doing the most?

____

____

____

(Form continued)

8. How do you go about finding what students are good at?

9. Would you rather try a lot of way-out teaching strategies or would you rather try to perfect the approaches that work best for you? Explain.

10. Do you like to teach with an overall plan in mind for the year, or would you rather just teach some interesting things and let the process determine the results? Explain.

11. A student is doing poorly in your class. You talk to her, and she tells you that she considers you to be the poorest teacher she has ever met. What would you do?

12. If there were absolutely no restrictions placed upon you, what would you most want to do in life?

An application is considered active when the Personnel Office has received (1) this employment application (completed and signed) along with the applicant information card, (2) placement office credentials (or letters of reference), and (3) all official transcripts.

A medical examination (at the applicant's expense) and a valid State Teaching Certificate will be required when employed.

Applications are placed in the active file from January 1 to December 31 of each year. Each applicant must notify the Personnel Office *in writing* by December 31 if they wish to have their application remain active during the next calendar year.

An on-site interview (at the applicant's expense) is required before hiring, unless specifically waived by the District.

PLEASE READ CAREFULLY BEFORE SIGNING

I certify that the information given by me on this application and any supplement is true and correct to the best of my knowledge. I understand that false statements on this application may result in termination of employment.

Date | Signature of Applicant

(Form continued)

(See Also: APPLICATION; CAFETERIA; CONTRACT; EDUCATION; INTERNSHIP; QUALIFICATIONS; STUDENT TEACHER)

CHAIRPERSONS

duties and responsibilities of...

1. Work with principal in overall development of general policies for department.
2. Organize and conduct department meetings.
3. Work with members of department in developing guides, conducting curricular studies and revisions, and defining instructional policies as further refinements of the program of the State and District offices.
4. Conduct inservice workshops within department when necessary.
5. Make recommendations of new texts and other instructional materials.
6. Make recommendations for departmental library of curriculum materials and professional books, and maintain a centralized departmental resource file.
7. Maintain file of departmental correspondence, catalogues and other related material.
8. Keep inventory and make distribution of text, supplies and equipment within department.
9. Assist in orientation and evaluation of new teachers and substitutes assigned to department.
10. Assist teachers of the department by necessary consultation, conferences and classroom visitations.
11. Prepare department budget and approve requisitions for department.
12. Coordinate work of department with that of other departments and services of the school (for example, testing, A.V. program).
13. Represent school in departmental matters that require contact with other schools or with district and state curriculum offices.
14. Handle departmental problems in connection with student, teacher, parent, public relations.
15. Develop year-end evaluation on the department and provide progress report to the principal when requested.
16. Administrative-faculty council:
    a. represent department on council
    b. provide liaison between departments
    c. provide liaison between principal and department members
17. Perform such other duties that may be assigned by the principal in connection with the life of the school.

18. Work with your department in making decisions as to master schedule and long-range curriculum developments.
19. Set up department goals for the year.
20. Assist the registrar with registration procedures.
21. Assist the Accreditation Committee in those areas concerning your department.

(See Also: BUDGET; DEPARTMENTAL MEETINGS; EQUIPMENT; FIELD TRIPS; INVENTORY; ORGANIZATIONAL CHART; PURCHASING; SUPERVISION)

CHALLENGED MATERIALS

policy statement on...

The Board believes that issues relating to the program of the Rock Township school system should be dealt with, whenever possible, by the Superintendent and his staff. When an individual or group confronts a Board member with a complaint or grievance, the Board member should withhold commitment or opinion until the matter has been reviewed by the Superintendent.

The Superintendent shall prepare regulations to deal fairly and effectively with complaints and grievances from the public about curriculum and resource materials.

procedures for...

1. Upon receipt of written complaint, an informal conference should be held with principal, teacher, and parent within ten (10) days of the receipt of the complaint.
2. If the issue is not resolved at the informal conference, the written complaint, together with a summary of the informal conference completed by the principal, should be forwarded to the Instructional Coordinator, who will then establish a District Review committee under his/her chairpersonship. This committee should include, in addition to the Instructional Coordinator, a department supervisor or chairperson, or a teacher from the affected area or level, and a parent representative (PIC or PTA Presidents' Council). Committee members should be drawn from schools other than the affected school.
3. Within fifteen (15) school days, the Committee will review the materials in question and will forward its findings to the Superintendent. The Superintendent will present these findings at the next regularly scheduled Administrative Council meeting for the Council's recommendations. All recommendations will be presented to the Board of Education for appropriate action, and the complainant notified of the action taken.

(See Also: ACADEMIC FREEDOM; BOARD OF EDUCATION; BOOKS; COMPLAINTS; CONTROVERSIAL TOPICS; GRIEVANCES; LIBRARY; TEXTBOOKS)

CHANGE

change of recorded information form...

OLD INFORMATION REGARDING CHILD (information currently in files):

Name: ______________________________________ Tel. #: ______________
last first middle Area Code-Number

Address: (street) ______________________________________

(city-state-zip) ______________________________________

Other Data (specifically, any other data currently in files that will be changed other than that recorded above:

____

____

NEW INFORMATION REGARDING CHILD (information to be changed in file):

Name: ______________________________________ Tel. #: ______________
last first middle Area Code-Number

Address: (street) ______________________________________

(city-state-zip) ______________________________________

Other Data (specifically, the information to be changed from that in old file):

____

____

Present Date: ______________ Date Change Is Effective: ______________

Person Recording Change: ______________________________________

Relationship to Child: ______________________________________

policy on change of address or telephone number...

The school must be notified when a change is made in the address or phone number of a child. It is important that these items of information are current at all times. Parents are required to notify the school within ten (10) school days of such a change and are required to complete a change of information form which will be available at every school.

policy on change of name...

Legal Name of Child on School Records:

It is necessary that a child's name on school records be the same as the name on his or her birth certificate. In the case of adoption, school authorities will then change the name upon seeing the court order. For purposes of identification, the child's stepfather's name will be recorded in parentheses on the permanent record.

(See Also: ACCIDENT; ASSIGNMENTS; COMPLAINTS; GRIEVANCES; NEW POLICY OR PROGRAM; REQUISITIONS, REPAIRS, AND REPLACEMENTS; TRANSFER; ZONES AND ZONING)

CHAPERONE

duties of chaperones at school activities...

1. Advisor:
   a. Check activity dates and inform teachers two weeks prior to event.
   b. See that sufficient chaperones will be on hand, and check to see that security personnel is hired.
2. Teachers' Responsibilities:
   a. Be at the activity 15 minutes prior to and remain 15 minutes after activity ends.
   b. Report to the advisor for duties, which may include one or more of the following:
      1. Help control entrance area. Please be at the entrance—check I.D.'s, check late passes, see that any student under the influence of liquor (smell) is not permitted to enter. Police should assist in this area.
      2. Check bathroom at regular intervals. If someone is abusive, call the police.
      3. Circulate inside of gym—check students for smoking, drinking or any other behavior that may be detrimental or annoying to others.
      4. Check doors to see that they are properly secured.
      5. In the event that there is only one security person, check the parking area. NOTE: If you find students loitering after the event starts, call the police department to assist in checking this area at reasonable intervals.
   c. If you're not able to serve, it is your responsibility to get a substitute in sufficient time (at least one week prior to event) and report this change to the advisor in charge. It should be understood that a teacher is preferred for obvious reasons.

request for parent volunteer chaperone...

Dear Parents,

We could use your assistance.

Throughout the school year, we plan various activities for our students. These activities range from sports to social events such as dances and school socials. While the faculty and staff are most generous in donating their personal time to help supervise these activities, we are still in need of chaperones at various times throughout the year.

Therefore, we are calling upon our "number one" school resource—you, the parents of our students. If you can see your way clear to volunteer to help chaperone these events, we can promise that you will receive adequate guidance in what to do, will be performing an invaluable service to the school, and will have fun as well.

Can we count on you? If you can, take a moment to fill in the information below and return it to the school via your child. We look forward to seeing you at our school functions.

Sincerely,

John Benson, Principal

YES, I would like to volunteer to chaperone some school activities.

Name: ______________________________ Tel. #: ______________

Activity Preferred: ______________________________

responsibilities of chaperones...

First, let me say that we are very thankful that you have volunteered to serve as chaperone for:

1. ______________________ on ______________________
   Activity Date
2. ______________________ on ______________________
   Activity Date

Your duties include the following:

1. See that each student has a permission slip signed by his/her parents and has paid for the trip.

   Note: All monies collected must be turned in to Mrs. Jones. The form (receipt) must be secured from her prior to collecting. Chaperones will be held accountable for all monies collected.

2. See that each student is on board the bus. Take a count and check individual names against the permission blanks when necessary. This must be repeated each time students are released from the bus and are boarding the bus.

3. See that all bus regulations are followed:
   a. No smoking or walking in bus.
   b. Behavior must comply with all directions given by the bus driver and chaperones.
4. Student behavior at games must reflect respect for others and sportsmanship. No booing and cat-calls should be tolerated.
5. Any student who does not comply should be warned that all future privileges will be removed and are subject to disciplinary action by the administration.
6. After returning to school, chaperones must see that all students are accounted for and have left the premises.

I have read the statements above and am willing to assume all responsibilites of carrying out each provision specified.

________________________ ______________

Signature of Chaperone Date

(See Also: APPRECIATION; DANCES; OPEN HOUSE; P.T.A.; TRIPS; VOLUNTEERS)

CHILD ABUSE

special note...

The following memorandum is an excellent example of one state Department of Education's guidelines on child abuse. Virtually every state has enacted similar legislation that may be incorporated into the policy of a school system. It is presented here in its entirety for your consideration.

TO: District Superintendents and Principals
FROM: George M. Pauls, Superintendent of Education
SUBJECT: 1. Department of Education-Department of Social Services Working Agreement
2. Implementation of Act 261 (H.B. #28) Mandatory Reporting of Child Abuse

This is a reminder that our memorandum dated November 21, 1984 be implemented in accordance with the law and our agreement with the Department of Social Services.

Please discuss this memo with your teachers so that they are aware of this matter.

Section III of our working agreement, Procedures for Case Referrals, permits the principal to directly contact the Public Welfare Division, Applications Unit, and with the agency's district office.

A copy of every referral for child abuse must be sent to the office of Instructional Services for reporting purposes and any follow-up that may be necessary.

1. Working Agreement

   The Department of Education and the Department of Social Services have completed the attached working agreement in relation to service to pupils.

   Special Services in our department and the services of the Public Welfare Division are described to acquaint respective staffs with the kinds of help offered to pupils and their families. This is followed by a brief description of how services between the two departments will be initiated and followed through.

   The district offices, Special Services, and the schools will be concerned with implementing this working agreement and the state office is available for any needed interpretation.

2. Act 261, Mandatory Reporting of Child Abuse and Its Implementation

   On June 7, 1984, Act 261 was passed which made it mandatory for school teachers, registered nurses, social workers, among others, to report to the Department of Social Services instances of child abuse and neglect.

   The agreement between the Department of Education and Department of Social Services describes how such reporting shall be made by teachers, registered nurses and social workers in the Department of Education.

   In December 1984, the Department of Social Services' brochure will be distributed by the Department of Education. This gives additional interpretation of Act 261 which holds persons who report immune from liability.

   Each district and school is encouraged to become familiar with this law and to effect means for its implementation locally.

Copies of Act 261 and the working agreement with the Department of Social Services may be secured from the Special Services Branch, State Office. The State Office is happy to serve as consultant in reference to both of these concerns.

INTER-AGENCY AGREEMENT BETWEEN PUBLIC WELFARE DIVISION DEPARTMENT OF SOCIAL SERVICES AND OFFICE OF INSTRUCTIONAL SERVICES, SPECIAL SERVICES BRANCH, DEPARTMENT OF EDUCATION

I. GENERAL FUNCTIONS

A. *Public Welfare Division, Department of Social Services*

   The Department of Social Services is charged by law to maintain and improve family life, to safeguard the welfare of children, and to prevent delinquency. In carrying out this legal mandate, the following services are provided to families and children by social workers of the Department of Social Services.

   1. Counseling of parents and relatives in the care and supervision of children and in improving family life.
   2. Protection of children from parental neglect, abuse, and cruelty through investigation of and action on complaints regarding child neglect and abuse. Immediate protective services are provided in situations of child abuse and extreme neglect.
   3. Placement, supervision, and financial support of children who need temporary care away from their families, in suitable foster boarding homes.
   4. Placement of children without permanent parental ties in suitable adoptive homes.

5. Help to the unmarried mother in planning for herself and her child.
6. Provision of temporary emergency shelter care for the child who is in need of such care.
7. Purchase of specialized group care, such as offered by the Salvation Army Facilities for children who cannot remain in their own homes or be placed in foster family homes.
8. Purchase of family or group day care for children of needy families.
9. Provision of financial assistance including costs of medical care to needy families and children.
10. Provision of food stamps for marginal income families not needing financial assistance whose food budget needs further supplementation.
11. Provision of homemaker services to families in emergencies when the mother is temporarily incapacitated or absent from the home.

B. *Special Services, Department of Education*

The Special Services helps pupils through the following:

1. *Guidance and Counseling Program*

   General guidance activities and counseling services are provided to all students in each school. There are procedures in each school for identifying and referring pupils who need additional assistance.

2. *Health Program*

   School health procedures and practices are established for the purpose of: (a) finding children with health needs; (b) following up on children in need of care; interpreting health conditions and providing health guidance, through contacts with children, parents and community agencies; (c) communicable disease prevention and control; and (d) providing emergency care for the sick or injured.

3. *Psychological Program*

   Under the direction of the School Psychologist, selected pupils with learning and/or behavior problems are given examinations to determine reasons for present performance and suggest remedial measures or recommend referrals to programs in special services or to community resources.

4. *School Social Work Program*

   Social case work service is offered to selected pupils whose social and emotional adjustment interferes with learning, association with teachers and classmates, attendance, or participation in school-centered activities. A close working relationship also is maintained with the family and school personnel; referrals are made to community resources when indicated.

5. *Special Education Program*

   Classes exist in limited number for the mentally retarded, emotionally disturbed, physically handicapped, and for pupils with other learning difficulties. Candidates must meet admission requirements of the particular program and may be referred by school personnel, parents or community agencies.

6. *Speech and Hearing Program*

   The major functions are to: (a) assess or appraise the speech, hearing and language performance of pupils referred; (b) provide remedial services within the school setting for individuals found to have handicapped impairments. Cooperative and coordinated efforts are made with other disciplines to fulfill these goals.

Special Services personnel are assigned to state, district and school staffs. The Special Education teachers and counselors are assigned to particular schools. Psychological examiners, school social workers and speech-hearing specialists serve schools from their district offices. There is representation of all the Special Services personnel at the state office.

II. WORKING RELATIONSHIPS

A. *The Role of Special Services, Department of Education in Relation to the Public Welfare Division*

1. If school personnel need to know whether a family is receiving Public Welfare Services, this is ascertained by asking the pupil and/or his parents. Policies do not allow for the release of lists of Public Welfare Division recipients.
2. Where school personnel need assistance in working with a child known to the Public Welfare Division, the agency may be contacted for: (a) exchange of information, and (b) coordination of general planning between the school and agency.
3. If the service of any of the Special Services is needed to help implement planning regarding school adjustment problems of a child known to the Public Welfare Division, a school referral shall be made on the appropriate form to the District Office, Intake, Special Services.
4. When a School Social Worker is assigned a case which is known to the Public Welfare Division, determination is made in cooperation with the Public Welfare Division as to how service to the child can best be implemented in relation to his school adjustment problems.

B. *The Role of the Public Welfare Division in Relation to Special Services, Department of Education*

1. When visiting the school, the Public Welfare Social Worker shall make initial entry to the school through the principal, who will determine the future pattern of contact with school personnel. However, the principal remains responsible for the administration of all of the programs and activities in the school.
2. The Special Services field staff may be contacted directly at the District Office, Special Services.
3. The Public Welfare staff shall take responsibility for giving information to Department of Education staff about the kind of services it can provide on an individual situation.
4. The Public Welfare Division will not assume duties that are the responsibility of the child's parents, but will help the parents or foster parents to assume this.
5. The school shall make every effort to assess a child's learning problems and to resolve the difficulty at the school level. However, where the problem is chronically related to the home, the Public Welfare Social Worker may expect to become involved in working with the school.

6. Public Welfare staff shall not be expected to secure specialized information for educational planning for a child known to the agency. However, if such information is already available to the Division, the agency may release such information.

III. PROCEDURES FOR CASE REFERRALS

A. *Referrals from Special Services, Department of Education to the Public Welfare Division*

1. Where services to a pupil or family seem indicated, the school makes a referral on the Department of Education form to Special Services, Intake, District Office.
   a. In a crisis situation concerning abuse and neglect, direct contact shall be made with the Public Welfare Division, Applications Unit, and with the agency's district office. This shall be followed immediately by a written referral on the appropriate form to Special Services District Office, with a copy of the referral being sent to the Public Welfare Division.
2. Disposition of referrals from schools is made by Special Services, Intake, District Office, in one of the following ways:
   a. Clearance with, or referral of the case to the Public Welfare Division.
   b. Case conference with the Public Welfare division regarding disposition.
   c. Assignment of the case to one of the programs in the Special Services, preferably School Social Work, for an indicated service.
3. The district staff of Special Services shall make referrals through the District Office, Special Services Intake to the Public Welfare Division.
4. Intake, Special Services, District Office shall submit a copy of the form with the transmittal memo when referring a pupil to Public Welfare Services.

B. *Referrals from the Public Welfare Division to Special Services, Department of Education*

1. Requests for assistance from a school or district office are made in writing to the District Office, Special Services, with most referrals being concerned with assistance on a school centered situation.
   a. A copy of the request for assistance shall be sent to the principal of the school the pupil attends.

(See Also: ACCIDENT; BOARD OF EDUCATION; CHILD STUDY TEAM; CORPORAL PUNISHMENT; DOCTORS; POLICE; RESOURCE TEAM)

CHILD STUDY TEAM

referral for possible classification form...

(Complete in triplicate. Retain one copy for school files and forward two copies to Unit Child Study Team Administrator within seven (7) days of parental approval.)

Copy of In-School Intervention Plan Materials must be attached.

Date ______________________

Student ________________ School ________________ Date of Birth ____________

Address ____________ Grade ________ Teacher/Guidance Counselor ________________

Telephone ________________ Parent/Guardian ________________________

Parent Notification of Referral.

1. Conference with parent/guardian was held on ____________ by ________________

2. Reasons for referral: ____

3. A copy of the reasons given for referral and of Due Process Procedures were discussed with the parent/guardian on ________________________________

Signatures of: Classroom Teacher/Guidance Counselor ________________________

Principal ________________________

Date ________________________

____ I am aware of this request and have discussed and received a copy of the reasons for the referral and of my rights under Due Process.

____ I do not wish my child to receive this service.

Date ________________ ________________________

Parent/Guardian

FOR OFFICE OF PUPIL PERSONNEL USE

Date Received: ________________ Assigned to: ________________________

EVALUATION TO BE COMPLETED BY: ________________________________

(Sixty (60) Calendar Days from Date of Referral)

request for in-school intervention plan form...

(Complete in triplicate. Copies for Assistant Principal, Guidance Counselor, and Student file.)

Initiated by ______________________________ Date ________________________
Signature

Student ________________ School ________________ Date of Birth ______________

Address ________________ Grade ________ Guidance Counselor ________________

Telephone ______________________ Parent/Guardian ________________________

Attendance Record Last Three Years: Absent _____ Tardy _____ Grades Repeated _____

If transfer student, name of previous school system. ______________________________

Reason for Request: ______ Academic Progress ______ Attendance
______ Emotional Adjustment ______ Peer Relationships
______ Speech and/or Hearing ______ Behavior

Statement of Problem: (Give facts only.) ____

____

____

____

____

____

Previous Actions Taken: (Give summary of actions taken, including parent conferences. Be prepared to document if necessary.)

____

____

____

____

____

____

____

____

____

(Form continued)

request for in-school intervention plan form (cont'd)

Previous Services: (Please check and give dates where possible.)

_____ Psychological Evaluation _____ Special Class

_____ L.D.T.C. Evaluation _____ Supplemental

_____ Speech Evaluation _____ Title I

_____ Social Assessment _____ Compensatory Education

_____ Resource Teacher _____ Reading _____ Math _____ Science

Copies of Progress Reports must be attached when available.

Health Report:

Vision _______________ Date _______________

Hearing _______________ Date _______________

Nurse's Comments:

____

____

____

____

INTERVENTION PLAN

Discussed with: ☐ Reading Resource ☐ L.D.T.C.

☐ Math Resource ☐ Social Worker

☐ Speech ☐ Psychologist

☐ Subject Teacher ☐ Assistant Principal

No testing will be done at this point by C.S.T.

☐ Other (Specify) _______________ ☐ No further action required.

Date _______________ Signatures: _______________

Guidance Counselor

____

Assistant Principal

(Form continued)

(See Also: COUNSELING; FAILURE, IDENTIFICATION; INDIVIDUALIZATION; NURSE; OBSERVATIONS; PERMANENT RECORDS; RECORDS; REFERRAL; REPORTS; RESOURCE TEAM; SPECIAL EDUCATION; SUPPLEMENTAL INSTRUCTION)

CITIZENSHIP

examples of guidelines in student handbooks...

1. Will arrive at school by 8:25 a.m. each day.
2. Will exercise good manners in classroom, library, lunchroom—in fact, everywhere.
3. Never leave the classroom without permission of the classroom teacher, except in an emergency.
4. Pass immediately to his or her class.
5. Use the sidewalks upon entering the school grounds—will not walk across the grass.
6. Cover, take good care of, and pay for any textbooks that are damaged or lost.
7. Leave the building or go to practice immediately after school. LOITERING IN THE BUILDINGS IS FORBIDDEN.

A GOOD CITIZEN WILL

1. Go directly to his or her classroom at 8:25.
2. Go to his locker no more than four times a day—before going to first period class, before lunch, after lunch, and after school.
3. Exercise good manners in classrooms, library, cafeteria—in fact, everywhere.
4. Never leave the classroom without first obtaining a blue I.D. slip or a hall pass from the teacher, or will never leave the building without first obtaining a "Permit to leave the grounds" from the office.
5. Pass immediately to the next class; he does not ask the teacher for a conference at that time; he sees the teacher during the "special help period."
6. Wait for the teacher to dismiss the class at the end of the period.
7. Use the sidewalks upon entering the grounds, not cut across lawns.
8. Cover, take good care of, and pay for any textbooks that are damaged or lost.
9. Leave the building or go to an activity immediately after school. Loitering in the hallways after school is strictly forbidden.

The majority of our students have little need for a system of penalties for misconduct. Many are good school citizens because they want to be good citizens. However, the unfortunate fact is that there is a small number of students, who, because of their patterns of behavior, cause school regulations to be made. With these opposing factors at work it becomes necessary to devise a plan of evaluation of school citizenship and report this evaluation to all parents by using a classroom attitude grade in each class, and a citizenship grade for non-classroom conduct.

The grade in citizenship is determined by using demerits. For various cases of misconduct demerits may be given to students by any member of the staff. At the beginning of each nine weeks grading period all students begin with no demerits, entitling them to an A. As the classroom teacher accumulates demerits, the class attitude grade for just that class deteriorates according to the schedule below. The same applies for demerits turned into your homeroom teacher for conduct outside the classroom.

No demerits – A in citizenship

1 demerit – B in citizenship

2 demerits – C in citizenship

3 demerits – D in citizenship

4 demerits – F in citizenship

More than 4 demerits – F in citizenship

An excessive number of demerits may lead to possible suspension (in-school or out) or expulsion.

(See Also: ACHIEVEMENT; ALTERNATE SCHOOL PROGRAM; BEHAVIOR; BOARD OF EDUCATION; DEMONSTRATIONS; HONOR ROLL; NATIONAL HONOR SOCIETY; RIGHTS AND RESPONSIBILITIES; STUDENT COUNCIL (GOVERNMENT))

CLASS

class rolls and record books...

A great deal of time and effort have been given in trying to balance class numbers. Students must not be allowed to shift from one section of a class to another. Under no circumstances should a student's schedule be changed without approval and knowledge of the office. It is not advisable to put names in your roll books until all classes have been stabilized. Use the temporary roll for the first few days. When the roll books are filled in, they should be completed in detail, including the top of the page and the spaces for the daily dates. BE SURE THAT ALL STUDENTS ENTERING YOUR CLASS AFTER THE ROLL HAS BEEN ESTABLISHED ARE ADDED AND THAT STUDENTS WHO DROP YOUR CLASS ARE DELETED FROM YOUR CLASS ROLL IN ORDER THAT GRADE REPORTING TO THE COMPUTER WILL BE ACCURATE.

CLASS RECORD BOOK

This book is a record for your marks/grades. Be consistent in keeping a record that will provide information you can give to parents at evaluation times during the school year. Parents may have questions, so a complete consistent record will provide you with information for these conferences.

Although fewer letter grades are presently being used, there is still a need for regular evaluation to check on the progress of the child. The record book should show a large enough sampling so the work of the child can be evaluated in terms of the progress being made for report cards and conferences with parents.

class schedules...

Teachers are asked to note and follow the suggestions in the Rock Township Public School system Curriculum Guide for each subject area. This provides a scope and sequence plan for each subject. Teachers are encouraged to correlate instructional units and areas when possible. The system Curriculum Guide is constantly being reviewed and updated through the work of the Curriculum Committee in each subject area.

Teachers will be asked to prepare three copies of their Daily Program schedule once it is set (one for the office, one to be posted in the room, and one for the plan book).

(See Also: ACADEMIC FREEDOM; ADULT EDUCATION; CLEANUP; CONTROVERSIAL TOPICS; CURRICULUM; CUTTING; DISCIPLINE; ELECTIVES; GRADES; HOMEWORK; LESSON PLANS; OBSERVATIONS; SUBSTITUTE TEACHER; TEXTBOOKS)

CLEANUP

guidelines for...

Although we have custodians to do the cleaning and maintenance of the school building, each teacher is responsible for the care and cleanliness of the room as it pertains to book storage, shelves, teacher's desk, etc.

Teachers are asked to make provision or provide procedures to take care of the following:

1. Students should pick up all paper, pencils, etc., from the floor around their desks at the end of the school day.
2. Students should remove everything from the tops of their desks at the end of the school day. Books and personal items should be picked up from the floor at the end of the day.
3. Teacher should check on keeping shelves, tables, desks, etc., in an orderly manner at the end of each school day. Teacher's desk should be tidied up before leaving school for the night.
4. Teacher should close all windows when leaving the room at the end of the school day.
5. Please use discretion on taping things to the walls or chalkboards in the classrooms. Items taped to the walls or windows with masking tape should not be left too long as the glue will separate from the tape and deface the wall, boards, etc., after a period of time. Taping to chalkboards *can ruin them by taking off coating finish.*
6. Teachers—be sure that outside doors lock behind you when you leave the building. (*The doors close, but often do not lock. Please check them.*)
7. Students should be encouraged to respect the building as part of their civic responsibility and respect for public property. Please note the following:

a. There is absolutely no need for writing on or defacing any part of the building, equipment, or grounds. Violations of this will be dealt with through the principal's office.

b. Students should clean off their shoes and boots before coming into the building in wet and muddy weather.

c. No writing or marking on desks or walls.

8. Rooms with carpet—Teachers need to use good judgment and care in the use of glue and clay. It is very hard to get out of the carpet.

policy on...

CLASSROOM HOUSEKEEPING

Teachers are expected to use ceiling lights any time they are needed. The lights should be turned off when you are leaving the room or when otherwise not needed. Caution should be exercised to see that the best available light (natural or artificial) is provided for the students at all times. If you are leaving a room at the end of a class period, please turn off the lights. If the room is to be used the next period by another teacher, it is a simple matter for this teacher to turn them on if needed.

Always attempt to keep the best lighting. The last teacher to use any room for the last time during the school day should see that all windows are closed.

WHEN THE AIR CONDITIONING IS IN USE ALL CLASSROOM WINDOWS AND DOORS SHOULD BE KEPT CLOSED.

(See Also: ANIMALS; BUILDING; CAFETERIA; CUSTODIAL SERVICES; LAVATORIES; STRIKES; VANDALISM**)**

CLERICAL SERVICES

application for clerical position...

CLERICAL APPLICATION

INSTRUCTIONS:

All responses are to be handwritten in ink. When all questions have been answered, the completed form should be returned to the Personnel Office. Please attach a resume if available. Applications are held for a period of 90 days and then declared inactive. If applicants wish to remain active, they must notify the Personnel Office in writing.

APPLICATION OF:

NAME: ____________________________________ PHONE: ____________
(First) (Middle) (Last)

____________________________________ ____/____/____
(Present Address) (City) (State) (Zip Code)

POSITION YOU ARE APPLYING FOR: ____________________________________

ARE YOU A HIGH SCHOOL GRADUATE? ______ DATE OF GRADUATION: __________

Name of High School: ____________________________________

HAVE YOU ATTENDED COLLEGE? _____ Dates Attended: ____________________
(from) (to)

Name of College: ____________________________________

Please check business training courses you have had, indicating number of years in each subject:

☐ Typing ______ Years ☐ Secretarial Practice ______ Years

Approximate TYPING Speed? ________

☐ Shorthand ______ Years ☐ Bookkeeping ______ Years

Approximate SHORTHAND Speed ________

Other training appropriate to the position applied for: (please specify)

____

____

PREVIOUS WORK EXPERIENCE: (list chronologically)

Employed By	Title or Nature of Job	Dates of Employment From	To

(Form continued)

application for clerical position (cont'd)

HAVE YOU EVER BEEN DISCHARGED FROM A POSITION YOU HAVE HELD? ________

If answered YES, please explain (include job title and date): ________________

____

REASON FOR LEAVING LAST EMPLOYMENT: ________________________

____

REFERENCES:

Name	Mailing Address	Occupation

WHEN COULD YOU BEGIN WORK? ________________________

FURTHER COMMENTS: ________________________________

____

____

____

Date: ______________ ________________________

(Signature of Applicant)

-------------------- FOR OFFICIAL USE ONLY --------------------

Interviewed for:	Building	Date/Time	Initials

WE ARE AN EQUAL OPPORTUNITY EMPLOYER AND FOLLOW FAIR EMPLOYMENT PRACTICES.

(Form continued)

memo to faculty concerning clerical services...

TO: Faculty and Staff
FROM: J. Benson, Principal
RE: Secretarial and Clerical Services

The secretary does a variety of work tasks to help in the smooth operation of the school. Her workload and hours are basically office clerical work, but she does a variety of work which is also helpful to the teachers, such as:

1. handling all school lunch money
2. setting up the Cumulative Folders for new students and first graders
3. putting pictures in folders, recording standardized tests, and getting the folders set up by room in the fall
4. helping with some library work

Please do not ask the secretary to take on classroom work, typing, or projects for you. If you feel it is necessary, please see the principal first and discuss it with him. All of the secretary's work is assigned by the principal.

(See Also: ADDRESS; ATTENDANCE; BULLETIN; DISTRIBUTION OF MATERIALS; MEDICAL FORMS; SECRETARY; TYPISTS; XEROXING)

CLOSE OF SCHOOL

emergency closing procedures...

SPECIAL DISMISSAL PROCEDURES

A. IN ORDER TO ENSURE A SAFE AND RAPID DISMISSAL, THE FOLLOWING PROCEDURES AND ASSIGNMENTS HAVE BEEN DEVELOPED. THE COOPERATION OF THE ENTIRE FACULTY IS IMPERATIVE FOR ITS SUCCESS.

B. GENERAL INFORMATION:

1. No students are to be sent to the library or out of any classroom without a pass from a teacher.
2. Bathrooms will not be open during periods 6 and 7.
3. Once students are outside, all interior doors (excluding main doors) will be chained.

C. At the beginning of period 7 until the end, the following staff are assigned below:

FIRST FLOOR:

Mr. Hendric .... EXIT 11 (Near Room 90)
Mrs. Gyre .... EXIT 10 (Near nurse's office)
Mr. Rad .... EXIT 7 (Gym corridor)
Mr. Karlin .... EXIT 8 (Near side parking lot)
Mr. Ames .... EXIT 1 (Main door)

Mr. Falke ....EXIT 4 (Near Room 113)
Mrs. Danielli ....EXIT 2 (Across from guidance)
Miss Gron ....EXIT 3 (Near Room 108)
Mrs. Jaczyk ....EXIT 6 (Near Room 108)
Mr. Funiell ....EXIT 5 (Near Room 113)
Mrs. Parsons ....EXIT 12 (Near Room 94)

SECOND FLOOR:

Mrs. Van der Mere

OUTSIDE:

Mr. Leon ....SIDE PARKING LOT
Mrs. Weberson...............................FRONT PARKING LOT
Mr. Chancellor..............................FRONT PARKING LOT
Mrs. Hunter ....FRONT OF BUILDING

public notification of close...

TO ALL PARENTS:

If it becomes necessary to close school for any reason (for example, inclement weather, boiler breakdown, etc.), you will be notified of the closing in the following manner:

1. At 7:00 a.m. all Township fire sirens will sound for a period of two minutes. This signal will be repeated at 7:10 a.m. and at 7:20 a.m.
2. Announcement of the school closing shall be reported over radio stations KLMN (107.5 AM) and WXYZ (98.7 FM) starting at 6:00 a.m. and continuing through 9:00 a.m.

It is important that you refrain from calling the Board of Education, the police, or the fire department for information regarding school closings, as these lines must be kept open to handle emergency situations.

Your cooperation and understanding in this matter is greatly appreciated.

Sincerely,

(See Also: DISMISSAL PROCEDURES; EMERGENCY; FIRE DRILLS; WEATHER ALERTS)

CLUBS

chartering of clubs...

1. The Constitution of the R.T.H.S. Student Association provides for the chartering of clubs as follows:

   a. No group of students will be considered an R.T. High School club unless it has first obtained a charter.

b. To obtain a charter, a club must prepare in duplicate a constitution and by-laws, which make provision for the election of members, officers, purposes, and termination of membership. They should also submit a plan of work for the year, the amount of dues to be collected, or any plans for obtaining money other than by dues. Two copies of this should be made, one for the Principal, and one for the Student Council. When approved, the charter will be issued.

c. The charter of a club may be renewed subsequently by submitting to the Principal and the Student Council before October 1 a program and budget for the year, and any amendment to the constitution and by-laws. When approved, the charter will be renewed.

d. Each club is to abide by the rules of the Department of Education in regard to collection and disbursement of funds.

2. Student clubs are to be divided into four categories. They are:

   Group I: Sponsored by the Administration
   - Student Government
   - Class
   - Athletic Committee

   Group II: Co-curricular Clubs

   Group III: Chartered Clubs

   Group IV: Outside Clubs

3. A faculty member shall be appointed by the principal to act as coordinator for club meetings and to work closely with the bulletin board committee.
4. Definite bulletin boards shall be designated for club announcements and posters. Posters will not be allowed on any other part of the campus. Posters must be initialed by the principal or vice-principal or the advisor of the Good Citizenship Committee within 48 hours after the announced event.

club financial procedures...

According to our State Law, all clubs and organizations sponsored by any public school must keep funds in a central bank account under the direct authority of the school Principal. The Uniform Accounting System for Local Schools in the state was established and arranged so that school officials may adequately account for financial operations for which they are responsible. Rock Township High School, in complying with this state-wide directive, has established the following procedures for club accounts:

1. All clubs should have a responsible treasurer to work in cooperation with the sponsor on financial matters.
2. Each club or organization is to be issued a receipt book and a money envelope at the opening of the school year. All money received from any source should be receipted in this receipt book. The receipts should be totaled each day and the money (which

should equal the total of receipts written that day) should be enclosed in the money envelope and turned in to the Bookkeeper's Office before 3:00 that day. The date, amount, and purpose should be recorded in ink on the outside of the envelope leaving the last two columns blank.

3. Money will be checked by the Bookkeeper and a receipt will be issued from the Master Receipt Book. Envelopes will be placed in the sponsor's mailbox at the end of each day.
4. Purchases should be made using the procedure mentioned in this handbook. No check can be issued unless properly documented, as explained.
5. All receipts and expenditures should be recorded daily in proper form by the club treasurer (or in the case of the person from whom the money is received, the receipt numbers and the amount). This information is to be taken from the receipt book.
6. Expenditures are to be recorded on this form when a purchase order is approved by the principal. When the merchandise is received, any necessary adjusting entry should be made for shipping costs, etc., before turning the invoice in to the Bookkeeper's Office.
7. The balance should be recorded after each entry and should be reconciled with the monthly statement issued by the Bookkeeper.
8. All financial records should be retained on file and should be turned in to the Bookkeeper's Office at the end of each school year for audit.

(See Also: ADVISORS AND ADVISORY COMMITTEES; CHAPERONE; DANCES; FEES, FINES; FUNDS AND CHARGES; MEETINGS; MONEY: PERMISSION SLIPS; STUDENT COUNCIL (GOVERNMENT); YEARBOOK)

COLLEGE

college prep course outline in student handbook...

THE DISTRICT'S COLLEGE PREPARATORY COURSE

If you are planning to attend college, the Board of Education has established these college prep studies which includes those required by law.

4 years of English, Math and Physical Education

3½ years of Social Studies

at least 3 years of a foreign language

2 years of science

1 year of fine, practical performing or creative art

1 year of career education taken anytime within grade 9–12

The college prep course also requires that you be enrolled in a 7-period day, and that honor students will be enrolled in advanced courses as available.

teacher guidelines for involvement of college students...

STUDENTS FROM THE STATE COLLEGE

At various times we become involved with students from the college. This involves student teachers, teacher assistants, special projects, etc.

Do not make arrangements on your own with students from the college to come or be in your classroom. Any such participation by students from the college—regardless of the activity—is to be channeled through the appropriate college office and approved by the public school central office ahead of time. This procedure is very definite, and we need to follow it. Please keep this in mind if you are approached by college students or college instructors requesting placement.

Specific instructions relative to student teachers, teacher assistants, etc., will be given out at the time any of these students are assigned to us.

(See Also: ADULT EDUCATION; INTERNSHIP; QUALIFICATIONS; STUDENT TEACHING)

COMPLAINTS

complaint form...

NAME: ______________________ DATE: ______________________

POSITION (student, teacher, parent, etc.) ______________________

WHERE MAY YOU BE REACHED: ______________________

EXPLAIN NATURE OF COMPLAINT: ______________________

____

____

____

____

SIGNATURE: ______________________

notice concerning complaints...

We recognize that from time to time situations may occur that engender legitimate complaints on the part of students, teachers, parents and/or community members relative to the school and/or its operations.

We believe that complaints must be aired in order that all sides of the issue may be heard and a rational solution formulated.

Anyone having a complaint, therefore, is encouraged to file a complaint form (obtainable in every school) with the main office of the school or (if the complaint does not concern a single school) with the secretary of central administration. All complaint forms must be signed by the person originating the complaint.

Complaint forms will be read by persons in charge, and the complainant will be contacted for further information, discussion or resolution of the difficulty.

(See Also: ACCIDENT; BEHAVIOR; CHILD ABUSE; CONTROVERSIAL TOPICS; DEMONSTRATIONS; DUE PROCESS; GRIEVANCES; POLICE; QUESTIONS; WARNING NOTICES)

CONFERENCES

conference report summary sheet...

Conference Reports:

Date: ______	Present: ______

Date: ______	Present: ______

Date: ______	Present: ______

Date: ______	Present: ______

Date: ______	Present: ______

memo on department conferences...

TO: ALL TEACHERS & DEPARTMENT COORDINATORS
FROM: J. Benson, Principal
RE: Department Conferences (7:45–8:15)
Department Coordinators' Meetings (7:45–8:15)

Department conferences have been scheduled on the dates listed below. All teachers must attend. Teachers who are on late schedules are to follow a regular schedule on these days.

Dates	Room Assignments	
September 17		
October 15	Science	Room 100
November 19	Math	Room 214
December 17	Foreign Language	Room 112
January 14	Social Studies	Room 200
February 18	Language Arts	Room 102
March 18	Health/Physical Ed.	Boys' Gym Office
April 15	Activity Arts	Room 95
May 20		

Department coordinators' meetings in the Principal's Office will be held on the following days:

September 15	January 12
October 13	February 16
November 17	March 16
December 15	April 13
	May 18

(See Also: ADVISORS AND ADVISORY COMMITTEES; CHILD STUDY TEAM; COUNSELING; DUE PROCESS; EVALUATION; GUIDANCE; INTERVIEW; OBSERVATIONS; RESOURCE TEAM)

CONFIRMATION

conformation form (all purpose)...

DATE: ______________________ SCHOOL: ______________________

FROM: ____

TO: ____

THIS SHALL CONFIRM THE FOLLOWING: ______________________

____

____

COMMENTS: ____

____

____

Signature: ______________________

letter of confirmation...

Dear Jean,

This shall confirm our appointment on October 9 at 1:30 p.m. at which we shall discuss ways in which the P.T.A. can become more positively involved in school activities.

It is my understanding that you will be accompanied by your vice-president, Mrs. Ada Schottle. While you are free, of course, to bring anyone you feel may make our meeting more productive, I do request that you inform me if more than five (5) people will be attending in order that suitable arrangements may be made.

I look forward to our meeting with great enthusiasm.

Sincerely,

(See Also: ACCEPTANCE; DISTRIBUTION OF MATERIALS; DUE PROCESS; ENROLLMENT; INFORMATION; INVENTORY; PROGRESS REPORT; STUDENT RECORDS; TRANSFER; WARNING NOTICES)

CONTRACT

data for issuance of contracts form...

School ______________________ School Year ______________________

Teacher ______________________ Certificate Number ______________________

Address ______________________ Cert. Expiration Date ______________________

1. Highest Degree ______________ ______________________
   (Year Earned)

   B.S. Degree Major(s) ______________ Minor(s) ______________

   M.S. Degree Major(s) _____ Minor(s) _____

2. Teaching Assignment ______________________________

3. Total Q.H. credits earned in last 6 years: ________
4. Total Q.H. credits approved beyond last degree for advancement on salary schedule: ________

5. Educational step on salary schedule: ________

6. Outside Exp: _____ + Dist. Exp: _____ =
   Exp. Step on Sal. Sched: ________
   (7 yrs. max.)

7. Index determined by 5 and 6 above: ________

8. No. of yrs. on this index (include yr. represented by this data sheet): ________

9. Salary determination by salary schedule (part-time fraction ________): $________

10. Total previous career increments ______________. $________
    (Years awarded)

(Form continued)

data for issuance of contracts form (cont'd)

11. Career increment this year: YES NO (Circle One) .05 × ________ (Base) $________
12. TOTAL SCHEDULE SALARY $________

Extra Compensation

Extracurricular:

Position ________	Position ________	Position ________
% ________	% ________	% ________
Yrs. allowable in this position ________ (prev. exp.)	Yrs. allowable in this position ________ (prev. exp.)	Yrs. allowable in this position ________ (prev. exp.)
Salary Schedule Exp. Step ________ (not $ amt.)	Salary Schedule Exp. Step ________ (not $ amt.)	Salary Schedule Exp. Step ________ (not $ amt.)
Extracurricular Pay $________	Extracurricular Pay $________	Extracurricular Pay $________

Extra Days: Base Teaching Salary: ________ divided by 182 × number of extra days: ________ = $________.

Extra Class: Base Teaching Salary: ________ divided by ____ = $________.

TOTAL EXTRA COMPENSATION $________

TOTAL SALARY $________

________ (Teacher's Signature) ________ (Principal's Signature) ________ (Date)

partial contracts guidelines...

1. All partial contracts are paid on sixths.
2. If a teacher is teaching:

   one class—1/6
   two classes—2/6
   three classes—3/6
3. If a teacher is teaching four classes, he or she will receive credit for planning period and move to a 5/6 contract.
4. A teacher on 5/6 contract receives full benefits:
   a. 10 days sick leave
   b. Blue Cross/Blue Shield
   c. Life Insurance
   d. Workman's Compensation
   e. Teacher's Retirement
5. A teacher with 3/6 contract or less receives partial benefits:
   a. 10 days sick leave

10–3-hour days	3/6 contract
10–2-hour days	2/6 contract
10–1-hour day	1/6 contract

   b. Workman's Compensation
   c. Teacher's Retirement

preliminary statement on master contract...

THIS AGREEMENT, MADE AND ENTERED INTO THIS ____ day of ________, 19______, by and between the ______________________________, of the State of ______________________, hereinafter referred to as the Employer; and ______________________________, hereinafter referred to as the Union, shall be effective as of the ______ day of ____________________, 19______, and remain in effect from year to year hereafter unless changed or terminated in the manner prescribed herein.

sample teacher's contract...

TEACHER'S CONTRACT

The School Board of Rock Township, in the State of ____________________, enters into this agreement with ______________________________, of ______________ ____________________, a legally qualified teacher, who agrees to serve in the following assignment in the Rock Township Public Schools.

Assignment: ____

____

____

____

Other specified duties: ____

____

____

This contract shall be in effect for ____ days of employment for the school year 19__-19__, beginning on or about ____________, and shall be terminated on or about ____________.
Teacher's Salary ____
($____________).

Rock Township Public Schools:

____________________	____________________
Teacher	President
____________________	____________________
Date	Date
	____________________
	Clerk
	____________________
	Date

(See Also: ACCEPTANCE; APPLICATION; BOARD OF EDUCATION; DUE PROCESS; GRIEVANCES; INTERVIEW; MEDIATION; NEGOTIATIONS; NON-RENEWAL OF CONTRACT)

CONTROVERSIAL TOPICS

policy on...

Free discussion of controversial issues is the heart of the democratic process. Freedom of speech and free access to information are among our most cherished traditions. It is the responsibility of the schools to prepare pupils to understand these democratic practices and to use them wisely.

The schools do not teach controversial issues, but rather provide opportunities for their study. For the public schools, policy on controversial issues is defined in terms of the rights of pupils rather than in terms of the rights of teachers. The pupil has four rights to be recognized.

1. The right to study any controversial issue that has instructional significance and concerning which (at his level) he should begin to have an opinion.
2. The right to have access to all relevant information, including the materials that circulate freely in the community.
3. The right to study under competent instruction in an atmosphere free from bias and prejudice.
4. The right to form and express his own opinion on controversial issues without thereby jeopardizing his relations with his teacher or the school.

The Board expects each teacher to control the approach to controversial issues in the classroom so that they are presented in an impartial, unemotional, and unprejudiced manner as possible and to refrain from using his classroom privileges and prestige to promote a partisan point of view.

(See Also: ACADEMIC FREEDOM; CURRICULUM; DISTRIBUTION OF MATERIAL; NEW POLICY OR PROGRAM; PHILOSOPHY)

CORPORAL PUNISHMENT

special note...

A number of states prohibit corporal punishment in any form, while it is allowed by law in others. The following entries are representative of both viewpoints.

guidelines for corporal punishment...

1. **Definition.** Chastisement inflicted on the body in order to cause physical pain, usually with the professed purpose of modifying behavior.

2. **Method of Punishment.** One swat, with a wooden paddle not more than one-half inch in thickness nor more than fourteen ounces in weight, upon the buttocks. Students must bend over and touch his toes (eliminates danger of hitting the spine). Paddling must be done by the same sex.
3. **Punishable Offenses.** Students are paddled for using profanity, vulgarity, disrespect, and bold and open defiance to lawful authority.
4. **Who May Paddle.** The principal, assistant principal, dean of students, or the teacher are those who may paddle students. No other person may do so, including the parent. Teachers are only allowed to do so in case of physical attack.
5. **Students Who Are Exempt.** Those students who have psychological or medical problems are not to be paddled. Parent is responsible for notifying the school of any valid reason for exempting his child from paddling and must supply any necessary documentation.
6. **Due Process.** Must consist of notice, evidence and response. "Notice" means informing the student of the rule that is broken and telling him of the penalty. "Evidence" means telling the student why he has been charged. "Response" means giving the student a chance to tell his version of the involvement.
7. **Witness Must Be Present.** A witness must hear the notice, evidence and response before the punishment is administered.
8. **File a Report.** A brief report must be placed in the student's file and in a general discipline file immediately after the paddling. All such evidence in the student's file is destroyed with termination of enrollment.

handbook disclaimer of corporal punishment...

CORPORAL PUNISHMENT

You are protected from corporal punishment by school employees except under these four conditions when such force is considered "reasonable and necessary (1) to quell a disturbance, (2) to obtain possession of weapons or other dangerous objects, (3) for the purpose of self-defense, and (4) for the protection of persons and property."

(See Also: BEHAVIOR; DISCIPLINE; DUE PROCESS; PRINCIPAL; REFERRAL; VICE-PRINCIPAL)

COUNSELING

definitions for parent flyer...

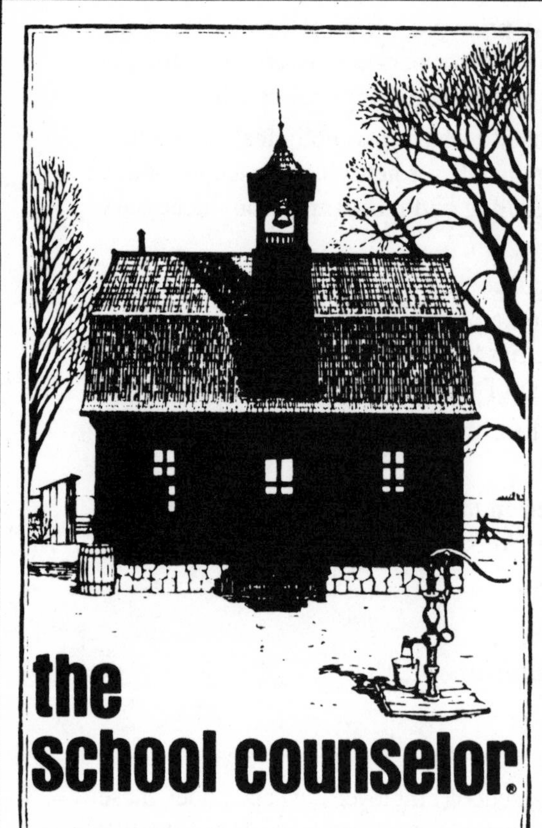

What Is Counseling?

It is . . .

Visiting individually with students.

Involvement with students in groups.

Consultation with administrators.

Working with teachers to meet a student's needs.

Meeting with parents.

Collaboration with community agencies and others.

What Is Guidance?

Guidance refers to informational services provided by counselors, ranging from how to prepare a child for his first day of elementary school to applying for college or a job. It involves more information giving than anything else.

Whom Do Counselors Work with in a School?

Students

Parents

Teachers

Administrators

Community

Anyone who can assist in helping a student reach his or her fullest potential.

duties and assignments of...

1. Guidance and Counseling Programs

   The counseling department will be responsible to create various guidance and counseling programs to meet the needs of the various interest groups on campus such as the college, vocational, business, military and other interest groups.

2. Assignments of Students to the Counseling Staff

   The counselors will prepare the counselor-student list during the fourth quarter. Assignments will be based on the counselor's area of responsibilities, for example, college-vocational-business, sophomores, etc.

19XX-XX: Mr. Robert Hyers, Department Chairperson

Coordinator of testing (SAT, National Merit)
Coordinator of OEO-ESAA Project
Coordinator of CETA Programs
Chairperson–Accreditation Committee (19XX-XX)
Counselor for half of Sophomore class + 25 Juniors

Mr. Thomas Wells

Counselor of Sophomores + 25 Juniors
Varsity Football Coach
Coordinator–military programs
Sophomore Class Advisor
In-coming Sophomore Class Orientation

Mr. Henry Calbreth

Counselor of Non-College Prep Junior and Senior Students
Coordinator of business-technical-vocational post-high school programs
Apprenticeship Programs
Post-high school military programs

Mr. James Lincroft

Counselor of Junior-Senior College Prep Students
Varsity Basketball Coach
Driver Training Coordinator
Coordinator of College Representatives
In charge of college catalog filing

Mrs. Barbara Dean

Counselor of Junior-Senior College Prep Students
Financial Aids Coordinator
Senior Class Advisor

Mrs. Cynthia Moore

PIP

Mr. Donald Martin

Campus Counselor

explanation for parents...

Some things an Elementary Guidance Counselor does:

Helps students—

- Understand his/her abilities and limitations
- Adjust to a new school
- Find answers to his/her concerns
- Learn to make decisions
- Develop skills in getting along with others
- Achieve more in school

Talks with you about your child's—

- Progress in school
- Abilities and limitations
- Growth and development

Assists teachers in—

- Understanding and meeting individual student needs
- Providing classroom guidance in such areas as self-understanding, decision-making, and values
- Finding special help for students when needed
- Planning units on guidance-related topics

Consults with parents and teachers in private conferences about their children

Coordinates referrals to school and community agencies when school personnel and parents agree this is needed

Talks with children individually or in small groups. The child may request the counseling or may be referred by parents or teachers. Counseling is a voluntary service—no child is required to talk with the counselor.

open letter to parents...

Dear Parents...

Do you sometimes hear your kids say things like, "Why do I have to go to school?" or "When I take tests, I get scared!" or "When I'm worried, I can't think at school. I'm just dumb!" If you do, then maybe the school guidance counselor can help.

"But," you say, "what is a guidance counselor? How does a counselor work in school? When is the counselor at school? How can I get hold of a counselor?"

For some answers, read the attached flyer. Better yet—call your school and make an appointment to sit down and visit with the counselor. We bet that you'll enjoy the experience and that you'll come away with a better knowledge of how to help us help your child.

(See Also: ABSENTEEISM; BEHAVIOR; CAREERS; CHILD STUDY TEAM; CONFERENCES; GUIDANCE; IDENTIFICATION; PERMANENT RECORDS; SCHEDULE; WARNING NOTICES)

COURSES

course requirements...

One (1) Science Course in Grades 10–12

Drivers' Education–1/2 unit required

Required for Graduation:

Required courses	15 units
Electives	8 units
Total	23 units

Any student moving to Rock Township from a school that required twenty (20) units for graduation will have his requirements for graduation adjusted on the basis of time left on Rock Township Public Schools.

Entering from out of system as a 10th grade student	22 units
Entering from out of system as a 11th grade student	21 units
Entering from out of system as a 12th grade student	20 units

All graduation requirements will be reviewed annually.

Any fractional credit that a student earns may be combined with any other fractional credit and count toward graduation or for promotional purposes.

One year or unit of foreign language is counted even if a student does not pursue a second year of the program.

Any subject offered in grades nine through twelve that meets for a minimum of one-hundred twenty (120) clock hours of recitation is successfully completed by the student enrolled in class must carry a unit of credit.

No student in grades 9–12 will be utilized as a teacher's assistant except in the library, and there he/she must follow an outlined independent study program in order to earn a unit of credit.

Students may elect to work in the Office Assistant Program which is designed to give on-the-job experiences. Students enrolled in business programs will receive priority consideration. One unit credit per year will be given.

courses acceptable for salary improvement form...

____

Name

COURSES ACCEPTABLE FOR IMPROVEMENT ON SALARY SCHEDULE

Rock Township Public Schools

			CREDITS EARNED				
APPROVED BY	DATE	NAME OF COURSE	QTR HR.	SEM. HR.	COLLEGE	GRAD. HR.	UNDER GRAD. HR.

credit for courses...

CREDIT FOR OTHER COURSES

Occasionally, students with certain abilities and needs are given a special program of study in school. This program, known as a "Plan B," is only given to you if your educational needs are not being met in regular courses.

Should you need to have a "Plan B" developed for you, you will need the approval of your guidance counselor, department supervisor, and ultimately the Board of Education.

CREDIT FOR SUMMER SCHOOL COURSES

Generally, you should take normal course offerings in the district. However, you can get permission to make-up or accelerate credit under certain conditions.

You can attend summer school and receive credit as long as you get your principal's permission. The grades you get, however, are not calculated into your class rank.

You can also be instructed by a certified tutor if the courses you want are unavailable in summer school, as long as you get your principal's permission. Again, the grades in such courses cannot be calculated into your class rank. Also, you must submit your grades in writing, signed by your tutor, by September 1.

If you want to take 120 hours of (full-year) courses in summer school you must get your principal's permission. These courses will be calculated into your class rank and will count toward graduation.

dropping a course...

POLICY: While there is no specific statement, past and present practice is such that "any student who drops a course after the probationary period (deadline set for changing of courses) is dropped with an "F."

The rationale is based on two reasons:

1. The student was given a probationary period within which to make an assessment and, therefore, should be held accountable for his decision thereafter.
2. Failure to apply some standard may result in irresponsible action that would be detrimental to the student as well as create a bookkeeping problem that cannot be adequately handled with the limited staff on hand. (This is further complicated because we are on computer schedule.)

Exceptions, however, have been granted under the following conditions and guidelines:

1. Teacher recommendation is based on evidence that circumstances were not *entirely* dependent upon student initiative or effort.
2. The entire department and/or a committee designated to handle such affairs concurs (majority vote) that the exception should be considered and/or granted.

(See Also: ADULT EDUCATION; CLASS; CURRICULUM; ELECTIVES; GRADES; MINI-COURSES; SUPPLEMENTAL INSTRUCTION; WARNING NOTICES)

CURRICULUM

application for new curriculum offering...

-APPLICATION FOR NEW ACTIVITIES, ADDITIONAL CURRICULUM OFFERING, OR SPECIAL PROJECTS-

This form shall be completed for any extension of curriculum, extra curricular activity, or special projects that commit the school board to additional expenditures of either a short term or long range nature. This form is primarily designed to give a clear understanding of the change to take place as to need, procedure, management, measurable values, and the short and long term financial obligation. The outline is condensed, without sufficient space for writing or developing details, but it is expected that in the writing process the director, principal or other administrator requesting the change shall complete and expand all applicable areas as completely and accurately as possible using whatever space is needed. The completed request shall be sent to the assistant supervisor, business manager, superintendent, and in some cases to the school board, for approval.

Approved by: Approved by:

________________________ ________________________

Superintendent Date Assistant Superintendent Date

________________________ ________________________

School Board President Date Business Manager Date

SECTION I - GENERAL INFORMATION OUTLINE

TITLE: ________________________

PROPOSER: ________________________ BUILDING ________________

PARTICIPANTS, if known: ________________________

NUMBER OF ADULTS SERVED: ________________________

NUMBER OF STAFF SERVED: ________________________

	1	2	3	4	5	6	7	8	9	10	11	12
NUMBER OF STUDENTS SERVED - By Grade:												
NUMBER OF HANDICAPPED SERVED - By Grade:												

CERTIFIED AND PROFESSIONAL STAFF (by grades) TO BE EMPLOYED AND THE ESTIMATED TOTAL HOUR/MONTHLY, OR CONTRACTED TIME TO BE EMPLOYED: ________________

SUBJECT SPECIALIST: Media, Counselor, Evaluators, Other--Name. Number to be employed and estimated time: ________________________

NONCERTIFIED - Secretarial, Artist, Photographer: List positions and estimated time: ____________

If this involves no new staff, explain realignment.

SECTION II - NARRATIVE

NEEDS AND OBJECTIVES - Subsection 1.

A. Statement of Needs: Explain in general terms and in specific terms why the students and the district need this activity. If relevant research is available, please include it.

B. Population: Describe population to be served: children, parents, numbers, etc.

C. Process Objectives: Arrange a calendar of events, in sequence, and indicate who is responsible to do what activity, by what time, and how it will be assured of being done.

D. Performance Objectives: Write the major outcome of the project and how it will be measured in terms of student performance, parent response, behavior change, improvement, tests, or whatever else is appropriate for the goal. Include samples, examples, etc.

OTHER COMMENTS BY PROPOSERS OF ACTIVITY –

SECTION III - BUDGET-EXPENDITURES OUTLINE - PART A

(Complete only account categories that will be used, but itemize carefully and accurately. Use another sheet(s) to allow adequate space.)

ACCT. NO. AMOUNT

200 - SALARIES
Professional Time: $________
(Name positions and give names, if know.)

Noncertified Time: $________
(Name positions and give names, if know)

220 - TEXTBOOKS $________

230 - LIBRARY AND AUDIOVISUAL $________

240 - MATERIALS AND SUPPLIES $________
(Use current catalog or contact supplier; be accurate as possible.)

Quantity	Item	Supplier	Cost Each	Total Cost

250 - TRAVEL
__________ miles x $.15 per personal vehicle $________
Commercial travel; describe $________
Per Diem:
Meals @ $10.00 per day maximum, in-state $________
$15.00 out-of-state $________
Rooms @ $16.00 per night maximum, in-state $________
Actual - out-of-state $________

253 - CONTRACTED SERVICES $________
(List special service, lectures, etc. to be given and names, if known. Rate of charge.)

300 - ATTENDANCE SERVICES COSTS $________

410 - HEALTH SERVICE COSTS $________

500 - PUPIL TRANSPORTATION COSTS $________

600 - OPERATION OF PLANT COSTS $________

700 - MAINTENANCE OF PLANT COSTS $________

800 - FIXED CHARGES
Total Salaries - $________ x .0585 social security $________
Total Teachers Salaries - $________ x .04 teacher retirement $________
(If during school year)
Other, list $________

900 - FOOD SERVICE COSTS $________

1000 - STUDENT BODY ACTIVITIES $________

1100 - COMMUNITY SERVICES - RECREATION $________

1220 - REMODELING $________

1230 - EQUIPMENT $________

SECTION III - SUMMARY - PART B

PUBLIC SCHOOL

Budget Period ______________

EXPENDITURE ACCOUNT		EXPENSE CLASSIFICATION							
		SALARIES							
Classification	Acct. No.	Professional	Non Professional	Contracted Services	Materials and Supplies	Travel	Equipment	Other Expenses	Total Expenditures
(1)	(2)	(3)	(4)	(5)	(6)	(7)	(8)	(9)	(10)
1. Administration	100								
2. Instruction	200								
3. Attendance Services	300								
4. Health Services	400								
5. Pupil Transp. Services	500								
6. Operation of Plant	600								
7. Maintenance of Plant	700								
8. Fixed Charges (except 830)	800								
9. Leasing of Facilities	830								
10. Food Services	900								
11. Student Body Activity	1000								
12. Community Services	1100								
13. Remodeling ($2,000 or less)	1220C								
14. Capital Outlay (Equipment only)	1230								
15. TOTAL EXPENDITURES									

SECTION III - EXPLANATION OF INCOME - PART C

INCOME

Local Taxes: $__________

State Reimbursement: $__________

Local Fees: $__________

Sales of Material or a Service: $__________

Federal Grants: $__________

Other: (Gifts, etc.) $__________

TOTAL $__________

sample introduction to a new curriculum document...

This document, like any curriculum document presented for the first time, is to be considered a working paper for the first year. During that time, teachers are to use it, make notes on what worked well, what did not, and suggestions for revisions. After a year's trial the document will be revised on the basis of teachers' input and thereafter considered "official."

(See Also: ADULT EDUCATION; CLASS; CONTROVERSIAL TOPICS; COURSES; ELECTIVES; GRADES; MINI-COURSES; SUPPLEMENTAL INSTRUCTION; WARNING NOTICES)

CUSTODIAL SERVICES

duties of...

1. What they are expected to do
   a. Clean lavatory rooms, rest rooms, auditorium and offices occupied by some of the "overhead"
   b. Campus–weeding, watering, planting
   c. Repairs–of a simple nature which do not require a state or county plumber, carpenter or painter
2. What they should *not* be asked to do
   1. Sweep and (or) dust inside the classrooms
   b. Run errands for the teachers

The custodians are civil service employees of the state and are on a 40-hour work week. They have the same holidays, sick and vacation leaves as the other civil service employees.

Any overtime request to complete *any work must be cleared by the administration, who must clear with the District Office*.

request for custodial services form...

DATE: ____________________

PERSON INITIATING REQUEST: ____________________

DATE SERVICES REQUIRED: ____________________
(month) (day) (year) (day of week) (times)

NATURE OF CUSTODIAL SERVICES REQUIRED: ____________________

____

____

FOR WHAT ACTIVITY(S): ____________________

____

____

WILL MORE THAN TWO CUSTODIANS BE REQUIRED? YES ( ) NO ( )

IF "YES," EXPLAIN: ____________________

____

____

APPROVED BY: ____________________ DATE: ____________________

COMMENTS: ____________________

____

____

(See Also: APPLICATION; BUILDING; CLEANUP; DANCES; EQUIPMENT; INVENTORY; KEYS; MAP OF THE SCHOOL; REQUISITIONS, REPAIRS, AND REPLACEMENTS; USE OF FACILITIES; VANDALISM; WORK)

CUTTING

form for detection of students cutting class...

To use the following form, teachers record absences from class in the space for the appropriate period. At the end of the school day, these names are checked against a daily attendance list. The names of those students absent from class but not on the absentee list are circled, and the main office checks into their whereabouts.

CLASSROOM ATTENDANCE

(Cut Sheet)

TEACHER'S NAME ______________________ DATE ______________

Period 1	Period 5
Period 2	Period 6
Period 3	Period 7
Period 4	

HALL PASS RECORD

Name	Destination	Time left	Time returned

policy statement on...

CUTTING may be defined as an unacceptable absence from school or class(es) and/or assigned location(s) as a result of a deliberate and willful action on the part of the student.

Each school in the district will establish procedures for the detection of cutting and implement them on a daily basis.

Students found to be cutting an assigned location (that is, class, lunch, study hall, etc.) are liable to disciplinary action on the part of the school. This disciplinary action may include but will not be limited to notification of parents, detention, assignment to the Alternate School Program, and, in severe cases, referral to juvenile authorities.

(See Also: ABSENCE; ABSENTEEISM; BEHAVIOR; COURSES; DETENTION; DISCIPLINE; PASSES; RETENTION)

DANCES

guidelines for student conduct...

Students attending related school activities such as school dances, athletic events, plays, etc., are subject to all school regulations and are expected to conduct themselves properly at all times. Any student involved in disorderly conduct, possession of alcohol, drugs, fighting, smoking in prohibited areas, improper dress, etc., will be subject to strict discipline and possible suspension. Class sponsors, student leaders, and faculty members involved in school-related activities are to work closely with the assistant principal in charge of student activities. These activities are essential components of school life. We will not allow a few unruly students to spoil these activities for the majority of our students who have the right to enjoy them.

school rules for dances...

1. Students pay an admission to be admitted to a school dance.
2. Once a student leaves the dance, he may not be re-admitted.
3. All school and state laws pertaining to users of alcohol, tobacco or other harmful drugs are in effect.
4. Proper conduct is required at all times.
5. Dress restrictions may be placed on certain dances such as Prom or Homecoming.
6. School dances will be chaperoned by teachers and a uniformed police officer. They are in charge of the building during a dance and are to be obeyed at all times.
7. Guests will be admitted to three dances during the school year—Homecoming, Snowball Dance and the Prom. You must secure a pass from a principal—no exceptions. Non-students may not attend any other school dances.
8. Dances must be scheduled in the principal's office at least two weeks in advance.
9. Students must show I.D. card for school-sponsored dances.

(See Also: ADVISORS AND ADVISORY COMMITTEES; CHAPERONE; DANCES; FEES, FINES, FUNDS AND CHARGES; MEETING; MONEY; PERMISSION SLIPS; STUDENT COUNCIL (GOVERNMENT); SUPERVISION**)**

DEMONSTRATIONS

policy and guidelines for...

In the best interest of all students, the following criteria must be met by individuals and groups who anticipate participation in any demonstration:

Off Campus

Parental request should: (a) note reason or reasons for request, and (b) designate specific time of departure from school. Note: Students should not return to the campus on the same day.

On Campus

Demonstrators will: (a) not be permitted to cut classes for the purpose of demonstrating or loitering, and (b) not disrupt the normal operation of classes or the school.

NOTE: ANY VIOLATIONS OF THE ABOVE WILL BE DEALT WITH UNDER THE POLICIES SPECIFIED BY THE SCHOOL CODE.

(See Also: ACADEMIC FREEDOM; CONTROVERSIAL TOPICS; STRIKES; VANDALISM**)**

DEPARTMENTAL MEETINGS

message in teacher handbook...

Tuesday afternoons after school hours should be reserved for departmental meetings here at Rock Township High School. These meetings are usually held in the particular departmental office and start at 3:15 p.m.

These meetings are not held every Tuesday, but as needed. Teachers are asked to provide in-put into these meetings whenever possible. Various activities of a departmental nature will be conducted at this time that could not ordinarily be handled during the school day.

No time limit is set on these meetings, but they will only be for as long as is necessary for the completion of necessary business. As professional people, your cooperation is requested on this as it is impossible to know just how long they will run each time. We will all try to get the work done as quickly as possible, and usually a departmental meeting will be concluded by 4:15 p.m.

notice of...

ROCK TOWNSHIP HIGH SCHOOL

Notice of Departmental Meeting

To: ALL MEMBERS OF THE ____________________ DEPARTMENT

From: ______________________________, Departmental Chairperson

Re: Departmental Meeting

WHEN: ______________________________TIME: __________

AGENDA: ____

____

____

____

DATE OF THIS NOTICE: ______________________________________

(See Also: CHAIRPERSONS; FACULTY MEETINGS; OBJECTIVES)

DETENTION

detention notification form...

Date of This Notice: ______________________________________

Name and Grade of Student: ______________________________________

(last) (first) (initial) (grade)

HAS BEEN ASSIGNED DETENTION ON: ______________________________

(day) (full date)

REASON: ____

____

PLACE DETENTION IS TO BE SERVED: ______________________________

PERSON ASSIGNING DETENTION: ______________________________

(Note: Detention is served from 3:15 p.m. until 4:00 p.m. Late buses are available at that time and leave school at approximately 4:15 p.m. for those who normally use bus transportation.)

SIGNATURE OF TEACHER/ADMINISTRATION: ______________________

SIGNATURE OF STUDENT: ______________________

SIGNATURE OF PARENT: ______________________

examples of messages from student and teacher handbooks...

Detention will be held every day from 3:20 to 4:10. Teachers will assign detention to students for being tardy three times during the nine-week period or the first offense for skipping. **Do not assign detention for other reasons.** Teachers will be responsible for informing students of detention to be served, making sure to tell the student the **date, time and place** of detention. It is best to give the student 24 hours' notice of detention to be served. Once the student has been informed of detention to be served, fill out a form, have the student sign it, and turn in the form to the attendance secretary.

Detention for misbehavior in your class or homeroom will be left up to you. Students who ride buses should be allowed to make up their detention the following night. This will give them the necessary time to make arrangements for a ride home. Students with medical or dental appointments should be excused until the following day to make up their detention.

Students may be asked to stay after school for special help, to work off demerits, or for teacher and central detention. Students are expected to tell their parents twenty-four hours in advance of the date they will be staying after school. All students are responsible for reporting at the time and place designated. Those not reporting to central detention may warrant school suspension.

(See Also: ALTERNATE SCHOOL PROGRAM; BEHAVIOR; CUTTING; DISCIPLINE; DUE PROCESS; FIGHTING; REFERRAL)

DISCIPLINE

explanation of discipline procedures for students...

Various discipline measures are used in the district for different types of student behavior. The discipline actions given for various types of student behavior are outlined below.

If you are guilty of certain offenses you will be immediately referred to school administrators for either assignment to ASP, suspension or expulsion from school. If appropriate, school administrators will contact the proper authorities.

Other disciplinary actions are handled by teachers directly with the student, in consultation with the student's parents. Frequent offenders are referred to school administrators.

1st Offense — conference with an administrator, referral to guidance counselor and office detention

2nd Offense — assignment to ASP for 3 days

3rd Offense — loss of course credit

4th Offense — referral to attendance officer for truancy investigation and court proceedings

guidelines for teacher handbook (first example)...

In all discipline use good judgment and do not act too hastily.

The teacher should make every effort to establish good discipline and respect from the very first day. It is very easy to become more lenient if necessary, but almost impossible to establish respect and discipline once the students have gotten away from you. You will not do an effective job of instruction until proper respect, discipline, and organization have been established.

Good discipline is the establishment of a working relationship for each other. The child must respect the teacher as the instructional leader in the classroom—the person who is in charge of leading and directing the activities in the room. The child does not need to fear the teacher, but *must* respect the teacher. The child needs to respect his fellow classmates, the building, other adults, and the equipment and materials which have been provided for his use. We can work toward establishing this respect by providing the leadership, careful planning of all activities, promptness at all times, and continuity from day to day so the child knows what is expected of him.

Good discipline is not continually nagging, screaming, yelling, or hitting a child. Good discipline is not instilling fear in students. These things only tend to make a situation that does not provide a good instructional atmosphere.

Teachers should refrain from any action, such as hitting a child about the face or head, striking with an object, pulling hair or ears, etc., that could cause injury to the child. These things—which are usually done in an emotional state or in haste—are very hard to defend as necessary to parents or to the instructional program.

The principal is ready to help in any discipline problem. Please do not threaten students with "sending them to the principal" as an everyday means of controlling a class or individual student. This soon loses its effectiveness.

If it is necessary to send a child to the office, please try to let me know ahead of time about the problem. It is quite demoralizing for a student to come to the office and find that I already have information as to why he is there.

Students are expected to take part and do the best they can with a cooperative attitude in music classes, physical education, etc. A student should not be removed from these classes because of his attitude and effort—this may be what the child wants. Any specific problems should be discussed with the principal ahead of time before sending the child from the class. Any problems of this nature should be discussed on an on-going basis with the principal so that every effort can be made to help the child before the action of sending the child out of class.

It is of questionable value to have students sit in the halls for strictly disciplinary reasons. It may be necessary to remove the child from the classrooms at times, but this can be done in better ways then just sitting in the hall. Students should not be put in the storerooms for work. The teacher cannot supervise the child in the hall or these rooms and is still responsible for the child. The work accomplished in these situations questions the merit of this action.

Students are to respect and obey the person on duty, regardless of who it is. Students who "talk back" or show disrespect for teachers or other adult workers will be dealt with through the principal's office.

Discipline problems in the room can be avoided by:

1. Always being well planned.
2. Being back to your room at the end of the recess or noon period to meet the students when they come in. (This is very important.)
3. Letting the children know ahead of time what is expected of them.
4. Being consistent and uniform from day to day in dealing with the students.
5. Being fair with all students.
6. Setting policies and procedures in the room and following them.
7. Setting schedules for work and following them. If classes are run hit and miss, students will learn to operate in the same way.
8. Being well organized so you have materials, equipment, etc., ready for the class session. It should not be necessary on a regular basis to leave the room for ditto work, materials, equipment, etc.

guidelines for teacher handbook (second example)...

1. All teachers must be consistent in following school rules and policy guidelines. We must be accountable to students, parents, and other faculty and staff members, just as they must be accountable to us.
2. Teachers must be the initial disciplinarians. Document disruptive incidents (date, period, nature of incident) and action or actions taken by person making the referral.
3. Teachers should make students aware of course objectives for quarter, semester and/or year so student will have an understanding of what will be required of him.
4. Teachers are accountable to students and parents for the education of the youngster. Students, in turn, are responsible for cooperating and educating themselves.
5. If a teacher deprives a student of his rights (to be informed, educated, etc.), the student has a right to question why and seek to remedy the situation. The teacher (like the student and administrator) is accountable to all the other partners in the process of education.

policy statement on...

Our policy on discipline is directed to the advancement of reformative and preventive discipline with emphasis upon the role of self-discipline in a democracy and in keeping with the school philosophy.

No single set of suggestions can provide ways and means of meeting the variety of disciplinary situations which arise—every disciplinary situation differs in some way. At the same time, there are certain general procedures which can serve as a starting point.

1. Recognize and eliminate possible sources of trouble before they have a chance to develop. Be alert to all danger signals that indicate some maladjustment: (a) emotional problems, (b) home problems, (c) know the pupils and parents as early as possible.
2. Maintain a high standard of teaching (well-planned lessons, well-organized and smoothly functioning classroom standards and rules).
3. Inform students early of what is expected of them. Expect the best.
4. Establish and maintain favorable study conditions that are free of distractions and misbehavior.
5. Provide opportunities for training of self-control. As self-discipline develops, disciplinary problems will decrease.
6. Establish and maintain a healthy relationship with pupils. Be pleasant and friendly, but not chummy. Be firm but fair.
7. Provide for individual differences in organizations, assignments, participation, and evaluation.
8. Create and preserve the conditions essential to the orderly progress of the school.
9. Administration, teachers, and parents must be together and support each other 100 percent in matters of conduct control (school policies).
10. Discipline everywhere in the school is the responsibility of each teacher.
11. A disorderly room invites disorderly behavior.
12. Cheating is not to be condoned. A student giving or receiving help automatically receives a zero. A notice is sent to the office immediately.

procedures for disciplinary referral notice...

When classroom teachers issue a disciplinary referral notice, it will be handled by one of the administrators who will confer with the student and, if necessary, the teacher as well as the parents. A statement describing the disposition of the problem will be added to the notice to the parents and a copy of the document will be mailed to the parents. The teacher will also receive a copy of the referral and the third copy will be inserted in the student's folder. Notices to parents, or occasionally a letter, advising parents of their son's/daughter's transfer to the alternate school class or suspension from school will include a copy which is to be signed and returned to the school in the envelope provided.

(See Also: BEHAVIOR; CORPORAL PUNISHMENT; DRUGS; DUE PROCESS; EXPULSION; GAMBLING; LAVATORIES; PASSES; REFERRAL; TARDINESS AND TRUANCY; WARNING NOTICES)

DISCRIMINATION

policy statement...

The Board of Education condemns prejudice in any form. Discrimination based on race, creed, sex, or national origin has no place in any public school system and will not be tolerated in ours. The Board affirms that such discrimination shall play no part in any action taken by the Board or employees of the Board in the performance of their duties. The Board further affirms that any complaints of discrimination or prejudice brought to the Board's attention will be handled in a judicious manner through the District's affirmative action officer and/or the Board of Education.

(See Also: ACADEMIC FREEDOM; APPLICATION; BIDS; BOARD OF EDUCATION; CITIZENSHIP; DUE PROCESS; GRIEVANCES; OPENING PROCEDURES; PHILOSOPHY; RELIGION; USE OF FACILITIES)

DISMISSAL PROCEDURES

guidelines for teachers...

At all dismissal times—recess, noon, and end of the day—the teacher should dismiss the room in some orderly fashion. Establish a procedure for this. This is necessary to avoid confusion in the halls and avoid disruption of other classes.

Each teacher should see the class to the proper exit. Set a definite procedure on this when school starts and follow it each time.

Dismissal time for all students at the end of the day is 3:15. Please do not dismiss early as this becomes a disruption for other classes. Keep your rooms/classes until the designated time. Likewise, make it a procedure to be well planned so you are ready to dismiss your class at the assigned time.

Under no conditions should students or a student be dismissed from any class until the end of the period unless there is an emergency. Classes or individuals are to be dismissed as the bell rings designating the termination of the class. Only by adhering to the above regulation can we avoid confusion and disruption. Also, please do not excuse students from your classroom to work on other projects or for some other teacher.

of students for medical reasons...

Plan all dental, medical, and other appointments for a time after school is dismissed.

A student excused for a dental or medical appointment must bring satisfactory evidence that he has an appointment, such as a note from parents or an office appointment card. The permit to leave the grounds, which is issued to the pupil who has an appointment, must be signed by the doctor and the parent.

(See Also: ASSEMBLIES; BOMB THREATS; CLOSE OF SCHOOL; DUTIES; EARTHQUAKE)

DISTRIBUTION OF MATERIALS

checkoff list...

Please read the attached material and pass it on to the next person on the list.

Your comments WILL (   ) WILL NOT (   ) be needed.

NAME: ____________________

NAME: ____________________

NAME: ____________________

NAME: ____________________

NAME: ____________________

NAME: ____________________

---

policy statement on...

Any material which is not related directly to school matters must have the superintendent's approval before distribution to employees or students.

routing slip...

ROUTING SLIP

ITEM__________

Name	: :	
	: :	Action
	: :	Approval
1	: :	Concurrence
	: :	File
2	: :	Information
	: :	Investigate and Advise
3	: :	Note and Forward
	: :	Note and Return
4	: :	Per Request
	: :	Recommendation
5	: :	See Me
	: :	Signature
6	: :	Reply for the Signature of:
7	: :	

REMARKS:

FROM:

Name: Date:

(See Also: **ADVERTISING; CLERICAL SERVICES; CONTROVERSIAL TOPICS; INFORMATION; SECRETARY; TYPISTS; WARNING NOTICES; XEROXING)**

DOCTORS

physical examination by school doctor form...

Dear Parent:

In accordance with State Law, the school doctor will be conducting a physical screening of students in Grades 1, 5, 8 and 11 during the coming school year. You will be notified of any condition which might need further attention by your family doctor.

You may, if you wish, have your child examined by your family physician at your own expense. Please have your private physician complete this form, which should be returned to the school nurse at the school your child will be attending in September.

If the form is not completed and returned to the Health Office by September 30, your child will be screened by the school doctor.

Name: ______________________ School: ______________________

Address ____

	NORMAL	ABNORMAL–SPECIFY
Skin		
Eyes		
Ears		
Nose		
Throat		
Teeth		
Heart		
Lungs		
Abdomen		
Nutrition		
Blood Pressure and Pulse		
Complete Urinalysis		
Nervous System		
Hernia		
Orthopedic Defects (specify)		
Height		
Weight		

Date of Examination______________ ______________________

Private Physician's Signature

school physician's report...

Significant Findings of Medical Examination

Name of Student ____________________

School ____________________ Grade __________

Name of Parent ____________________

Address ____________________ Phone __________

Physical findings that are of significance to the school: ____________________

____

____

____

____

Recommendations to the school: ____________________

____

____

____

____

Is student capable of sports competition? Yes _____ No _____

Should there be restrictions? Yes _____ No _____

Remarks:

____________________ M.D.
Signature of Physician

Date ____________________

Address ____________________

Phone ____________________

(See Also: ABSENCE; ACCIDENT; DRUGS; EMERGENCY; HEALTH; ILLNESS; MEDICAL FORMS; MEDICATION; NURSE; X-RAYS)

DRESS

samples of statements on dress from student handbooks...

We take pride in the appearance of our students. Your dress reflects the quality of the school, of your conduct, and of your schoolwork.

All students are expected to dress and groom themselves neatly in clothes that are suitable for school activities.

BOYS:

1. Most boys' clothing is acceptable for school wear as long as it is neat and clean and of proper fit.
2. Socks must be worn at all times.
3. Obscene or vulgar clothing of any kind may not be worn.

GIRLS:

1. Most girls' clothing is acceptable for school wear as long as it is neat and clean and of proper fit.
2. To provide a modest appearance, leotards or panty hose should be worn with short skirts or dresses.
3. Socks or stockings must be worn at all times.
4. Obscene or vulgar clothing of any kind may not be worn.

Students are expected to dress in a clean, neat, modest and safe manner at all times. Dress that tends to disrupt the class or contributes to a safety hazard in class will result in a telephone call to parents asking that they bring a change of clothing for their son/daughter.

(See Also: ACCIDENTS; BOARD OF EDUCATION; DANCES; RIGHTS AND RESPONSIBILITIES; SAFETY**)**

DRINKING OF ALCOHOLIC BEVERAGES

policy statement...

A student who uses or possesses narcotics, hallucinogens, drugs, stimulants or alcohol at school or school functions, or appears at school or school functions showing evidence of having used narcotics, hallucinogens, drugs, stimulants or alcohol may be suspended from school.

A student who uses or possesses narcotics, hallucinogens, drugs, stimulants, or alcohol away from school or its functions may be suspended pending a parental conference.

Disciplinary action may include the loss of participation in extracurricular activities, the loss of all privileges and any other action deemed necessary. Flagrant offenders who are considered a detrimental influence to the moral well being of the student body may be suspended from school.

(See Also: BEHAVIOR; BUILDING; DRUGS; HEALTH; MEDICATION; NURSE; USE OF FACILITIES)

DRIVING

message in student handbook...

GETTING A DRIVER'S LICENSE DURING SCHOOL

If you reach 17 years of age and want to obtain your driver's license, you should notify the office at least one day in advance, go directly to the Motor Vehicle station from your home in the morning and then return promptly to school with a note from your parents explaining your lateness.

requirements and description of courses...

State Department of Public Instruction Requirement for Graduation—The state department requires a minimum of 30 classroom hours as a requirement for high school graduation. Course 0500 meets this requirement.

Requirement by State Law for a Driver's License Test—State statutes permit students between the ages of XX and XX to take a driver license on-street test if they have completed a minimum of 30 hours of classroom instruction and an equivalent of six hours of in-car instruction. Students must have a certificate issued by the State Department of Public Instruction stating that such work has been completed. A student may earn this certificate by completing courses 0500 and 0501. At the age of XX, license tests are permitted without driver education training. In all cases, the testee must have a valid State Instructional Permit in order to be tested. The permit is issued only when the student has passed a written test. Most insurance companies offer a reduced rate if the student has a driver education completion certificate.

0500 Driver Education—classroom—¼ Credit

Open to Grades 10, 11, 12

Offered during the normal school day; no cost; Grading—Pass/Fail

This course is designed to include 68 hours of instruction in traffic law, vehicle function and maintenance, car insurance, defensive driving, etc.

0501 Driver Education—Classroom—¼ Credit

Open to Grades 10, 11, 12

Offered during the normal school day; Cost—$30.00; Grading—Pass/Fail

This course is designed as a laboratory course consisting of 13 hours of driving simulation, nine hours of multiple-vehicle driving range, two hours of on-street instruction and the National Safety Council's Defensive Driving Course. This course is offered concurrently with course 0500. All students are enrolled in both Driver Education 0500 and Driver Education 0501 unless special arrangements are made with a principal.

(See Also: ACCIDENT; AUTOMOBILES; BUS; FIELD TRIPS; PERMISSION SLIPS; TRAVEL; TRIPS; VOUCHER)

DRUGS

"legal" drugs in school...

UNDER VERY SPECIAL CIRCUMSTANCES, IT MAY BE NECESSARY FOR THE PARENT TO WORK OUT A PROGRAM OF ACTION WITH THE SCHOOL ADMINISTRATOR AND THE SCHOOL NURSE, BASED ON WRITTEN ORDERS FROM A PHYSICIAN, SAFE STORAGE IN A LOCKED FACILITY IN THE SCHOOL, AN AWARENESS OF DRUG CONTENT, AND A LIABILITY RELEASE FOR THOSE CONCERNED WITH DISTRIBUTION OF THE DRUG WHILE THE STUDENT IS IN SCHOOL, SUCH RELEASE TO BE SIGNED BY PARENTS OF STUDENT.

GENERALLY, SINGLE DOSES WILL BE PLACED IN SINGLE ENVELOPES (i.e., 1 DOSE PER DAY WOULD REQUIRE ONE SEPARATE ENVELOPE). THE STUDENT'S NAME AND TYPE OF MEDICATION WILL APPEAR ON EACH ENVELOPE AND THE ENVELOPE WILL BE DELIVERED TO THE SCHOOL SEALED, AND A SIMILAR PROCEDURE WILL BE FOLLOWED IN THE EVENT THAT MORE THAN ONE DISTRIBUTION OF DRUGS IS TO BE MADE IN A SINGLE SCHOOL DAY. THE ENVELOPE SHOULD BE DATED WITH THE DATE INDICATING THE DAY ON WHICH THE DRUG IS TO BE DISTRIBUTED.

THE PARENT OF THE STUDENT WILL BE RESPONSIBLE FOR PLACING THE CORRECT DOSAGE IN THE DAILY ENVELOPES AND ONLY IN EXTREME CASES WILL A TEACHER DO ANY ACT IN FURTHERANCE OF DISTRIBUTION OTHER THAN HANDING THE STUDENT THE ENVELOPE BEARING HIS NAME WHICH CONTAINS THE MEDICATION FOR THE DATE INDICATED.

symptoms of drug abuse in students (for educators)...

GENERAL SIGNS OF POSSIBLE DRUG ABUSE

A. Mild symptoms:

1. loss of interest in friends, job, schoolwork
2. ups and downs of excitement and depression
3. sudden flares of anger
4. careless about appearance
5. furtive actions
6. long secret phone calls

7. long periods alone in bedroom or bathroom
8. inappropriate wearing of sunglasses even at night (to hide dilated or constricted pupils)
9. long sleeves worn constantly (to hide needle marks)
10. inordinate disappearance of money and requests for money

B. More serious symptoms:

1. yawning a great deal
2. suffering cramps and vomiting
3. blood spots on sleeves
4. sores on arms or legs
5. significant weight loss and loss of appetite

SPECIFIC SYMPTOMS AND BEHAVIOR OF DRUGS AND NARCOTICS

A. *Barbiturate* (commonly known as "sleeping pills") *Users*:

1. Behave like drunks, mental disorientation and physical incapacity, intoxication
2. Stagger around, falling asleep, depressed
3. Judgment and motor coordination impaired
4. No alcohol odor
5. Reaction time, visual perception, attention affected even by small doses

   Long-range effects serious: addictive with painful withdrawal symptoms; overdose common, can lead to death.

B. *Amphetamines* (speed, pep pills, dexies, ups, bennies, drivers):

1. Larger than normal doses induce feelings of euphoria, exaggerated alertness, actual intoxication. (Normal dose keeps you peppy and awake.)
2. Initial stimulus can bring on aggressiveness, false self-confidence
3. Overdoses lead to blackout, exhaustion, schizophrenic symptoms (hallucinations, erratic behavior, gibberish writing)
4. Highly dangerous combination–pills and alcohol

C. *Marijuana* (pot):

1. Stimulation and animation (early stages–loud bursts of laughter, emotionally unstable, exhilarated, talkative, giggly)
2. Later stages–appears stuporous, depressed
3. During ALL stages–dilated pupils
4. Cigarettes are greener than tobacco and are tucked in at both ends—characteristic "sweet" odor like alfalfa or hay or burned rope. Can be taken into the body in many ways—chewing, sniffing, drinking, candy for eating, smoking

5. Time and space distorted
6. Sights and sounds exaggerated
7. Becomes intoxicated, walks unsteadily, sees fuzzily, acts stupidly
8. Liable to be highly suggestible—experience false courage

D. *LSD* (odorless, colorless, tasteless):

1. Dilation of pupils
2. Highly emotional, shifting moods, laughing and crying uncontrollably
3. Sometimes becoming terrified–panic–severe depression often with suicidal thoughts and attempts
4. Can become totally unresponsive to environment– "freak out"
5. Can become irrational and have a psychotic incident– "bad trip", may try to kill self or others
6. Hallucinations, delusions, illusions: objects and sounds distorted and/or accentuated; faces melt away; bodies merge with walls; solid items pulsate (these perceptual changes called "psychodelic")
7. Distortion of time sense
8. Intensification of sensations

Unusual effect: symptoms can recur with original intensity weeks or months after initial dose without intervening subsequent doses.

Chronic side effects on users—highly damaging to brain and chromosomal structure

E. *Glue Sniffers* (paint and other volatile chemicals):

1. Retains odor of substance on breath and clothes
2. Swollen, inflamed mucous membranes in mouth, nose and throat
3. Watery eyes, double vision, ringing in ears, dizziness
4. Initial stage—tingling sensation in head, feeling of exhilaration. Continued inhalation leads to a state similar to alcoholic intoxication

Danger—organic solvents present in plastic cements: brain damage–mental deterioration; affect liver and kidney action; interfere with blood-forming function and bone marrow.

F. *Narcotics* (heroin, morphine, codeine, methadone, cocaine, etc.):

1. Heroin: works immediately in body

physiological:
a. circulation and respiration slowed
b. blood pressure lowered
c. metabolic rate reduced
d. dehydration, loss of appetite, loss of weight

psychological:
a. euphoria, sense of well being and contentment
b. gets "thrill," "kick" or "jolt" immediately after drug enters the blood stream—this sensation is what drives person back for more

c. body builds tolerance so subsequent doses must be larger to obtain the same result and desired effect

withdrawal symptoms quite severe:

morphine, codeine, methadone, cocaine are all substitutes for heroin and are all addicting (methadone being medically used as an antidote for heroin)

(NOTE: This information was prepared from *Drug Abuse*, published by the California State Department of Education.)

(See Also: BEHAVIOR; DOCTORS, EMERGENCY; HEALTH; MEDICAL FORMS; MEDICATION; NURSE; POLICE; SMOKING)

DUE PROCESS

special note...

That due process be followed in every case involving legalities in the public schools is not only morally desirable, but, in terms of our increasingly legalistic society, it is fast becoming a survival skill for school administrators. The following forms are representative of all stages of "due process" required for a student. They are presented in order of their occurrence in the process. Taken as a whole, they represent a fine example of "due process" for any school.

WRITTEN CHARGE AND REQUEST FOR EXPULSION

TO: ______________________________ ______________

(Superintendent) (Date)

______________________________ ______________________________

(Parent or Guardian) (Address)

______________________________ on ______________

(Name of Student) (Date of Birth) (Date)

engaged in the following misconduct:

____

____

____

This misconduct constitutes a violation of validly adopted student conduct rule(s) and/or State Law which in summary state(s):

____

____

____

In my opinion, the misconduct cited requires that this student be expelled from the school

system until ______________ because ______________________________

(Date)

____

☐ This student is enrolled in special education, including any L.D. Program.

I, therefore, request that you initiate proceedings necessary to accomplish this expulsion. At this time:

☐ I have not and do not presently intend to suspend this student pending your determination.

☐ On ______________, I suspended this student in accordance with State Law until you

(Date)

either dismiss this charge or complete your determination following a hearing on this charge because I have reason to believe that this student must be removed from school immediately in order to prevent or substantially reduce the risk of:

1. Interference with an educational function, or school purposes; or
2. A physical injury, or illness to himself/herself, other students, school employees, or visitors to the school.

______________________________ ______________________________

(Signature) (Title)

______________________________ ______________________________

(School) (Date)

WRITTEN NOTIFICATION OF RIGHTS TO PARENTS/GUARDIANS

DATE: ____________________

RE: ____
(Name of Student) (Age)

____
(School)

TO: Mr. & Mrs.______________________________ and ____________________
(Parent, Custodian or Guardian) (Student)

____
(Address)

1. RIGHT TO HEARING

______________________________, ____________________, ______________

__________ has requested that ______________________________________ be

expelled from ______________________________ until ____________________.
The Superintendent of Schools has determined that there are possible grounds for investigation and has appointed me as hearing examiner in this matter. Before this penalty can be invoked, one or all of you may request a hearing on the alleged misconduct which prompted this request for expulsion.
IF YOU DO NOT REQUEST SUCH A HEARING WITHIN TEN (10) CALENDAR DAYS FROM THE DATE YOU RECEIVE THIS NOTICE, YOUR LEGAL RIGHT UNDER STATE LAW TO CHALLENGE THIS PROPOSED EXPULSION IS LOST AND THE EXPULSION OF ____

FROM SCHOOL ATTENDANCE UNTIL ____________________ BECOMES AUTOMATICALLY EFFECTIVE.

2. WAY TO REQUEST HEARING

If one or all of you desire a hearing on this proposed expulsion, you must put your request in writing and deliver it in person or by certified mail within ten (10) calendar days to: ______

____,

(Form continued)

WRITTEN NOTIFICATION OF RIGHTS TO PARENTS/GUARDIANS (cont'd)

3. ALLEGED MISCONDUCT AND STUDENT CONDUCT RULE VIOLATED

The expulsion of ________________________________ has been requested because on

______________________ he/she engaged in the following misconduct:

____

____

____

This misconduct constitutes a violation of the validly adopted student conduct rule(s) and/or State Law ______________________ which in summary state(s):

____

____

____

4. SUMMARY OF EVIDENCE AGAINST STUDENT

a. If you request a hearing, ____ or a representative will offer the written or oral testimony of:

______________________________	______________________
(Name)	(Title)
______________________________	______________________
(Name)	(Title)
______________________________	______________________
(Name)	(Title)

You would have the opportunity to examine written statements of these witnesses prior to the hearing. They believe this testimony and other evidence will prove that your child did commit the misconduct alleged and that the proposed expulsion is necessary.

(Form continued)

5. RIGHT TO EXAMINE RECORDS AND AFFIDAVITS OF WITNESSES
You may, if you wish, examine or have your attorney or other representative examine your student's academic records, disciplinary records, and the affidavits and written information listed above, in making the decision whether or not to request a hearing, and in preparation for the hearing, if requested.

6. DESCRIPTION OF PROCEDURE TO BE USED IF HEARING IS REQUESTED
a. If you request a hearing, I will notify you of the time of the hearing within two (2) days after receipt of your request. The hearing would be held no sooner than two (2) school days nor more than five (5) school days after your request. The hearing would be held at _______

____

b. You may be represented by an attorney or any other person in preparation for the hearing. An attorney may also represent the person requesting the expulsion.
c. The hearing would not be open to the public. Witnesses would be in the room only while testifying. Testimony would be under oath. The student will attend the complete hearing unless temporarily excluded by agreement between the hearing examiner and parents.
d. Sequence of events at the hearing would be:

1. Opening statement by hearing officer.
2. Statement of the position of the person requesting the expulsion.
3. Statement of the student's position, if the student or parent desires that this be done.
4. Presentation of witnesses and evidence by the person requesting the expulsion with right of student to cross-examine witnesses.
5. Presentation of student's witnesses and evidence, if any, with right of person requesting expulsion to cross-examine student's witnesses.
6. Rebuttal or additional information on behalf of person requesting expulsion, if any.
7. Rebuttal or additional information on behalf of student, if any.
8. Hearing officer's clarification questions, if any.
9. Closing remarks by each side and the hearing examiner.

e. The record of the hearing will be made by________________________________
f. The student need not testify at the hearing. No inference will be drawn from a decision not to testify. If the student elects to testify, the student would be subject to cross-examination by the person requesting the expulsion.
g. After the hearing, the hearing examiner would send written findings and a recommendation of appropriate punishment, if any, to the Superintendent. The Superintendent would then decide what action, if any, should be taken against the student. If you were not satisfied with the decision of the Superintendent, State Law provides for the appeal of the Superintendent's determination to the school board and appeal of the school board's determination to the courts.

____
(Hearing Examiner)

(Form continued)

NOTICE OF HEARING

____
(Date)

TO: ______________________
(Name of Student)

____
(Parent(s), Guardian or Custodian)

____
(Address)

This notice acknowledges receipt of a written request for a hearing concerning the proposed expulsion of ______________________

from ______________________.

In response to this request, the hearing has been scheduled for __________.M. on __________, __________, 19______, at __________

______________________.

Please advise me as soon as possible of the names of any witnesses you want to have testify on your behalf at the hearing so that I can assist you in securing their attendance at the hearing.

If you will be represented at the hearing by an attorney or other representative, I request that this attorney or representative contact me as soon as possible so that I can advise the person as to the nature of this proceeding and the manner in which the hearing will be conducted.

Please contact me at ______________ if you have any questions.
(Telephone)

____
(Hearing Examiner)

(Form continued)

HEARING EXAMINER'S FINDINGS AND RECOMMENDATION

____
(Date)

TO: ______________________________ (Superintendent)

On ____________________, ____________________ a hearing was held in Room
(Day) (Date)

________, of ______________________________ located at

______________________________, at ________ o'clock ________.M.,

for the purpose of considering the matter of the proposed disciplinary action against:

____

Those present at the hearing for or representing the person requesting the expulsion were:

____

____

____

Those present for or representing the student were:

____

____

____

______________________________, called the following witnesses:

____

____

____

and offered the following evidence in written form:

____

____

____

These witnesses (were) (were not) cross-examined by the ______________________________.

The student or his/her attorney or representative called the following witnesses:

____

____

____

and offered the following evidence in written form:

____

____

____

These witnesses (were) (were not) cross-examined by ______________________________.

(Form continued)

WRITTEN NOTIFICATION OF RIGHTS TO PARENTS/GUARDIANS (cont'd)

On the basis of the evidence presented, I make the following findings:

____

____

____

____

____

____

____

____

Additionally, I find that the misconduct of ____________________

(violated) (did not violate) the following validly adopted student conduct rule(s) of the ______

____________________ and/or provision(s) of State Law:

____

____

____

On the basis of the above findings, I recommend that this matter be disposed of as follows:

____

____

____

____

This recommended disposition meets the needs of the school corporation in that:

____

____

____

This recommendation disposition meets the needs of ____________________
(Student)

in that:

____

____

____

____
Hearing Examiner

(Form continued)

NOTICE OF SUPERINTENDENT'S DETERMINATION

____
(Date)

TO: ______________________________
(Name of Student)

____
(Parent(s), Guardian or Custodian)

____
(Address)

On ______________, a hearing was held at ________.M. in Room ________

in ______________________ located at ______________________

______________________, for the purpose of considering proposed disciplinary

action against ______________________________.

On ______________, the hearing examiner, ______________________
sent me findings and a recommendation of proposed disciplinary action. A copy of this document is attached.

After considering these findings and recommendations, I have made the following

determination concerning the proposed expulsion of ______________________

____

____

____

____

____

____

One or all of you can appeal my determination to the school board by personally delivering or mailing by certified mail, a written notice of appeal to the Superintendent at ________

______________________________,

within 30 calendar days following the postmark of this notice.

If any or all of you decide to appeal my determination, the punishment stated above shall continue in effect unless you appeal my determination and the school board takes action to delay the implementation of my determination. A request to postpone the implementation of my determination should be directed to the person designated above to receive the written notice of appeal.

____
(Superintendent)

(Form continued)

(See Also: ACADEMIC FREEDOM; APPLICATION; BOARD OF EDUCATION; CERTIFICATION; CHILD STUDY TEAM; CONTROVERSIAL TOPICS; EVALUATION; EXPULSION; GRIEVANCES; MEDIATION; NEGOTIATIONS; NON-RENEWAL OF CONTRACT; OBSERVATIONS; REFERRAL; RETENTION; RIGHTS AND RESPONSIBILITIES; SUSPENSION)

DUTIES

duty assignment form...

DUTY ASSIGNMENT ROSTER

19__-19__

Teacher's Duty	1	2	3	PERIODS 4 A	B	C	5 D	E	6	7
*Denotes Lunch Duty Teacher in Charge										

sample of duties from a job description...

ACCOUNT CLERK, DUTIES

1. Has charge of the Finance Office under the supervision of the second vice principal.
2. Is responsible for the collection, balancing and depositing of all school monies:
   Cafeteria lunch collection
   State collection (workbooks, lost books, transcripts, driver education fees)
   Local school accounts (class & chartered club dues, money raising, etc.)
3. Maintains accurate records of all business transactions.

4. Prepares monthly and annual Principal's Financial report and submits to:

   District Superintendent
   State Superintendent
   Board of Education
   Department of Accounting & General Services

5. Is responsible for checking invoices charged against purchase orders issued by class and club treasurers; paying bills according to specific procedures.
6. Prepares refunds to students due to releases; maintains detailed student roster and keeps records of all pupil accounts of fees.
7. Prepares payrolls for testing supervisors, proctors and others hired through school funds.
8. Instructs and advises student treasurers on matters relative to school and club finances.
9. Maintains accurate record of allotments; expenditures and balances of all state appropriations allocated to the school for textbooks, supplies, equipment.
10. Prepares and types state purchase orders.
11. Performs other miscellaneous duties.

(See Also: ADVISORS AND ADVISORY COMMITTEES; AIDES; ASSIGNMENTS; DANCES; DISMISSAL PROCEDURES; HALLS AND HALL DUTY; KEYS; LUNCH AND LUNCH DUTY; STUDY HALL; SUPERVISION)

EARTHQUAKE

policy and procedures for...

During an earthquake when inside the school building, the following procedures will be initiated:

1. The teacher, or other person in authority, implements Action DROP.
2. Try to avoid glass and falling objects. Move away from windows where there are large panes of glass and out from under heavy suspended light fixtures.
3. Implement Action LEAVE BUILDING when the earthquake is over. Special consideration should be given to exit routes, as some older schools have heavy architectural ornaments over the main entrances. *DO NOT RUN, particularly on stairways.*
   a. Do not return to buildings for any reason until they have been declared safe by qualified persons.
   b. Guards should be posted at a safe distance from all building entrances to ensure that no one re-enters the buildings.
4. Do not light fires in school buildings after an earthquake until declared safe by the fire department.
5. Avoid touching electrical wires which may have fallen to the ground.
6. Render first aid if necessary.
7. Take roll. Teachers to develop procedure for quick rolling taking. Initiate a search for any student found to be missing.
8. Notify utility companies of any break or suspected break in pipes or lines.
9. If possible, notify the School District Civil Defense Coordinator, or other appropriate school official. Request assistance as needed, through normal school channels.
10. When damage to buildings is apparent, the Principal will determine the advisability of closing the school. If necessary, he will procure the advice of competent authority about the safety of the buildings.

During an earthquake when on school grounds outside of buildings, the following procedures will be initiated:

1. Move away from buildings, trees, and exposed wires.
2. The teacher, or other person in authority, implements Action DROP.
3. The safest place is in the open. Stay there until the earthquake is over.
4. *DO NOT RUN*!
5. Follow procedures 4 through 10 under "Inside School Building" above.

During an earthquake while riding on the School Bus, the following procedures will be initiated:

1. If possible, the bus driver will pull to side of road away from any buildings and issue command "DROP." On hilly roads, the side of the road may not be the safest place, so the bus driver should quickly consider the terrain before deciding where to stop.
2. Set the brakes.
3. Turn off the ignition.
4. Wait until the earthquake is over.
5. Follow procedures 5 through 7 under "Inside School Buidling" above.
6. After the earthquake if enroute to school, continue to school; if taking students home, continue on route.

During an earthquake while walking to and from school, the following actions should be taken:

1. Stay in the open. It is the safest place.
2. Move away from buildings, trees, and exposed wires.
3. *DO NOT RUN*!
4. After the earthquake, if on the way to school, continue to school; if on the way home, continue home.

student directions in student handbook...

In the event of an earthquake, please abide by the following guidelines:

a. Students should be kept calm and no one should leave the buildings until directed to leave over the PA system.
b. Immediate cover can be taken under a table so that student will be protected from falling objects from the ceilings.
c. In the event that a large structure is falling within one part of the classroom, the teacher must make a determination to shift to the other side of the classroom.
d. The evacuation of the building may be called for soon after the quake subsides. In this event all students will be asked to move towards the open field in an orderly fashion.

Note: Extreme caution must be exercised in taking note of fallen electrical lines which may be hazardous or moving close to buildings that may be hazardous.

e. No student should be allowed to move his or her car. All roads should be kept clear. In all cases, teachers must assume the responsibility of the students' safe conduct and control.

f. Second and Third Floors—Before coming down the stairs, some effort should be made in checking to see whether the stairway is safe in order to move from that building. A second stairway could be used in the event that one is not useable.

g. DO NOT RUN!

(See Also: ACCIDENT; DISMISSAL PROCEDURES; DOCTORS EMERGENCY; FIRE DRILLS; NURSE; POLICE; WEATHER ALERTS)

EDUCATION

objectives of education...

WE BELIEVE THAT EDUCATION SHOULD:

1. Provide students with the basic learning tools necessary to enable them to assimilate knowledge for the rest of their lives.
2. Provide students with a knowledge and appreciation of their heritage.
3. Provide students with the awareness that change is inevitable, and that change must be a factor in planning and organizing.
4. Provide students with an environment in which to learn the responsible use of freedom. Students must learn that each personal decision has a result.
5. Provide students with the opportunity to accumulate and accentuate such personality characteristics as integrity, responsibility, morality, dependability, initiative, self-discipline, and leadership.
6. Provide students with the knowledge of the importance of participating in and preserving the democratic process.
7. Promote a concern for improving life by working toward a solution of community problems.
8. Provide differentiated and varied curriculum offerings and an environment in which a student can work toward the highest possible fulfillment of his/her potential.
9. Accept responsibility for educating all youth regardless of individual differences—intellectual, physical, personal.
10. Provide students with an opportunity to develop an appreciation for aesthetic qualities that contribute to a rich and full life.

11. Provide training and skills for entrance into the world of work, including opportunities in vocational, college preparatory, and general education.
12. Provide students with the opportunity to develop skills and attitudes that will enrich their leisure time now and in the future.
13. Provide each student with a recognition of his/her self-worth and respect for others.

parent notification of review of educational plan...

Date: ______________________________

ROCK TOWNSHIP PUBLIC SCHOOLS

ANNUAL REVIEW OF EDUCATIONAL PLAN

The policy of Rock Township Schools is to review annually the education plan of each child receiving special services.

The proposed date for the review of your child's plan is: ______________.

If the scheduled time is not convenient, please contact your school immediately so that another time can be arranged.

Sincerely,

____

____
(telephone number)

(See Also: EVERY OTHER HEADING IN THIS BOOK, SINCE EVERYTHING HERE RELATES TO THE MASTER TOPIC OF EDUCATION)

ELECTIVES

sample elective course descriptions...

0310 Microcomputers and Business Machines—½ Credit

Open to Grades 11, 12

This course is designed to teach student to operate the Apple II computers (programmed for word processing and data processing), electronic calculators, ten-key adders, dictating and voicescription equipment. Simulated work on office forms is provided through a machines practice set. Juniors who are planning to take Office Education are recommended to take this course. (Prereq: Typing I or presently enrolled in 0302)

1113 Pre-Calculus—1 Credit

Open to Grade 12

This course is designed for students in the areas of science, engineering, medicine, etc., so they can be prepared to start their college training with the calculus; this is the function of the Pre-Calculus course. The course begins with the language of mathematics and proof by induction. We then study vectors and apply this to the fields of Algebra and Geometry; included is a study of exponential function and a complete study of the circular function. (Prereq: Advance Algebra I)

0600 French I—1 Credit

Open to Grades 9, 10, 11, 12

This course is designed as an introduction to the French language. It acquaints the student with the areas of listening, speaking, reading and writing while taking a look at France in depth. Emphasis at this level is placed on the listening-speaking areas; however, reading and writing will be introduced. This will be accomplished through the use of basic dialogues, exercises, narratives and special projects dealing with a comparative look at the student's own culture and the French culture. It is expected that the student shall be able to communicate at the elementary level in a French speaking situation such as in the restaurant, hotel and airport.

(**See Also:** ADULT EDUCATION; CLASS; COURSES; CURRICULUM; GUIDANCE; MINI-COURSES; SCHEDULE; TRANSFER)

ELEMENTARY EDUCATION

elementary instructional materials chart...

The following supplies are needed for each child at each grade level and may be purchased at various stores throughout the County.

FIRST YEAR	Approximate Price
Crayons (Buy only one)	$ .99
Prang-Kantroll (Semi-Pressed) #937-8	
Binney-Smith-Besco Anti-Roll (Semi-Pressed) #10-B	
Milton Bradley Tru-Tone No-Roll (Semi-Pressed) #9157	
Pencil, Dixon No. 308 or Eagle No. 245	.20
Scissors, round point	.85
Handwriting Tablet, Zaner-Bloser #1	.75

SECOND YEAR	
Crayons (Buy only one)	.99
Prang-Kantroll (Semi-Pressed) #936-16	
Binney-Smith-Besco Anti-Roll (Semi-Pressed) #20-B	
Milton Bradley Tru-Tone No-Roll (Semi-Pressed) #9196	
Pencil, Dixon No. 304 or Eagle No. 283	.20
Scissors, round point	.85
Handwriting Tablet, Zaner-Bloser #2	.75

THIRD YEAR	
Crayons (Buy only one)	$ .99
American Crayon-O4X, Lift-Lid Box	
Crayola No. 161, Lift-Lid Box	
Milton Bradley No. 16, Wax	
Paints (Buy only one)	2.37
Prang–#7 (Special)	
Artista–#O4W (Semi-moist whole pans and one brush)	
Also–whole pan refill–white	.20
Scissors	. 85
Handwriting Tablet, Zaner-Bloser #3	.75
Glue, Elmers	.88

FOURTH YEAR	
Crayons (Buy only one)	$ .99
American Crayon No. 323	
Crayola No. 24	
Crayrite, Milton Bradley, No. 924, Lift-Lid Box	
Official Letter Pad (Westab)	.85
Paints (Buy only one)	2.37
Prang, #7 (Special)	
Artista–#O4W (4 semi-moist whole pans and one brush)	
Also–whole pan refill–white	.20
Scissors	.85
Glue, Elmers	.88

FIFTH AND SIXTH YEAR
(This information does not apply to sixth grade students at middle/junior high schools.)

Crayons (Buy only one)	$ .99
American Crayon No. 323	
Crayola No. 24	
Crayrite, Milton Bradley, No. 924, Lift-Lid Box	
Official Letter Pad (Westab)	.85
Paints (Buy only one)	2.37
Prang–Ovl. 8 (8 semi-moist half pans and one brush)	
Artista–#080 (9 semi-moist half pans and one brush)	
Also–half pan refill–white	.20
Ruler	.29
Scissors–Pointed	.85
Glue, Elmers	.88

guide to beginning elementary students and parents...

GUIDE FOR BEGINNERS

Prepared by First Grade Teachers

First Graders, you should know how to:

1. Dress yourselves completely and independently.
2. Tie your own shoes and parkas.
3. Put on and take off your wraps and overshoes.
4. Use a handkerchief.

Boys and Girls, have you established good health habits?

1. Do you go to bed by 8:00 or 9:00 p.m.?
2. Do you brush your teeth?
3. Do you keep your face and hands clean?
4. Do you help yourself at toilet time?
5. Do you wash your hands after toilet?
6. Do you keep your hair combed?

Will you bring to school the first day:

1. a wide line tablet?
2. two No. 2 pencils?
3. a small plastic bottle of white glue?
4. a rubber eraser?
5. a box of 8 crayons (large size if available)?
6. a package of tissues?

Mother and Father, will you:

1. Return Certificate of Immunization form properly signed as required by law?
2. See that your child knows the way to and from school?
3. See that the rubbers or overshoes are large enough and marked; that the mittens are marked and clipped to keep them with the coat?
4. Prepare your child to remain in school without you?
5. Acquaint your child with books by taking him or her to the library and bookmobile?
6. Acquaint your child with the use of scissors?
7. Acquaint your child with many social experiences, such as a visit to a farm, zoo, bakery, etc.?
8. Have your child memorize your telephone number?

After school begins:

1. Expect little of your child the first 9-week period. It is a time of orientation and adjustment. Your child will show little progress. The most progress will be evident after the first semester. For this reason no grades are given the first nine weeks; it is a readiness period.
2. Encourage your child. Be generous with praise.

(See Also: **ASSEMBLIES; ENROLLMENT; INFORMATION; KINDERGARTEN; LAVATORIES; PERMANENT RECORDS; RECORDS; REGISTRATION; REPORT CARDS; RETENTION; SPECIAL EDUCATION; STUDENT RECORDS; WRITING; ZONES AND ZONING)**

EMERGENCY

emergency information sheet...

TO ALL PARENTS/GUARDIANS:

The information you are about to supply on this form could be of vital importance to your child. In the event of an emergency situation in school (that is, serious accident/illness) requiring more than normal first aid procedures, we will use the information on this sheet in the treatment of your child. Therefore, please take some time NOW to fill out this form and make certain that it is returned to school via your child as soon as possible.

Student's Name: ______________________________ Today's Date: __________
Last First Initial

Address: ______________________________

____

Student's Birth Date: ____________________ Grade: ______ Home Room: ______

SPECIAL MEDICAL DATA

Place here any special medical data (that is allergies to medications, special blood type, physical condition requiring special handling, etc.) which the school should know during emergency situations.

____

____

____

PARENTS/GUARDIANS

If you cannot be reached at home, where may we reach you?

MOTHER: ______________________________
(Name if different from child's name)

____
(Address and Telephone Number)

FATHER: ______________________________
(Name if different from child's name)

____
(Address and Telephone Number)

PLEASE list the names, addresses and telephone numbers of at least two (2) relatives or neighbors/friends who will assume temporary responsibility and care of your child in the event you cannot be reached.

1. ______________________________

____

2. ______________________________

____

(Form continued)

emergency information sheet (cont'd)

NAME, ADDRESS AND TELEPHONE NUMBER OF THE CHILD'S DOCTOR:

____

____

FILL IN AND SIGN

To Rock Township Public Schools:

In the event of serious accident or illness concerning my child, I understand that the school will try to contact me using the information supplied above. If the school cannot reach me, I hereby authorize the school to contact the doctor indicated above and follow his/her instructions. If the doctor cannot be reached, I then authorize the school to take whatever steps and make whatever arrangements they deem necessary for the health, security, and comfort of my child.

SIGNATURE OF PARENT/GUARDIAN:______________________________

DATE OF SIGNATURE:______________________________

teacher information on emergency drills...

EMERGENCY DRILLS (FIRE & TORNADO)

Fire drills will be held intermittently throughout the school term. It is of extreme importance that each and every fire alarm situation be treated as the real thing. Emphasize this to your class along with instructions regarding the proper procedure to follow.

LOCATION	ROOMS
West entrance by Room 111	110, 111, 112
West entrance by Room 113	113
North entrance by Room 114	114
E. entrance thru Auto Shop	120, 121, 122, 123, Auto Shop, Wood Shop
E. entrance by DECA store	130, 131, 132, 135
E. entrance by Home Ec.	133, 134
NW entrance to Academic Wing	200, 201, 202, 203, 204, 205, 206, 207, 208, 219, 220
NE entrance to Academic Wing	209, 210, 211, 212, 213, 214, 215, 216, 217, 218, Human Resource

LOCATION	ROOMS
N. entrance on 1st floor by Music Department	300, 301, 302, 303, Math Resource, Science Resource, 304, 305, 306, 307, 308
N. entrance on 1st floor by Electronics Room 122	309, Bus. Ed., 310, 311, 312, 313, 314, 315, 316, 317, 318, 319, 320
Commons entrance	Commons area, library
South entrance to gym	Gymnasium area
South entrance to pool	Swimming pool
South entrance to locker area	Phy. Ed. locker areas

Procedure:

1. Anytime the fire alarm rings, it's essential that we assume it's the real thing. To do otherwise is inviting disaster.
2. Students and teachers should go immediately to the designated exit.
3. Do not congregate near the exit areas. Go directly to parking areas, street or other applicable area.

During tornado drills, students are to pass directly to either the fallout shelter or a north-south school corridor. The best safety position is one in which the person kneels on the floor with head resting on knees and hands over the head.

(See Also: ACCIDENT; BOMB THREATS; CHILD ABUSE; DEMONSTRATIONS; DOCTORS; EARTHQUAKE; EMERGENCY; FIRE DRILLS; NURSE; SAFETY; STRIKES; WEATHER ALERTS)

ENERGY

energy impact form...

This form is designed to assist the local School District in providing statistical data essential to apply for coal impact or other special funds that may be available due to school enrollment growth based upon energy exploration and development.

The information is purely voluntary on the part of parents and the school stresses the point. It is appreciated as a help to us and will be used only for documentatin of statistical information; the end result would provide better educational services. It will not be used in any way to solicit parents personally or to pass privileged information to others for personal or business gain. Only one form need be completed for all children in the family, at any building of the parent's choice when registering children.

Assistant Superintendent

****

DATE: ______________________________

NAME OF PARENT(S) ____

CURRENT ADDRESS __________________________ PHONE NO. ____________

LENGTH OF TIME AS A SCHOOL DIST. RESIDENT ___________________________

LAST RESIDENCE PREVIOUS TO HERE ________________________________

CHILDREN:	Name	Age	School Enrolled	Grade

emergency impact form (cont'd)

ANTICIPATED LENGTH OF STAY IN DISTRICT (if known) ____________________

MAJOR EMPLOYMENT OF PARENT(S)-Check one:

_____COAL INDUSTRY EMPLOYMENT–Example: miner; heavy equipment operator; managers; office personnel, etc.

Job Title ____________________

Company ____________________

_____OIL AND GAS INDUSTRY EMPLOYMENT–Example: driller; exploration and survey crewman; oil and gas lease/minerals purchase representatives, etc.

Job Title ____________________

Company ____________________

_____OTHER ENERGY INDUSTRIES EMPLOYMENT–Example: Uranium; Solar; Federal Employment–directly related to planning, environment, leasing; other.

Job Title ____________________

Company ____________________

COMMENTS: ____________________

____

____________________ ____________________

Parent Signature (optional) Building Principal (completed by)

(Form continued)

(See Also: AUTOMOBILES; BUILDING; BUS; MONEY; USE OF FACILITIES; WORK**)**

ENROLLMENT

district-wide enrollment form...

ENROLLMENT AS OF____________________, 19_____

GRADES	THOMAS	GLENVIEW	SCHOOLS HALLEY	MARTIN JHS.	HIGH
1	_____	_____	_____	_____	_____
2	_____	_____	_____	_____	_____
3	_____	_____	_____	_____	_____
4	_____	_____	_____	_____	_____
5	_____	_____	_____	_____	_____
6	_____	_____	_____	_____	_____
7				_____	_____
8				_____	_____
9				_____	_____
10					_____
11					_____
12					_____
TOTALS	_____	_____	_____	_____	_____

TOTAL ELEMENTARY (Thomas, Glenview, Halley): ____________________

TOTAL JUNIOR HIGH SCHOOL: ____________________

TOTAL HIGH SCHOOL: ____________________

TOTAL ENROLLMENT (ALL SCHOOLS): ____________________

DATE OF PREPARATION: ____________________

PREPARER: ____________________

instructions to schools on enrollment procedures...

AUGUST 25–SEPTEMBER 12

REGISTRATION AND ENROLLMENT ACTIVATION

1. ALL SCHOOLS K–12 (Includes Special Education)
   a. All new enrollees through September 12 will have an entry date of September 3 and an E entry code. Effective September 15, use actual date of enrollment and correct entry code.
   b. Parent or student will complete all items in Section I except shaded areas. School will complete shaded areas in Section I and II; leave Residence Code, Field 10, blank.
   c. Refer to Code Card for correct primary language and Tuition Status codes.
   d. If student lives with someone other than parent, Field 15, Item 5, see procedures for District Tuition of Request for Tuition Waiver in Records Handbook.
   e. There must be an enrollment activation card for EVERY student enrolling through September 12. After that date destroy all pre-printed cards and send blank cards to Mr. Kane.
2. ELEMENTARY SCHOOLS K–6
   a. Handcarry original copies of registration to Pupil Accounting, Records Building or to Elementary Education, 2nd Floor, Administration Building, daily *before 4:00 p.m.*
   b. Separate pre-printed from unprinted activation cards, handcarry to Pupil Accounting or to Elementary Education, 2nd Floor, Administration Building, daily from September 3 through September 12.
3. SECONDARY SCHOOLS 7–12
   a. Handcarry original copies of registrations to Pupil Accounting, Records Building, or to Mrs. Jakes, Secondary Education, 2nd Floor, Administration Building, daily *before 4:00 p.m.*
   b. Handcarry activation cards to Mr. Carson *daily*.

Retain all "no show" records until copies are requested from another school within or outside the district.

1. ELEMENTARY SCHOOLS K–6
   If no copies have been requested by the end of the quarter, follow the Student Records withdrawal procedure, pages 15–17, (Student Records section) in the Records Handbook and forward to the Student Records Center.
2. SECONDARY SCHOOLS 7–12
   If no copies have been requested within 60 days, follow the Student Records withdrawal procedure, pages 18–20, (Student Records section) in the Records Handbook and forward to the Student Records Center.

(See Also: ADDRESS; CLASS; ELEMENTARY EDUCATION; INFORMATION; PERMANENT RECORDS; REGISTRATION; STUDENT RECORDS; ZONES AND ZONING)

EQUAL EDUCATIONAL OPPORTUNITY

sample policy on...

NONDISCRIMINATION IN SCHOOL AND CLASSROOM PRACTICES

The Board of Education declares it to be the policy of this district to provide an equal opportunity for all children to achieve their maximum potential through the programs offered in these schools regardless of race, color, creed, religion, sex, ancestry, national origin, or social or economic background.

In order to achieve the aforesaid goal the Board directs the Superintendent to assume the responsibility of coordinating all implementing activities or delegating said responsibility to an Affirmative Action Officer. It shall be the duty of the Superintendent or the Affirmative Action Officer to prepare a plan specifying discrete areas of investigation, a method for conducting such investigation, and a date for reporting to the Board the results of such investigation.

The plan proposed for the investigation of School and Classroom Practices that promote equal educational opportunity shall be approved by the Board before it is implemented. In the development of said plan, representatives of the staff, student body, and community shall be involved. Every effort shall be made to ensure equal representation among those participating in the development of the plan with regard to race, color, creed, sex, national origin and ancestry.

(See Also: ADULT EDUCATION; BILINGUAL EDUCATION; COURSES; CURRICULUM; DUE PROCESS; EDUCATION; ELEMENTARY EDUCATION; GOALS; INDIVIDUALIZATION; PHILOSOPHY)

EQUIPMENT

multi-year plan for equipment replacement...

The following form is for your use in updating your multi-year plan for equipment. Please use the following guidelines in its preparation:

1. Form Format
   a. type all information
   b. prepare in triplicate
   c. use only forms provided; request if you need more.
2. General
   a. The form is for both elementary and secondary schools.
   b. Identify, in proper space, grade level (elementary) or department (secondary).

c. The principal must sign each plan.
d. Type in the year in which the original equipment was purchased.
e. Replacement Category—Check appropriate replacement category for each item:
   (1) "Obs."—Obsolete—no longer useful because of outmoded/outdated content or technology.
   (2) Lost—self-explanatory.
   (3) BER—Beyond Economical Repair.
f. Additions
   (1) List additional needs to existing program.
   (2) List additional needs due to new programs.
g. Unit Cost:
   (1) Use the unit cost figures for the current year and for all fiscal years thereafter. Do not include inflation index. We will adjust all figures for all years for inflation.
   (2) Total at bottom and at right—six-year requirement.
   (3) Round-off all figures to the nearest dollar.

EQUIPMENT REPLACEMENT FORM ATTACHED.

MULTI-YEAR PLAN
TO MEET EQUIPMENT NEEDS

DISTRICT ____________

Subject ____________

Grade (Elem.) ____________

Dept. (Sec.) ____________

School ____________

Principal ____________

Date ____________

DESCRIPTION	Yr. Acq.	Number of Units Needed					Unit Cost	AMOUNTS REQUIRED (To Nearest Dollar)						Total 6-Yr. Requirement
		Replacement			Additions									
		Lost	Obs.	B.E.R.	Add to Prog.	New Prog.		19 -	19 -	19 -	19 -	19 -	19 -	
TOTALS														

(See Also: BIDS; BUDGET; CUSTODIAL SERVICES; REQUISITIONS, REPAIRS, AND REPLACEMENTS; TELEPHONE; USE OF FACILITIES; WORK**)**

EVALUATION

consent form (for student evaluation)...

Student: ______________________ Date of Birth: __________

Parents: ______________________ Proposed Date of Evaluation: __________

Address: ______________________ Person(s) Requesting Evaluation: __________

Business Phone: ______________________ Phone Number of Person Requesting Evaluation: __________

Home Phone: ______________________

Statement of Problem/Reasons for Evaluation: ______________________

____

____

____

____

This evaluation procedure is necessary to determine the type and extent of special assistance that may be needed for your child. The evaluation recommended for your child includes the following areas:

______Psychological (intellectual assessment) ______Audiological (hearing)

______Educational (achievement) ______Physical Therapy

______Social ______Occupational Therapy

______Speech and Language ______Other

______Vision

If you have any questions regarding the specific procedures or purpose of this evaluation, please contact your child's school.

I understand the purpose of the requested evaluation and hereby *agree to* this evaluation ______, or *do not agree to* this evaluation ______.

Parent's Signature: ______________________ Date: __________

*Attach Parent Rights Booklets.

policy and procedures for professional evaluation...

I. General Aspects

A. Foundation:

In order that there is agreement with and common understanding of the specific tasks and duties for which the teaching staff member is responsible, the written job description for the position held by the teaching staff member will form the foundation of the evaluation. The teaching staff member's performance will be assessed in terms of the degree of excellence with which he/she carries out the specific duties and responsibilities set forth in the job description and the individual professional improvement plan. The annual written performance report shall constitute the composite evaluation and shall summarize performance reports, incident reports, the revised individual professional improvement plan and any other pertinent data which constitutes the total performance.

B. Criteria:

Explicit written criteria for determining the degree of excellence, with which the teaching staff member performs will be developed by the professional staff and shall include, but not necessarily be limited to relevant indicators of:

- Student progress and growth
- Professional knowledge
- Professional skills
- Instructional effects
- Professional activities
- Behavior as an exemplar

C. Methods of Data Collection:

Specific methods for collection of evaluation data will be developed for each position by the professional staff and shall include, but not necessarily be limited to:

- Observations
- Review of Personnel File, including a review of graduate courses, inservice courses, etc.
- Student progress
- Participation on PTA committees, inservices, curriculum committees, school committees, etc.

D. Data Collection:

The source of data may include professional staff, students, community members, and parents. The data obtained shall be collected and evaluated by properly certificated members of the professional staff.

II. Procedures

A. Notification:

1. At the beginning of their employment, all teaching staff members shall be given a copy of the policy and procedures relating to staff evaluation by the Assistant Superintendent for Personnel and/or Principal.
2. Principals shall review with their staffs the policy and procedures on evaluation by October 1 of each year.
3. Amendments to the policy or procedures will be distributed by the Administration within ten (10) working days after adoption or acknowledgment by the Board of Education.

B. Observations:

1. All teaching staff members, including those assigned to regular classroom duties and those not assigned to regular classroom duties, are subject to observations and performance reports.
2. Each observation shall be conducted for a minimum duration of one class period in a secondary school, and for the duration of one complete subject lesson in an elementary school.
3. Observations need not be limited to the classroom, but may be made on any or all scheduled assignments.

C. Performance Reports:

1. Each of the required two (tenure) or three (non-tenure) performance reports shall be followed within three school days by a conference between the staff member and the supervisor to discuss the performance report and recommendations concerning the employee's total performance. All recommendations must appear on the written performance report.
2. All performance reports must be in written form and made by appropriately certified personnel. The teacher's and supervisor's signatures must both appear on the performance report.
3. Immediately upon completion of the performance reporting process, copies of performance reports shall be distributed to the following:
   a. Assistant Superintendent (Personnel)
   b. Principal
   c. Teacher
4. The teaching staff member has the right to submit his/her written disclaimer of such performance report within ten (10) days following the conference. Such disclaimer is to be attached to each copy of the performance report.
5. "Report on Performance Reports" forms shall be completed by each school principal monthly and must be received in the Office of the Assistant Superintendent (Personnel) with the monthly reports.

6. The Superintendent of Schools or his designee shall be notified immediately when formal action is under consideration. (See Formal Action)

D. Schedule of Performance Reports:

Non-tenure

Three times annually, not less than one a semester

1. Deadline October 31st
2. Deadline December 31st
3. Deadline April 30th

Tenure

Two times annually, one each semester

1. Deadline February 10th
2. Deadline May 15th

E. Individual Professional Improvement Plan:

1. The individual professional improvement plan provides an opportunity to focus on specific aspects of the job description to continue professional growth. The plan is accomplished through a rational process where the supervisor and staff member meet and set objectives designed to continue professional growth for the staff member while aiding the staff of the building to fulfill district and state goals. This process provides for teacher input in the objective(s), establishes a time frame, considers the ways and means of attaining objectives, and involves the means of assessing the results.
2. The process is achieved through the following stages:
   a. Each staff member considers his/her objectives for the year. The objectives should center on teacher actions or behavior, not personality factors. The objective or objectives under consideration should be measurable and/or observable to the extent that the supervisor and staff member should be able to agree that the objective was accomplished or was not accomplished.
   b. The supervisor considers objectives for the year for the staff member (as outlined in *a).*
   c. The supervisor and teacher confer to determine the objectives, and mutually agree on the measurable and/or observable objectives. If the supervisor and teacher cannot mutually agree to objectives, then the teacher selects an objective and the supervisor selects an objective until a reasonable number of objectives is reached. "Reasonable" is defined as the amount of work that is manageable within a specified time frame.
   d. The teacher and supervisor then determine the implementation plan. This discussion considers the necessary materials, professional time, budgetary considerations, etc., that are needed to accomplish the objectives and a time frame for the completion of the objectives.

e. The teacher and supervisor should agree on how the success in completing the objectives will be evaluated. This discussion should clarify what is to be accomplished, where this will take place, when the objectives will be completed and how to clearly determine whether the objectives have been accomplished.

f. When the objectives have been defined, page 2 of the "Annual Written Performance Report" is completed. When the "Annual Written Performance Report" is completed, one copy will remain with the teacher, one will remain with the supervisor, and one will be sent to the Assistant Superintendent for Personnel for the Personnel file.

g. Data is gathered by the teacher and/or the supervisor throughout the year in the manner that was prescribed at the conference.

h. At the conclusion of the time frame, but in no event longer than one year from the setting of the objectives, the supervisor and the teacher meet to discuss the objectives.

   The conference should have two outcomes:

   a) A determination of whether or not the objectives were met (May 1st-June 30th)
   b) The re-establishment of objectives that were not completed and/or the setting of new objectives for the following year between May 1st and June 30th or September 15th for all teachers. Tenured teachers will work on a one- to three-year cycle.

NOTE: The process is more important than the outcome. It would be better to strive toward but only partially complete one challenging objective, than to complete five less meaningful objectives.

The supervisor evaluates the Individual Professional Improvement Plan on the Annual Written Performance Report and discusses the evaluation at the Annual Summary Conference.

III. Annual Summary Conference

(To be held before the written performance report is formally filed in the personnel file.)

SHALL INCLUDE, BUT NOT BE LIMITED TO:

1. Review of performance based on job description.
2. Review of progress toward objectives of the individual professional improvement plan developed at the previous annual conference.
3. Development of the objectives of the individual professional improvement plan for the next one (1) year cycle for non-tenure teaching staff members or for the next one to three (1-3) year cycle for tenure teaching staff members.
4. Review of available indicators of pupil progress and growth toward the program objectives.

5. Review of the annual written performance report and the signing of said report within five (5) working days of the review.
6. Relative to items 1 and 4—a discussion of (a) the evaluative procedure, (b) the evaluative criteria, and (c) the data collection methods to be followed in evaluating his/her performance.

IV. Annual Written Performance Report—Prepared by a Certified Supervisor Who Has Participated in the Evaluation of the Teaching Staff Member

The purpose of this report is to provide for the review of the total performance of the teaching staff member and shall include, but not be limited to:

1. Performance areas of strength.
2. Performance areas needing improvement based upon the job description.
3. An individual professional improvement plan developed by the supervisor and teaching staff member.
4. A summary of available indicators of pupil progress and growth, and a statement of how these indicators relate to the effectiveness of the overall program and the performance of the individual teaching staff member.
5. Provision for performance data which has not been included in the report prepared by the supervisor to be entered into the record by the evaluatee within 10 working days after the signing of the report.

PUPIL PROGRESS

The annual written performance report shall include a summary of available indicators of pupil progress and growth, and a statement of how these indicators relate to the effectiveness of the overall program and the performance of the individual teaching staff member. The answers to the following questions shall provide the data for the statements:

1. *Are the intended outcomes for the student(s) clear?*
   This refers to the students' understanding of the content they will study, their role during the learning process, and the behaviors that are expected at the conclusion of the activity(ies).
2. *Does the teacher monitor pupil progress and growth?*
   This refers to the proper monitoring to task analysis devices, teacher made evaluation devices, district monitoring devices, and State and standardized tests.
3. *What does the teacher do with the information?*
   This refers to analyzing the results of the student evaluation and implementing a program designed to provide for basics essential to continued student educational development in terms of student potential.

V. Formal Action—Under Consideration

The Superintendent of Schools or his designee shall be notified immediately when formal action is under consideration and the actions to be recommended decided jointly with the administration of the school or schools to which the teaching staff member is assigned. Some of the possible results of "formal action" are certification of charges, non-renewal of contract, withholding of an increment, withholding of a part of salary for contracted services not performed.

A. Performance Reports:

When a teaching staff member's performance report indicates one or more areas that are unsatisfactory, interim performance reports shall be made more frequently to monitor the implementation of suggested improvements.

B. Incident Conference and Reports:

Staff Actions Warranting Discipline—Should a member of the professional staff be involved in a situation which may warrant disciplinary action, his/her immediate supervisor or principal shall attempt to resolve the situation with a conference. The conference shall be held as soon as practicable. Following the conference, one or more of the following courses of action may occur:

1. The matter, if at all possible, shall be handled informally at the building level and closed without further action being taken.
2. A memorandum may be placed in the staff member's personnel file. The staff member may respond to the memorandum, in writing, if he/she so desires. The staff member's response will also be placed in the personnel file.
3. A letter of reprimand may be sent to the staff member and a copy placed in his/her personnel file. The staff member may respond to the reprimand in writing if he/she so desires. A copy of the response will also be placed in the personnel file.
4. The immediate supervisor or the principal may recommend to the Superintendent or his designee that more severe disciplinary action be taken against the staff member. Should this occur, the Superintendent or his designee may decide to hold a conference with the staff member involved and the staff member's immediate supervisor or principal. This conference shall be held as soon as practicable. Following said conference the Superintendent or his designee may direct that any of the procedures set forth in paragraphs 1, 2, and 3 above be followed or in the alternative, he may recommend the Board of Education that more severe disciplinary action be taken.
5. Should the latter occur, the Board or a committee of the Board may decide to hold a conference with the staff member, his/her immediate supervisor and/or principal and the Superintendent and/or his designee. This conference shall be held as soon as practicable. The staff member and the Association shall be notified of said conference. The staff member and one representative of his/her own choosing shall be permitted to be present at the conference.
6. Following said conference, the Board may direct that any of the procedures in paragraphs 1, 2, and 3 above be followed or in the alternative take the necessary statutory steps to withhold an increment or certify charges to the Commissioner of Education.

two examples of teacher evaluation forms...

CLASSROOM OBSERVATION AND CONFERENCES

DATE: __________ SUBJECT: ______________ STAFF MEMBER'S INITIALS __________

DATE: __________ SUBJECT: ______________ STAFF MEMBER'S INITIALS __________

DATE: __________ SUBJECT: ______________ STAFF MEMBER'S INITIALS __________

EVALUATION OF PROFESSIONAL STAFF

Name of Teacher ______________________________ School Year 19 ______

Schools ______________ Grade, Area, or Subjects Taught ______________

This form is designed to give a general, observable summation of a teacher's performance. The information can be used to plan areas of emphasis for staff improvement in the evaluation process. Column I: Y = Yes, S = To Some Extent, N = No, NA = Not Applicable.

COL. I CIRCLE	INSTRUCTION ITEM	COMMENTS/RECOMMENDATIONS
Y S N NA	1. Are opening activities well planned and smooth?	
Y S N NA	2. Are instructional objectives by the teacher readily apparent to the observer?	
Y S N NA	3. Do classroom activities clearly relate to instructional objectives presented by the teacher?	
Y S N NA	4. Are class activities well organized and effectively paced?	
Y S N NA	5. Is the classroom well managed and good discipline apparent?	
Y S N NA	6. Is teacher-pupil interaction positive and productive?	
Y S N NA	7. Does the instructor innovate, create, and use current information on the subject and approach to teaching?	
Y S N NA	8. Does the instructor attempt to provide and consider the variety of needs and differences in learning rates of students?	

Y S N NA	9. Are closing instructions (including assignment) clear and understandable?	
Y S N NA	10. Is the teacher's knowledge and understanding of the subject matter evident to the observer?	
Y S N NA	11. Does there appear to be meaningful learning taking place?	
Y S N NA	12. Are teaching techniques and procedures responsive to sound principles of learning?	
Y S N NA	13. Are variety of media and/or other resource materials used?	
Y S N NA	14. Is the classroom well-cared for, and are appropriate displays used?	
Y S N NA	15. Does the instructor participate in professional groups and in other ways actively involve him or herself in the general programs of the school and the student?	

(Additional data on times of conferences, contacts, evaluation forms and other items may be attached.)

EVALUATOR SUMMARY COMMENT TEACHER SUMMARY COMMENTS

Date
____
Bldg. Administrator Signature

Date
______________________________ ______________________________
Other Evaluator's Signature Staff Signature

(See Also: CHILD STUDY TEAM; GRADES; INTERNSHIP; LESSON PLANS; OBSERVATIONS; PIP; PROGRESS REPORT; RESOURCE TEAM; WARNING NOTICES)

EXAMINATIONS

examination schedules...

Tests are a teacher's prerogative. It is important, however, that any grade issued must be able to be substantiated. Common exams are daily, weekly, nine-weeks and semester-oriented. A test schedule will be followed at the end of each semester. Testing is required at these times unless an exception is approved by the principal.

FIRST SEMESTER

January 21–

8:00- 9:30	Period 7
9:30-11:00	Period 3
12:00- 1:30	Period 5
1:30- 3:00	Period 1

January 22–

8:00- 9:30	Period 2
9:30-11:00	Period 4
12:00- 1:30	Period 6

END OF YEAR

May 26–

9:00-10:30	Period 3
10:30-12:00	Period 5
1:00- 2:30	Period 7

May 27–

9:00-10:30	Period 2
10:30-12:00	Period 4
1:00- 2:30	Period 6

May 28–

9:00-10:30	Period 1

Make-up Tests

exemptions from examinations...

Perfect Attendance–A policy of exempting students from one mid-term and one final exam of their choice is in effect subject to the following:

a. To be exempt from an examination for perfect attendance, a student must have perfect attendance recorded in the homeroom teacher's register.

b. The student must also have perfect attendance in the class from which the exemption is requested. (No tardiness or absence from class allowed.)

c. Exemptions cannot be granted in any class where the student has a nine weeks' grade lower than "74."

d. The perfect attendance policy does apply to students transferring to our school if there is proof that the record was maintained prior to transfer and no time was lost between school during transfer.

e. Students sent to the Alternative School lose all exemption privileges.

All A's–Exemptions from semester exams will be granted in any subject in which the student has all nine weeks' grades of at least "92."

Transfer Students–A student who has been here six weeks or longer and brings all A's from another school and continues to make all A's here is eligible for exemption. Students who attend school in another system for 3–5 weeks of the nine weeks' period will have their transfer grades averaged with the grades they make here for the final nine weeks' grades. Those who attend for less than three weeks in another system will receive a nine weeks' grade on the basis of the work done in this system only. Students who attend school for six weeks or more in another system will receive their transfer grades as final nine weeks' grades. Transfer grades will be converted to our school's equivalency.

(**See Also:** ACHIEVEMENT; EVALUATION; FAILURE; GRADES; IDENTIFICATION; PROMOTION; REPORT CARDS; RETENTION; WARNING NOTICES)

EXPULSION

examples of messages in student handbooks...

SUSPENSION AND EXPULSION

Suspension, which is a function of the school administrator, and expulsion, which is a function of the local board of education, are serious disciplinary sanctions which may be imposed against you when it can be proved that you have "materially and substantially interfered with" the maintenance of good order in the school, and when, under procedures conforming with due process of law. Expulsion is permanent removal from the school rolls. Continued and willful disobedience, the habitual use of profanity or obscene language or injuring of individuals or of school property are causes for punishment and suspension from school. You can be suspended for something you have done off as well as on school property if school authorities can prove that such action is reasonably necessary for your physical or emotional safety and well being, or for the safety of other members of the school community. Certain rules governing suspension are designed for your protections:

1) The principal must report your suspension immediately to the superintendent.

2) The superintendent must report it to the school board at its next regular meeting.

3) Either the board or the superintendent may reinstate you before the board's second regular meeting after your suspension.

4) After that board of education meeting, only the board may continue your suspension or expel you.

In case of either suspension or expulsion you have the right to the following elements of due process:

1) A written statement of the charges against you and the grounds justifying the sanction to be imposed.

2) A hearing.

3) A means of effective appeal.

The following are your rights regarding hearings:

INFORMAL HEARING

Under ordinary circumstance you are entitled to the opportunity to demonstrate to the authorities that there is a case of mistaken identity or some compelling reason why you should not be suspended a full hearing; where school officials believe that you may be dangerous to yourself or others, you may be suspended for a short period. If the suspension is to be extended, you are entitled to a full hearing.

FORMAL FULL HEARING

Court and school law decisions have held that in any situation where a fundamental right may be denied, students must be afforded all appropriate elements of due process. This may apply in cases involving expulsion, a long-term suspension which exceeds 21 days, a short-term suspension in which the timing of the punishment is crucial for that particular student, prohibition against certain student activities, or other instance of a serious nature.

1) The hearing must be held within 21 days after the informal hearing.

2) You may be represented by a lawyer.

3) The hearing may be held by the board of education or by a hearing examiner appointed to them.

4) You are entitled to a translator where necessary.

5) You are entitled to the rudiments of an adversary proceeding. Courts have held that these rudiments may include the right to be presented with the names of witnesses against you and copies of the statements and affidavits of those witnesses, the right to demand that any such witness appear in person to answer questions, and the right to testify and produce witnesses on your own behalf. The precise nature of the hearing depends upon the circumstances of the particular case, such as the sanctions to be imposed or at what level the hearing is held.

6) A record must be kept of the hearing procedures. You are entitled, at your own expense, to a copy of that transcript.

7) The proceeding must be held with all reasonable speed.

If you are found innocent, you may request that any written entry referring to the incident may be expunged from your school records.

APPEALS

You may appeal a decision made by your school officials to the superintendent and the local board of education. If this is unsuccessful you have two more appeals within the school system—first, to the Commissioner of Education, and then (within 30 days after the Commissioner has made his decision) to the State Board of Education. You may appeal your case in court without going through the administrative procedures outlined above, but the court may require you to first exhaust those channels within the local and state school systems. Your local board of education also has this right of appeal.

STUDENT SUSPENSIONS & EXPULSIONS

The Rock Township School Board through formal action adopted a Student Suspensions and Expulsions policy during the spring of 1984. This policy provides a code prohibiting student misconduct in the following areas:

Rule 1 — Disruption of School
Rule 2 — Damage or Destruction of School Property and stealing or attempting to steal School Property.
Rule 3 — Damage or Destruction of Private Property and stealing or attempting to steal private property.
Rule 4 — Assault on a school employee.
Rule 5 — Physical abuse of a student or other person not employed by the school.
Rule 6 — Weapons and Dangerous Instruments.
Rule 7 — Narcotics—Alcoholic Beverages—Tobacco and Stimulant Drugs.
Rule 8 — Repeated school violations. (Failing to comply with direction of teachers, student teachers, substitute teachers, teacher aides, principals or other authorized school personnel.)

A procedural code for dealing with alleged violations was also adopted. The school district has a Short-Term Suspension (which suspends students up to ten school days) and a Long-Term Suspension or Expulsion (decision to seek suspension over ten days or expulsion).

Any chronic offender who has been suspended for a total of 10 school days during a semester by the principal shall appear for a hearing as soon as possible.

A copy of the complete policy is available for examination by students or parents in the Principal's office.

(See Also: BOARD OF EDUCATION; CHILD STUDY TEAM; DUE PROCESS; EMERGENCY; REFERRAL; RIGHTS AND RESPONSIBILITIES; SUSPENSION**)**

EXTRA-HELP

policy on...

A. Faculty members shall be available for extra help whenever a student requires it at a mutually agreeable time. As soon as your schedule has been determined, please inform your students as to the time, place, day of the week you will be available for this.

B. Teachers should keep a record of the pupils who attend.

C. Teachers must directly supervise any student who is coming early or staying after for extra help. Students coming in early must have a written pass from the particular teacher. *Students who are staying after period 7 may not be dismissed until 3:00 p.m. and then only when escorted to the main entrance by the teacher.*

(See Also: **ABILITY; CLASS; COUNSELING; DETENTION; GRADES; HOMEWORK; PROGRESS REPORT; PROMOTION; RESOURCE TEAM; RETENTION; SUPPLEMENTAL INSTRUCTION; WARNING NOTICES)**

FACULTY MEETINGS

agenda for...

TO: Faculty
FROM: J. Benson, Principal
RE: FACULTY MEETING

WHEN? Wednesday, December 19, 1984
WHERE? Multi-Purpose Room
TIME? 3:00 p.m.–4:00 p.m.
AGENDA:
1. Discussion of results of Iowa Tests—Mr. Benson
2. Explanation of Guidance Intervention Program—Mrs. Kroll
3. Changes in daily operations:
    a. new referral slips—Mr. Hastings
    b. bus schedule changes—Ms. Farrell
4. Review of discipline policies—Mr. Benson
5. Teacher Association business—Ms. Hargrave

SPECIAL NOTE: We will make every effort to keep to the time schedule listed above. We must, however, cover the topics in the agenda. Therefore, if we can start on time, we stand an excellent chance of ending on time.

message in teacher handbook...

FACULTY MEETINGS

Faculty meetings will take two forms: department chairperson initiated and principal initiated. Curriculum development, inservice education and communication-oriented activities will be the focal point of faculty meetings. Meetings start at 3:30 unless otherwise designated. All instructional staff members are required to be in attendance unless previous permission has been granted by the principal to be absent.

(See Also: BOARD OF EDUCATION; CHAIRPERSONS; DEPARTMENTAL MEETINGS; DUE PROCESS; MEETINGS; NEW POLICY OR PROGRAM)

FAILURE

policy on parent notification of potential failures...

Grades Are Earned

A letter grade is an evaluation of a student's performance in a given class, reflecting both the knowledge required and the effort expended in the quest for such knowledge. In short, a student *earns* the grade he/she receives.

Teacher's Obligations

The teacher's obligations in grading are:

a. To inform and explain to all students the evaluation process used by the teacher in determining a student's grade for the quarter and semester (that is, averaging of letter grades, point system, percentages, weighting of grades on homework, class work, quizzes, and exams, etc.)
b. To grade fairly and consistently within the guidelines established
c. To notify parent(s)/guardian(s) when a student is in danger of failing a course

Time Interval and Method of Notification

a. At the first indication of failure, a courtesy telephone call should be made to the parent(s)/guardian(s) of any student who is doing less than passing work.
   Option–a progress report may be sent home via the student providing for parent acknowledgment (signature). A copy should be sent to the student's counselor and a third suspense copy is to be kept by the teacher. If the signed copy is not returned in three days, or if there is reason to believe that the signature might be forged, a confirming phone call should be made to the parent(s)/guardian(s).
b. Deficiency notices for students who are failing, near failing, or doing work significantly below potential should be sent at the mid-quarter point as designated by the counselors.
c. When a student who was passing at the mid-quarter is in danger of failing due to last minute deficiencies, a phone call or progress report as described in section "a" should be made. The phone call is infinitely preferred over the progress report due to: (1) the personal nature of a phone call; and (2) the possibility that the student will be unreliable in delivering the message as requested.
d. When a parent contact has not been made despite the efforts of the teacher, the assistance of the student's counselor and/or the appropriate administrator should be sought.
e. A log or other notation should be kept of all efforts made by the teacher to inform the parent(s)/guardian(s) in the event that the parent/guardian complains about non-notification. When efforts have been made by the teacher as outlined above, there should be no repercussions for the teacher and the school.

This policy is designed to provide parents/guardians with sufficient notification to work with their child to minimize failures. There is no guarantee that the student will not fail, only that he/she has the chance to pass, and that the teacher cares enough to request parental assistance in working with and encouraging their youngster to pass.

three examples of failure notices...

STUDENT'S NAME	**ROCK TWP. HIGH SCHOOL** **Mid-Quarter Failing Notice**	DATE
CLASS-GRADE SOPH. JR. SENIOR		TEACHER
COURSE		COUNSELOR

NOTICE TO PARENTS

1. The student is presently in academic difficulty in this subject, and consequently in danger of failure.
2. We would like to inform you of this situation, and ask that you discuss this with your child.

CAUSE(S) FOR DEFICIENCY:

☐ ABSENCES ARE AFFECTING HIS GRADE
☐ ASSIGNMENTS NOT COMPLETED
☐ BEHAVIOR NOT ACCEPTABLE
☐ CUTS FROM CLASS AFFECTING HIS GRADE
☐ PARTICIPATION IS POOR
☐ TARDIES AFFECTING HIS GRADES
☐ BOOKS AND MATERIALS NOT BROUGHT TO CLASS
☐ STUDY HABITS NEED IMPROVING
☐ POOR TEST SCORES

RECOMMENDATION(S):

☐ MORE EFFORT
☐ CONFERENCE WITH TEACHER AND STUDENT THROUGH COUNSELOR
☐ AFTER SCHOOL HELP
☐ TUTORING

____

____

____

____

STUDENT'S HOMEROOM TEACHER ____________ STUDENT'S HOMEROOM ______

ROCK TOWNSHIP HIGH SCHOOL

Dear Parent Marking Period Ending ________

____ Grade ________

(Student)

____ is in danger of failing ____.

(Subject)

____ is doing passing work in ____________________, but is capable and should be urged to do better.

In order to improve this situation, he/she must:

____ take responsibility for bringing all necessary materials to class.
____ hand in assignments regularly and on time.
____ improve the quality of assignments.
____ take responsibility for finding out about, and making up all assignments missed because of absence, trips, etc.
____ give complete attention to the explanations and practice exercises in class.
____ study more diligently and pass more tests.
____ improve behavior in class.
____ put extra effort into improving skills in ______________________________
____ COME FOR EXTRA HELP.
____ complete a major project.
____ observe the safety rules.
____ dress for gym regularly.

Other comments: ____

____

____

____ Please telephone the Guidance Office (555-1234) for an appointment in order to discuss this more fully. If you prefer, you may arrange for a telephone conversation.

____ Please sign and return this to me. ________________________________

(Subject teacher/Date)

TO: ________________________ DATE: ________________
FROM: ________________________
STUDENT: ____________________ COURSE: ______________

Student's Performance

Academic Average Test Scores (Grades) – (A) (B) (C) (D) (F)

Assignments – (Satisfactory) (Late) (Not in) (Poor work) Incomplete)

Participation – (Satisfactory) (Poor) (None)

Comments:

Student's Behavior

Attendance – (Satisfactory) (Frequent absences) (Frequent cuts) (Frequent tardies)

Attitude – (Satisfactory) (Belligerent/Defiant) (Sullen) (Indifferent)

Comments:

Other Comments

STUDENT________________________
PARENT________________________

(See Also: ABILITY; ACHIEVEMENT; GRADES; PROMOTION; REPORT CARDS; RETENTION; SUPPLEMENTAL INSTRUCTION; WARNING NOTICES**)**

FEES, FINES, FUNDS AND CHARGES

fees and charges schedule (sample)...

Class Dues (required): A flat fee is charged for class dues. This money goes to the following accounts: Class Activities, $.75; Student Scholarship, $.50; Foreign Exchange Program, $.50, and Student Council, $.25 . . . . $ 2.00

Searchlight (optional): The Searchlight is the high school yearbook featuring all students' and the year's highlights $12.00

Student Athletic Ticket (optional): an athletic ticket admits you to all home high school athletic events. You also receive monthly copies of the *High Times*. This ticket cannot be purchased until the book fees have been paid. Duplicate tickets cost $1.00. . . . . $ 7.50

Individual Course Expenses: Some courses require extensive supplies for use in the lab or shop. Separate fees are charged for these items. Students in these classes are to purchase a supplies ticket from the finance office and the teacher will punch the correct amount as you use these materials in class. You must have the ticket before you will be given these materials in class.

financial obligation notice...

STUDENT FINANCIAL OBLIGATION NOTICE
AS OF
CLOSE OF SCHOOL JUNE 19

_______________ _______ $ _______
(Name of Student) (Grade) (H.R.) (Amount Owed)

For _______________________________
(Reason: Book damage, loss, library fine, etc.)

____
(Name of Teacher)

financial procedures for schools...

1. PURCHASES

   a. All purchases made in the name of the school must be cleared with the Account Clerk prior to purchasing.

      Note: Purchases made without first securing a purchase order will not be honored. In short, you may be held personally accountable for such purchases.

   b. Purchase orders initiated within a department will be made by the Department Head.

      (PROCEDURES FOR PURCHASING ARE APPLICABLE TO BOTH FACULTY AND STUDENTS.)

2. MONEY COLLECTION

   a. All money collected should be turned into the finance office daily before 1:30 p.m. This includes money collected by classes, clubs, workbooks, supplies, etc. The 1:30 p.m. deadline is to enable the finance office to prepare banking monies collected for the day.

   b. A receipt should be given if any money is collected.

3. MONEY RAISING ACTIVITIES

   a. Approval must be obtained from the District Superintendent and application must be made one month prior to activity date. See finance office for proper forms.

4. CASHING CHECKS

   a. No checks may be cashed by the school.

   b. Personal checks may be accepted for payments to school, only in the exact amount of the financial obligation. Checks must be made payable to the High School.

fund assignment form...

Date________________19____

Charge to:

GENERAL FUND ______ SUB ACCOUNT________________

HIGH SCHOOL ACTIVITIES FUND ______ SUB ACCOUNT________________

SPECIAL SCHOOL ACCOUNTS ______ SUB ACCOUNT________________

Pay to:

____

Address____________________________________

Attach approved vouchers to this jacket as evidence of expenditures.

Items	Amount

Signed by ____________________

Authorized Approval by:

Superintendent ____________________

Principal ____________________

fund raising policies...

PHILOSOPHY AND OBJECTIVES

While the primary objective is to raise funds for the benefit of students involved in the organization, all fund raising projects shall endeavor to provide as much educational benefits for the participants and the community as the nature of the project shall permit. To enhance the educational benefits to the students in the organization, those students shall be involved in the planning and implementation of the fund raising project.

POLICIES

1. All fund raising projects proposed by any High School organization, chartered club class, or affiliated booster club shall have the approval of the school administration prior to the undertaking of such a project.
2. Fund raisers involving a form of work or service project shall be encouraged.
3. The sale or re-sale of commercially prepared products (for example, candy sale, etc.) shall be prohibited.
4. No alcoholic beverages will be sold or served at any High School organization's fund raiser.
5. To keep booster club accounts from being confused with High School accounts, all fund raisers by boosters clubs, alumni association, or other non-student chartered organization shall use "BOOSTER" rather than "HIGH SCHOOL."

fund receipt form...

DISTRICT CASHIERS' FUND RECEIPT

SCHOOL:__________

Amount Disbursed $__

Purpose __________ Code

FUND/SCH	FUNC	OBJECT	AREA	AMOUNT
TOTAL				

Approved __________

Received Payment ____

Date __________

Month Day Year

school-related financial policies...

The following is the procedure to be followed for receipting and turning in money each day.

1. Never accept money from anyone without giving that person a receipt from the duplicate receipt book you have been issued. (This includes checks received by mail.) Be sure the receipt is correctly filled out showing name, receipt number, date, amount, and purpose.
2. Receipts for the day should be totaled and the teacher should make out the next receipt to him- or herself for the total amount. This receipt must balance with the money turned in. These daily receipt books will be checked at the end of the school year.
3. Money and the receipt for the total amount should then be enclosed in the money envelope, which should be filled out legibly and in ink, showing:
   a. Date
   b. Amount
   c. Purpose (Fund) – this is imperative
4. The money envelope is to be turned in to the Bookkeeper's Office *before* 3:00 or, if possible, at the Break.
5. The money will be counted in the Bookkeeper's Office and receipted in the Master Receipt Book. If there is any discrepancy between the teacher's figures and those of the bookkeeper, it will be noted in *red ink* on the money envelope. The envelope, with the receipt included, will be returned to the teacher's mailbox at the end of the day.
6. No money envelopes should be sent by students.
7. A receipt must be issued from one of these receipt books for *all* money collected in the name of Rock Township High School or of any subsidiary organization.

(See Also: BUDGET; DANCES; FREE LUNCHES; MONEY; PAYROLL; PURCHASING; TRAVEL; TRIPS; VOUCHER)

FIELD TRIPS

field trip permission slips (two examples)...

FIELD TRIP PERMISSION SLIP (To be signed/returned by parent for each field trip)

We understand the arrangement for taking your school group to ______________________________

____

We believe the necessary precautions and plans for the children's care have been made. We feel that reasonable vigilance in the care and supervision of the children during the trip will be exercised. Beyond this we will not hold the school or those supervising the trip responsible.

We hereby give consent for our child, ______________________________, to go on the trip to

____ ______________.

(place) (date)

____

(Parent's Signature)

FIELD TRIP PERMISSION FORM

My child has my permission to attend all teacher-supervised field trips and activities throughout the year, provided that I (or the foster parents) am informed of all such activities ahead of time.

Child's Name ____

Parent's Signature ____

Date ____

Telephone Number ____

It is my understanding that for field trips beyond reasonable walking distance of the school, private vehicles will be used to transport the children. I agree not to hold the driver of the vehicle responsible for any accident or injury that may occur while my child is being transported during the field trip.

____ ______________________________

Parent Signature Date

field trip request form...

FIELD TRIP REQUEST

NAME: ______________________ DEPARTMENT: ______________________

DATE(S): ______________________

NUMBER OF STUDENTS EACH DATE: ______________________

DESTINATION: ______________________

____

DEPARTURE TIME: ______________________

RETURN TIME: ______________________

METHOD OF FINANCING:

☐ STUDENT

☐ FUND RAISING*

*EXPLAIN: ______________________

____

____

TOTAL COST PER PUPIL: ______________________

HOW DO YOU PLAN TO PROVIDE ADEQUATE SUPERVISION? ______________________

____

____

APPROVAL OF DEPARTMENT COORDINATOR: ______________________

TO: All Teachers
FROM: John Benson, Principal
RE: Field Trip Procedures 1984–1985

1. Complete all information requested on the form entitled "Field Trip Request."
2. Submit this form to Mrs. Martin in the Main Office at least three (3) weeks in advance of the trip.
3. Once the trip has been approved/disapproved by the principal, you will be notified by Mrs. Martin.
4. If the trip has been approved you will receive three (3) copies of "Application for School Trip" which are to be completed and returned to Mrs. Martin at least two (2) weeks prior to the date of the trip.
5. At least three (3) days preceding the trip you are to submit to Mrs. Martin a "Class Trip Roster" in spirit master which will be duplicated and placed in every teacher's mailbox, as well as a completed "Field Trip Impact" form.
6. On the morning of the trip you are to submit to Mrs. Martin an up-to-date "Class Trip Roster."

RETURNING FROM A TRIP:

If students are not expected to return for regular buses, you are to survey the students and advise Mr. Walker as to the number of students who will be taking each of the late buses.

If arrangements have been made for parents to pick up their students after school, the teacher is to remain with and actively supervise the students until they have all been picked up.

If students will be returning before the close of the school day, they are to enter the building as a group with their teacher.

policies and procedures...

FIELD TRIP PROCEDURES:

a. Each June, department coordinators should submit a list of proposed field trips. Then early in the year submit your trip requests to Mr. Casey. You will be notified if your trip is approved. Once approved, you are to request a trip form from the office. This form must be submitted at least 3 weeks prior to the date planned.
b. Parental permission slips, available in the office, must be signed by a parent and turned in to the teacher at least one day before the proposed trip.
c. When any monies are involved, they should be collected by the teacher and turned in each day for safekeeping. All money should be collected at least two days before the trip. Requests for checks must be made at least one day before you need the checks.
d. In planning for a field trip, teachers will not purchase tickets, transportation, theater seats, etc., before receiving the money for these tickets from their students. Teachers will explain to their students when the trip is first proposed that paying

their share of the costs will constitute a firm commitment. The teacher must explain that the money cannot be refunded unless the refund would not impose an additional burden on the other students and/or the school.

e. Alphabetical lists of students must be turned in two days in advance. This will enable us to publish this list in the daily notices the day before the trip is scheduled.

f. The teacher in charge should obtain two copies of the daily notice on which this listing of students will be published. The day of the trip, the teacher in charge must send one of these daily notices to the office after roll has been taken on the bus. Please indicate those who are absent and send this list to the main office immediately before departure. The second list should be kept by the teacher for use during the trip.

Field Trip Policy

It is the belief of the Board that properly planned field trips that are an integral part of the program of classroom instruction are a valuable part of the learning experience. Plans for field studies or trips to various locations for the purpose of curriculum-related field studies shall be submitted to Central Administration by the principal for approval. The Board of Education also recognizes the practice of having its students participate in field trips that are extracurricular in nature. Permission of the Board must be obtained in advance for such trips.

(See Also: ACCIDENT; FEES, FINES, FUNDS, AND CHARGES; INSURANCE; PERMISSION SLIPS; SUPERVISION; TRAVEL; TRIPS)

FIGHTING

form for reporting...

STUDENT(S)
INVOLVED ______________________ Grade ________ Homeroom ________
______________________ Grade ________ Homeroom ________
______________________ Grade ________ Homeroom ________

TEACHER(S) REPORTING INCIDENT:
____
____

WHEN and WHERE did incident occur:
____
____

DESCRIBE what happened:
____
____

DESCRIBE TEACHER ACTION (include treatment of injuries, if any):
____
____

SIGNATURE OF TEACHER(S): ______________________________

DATE OF THIS REPORT: ______________________________

(See Also: BEHAVIOR; DETENTION; DISCIPLINE; HEALTH; NURSE; POLICE; PSYCHOLOGICAL SERVICES; REFERRAL; SUSPENSION)

FIRE DRILLS

complete fire drill policy and procedures...

PURPOSE:

The chief purpose of fire drills and procedures in a fire emergency is to ensure efficient, safe, and orderly exit to prevent the panic which has been responsible for the great loss of life in the major fire disasters of history. Speed in emptying buildings should be made secondary to the maintenance of proper order and discipline.

FIRE EXIT DRILLS:

Fire drills will be held monthly at varying times of the day and must be fulfilled to the highest degree of seriousness by the faculty, staff, and students.

These drills are mandated by State law, which reads:

"It shall be the duty of every principal or other person in charge of any public, private or parochial school or educational institution to hold not less than one fire-exit drill each month, during which drill the building shall be completely evacuated." (Sec. 9.8, Sub-Part B, Rules and Regulations of the Fire Marshall, amended 1964, Fire Exit Drills, Educational Occupancies.)

"Any owner, occupant, or other person having control over or charge of any building, structure, or other premises who violates any regulation of the fire marshall shall be fined not more than $500 or imprisoned not more than 30 days, or both." (Sec. 132-15 (in part) Revised Statutes, 1968, Penalty.)

PROCEDURES:

1. The fire alarm signal (bell) will be regularly used as the signal to start the drill. In the event of a malfunction, the emergency signal will be: 1st option—PA system buzzer (3 short buzzes), 2nd option—continuous manual hand bell ringing. In the event of need, all of the fire alarm options may be utilized. The recall bell used to signal the close of a fire drill will be a long blast (buzz) of the PA system and/or verbal notification.

2. Teachers must designate that the first person to reach any door should keep the door in an open position until all people have cleared the room.

3. While there are situations where the source of the fire is quickly identified and in its beginning stages and conditioned/automatic human reaction is to take immediate steps to extinguish it if an extinguisher is right at hand, fire fighting should always be made secondary to life/safety.

4. Each classroom group will move to a predetermined point that does not hinder fire-fighting operation by the fire department.

This fire drill movement to respective evacuation sites is a general operational procedure. In the event of an actual fire, good judgment in the selection of exit routes and evacuation site is imperative.

5. If a drill is called when pupils are going up and down the stairways, as during the time classes are changing, the pupils are to proceed immediately toward the areas indicated.

6. Walk rapidly! Do not run, push, or take several steps at a time on stairways or in corridors.

7. Everyone will be required to leave all buildings during a fire drill.

8. Absolutely no vehicles will be moved in a fire drill or actual fire. Any change of plan will be of emergency nature and will be communicated at that moment of need.

9. All safety and security aides and custodians will be directly responsible to the administration in helping to maintain free flow of exiting students, to keep driveway clear and accessible to fire fighting vehicles, and to assist in whatever other ways deemed necessary.

ADMINISTRATIVE CONSIDERATIONS:

A. Routine responsibilities:

1. It will be the duty of the administration to inspect all exit facilities daily in order to make sure that all stairways, doors, and other exits are in proper condition. Particular attention should be given to keeping all exitways clear and keeping stairs and fire escapes free from all obstructions and clear of any accumulation of any material whatsoever that may interfere with the rapid escape from the building.

2. Any condition likely to interfere with safe exit will be immediately corrected, if possible; otherwise, reported at once to the appropriate authorities.

3. It will be the duty of the administration to keep a monthly report of fire drills in the school files.

4. It shall be the duty of the administration to cooperate with the local fire department in all matters of fire safety, regulations, inspections, and conducting of fire drills.

5. Any other local requirements deemed necessary by the school authorities, or the chief of the fire department may be considered a part of this guide.

B. Actual Fire Responsibilities:

1. Notify Fire Department.

2. Notify Police Department.

3. Notify the District Office Civil Defense Coordinator, staff specialist, business and facilities.

4. Designate custodians to keep access roads open for emergency vehicles.

5. Notify utility companies of a break or anticipated break in utility lines or pipes. Inform Department of Accounting and General Services of action.

6. Determine whether ACTION GO HOME or any further action should be implemented.

In the event that ACTION GO HOME decision is reached, principal will notify:

1. District Superintendent
2. News media
3. Bus companies

(Students and staff should not return to the school until Fire Department officials declare the area safe.)

FACULTY CONSIDERATIONS:

1. Teachers will orient all students on the Fire Drill/Fire Plan Procedures and thereby ensure that students in every period know exactly what they are to do.

2. Teachers will be the last to leave classrooms in order that a check may be made that every student has left the classroom. She/he should then lock the door if possible (to prevent theft and pilferage).

3. While there is a general operational procedure for fire drill movement, each teacher is responsible for exercising good judgment in the selection of exit routes and evacuation site in the event of an actual fire.

4. Each teacher will be responsible for taking the student roll and grade book from the building during the fire exit drill. The registrar will be responsible for the school's register.

5. Each teacher will be responsible to account for and supervise his/her students upon arrival at the designated evacuation site. Any missing student should be immediately reported to the administration.

explanation of procedures in student handbook...

During fire drills, students are to pass directly to their assigned exit and not visit with fellow students until they are fifty feet from the building. Quiet and order are essential so that directions from teachers may be heard and quickly followed.

FIRE EXIT LOCATIONS

LOCATIONS	ROOMS
West entrance by Room 111	110,111,112
West entrance by Room 113	113
North entrance by Room 114	114
East entrance through Auto Shop	120, 121, 122, 123, Auto Shop, & Wood Shop
East entrance by Dist. Ed. store	130, 131, 132, 135
East entrance by Home Ec. Department	133, 134
Northwest entrance to Academic wing	200, 201, 202, 203, 204, 205, 206, 207, 208, 219, 220
Northeast entrance to Academic wing	209, 210, 211, 212, 213, 214, 215, 216, 217, 218, Humanities Resource
North entrance on 1st floor by Music Department	300, 301, 302, 303, Math Resource, Science Resource, 304, 305, 306, 307, 308

North entrance on 1st floor by Electronics Room 122	309, Bus. Ed., 310, 311, 312, 313, 314, 315, 316, 317, 318, 319, 320
Commons entrance	Commons area, library
South entrance to gym	Gymnasium area
South entrance to pool	Swimming pool
South entrance to locker area	Phy. Ed. locker areas

Procedure:

1. Anytime the fire alarm rings, it is essential that we assume it's the real thing. To do otherwise is inviting disaster.
2. Students and teachers should go immediately to the designated exit.
3. Do not congregate near the exit areas. Go directly to parking areas, street, or other applicable area.

(See Also: ACCIDENT; BOMB THREATS; DISMISSAL PROCEDURES; DOCTORS; EARTHQUAKE; EMERGENCY; NURSE; POLICE; WEATHER ALERTS)

FREE LUNCHES

lunch count slip (including free lunches)...

This slip is used for lunch count each morning. Take the count, fill out the form, and send it to the office each morning.

TEACHER____________________ Date________________

1. Students eating:
   a. Tickets/Cash ________________
   b. Free ________________
   c. Reduced ________________
2. Sack Lunches ________________
3. Going Home ________________
4. Absent ________________

Total Enrollment ________________

Adults Eating ________________

Tomorrow's Count (Students & Adults) ________________

lunch ticket reminder slip...

LUNCH TICKET REMINDER SLIP (Send home with child as his/her lunch ticket runs out)

____________________________________ needs a new lunch ticket:

________ meal/meals left as of ____________________
date

________ charges as of ____________________
date

policy on lost lunch tickets...

This constitutes quite a problem in that some students will change the name on tickets that have been either stolen or found. Encourage your students to take good care of their tickets because their loss can prove costly. The policy governing lost lunch tickets is as follows: Report all lost lunch tickets to the lunch cashier immediately. It is important that we know the day it was lost. The date of each lunch ticket is recorded on the Daily Program Card. We will use this information for determining how many lunches the student has coming. If the student does not report the loss of the ticket, we cannot give him or her credit beyond the first day of the reported loss.

(See Also: APPLICATION; CAFETERIA; FEES, FINES, FUNDS AND CHARGES; LUNCH AND LUNCH DUTY; MONEY; RECORDS)

GAMBLING

memo on...

TO: Faculty and Staff
FROM: J. Benson, Principal
RE: Gambling

Recently, there has been a rash of referrals to the office of students engaged in gambling on school grounds. Please remind your students that gambling on school grounds is not permitted by school policy. Also remind them that students caught gambling face prescribed penalties ranging from detention and notification of parents to suspension from school.

We must also remember that we, as educators, must set an acceptable example for our students. It is difficult to justify disciplinary action for a student caught gambling if such items as football pools and the like are openly circulated among the faculty and staff. We all entered education because we felt a need to help youngsters. Let us remember that and provide them with examples of what *we do* as well as what *we tell them to do*.

I know that I can count on you in this regard.

policy on card playing in school...

Card playing is permitted only under the following conditions: During small recess, lunch recess and enrichment period <u>if played in a classroom under the supervision of a teacher</u>.

In short, playing is *not* allowed during any class period including study halls. It also means that card playing is *not* allowed on the campus during the school day.

The reasons again are threefold:

1. A learning institution has the responsibility of providing a climate for learning. Card playing distracts from this climate.

2. As an educational institution, it is difficult to defend the position that card playing is the only alternative in keeping students occupied meaningfully; therefore, it is our responsibility to look for other alternatives.
3. There is no reasonable way in which we can distinguish between those who abuse the privilege (gambling) and those who play for pure recreation.

Your full cooperation will be appreciated.

(See Also: BEHAVIOR; BUILDING; DANCES; DISCIPLINE; LAVATORIES; MONEY; SUSPENSION)

GOALS

course goals (for a course in Composition)...

The student, through structured and intensive writing, will develop the ability to construct a sentence from its simplest form to its most complex.

Following mastery of sentence sense, the student will develop an ability to write a cohesive paragraph, which would include utilizing the techniques of development with fact, example, incident and reason. He would also work on narrative writing and the use of descriptive words.

The student who demonstrates mastery of basic techniques will be given advanced composition techniques, as in extended definition, critical essay, objective and subjective description, and narration.

goals for the classroom...

CLASS MANAGEMENT

a. Room
    1. Seating
    2. Temperature
    3. Outside noise
    4. Lighting
    5. Displays
    6. Ventilation
b. Teacher Organization
    1. Lesson plans—revised when necessary
    2. Let students know purpose of course
    3. Clarity of grading policies
    4. Clear objectives expressed to students
    5. Flexibility
    6. Punctuality
c. Discipline—Control
    1. Establishes proper student behavior

INSTRUCTOR SKILLS

a. Skills Relating to Individuals
   1. Receptive to different children and parents socially, economically, and intellectually
   2. Sensitive to child's physical needs
   3. Develops a sense of worth in students
   4. Receives and recognizes pupil responses and contributions in a positive manner
   5. Motivates students
   6. Students receive adequate oral and written feedback from teacher
b. Skills in Handling Students as a Group
   1. Uses resources to accommodate differences in children
   2. Adequately evaluates pupil progress
   3. Creates a positive and relaxed atmosphere
   4. Develops cooperation between students
   5. Flexible, creative, innovative
   6. Confers with students when necessary and appropriate
c. Skills in Using Different Modes of Instruction
   1. Involves student teachers and aides effectively
   2. Adapts subject matter to everyday life and life situations when feasible
   3. Uses flexibility in grouping
   4. Utilizes supportive staff, noncertified aides
   5. Makes use of centers—learning, resource, and interest
   6. Uses variety of instructional materials
   7. Paces instruction well—able to adjust tempo
d. Planning
   1. Sets and defines goals and objectives
e. Knowledge of Material
f. Specific Portions of Lessons
   1. Introduction
   2. Review of previous lesson
   3. Testing
      a. frequency
      b. validity
   4. Conclusion
      a. assignment—clarity, divergent, quality, variety
g. Questioning
   1. Divergent—lead to more questions
   2. Open ended
h. Speech Delivery
i. Emphasizes Communication Skills
j. Improves, Maintains, and Encourages Good Study Habits
k. Meets Goals and Objectives

PERSONAL CHARACTERISTICS

a. Personality
   1. Sense of humor
   2. Control of emotions
   3. Open minded

4. Consistent behavior
5. Self-confidence
6. Promptness

b. Physical
1. Health
2. Appropriate appearance

EFFORT TOWARD IMPROVEMENT

a. Resourceful
b. Innovative
c. Demonstrates self-improvement

INTEREST IN WORK

a. Personal Qualities that Demonstrate Interest in Work
1. Ambitious
2. Energetic
3. Enthusiastic
4. Reliable

b. Work Habits that Demonstrate Interest in Work
1. Is not unnecessarily absent from the classroom
2. Takes part in professional functions
3. Participates effectively in curriculum improvement
4. Cooperates in following school policies
5. Shows pride in teaching as a profession
6. Is prompt in meeting responsibilities

ABILITY TO WORK WITH OTHERS

a. Personal Qualities
1. Ability to relate to children and adults
2. Friendliness
3. Patience
4. Fairness
5. Considerate
6. Sincere
7. Tactful
8. Shows respect for others
9. Understands feelings of others

b. Professional Qualities
1. Cooperates with faculty and students
2. Gets along well with colleagues
3. Has rapport with students
4. Enjoys children and being around them
5. Interacts well with students
6. Sensitive to children's needs
7. Flexible
8. Accepts suggestions and/or criticism
9. Willing to share one's load of duties and obligations
10. Keeps parents informed of student progress

subject goals (for Mathematics—Grade 12)...

- Uses algebraic techniques and describes their relationship to the properties of real numbers.
- Calculates and interprets basic statistical measurements from a set of data.
- Calculates measures of dispersion and correlation of data.
- Explains relationships of the parts of a geometric figure and among geometric figures.
- Performs and describes geometric transformations.
- Describes ways that geometric properties and relationships are organized in a deductive system.
- Organizes geometric properties and relationships into deductive systems.
- Uses concepts from trigonometry and analysis to graph equations and inequalities and discuss these from a theoretical point of view.
- States the condition of the problem, introduces suitable notations, and determines whether the data is sufficient, consistent, and reasonable.
- Proves mathematical statements orally and in writing; writes alternate deductive justifications (proofs).
- Solves different problems using the same mathematical model and extends problems solved.

(See Also: ACHIEVEMENT; BILINGUAL EDUCATION; CAREERS; CLASS; COURSES; CURRICULUM; ELECTIVES; JOB DESCRIPTION; MINI-COURSES; OBJECTIVE)

GRADES

grading policies and procedures (three examples)...

Scale

A = 92–100; B = 83–91; C = 74–82; D = 65–73; F = 0–64

In averaging all grades, the median mark should be used for all grades that have been recorded as letter grades.

A = 96; B = 87; C = 78; D = 69

Grades are averaged numerically, and the average must be rounded off to the next highest number. All grades must be recorded numerically for recordkeeping purposes.

I = Incomplete (automatically becomes F if not removed prior to the end of the next grading period)

Grading Period and Averaging

The grading period will be nine weeks, four contained in the year. A minimum of five grades separately, randomly spaced will be required and recorded for each student. A comprehensive test is to be administered to all students in grades 9–12 at an appropriate time after the seventh week of each nine-week grading period on units covered during that grading period. Students should be informed twenty-four (24) hours before the test as to the weighted value of the test.

A standardized form, with room for individual comments, will be sent to parents of those students who have averages at the midpoint (the fifth week) of a grading period telling them their child is doing unsatisfactory work or working below potential. The teacher will be responsible for the progress report and will maintain a duplicate copy of each progress report which has been signed by the student showing receipt. Those reports are to be sent on all students with D's, F's, or who are dropping from previous averages.

GRADES: Marks in all subjects will be given according to the following alphabetical system:

Mark	Interpretation	Numerical Equivalency
A	Excellent	93–100
B+	Superior	89–92
B	Very Good	85–88
C+	Good	81–84
C	Satisfactory	77–80
D	Minimal Achievement–Passing	70–76
F	Failure	0–69

Mark	Interpretation
1	Excellent
2	Satisfactory
3	Improvement Noted
4	Improvement Needed
5	Parent Conference Requested

Averaging Letter Grades: It is generally agreed that quarterly marks or grades given students are wide-ranged teacher judgments of student proficiency and achievement. In view of this fact, it is recommended that all secondary teachers be given the leeway.

1. The teacher will inform the students of grading policies in the areas of:

a. Attendance

The school policies on excessive unexcused absences in which 20 absences in a semester normally will result in an automatic failure shall be rigidly enforced. In order to enforce this policy the following procedures must be followed:

1. The rule must be explained to the students by the teacher.
2. Parents must be notified in the early stages of cutting that such behavior may result in failure.
3. There must be a prior conference with parents about cutting.

4. Exceptions to this policy require a written note based on a valid reason, such as illness or family crisis.
5. Excessive absence due to illness or family crisis or other such extenuating circumstance may be made up.

b. Tardies
c. Participation
d. Discussions
e. Testing
f. Projects
g. Make-up work

2. Homework assignments shall be thoroughly explained in respect to grading and the relationship of such homework to in-class work.
3. Grading systems and the evaluation of these systems shall be left to the discretion of the individual teacher.

(See Also: ACHIEVEMENT; EXAMINATIONS; FAILURE; PERMANENT RECORDS; REPORT CARDS; SUPPLEMENTAL INSTRUCTION**)**

GRADUATION

graduation requirements...

Special Note: Graduation requirements may vary slightly from place to place.

The job of selecting the *right* course or courses is one that each student should carefully weigh and decide. Your concern and your ability to guide students to the proper sources (counselors, agencies, etc.) can be most helpful in helping the student to make his or her decision.

Credits for Graduation

Graduation is to be based on credits earned in grades 9–12. A total of 18 is required. Graduation from high school should signify the completion of a program that has been planned and carried out so as to meet as nearly as possible the needs of each student. These requirements must include the following:

English	4	credits
Social Studies	4	credits
Physical Education	1	credit
Mathematics	1	credit
Science	1	credit
Health	½	credit
Electives	6½	credits
Total	18	credits

Mathematics and Science requirements should be met any time in grades 9–11.

Prerequisites

Certain courses demand specific prerequisites and/or the teacher's or instructor's recommendation or consent. Each student has received a copy of the list. Study them carefully and be sure to observe all prerequisites in registering as you will not be given subjects of first choice if you fail to meet the requirements. Refer to "Course Descriptions" so you will know what to expect in the courses you choose.

The number of classes set up will be determined by the tally of this registration. Parents and students must understand that it is not possible to open up an indefinite number of sections in each course offered, and for this reason many classes will be closed as of the date the tally is made.

In cases where there is (1) conflict in scheduling; (2) prerequisites have not been met; or (3) a credit was earned for a certain subject in summer school, the student will be given a subject listed next, according to his or her choice.

Graduation requirements are established by the State Department of Public Instruction and the local Board of Education. Nineteen (19) credits are required. The specific graduation requirements are as follows:

1. **Mathematics**—One (1) unit of credit must be earned by the Class of '84; Two (2) units of credit must be earned by the Class of '85—in addition, each junior will be required to take a competency exam in basic mathematics. Any student not passing the exam will be required to take Applied Mathematics I and pass it in order to graduate.
2. **Social Studies**—Three (3) units of credit must be earned. These three units are to be divided as follows: One (1) unit of U.S. History; One (1) unit of World History; One-half (½) unit of elective, and One-Quarter (¼) units each of Economics and Government.
3. **Science**—Two (2) units of credit must be earned.
4. **Language Arts**—Four (4) units of credit must be earned. This will include the following requirements: One (1) unit of Grade 9 English or 0600 Grade 9 Basic English; One (1) unit of Composition; One (1) unit of Literature; one-half (½) unit of Oral Communications (Debate, Speech or Pinciples of Communication), and One-half (½) unit of Elective.
5. Physical Education—Two (2) credits must be earned. Every student in grades 9–12 is required to take a minimum of one (1) physical education course each quarter. Students must provide their own physical education uniform when needed. Fees are required for certain indicated courses. All students must taken one water-oriented course to meet graduation requirements.
6. **Electives**—A minimum of seven (7) electives are required for graduation. These courses should reflect a student's interest, abilities, and vocational goals.

Students who have questions on their graudation or credit status are urged to visit a counselor on this subject immediately.

(See Also: ACHIEVEMENT; ASSEMBLIES; BOARD OF EDUCATION; NEWSLETTER; NEWS RELEASES; PERMANENT RECORDS)

GRIEVANCES

definition of...

A grievance is a non-appealable complaint to management (except where a separate written complaint procedure exists to cover such areas as performance ratings) by an employee involving conditions of work, work relationships, or the interpretation or application of policies, rules and regulations which have been adopted to cover personnel practices and/or working conditions. A grievance must concern a matter that is subject to control of the administration.

procedures for...

Each step in this procedure is to give bonafide, fresh consideration to the grievance and is to be a separate review of the facts. Each official to whom the grievance is presented shall issue a decision independent of the persons who have issued previous decisions or who may issue later decisions regarding the grievance.

Formal Process–The formal process begins with the employee who is filing the grievance preparing a written statement containing his/her name, address and telephone number; school building, address, telephone number and name of principal; the condition, situation, being grieved and why; and the requested remedy. The written grievance must be signed and dated by the aggrieved.

STEP 1: An employee may present a grievance in writing at any time to his or her immediate supervisor provided that the term or condition of employment giving rise to the grievance still exists at the time the grievance is presented or did exist no more than 15 days prior to the time the grievance is presented. The employee shall discuss the grievance with his or her immediate supervisor. The supervisor will make every attempt to resolve the grievance. The employee may cancel Step 1 at any time and proceed to Step 2 within 10 days if he or she feels that the supervisor's attempts to resolve the grievance are unsatisfactory.

STEP 2: If the grievance is not resolved by Step 1 or if the employee does not feel free to discuss a grievance with his or her immediate supervisor as in Step 1 of the procedure, the employee may present the grievance in writing to the personnel director within five (5) days. The director shall within five (5) days respond in writing his or her decision to the aggrieved party.

STEP 3: If the aggrieved party is not satisfied with the decision of the personnel director, he or she may, within ten (10) days, submit a written copy of the grievance to the teacher-administrator board. The teacher-administrator board shall then have ten (10) days in which to set a date for a hearing.

STEP 4: Within twenty (20) days the teacher-administrator board shall have conducted a hearing, from which they have gathered enough testimony and/or other pertinent information on which to base its decision.

STEP 5: If, within ten (10) days from the hearing, the teacher-administrator board has been able to reach a majority decision on the grievance, it shall do so in writing to the employee. This decision is final and will be implemented unless civil court action is taken to delay it or set it aside. If within ten (10) days from the hearing the teacher-administrator board has not reached a majority decision, it shall notify the employee of his or her further rights.

STEP 6: If the teacher-administrator board could not reach a majority decision, the aggrieved shall have ten (10) days in which to present his or her grievance in writing to the Superintendent of Schools, who shall then review the grievance and relevant information and present his or her decision in writing to the employee, teacher-administrator board, personnel director, and the principal within ten (10) days. This decision is final, subject to court review if the employee files suit.

(See Also: BOARD OF EDUCATION; COMPLAINTS; CONTRACT; DUE PROCESS; MEDIATION; NEGOTIATIONS; WORK)

GUIDANCE

descriptions and messages concerning guidance (four examples)...

GUIDANCE PROGRAM

The elementary guidance counselor assists students in understanding their abilities and limitations, in adjusting to a new school, in finding answers to new concerns, in learning to make decisions, in developing skills in getting along with others, and in achieving more in school. The counselor also visits with parents concerning their child's progress in school, their child's abilities and limitations, and possible questions concerning growth and development. The counselor assists teachers in understanding and meeting individual students' needs, in sharing test results, and in finding special help for students when needed. The elementary guidance counselor consults parents and teachers in private conferences about their children. He or she coordinates referrals to school and community agencies when school personnel and parents agree this is needed. The elementary counselor visits with children individually and in small groups. The child may request the counseling or may be referred by parents or teachers. Counseling is a voluntary service—no child is required to talk with the counselor.

THE GUIDANCE DEPARTMENT

The purpose of the guidance department is to offer you assistance with the various problems you may face in school. You are encouraged to go to your guidance counselor for help at any time. Information on various occupations, the armed services, college and summer jobs is also available in the guidance offices.

GUIDANCE AND COUNSELING

Guidance services are provided and made available to all of us. Many services are provided through guidance without request; however, if you want to discuss a particular problem, you will always find receptive assistance in the Guidance Office.

You may go to the Guidance Office and make an appointment for a conference with the counselor, Mrs. Shaw. At times, teachers may make appointments for or refer students to the counselor for conferences.

An appointment is not always necessary in order to see the counselor, but permission from teachers in the form of a pass is desirable.

The guidance service is a "helping relationship" and it is hoped that students, parents, and teachers will avail themselves of this opportunity.

GUIDANCE

The staff of the Junior High includes a full-time guidance counselor. The counselor is available at all times to any student or parent desiring assistance with academic difficulties, school programming, vocational choices, or social problems. The use of these facilities is encouraged. Students may make appointments through personal contact with the counselor or through the office. The counselor also assists with the school testing program and the interpretation of results.

policies and procedures for counselors...

Program Changes

Counselors will process (through the registrar's office) student program changes according to program change guidelines as distributed to all teachers on September 5, 1984. These guidelines were established by the Rock Township High School's administrators.

Off-Campus Permit

a. Emergency and request from parents—permits will be distributed by the counselors.
b. Health (doctor, dentist and other health appointments and/or request) will be processed by the Health Aides. Please send student to the Health Room.
c. Excursion permits will be processed by the individual teacher in charge of the excursion.

Referrals

a. Counselors will accept referrals from faculty members dealing with student's needs, problems, etc.

b. Referrals will be accepted only on the official referral forms (available in the counseling complex). The teacher should keep the third copy when sending the referral for future reference.

c. The teacher should note action(s) taken regarding the referred student. Please document action taken by time, date and action results. FIRST LINE OF COUNSELING TO BE THE RESPONSIBILITY OF THE TEACHER INVOLVED.

d. The counselor will take immediate action on the referral. If immediate action is not possible, teacher will be informed immediately as to why there is a delay.

Notes and Referrals to Counselors

Please use the teachers-counselors boxes in the main office to send referrals/notes to the counselors.

Appointments (Students)

Students to sign up for appointments to see counselors during noninstructional time, such as recess. Counselors will call for student. Student is not to be released without an appointment unless deemed an EMERGENCY.

(See Also: ABSENTEEISM; BEHAVIOR; CAREERS, CHILD STUDY TEAM; CONFERENCES; COUNSELING; IDENTIFICATION PERMANENT RECORDS; SCHEDULE; WARNING NOTICES)

HALLS AND HALL DUTY

hall supervision guidelines...

The opportunity for the learning activity of our students is not restricted to the classroom, but to the total school plant. As teachers, we cannot restrict our responsibilities in our class, but must extend our influence beyond the confines of our classrooms. The effective school finds all teachers using every opportunity to serve as the counselor and director of learning. The individual teacher is expected to assume responsibility for his or her class for the entire period. We do not have the privilege of leaving a class unsupervised. Many teachers practice the procedure of supervising the dismissal of students as they exit from the classroom and simultaneously control the immediate area outside the classroom. This is a tremendous contribution to the general decorum of the school. Please do this!

Students are to leave the building by 3:50 p.m. unless they are participating in a school activity.

All teachers are expected to keep track of discipline in the halls during cafeteria passing, in the morning before homeroom, after school, and while the students are passing to and from classes. Check whistling, running, loud shouting, and boisterousness in any form. The library will be open at 8:00 a.m. for students wishing a place for supervised study.

student hall pass...

PERIOD ________ DATE ____________________

____________________ ________ was released from Room ________ to go to
Student's Name Grade

____ at ________ a.m. / p.m.

____
Teacher's Signature

Time released ________ a.m. / p.m.

____
Destination Teacher's Signature

(See Also: ASSIGNMENTS; DUTIES; LAVATORIES; LUNCH AND LUNCH DUTY; PASSES; SAFETY**)**

HANDBOOK

introduction in student handbook (two examples)...

Rock Township Junior High School, home of the "Mighty Rockets," is a proud school. "Enter to learn; go forth to serve." Many opportunities are available here to develop your interests and abilities if you will apply yourselves. The most important people in your lives during the adolescent age will be your parents, teachers, and spiritual leaders at your church. Listen to them; they deserve your respect.

Our faculty, highly competent and professional, is looking forward to working with each of you and assisting you in every educational adventure.

Make your junior high school years the most productive you have had. You have the power to determine your successes or failures. Good citizenship and honest endeavor to learn, a cooperative attitude with classmates and teachers, punctuality and thoroughness are some of the factors necessary for your success here and in life.

Let's make this year the best. "Success is fun."

Welcome to Larson High School and to the new and exciting experiences that will make your stay here happy and memorable.

This handbook has been prepared to tell you about our school. You will find the rules and regulations that govern our lives here at Larson High and make it possible for all of us to live, learn, work, and play together.

Read this booklet carefully **now**. Don't wait! Be sure you understand everything in it. Have your parents read it, too. If you have any questions about anything, see your teachers, advisors, guidance counselors, administrators, or other staff members. They will be happy to answer your questions.

Larson High School will be whatever you make it. Be proud of it. Take good care of it. Make this quotation from Abraham Lincoln your motto: "I will study and get ready and some day my chance will come."

introduction in teacher handbook...

Welcome to Towne Elementary School.

This Handbook is prepared to provide information on school policies and procedures for school personnel at Towne Elementary School. The Handbook is meant to supplement the School District Handbook and the School District Elementary Student Handbook with further information that directly affects the day-to-day operation of Towne Elementary School.

Please keep this Handbook readily available during the school year. I am sure that it will answer many questions for you. Any suggestions or recommendations for the improvement of this Handbook will be appreciated.

We are pleased to have you on our staff at Towne. This Handbook will help and assist you in your teaching duties at Towne. If there are any questions or concerns at any time, please feel free to see me.

James Harrison
Principal

policy on handbooks...

HANDBOOK, STUDENTS'

1. At the beginning of the school year, all teachers and students shall review the Handbook. Necessary corrections, clarifications or omissions shall be submitted immediately in writing to the Chairperson of the Handbook Committee.
2. The Handbook Committee will set up a group with the administration, appropriate committees, faculty and student personnel to review suggested revisions.
3. Responsibility for determining the content of the Handbook shall be with the Handbook Committee, not the Newswriting Class and Advisor. The class can do the layout and have the Handbook printed, but the content shall be determined by the Committee with administrative cooperation and approval.
4. Not later than May 10, the Handbook Committee will request updated material for inclusion in the Handbook for the following school year. Administrative, committee, advisory, department head, and other personnel concerned, shall submit such updated material in writing to the Handbook Committee chairperson no later than May 15.

(See Also: BOOKS; CALENDAR INFORMATION; INTRODUCTION; MAP OF THE SCHOOL; RIGHTS AND RESPONSIBILITIES; SCHEDULE; WRITING)

HEALTH

dental health report form...

DENTAL PLAQUE REPORT

School ________________

Dear Parents of ____________________:

The scores shown below indicate the percentage your child's teeth were plaque free on the dates they were checked as part of our dental health program at school.

The goal is to get 100% of the plaque removed every day in order to prevent tooth decay and gum disease. You are urged to encourage your child to continue the correct daily care of his/her teeth as has been demonstrated at school. It is highly recommended that you have some disclosing tablets or fluid available at home so that you and your children can tell if you are removing all of the plaque from the teeth each day.

Remember that tooth decay and gum disease are the most prevalent diseases in the United States, but they are also among the MOST PREVENTABLE.

____

School Nurse

Plaque Score ________ Date ________ Plaque Score ________ Date ________

health room policies...

a. A student who complains of not feeling well is sent to the health room with an "Out of Class Pass" stating reason for referral. The student takes the "Out of Class Pass" back to the same class if he returns to class. If he does not return to the same class, the "Out of Class Pass" will be left in the teacher's box.

b. A log of students reporting to the health room will be kept in the health room each day with the student's name, time reported to health room, complaint, disposition, and time left. This log is available for reference to teachers and counselors.

c. No student will be allowed to rest in the health room more than one period. If he needs to rest longer, he will be sent home. A "Permit to Leave Campus" will then be issued. This permit, signed by a doctor, dentist, parent or guardian, is to be presented to the attendance office immediately upon the student's return to school.

   Note: Should circumstances make it necessary for the student to remain in health room more than one period, teachers will receive information to this fact on the "Health Room Referral Form" signed by the nurse.

d. Students referring themselves to the health room during recess or lunch period will return to class with a "Health Room Referral Form" or be notified with same.

e. If a student is absent due to a contagious disease, he must present a doctor's certificate upon his return to school before he can be admitted to class.

f. Under no circumstances will medication be dispensed to students nor ointments or antiseptics be applied to cuts or sores.

g. If possible, all first aid is to be rendered in the health room. If it is impossible to do so, send for the nurse immediately.

health screening report...

____________________ date

Dear Parent:

Your child, ____________________, has had a health screening assessment by the school nurse. This does not take the place of a physical examination by a family physician but serves the statutory requirements for school entrance.

____

School Health Nurse

FINDINGS:

☐ Your child should be seen by your personal physician. A referral form has been enclosed for that purpose.

hearing loss report...

Date ________________________

Re: _________________________
(Name of Student)

Dear Parent,

Your child appears to have a high tone hearing loss in ____________________ ________ ear(s). If he/she has not already been examined by a doctor regarding this problem, it should be done.

This type of hearing loss may have been caused by a disease or a loud noise. Some of these loud sounds are gunshots, loud mechanical noises, such as jet aircraft, snow machines, high volume rock music, etc. Ears may be protected from some of these loud sounds by using ear plugs or wearing ear muffs. You should consult your physician regarding the use of these protective devices.

Because this hearing loss may become progressive, we would recommend your child have a hearing test each year. This may be done at school by the school nurse upon your request.

____

School Nurse

____

School

student physical assessment by school nurse form...

Certificate of
STUDENT PHYSICAL ASSESSMENT BY SCHOOL NURSE

Student's Name ______________________ Birthdate ____________

School ______________________ Grade ____________

Parent's Name ______________________ Home Telephone ____________

Address ______________________ Work Telephone ____________

Parent present at examination? ____________

PHYSICAL ASSESSMENT

Nose and Throat ____________	Height ____________
Mouth ____________	Weight ____________
Teeth ____________	Vision ____________
Heart ____________	Color Vision ____________
Lungs ____________	Temperature ____________
Posture (including Scoliosis) ____________	Pulse ____________
Skin ____________	Respiration ____________
	Blood Pressure ____________

Comments: ______________________

O = No Defect   √ = Defect Found   √√ = Requires Immediate Attention

Tuberculosis Test (Required by State Department of Education Rules and Regulations)

Date ____________ Results ____________

Able to participate in usual school activities? ______________________
(Yes or No–State Any Limitations)

This physical assessment does not satisfy requirement for State High School Activities Association.

Date of Assessment ____________ Signed ____________
School Nurse

(See Also: DOCTORS; DRUGS; EMERGENCY; ILLNESS; MEDICAL FORMS; MEDICATION; NURSE; PSYCHOLOGICAL SERVICES; SAFETY; SICK LEAVE; X-RAYS)

HOMEWORK

criteria for homework assignments...

There is no rigid policy on the matter of homework because of the varying conditions in schools and homes. Worthwhile homework assignments can extend learnings begun in the classroom, build independent study habits, and encourage children to think and work creatively outside of school. On the other hand, it is doubtful whether giving large amounts of homework is an important and useful means of promoting educational growth in elementary school children. The following guidelines and criteria for homework assignments take into account mental health, as well as intellectual aspects. Observance of these principles will make homework more effective and profitable.

Criteria for Homework Assignments

When considering homework assignments, the following criteria are important:

1. Does the assignment serve a valid educational purpose?
2. Is the assignment reasonable and consistent with the child's abilities, needs, and interests?
3. Does the homework assignment interfere with other worthwhile activities in which the child might engage while out of school?
4. Will the assignment extend the child's knowledge without fostering discouragement and resentment?
5. Does the pupil understand what is to be done? Is the assignment clear?
6. Is the length of the assignment reasonable—a maximum of thirty minutes for primary and one hour for intermediate grades?

homework for absent student form...

TEACHER ______________________________ DATE ________________

STUDENT ____

HOMEWORK FOR (NUMBER OF DAYS) ________________________

ASSIGNMENT IS: ____

____

____

____

____

message concerning homework in teacher handbook...

Homework, to be beneficial, should be of such a nature as to help the child in his or her progress in school. Homework is not something given solely for the purpose of giving the child something to do at home.

Homework could constructively include any of the following:

1. Completion of assignments, work, etc., started in school. (The student should fully understand the work before it is sent home to finish and the teacher should check on this.)
2. Drill or practice work needed by the student.
3. Individual projects for self-growth in special areas.

Suggested amounts of time for homework:

Fourth Grade – 15 minutes

Fifth Grade – 30 minutes

Sixth Grade – 45 minutes

(See Also: ASSIGNMENTS; CLASS; EXAMINATIONS; GRADES; REPORT CARDS; UNDERACHIEVERS; WRITING**)**

HONOR ROLL

criteria for honor roll compilation...

HONOR ROLL WORKSHEET

The honor roll calculation performed at the Computer Center is based on the number of hours a student spends in a class each week. If a student is scheduled for five hours a week in English and five hours in Wood Tech, these two classes would receive equal consideration in computing the honor standing. A Physical Education class which meets two hours a week would receive only 2/5 as much consideration as the above classes. An Auto Body class which meets ten hours a week would receive twice as much consideration as the five-hour classes. Basically, the rule of thumb is that the classes receive the following numerical consideration:

1. Any class that meets two hours a day for a week = 10
2. Any class that meets one hour a day for a week = 5
3. Physical Education classes meeting two hours per week = 2
4. Jazz Ensemble classes meeting three hours per week = 3

Let's work the following examples:

Student A Report Card		HRS/WK	×	Honor Points	=	Total
Auto Mech I	A	10	×	4	=	40
Am. Studies	C	5	×	2	=	10
Handball	B	2	×	3	=	6
Vot. Rights	D	5	×	1	=	5
Jazz Ensem.	B	3	×	3	=	9
Media	F	5	×	0	=	0
		30				70

Honors Standing is 2.333 — 30/70.000 = 2.333

Student B Report Card		HRS/WK	×	Honor Points	=	Total
Var. Winds	A	5	×	4	=	20
Mod. Office	B	5	×	3	=	15
Sec. Office	A	5	×	4	=	20
Shorthand II	B	5	×	3	=	15
Composition	C	5	×	2	=	10
Slimnastics	B	2	×	3	=	6
		27				86

Honors Standing is 3.185 — 27/86.000 = 3.185

By using this system, an hour spent in class in any area receives equal consideration with an hour spent in any other department in the school.

Senior Honors: Graduating students with at least a 3.0 average are graduated with honors. Students with an average of 3.5 or above are graduated with high honors. The top 1% of the graduating class are declared highest honor graduates. All honor students have the privilege of wearing a gold honor cord on their graduation gowns. Members of the National Honor Society have the privilege of wearing a white tassel on their caps (3.5 average).

explanation of honor roll in student handbook...

HONOR ROLL

To qualify for honor roll you must obtain a "C" grade or better and obtain these specific quality points if taking the following number of subjects:

6 subjects = 36 points

7 subjects = 42 points

You will be awarded a school certificate in grades 9–12 if you make three quarters honor roll for the school year.

You are not eligible for honor roll if you get a failing grade in any subject.

To arrive at the number of quality points you have earned, you add up the quality points for each letter grade you received. The quality points for each letter grade are:

Letter Grade	Quality Points
A	8
B+	7
B	6
C+	5
C	4
D	2
F	0

HIGH HONOR ROLL

To qualify for high honor roll you must obtain a "B" grade or better and obtain the total quality points specified below if taking the following number of subjects:

6 subjects = 46 points

7 subjects = 54 points

You will be awarded a school letter in grades 9–12 should you make three quarters high honor roll and one quarter honor roll for the school year.

NATIONAL HONOR SOCIETY

The National Honor Society is a group of students selected by the faculty on the basis of scholarship, service, leadership and character. Membership is limited to 15 percent of the senior class and 10 percent of the junior class.

Senior candidates must have at least a "B" average and have a member of the student body for one full semester. Junior candidates must have a "B+" average. If you fall below the standards which were the basis for your election into the Society, you may be dropped from the club.

explanation of honor roll in teacher handbook...

An Honor Roll is compiled and published at the end of each nine-week period. Homeroom teachers will be provided with the proper forms on which you will list the names of your students in your homeroom who meet the requirements for highest honors, high honors, and honors. Names of the students should be in alphabetical order, first name first, such as John Doe. Seventh grade homeroom teachers will use the pink form for reporting, eighth grade homeroom teachers will use the yellow form. These forms should be turned in to the office within two days after the grading period. Please post a copy of the Honor Roll in your homeroom, or go through it with the students *before* you hand it in to the office in order that errors may be found before it is sent to the *Rock Township Daily News*. All subjects which receive a grade of A through F will count in figuring the Honor Roll. Physical Education plus its related areas, Health and First Aid, are to be considered one course. In this case, average the two grades using the higher grade when a half is involved. Any student receiving an "F" in Citizenship will be ineligible for the Honor Roll regardless of his or her other grades.

(See Also: ACHIEVEMENT; AWARDS; CITIZENSHIP; NEWSLETTER; NEWS RELEASES; REPORT CARDS; STUDENTS' RECORDS)

IDENTIFICATION

policy on...

Each student will be issued an I.D. Card. This is a very important card and the student is urged to take good care of it. The card will be used for general identification purposes, to indicate if a student purchased a Searchlight and to indicate that a student has paid for his or her activity ticket and is to be admitted free to all school athletic events. If your card is lost or destroyed, it will cost $1.00 for it to be replaced.

sample I.D. card...

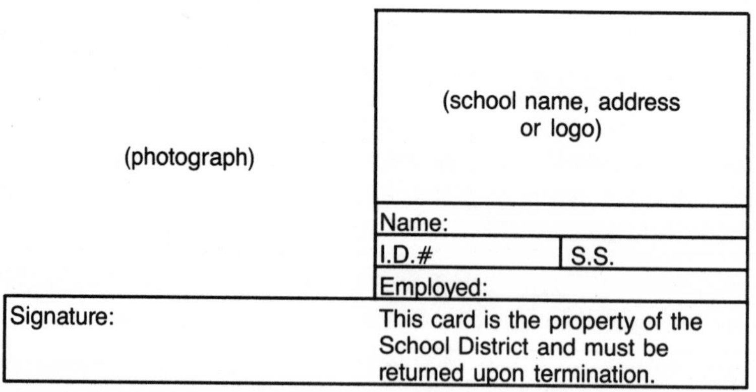

(school name, address or logo)

(photograph)

Name:

I.D.# | S.S.

Employed:

Signature:

This card is the property of the School District and must be returned upon termination.

Special Note: The above card would be for an employee of the district. With small changes, it could apply to students as well. This can be made up as a form, filled out, a photo attached, and the entire sheet copied and laminated for a sturdy I.D. card.

(See Also: BUS; CERTIFICATION; DANCES; HANDBOOK; ORGANIZATIONAL CHART; REGISTRATION; VISITORS)

ILLNESS

form for reporting employee illness...

DATE: ____________________

NAME: ______________________________ S.S.#: ____________________

POSITION (if teacher, give grade and/or subject): ____________________

DATE(S) ABSENT: ______________________________

____

NUMBER OF SCHOOL DAYS CONSECUTIVELY ABSENT: ____________

REASON FOR ABSENCE: ______________________________

____

WAS A PHYSICIAN CONSULTED: (   ) YES   (   ) NO

IF "YES" GIVE NAME AND ADDRESS OF DOCTOR: ____________________

____

NOTE: For absences beyond three (3) consecutive school days, a certificate from the attending physician may be required. If you have such a certificate, please attach it to this form.

SIGNATURE: ______________________________

(See Also: ABSENCE; DOCTORS; HEALTH; MEDICAL FORMS; MEDICATION; NURSE; X-RAYS**)**

INDIVIDUALIZATION

complete IEP plan form...

INDIVIDUALIZED EDUCATION PROGRAM PLAN

I. Identifying Information:

Student's Name: ____________________ School Year: ____________________

Date of Birth: ____________________ Grade/Program: ____________________

School Building: ____________________

II. IEP Planning Participants: Signatures:

Case Manager/Team Leader	____________________
Local Education Agency Representative (Principal or Special Education Administrator)	____________________
*Parent, Guardian, or Surrogate Parent	____________________
Classroom Teacher(s)	____________________
	____________________
Other Special Education Personnel	____________________
Student (where appropriate)	____________________
**Evaluator	____________________
Other	____________________
	____________________

*If the parent, guardian, or surrogate parent does not attend, documentation of attempts must be recorded.
**Must attend if student is newly identified as exceptional.

III. *Student's Present Level of Functioning
(Summary of student's strengths and weaknesses—to include observation and diagnostic testing.)

*Considerations may include academic, emotional, self-help, social, medical, communication, psychomotor, vocational, etc.

(Form continued)

complete IEP plan form (cont'd)

IV. Related Services (therapies, counseling, transportation):

Type(s) of Therapies: ______ Time/Sessions/Wk: ______ Personnel: ______
(OT, PT, Coun., etc.) (aide, therapist, etc.)

Type(s) of Therapies: ______ Time/Sessions/Wk: ______ Personnel: ______

Type(s) of Therapies: ______ Time/Sessions/Wk: ______ Personnel: ______

Transportation (if plan requires special arrangement, vehicle adaptation, or personnel):

Foster Care (if applicable):

Foster Parent's Name and Address: ______

Has the foster home been approved? YES ______ NO ______

V. Adaptive Physical Education (only include when adaptations are necessary):

______

______

______

______

VI. Special Services Program(s) Recommended (Special Class, Speech Pathology, Learning Disabilities, etc.):

Program(s): ______ Starting Date: ______ Length of Time in Special Service(s): ______

Program(s): ______ Starting Date: ______ Length of Time in Special Service(s): ______

Program(s): ______ Starting Date: ______ Length of Time in Special Service(s): ______

Program(s): ______ Starting Date: ______ Length of Time in Special Service(s): ______

Program(s): ______ Starting Date: ______ Length of Time in Special Service(s): ______

VII. Additional Considerations (school or community extracurricular activities suggested or necessary to implement this plan):

Type(s) of Activity: ______________________ Advisor: ______________________

Type(s) of Activity: ______________________ Advisor: ______________________

Type(s) of Activity: ______________________ Advisor: ______________________

VIII. Parent Involvement (describe type and amount of parent involvement necessary to implement this plan):

IX. *Regular Education Program (describe any special adaptations or instructions necessary to implement this plan):

Extent to which child will participate in Regular Education Program:

*All teachers are to receive a copy of the student's IEP.

individual instruction attendance record...

Month ______________ 19 ______

Pupil ____ School ____________ Grade ______

Address ______________________________________ Parent's Name ________________

Signature of Instructor ______________________ Subject or Subjects ________________

Instructor's Address ____

TIME SCHEDULE

WEEK Beginning Sunday	Date	Monday Date	Monday Hrs.	Tuesday Date	Tuesday Hrs.	Wednesday Date	Wednesday Hrs.	Thursday Date	Thursday Hrs.	Friday Date	Friday Hrs.	Total Hrs.

TOTAL NUMBER OF HOURS FOR THE MONTH:

When listing the hours under "Daily" and "Total" Hours, please be sure that you show no fraction other than ½. If the fraction involved is ¼, please save it until you can show a fraction of ½ hour.

This report must be accurate. Please check your calendar for all dates to be listed under "Time Schedule."

IMPORTANT:

Attendance and Progress forms must be submitted, each in DUPLICATE, to Central Administration. DO NOT hold forms for several months. Return no later than five (5) school days after the end of the month during which instruction has been given. All attendance for any one month must be recorded on one sheet. PLEASE DO NOT MIX MONTHS.

individual instruction progress report...

Month ______________________ 19 ______

Pupil ______________________________________ School ______________ Grade ______

Address ____

Signature of
Instructor ______________________________________ Subject or
Subjects ______________________

EACH AREA BELOW SHOULD BE COMPLETED IN DETAIL:

SUBJECT: (reading, arithmetic, etc.–pg. numbers and skills being worked on, etc.)

TEACHER'S PROCEDURES: (teacher-made materials, methods and techniques used and which work best with student, tests given and items of interest)

STUDENT'S PROGRESS: (academic progress, attitude and physical condition)

FURTHER RECOMMENDATIONS:

GRADE FOR MONTH:

TERMINATION: (date of return to regular classes, or moved, or date when instruction terminated, reason for, etc.)

request for IEP meeting...

TO:
FROM:
RE:

Date: ____
Student: ____
Birthdate: ____
Teacher: ____
Please plan to meet in ______________________________ on
______________________ at ______________________ for
a conference relative to the above-mentioned student.

(See Also: BILINGUAL EDUCATION; CHILD STUDY TEAM; COURSES; ELECTIVES; RESOURCE TEAM)

INFORMATION

destruction of file information...

Dear Parent/Guardian:

Our Public Schools must maintain the following information on your child _____.

a. name
b. address
c. phone number
d. grades
e. attendance record
f. classes attended
g. grade level completed
h. any type of special services received and for how long (for example, Speech Therapy from November 1984 to October 1985)

Since all file information cannot be kept indefinitely, we are asking you to indicate whether you would want your student's complete file for your records or if you want us to destroy the record. You may need some of the file information for social security, taxes, or other purposes.

Attached is a list of what might be in your child's folder. Please check those items you want and return the form to me. If you have not returned the form one month after the date of this memo, the file will be destroyed.

Sincerely,

_______ Send complete file.

If in file, send the following:

_______ Annual Report(s)
_______ Individual Education Plan(s)
_______ Program Summaries
_______ Special Services Record
_______ Evaluation Write-ups
_______ Pre-post Test Sheets
_______ Vocational Evaluations
_______ Case Histories
_______ Child Study Team Forms
_______ Evaluation Consent Form(s)
_______ Communication Form
_______ Exchange and Release of Information Form
_______ Field Trip Form
_______ Media Release Form
_______ Resource Team Information
_______ Medical Release Form
_______ Medical Reports
_______ Physical Evaluation Form
_______ Audiology Report
_______ Correspondence
_______ Referral Form
_______ Record of Inspection
_______ ______________________________
_______ ______________________________
_______ ______________________________

_______ Please destroy the complete file.

______________________________ ______________

Signature of Parent/Guardian Date

employee information update form...

Mr.
Mrs.
Miss ______________________________ ______________________
Please print–last name, first name, initial Social Security Number

______________________________ Phone ______________
Address

____
City State, Zip

☐ Male ☐ Married
☐ Female ☐ Unmarried

Position: ______________________________

Location ______________________________

Supervisor ______________________________

Grades or Subjects taught ______________________________

I want to insure my dependents if proven eligible: ☐ yes ☐ no

Number of children under 18 years of age: ________

IN CASE OF EMERGENCY, NOTIFY (THIS MUST BE FILLED IN)

______________________________ ______________
Name Relationship to You

______________________________ ______________
Home Address Home Phone

____
City State Zip

______________________________ ______________
Business Address Business Phone

______________________________ ______________
Family Doctor Address Phone

______________________ ______________
Date Signature

inner-office personnel information form...

Certified ______ Non-Certified ______

Name ______
(Print as it appears on Soc. Sec. card)

Address ______

Building ______ Phone ______

Birth Date ______ Marital Status ______

No. Dependents ______ Soc. Sec. No. ______

W.H. Add-on ______ Education (Last Grade Completed) ______

Date Employed ______

Position ______ Acct. No. ______

Contract $______ Monthly Rate ______

Hourly Rate ______ Work Wk.(No. Hrs.) ______

Date of First Pay Check ______

Schedule of Payment
10 mos. ______
12 mos. ______
Bi-weekly ______

Travel Allowance ______

Health Insurance
Single ______
Family ______
T. End. ______

Term Life Ins. ______

Retirement
Teacher ______
N.D. Public Employee ______

State Income Tax ______

Credit Union ______

Wn. Nat'l. ______

Annuity ______

Other ______

______
Supervisor Date

______
Personnel Dept. Date

permission for release and/or exchange of information form...

NAME: ______________________________

BIRTHDATE: ______________________________

I hereby consent to the release and/or exchange of all pertinent medical, psychological, and educational information on the above-named person. I understand that the information thus obtained will be treated in a confidential manner.

Information released by: ______________________________
Name of Agency

____
Name and Title of Representative

____
Street Address

____
City and State

Information released to: ______________________________
Name of Agency

____
Name and Title of Representative

____
Street Address

____
City and State

______________________________ ______________
Signature of Parent or Legal Guardian Date

____
Street Address

____
City and State

student information sheet...

Student Grade: ________
Student Homeroom: ______

STUDENT INFORMATION SHEET

(Please print)

STUDENT NAME ______________________________ BIRTH DATE ________
Last First Middle Month-Year

STUDENT ADDRESS ______________________________
House Number and Street

____
City or Town State Zip Code

STUDENT PHONE NUMBER ___ Sex ______ Year Grad. from High School ______

FATHER'S NAME ______________________________ LIVING ______
Last First Middle Yes or No

ADDRESS IF DIFFERENT______________________________

MOTHER'S NAME ______________________________ LIVING ______
Last First Middle Yes or No

ADDRESS IF DIFFERENT______________________________

GUARDIAN'S NAME ______________________________
(if not living with parents) Last First Middle

MAILING ADDRESS–if different

____

____

Name and address of last school attended

____

____

PLEASE COMPLETE ALL INFORMATION. THANK YOU.

(**See Also:** ADDRESS; DISTRIBUTION OF MATERIALS; ELECTIVES; ENROLLMENT; HANDBOOK; IDENTIFICATION; MAP OF THE SCHOOL; OPENING PROCEDURES)

inquiry communications form...

Steps	Areas
1	Pre-referral a. investigating alternatives b. consultation c. classroom observation
2	Referral
3	Evaluation reports and communication
4	IEP process & communication
5	Placement
6	Continuing program review
7	Dismissal

EDUCATIONAL PROGRAM PLANNING
COMMITTEE PROCESS

Case Initiator: ____________________

Student: ____________________

Year: ____________________

School: ____________________

Step	Date	Persons Involved	Reasons for Contact	Comments

(See Also: ADDRESS; BIDS; BUSINESS; ENROLLMENT; HANDBOOK; QUESTIONS)

IN-SCHOOL SUSPENSION

(See: ASP (ALTERNATE SCHOOL PROGRAM); EXPULSION; SUSPENSION)

IN-SERVICE

in-service professional training form...

NAME ______________________________ BUILDING ______________________________

IN-SERVICE PROFESSIONAL TRAINING FORM

Date (Mo., Day, Yr.)	Hours earned In-service	Name of In-service Training Program	Other Descriptions or Consultant	Administration Approval Initial

policy on...

IN-SERVICE PROGRAMS FOR DISTRICT STAFF

It is the purpose of the Board to provide staff opportunities to develop those skills necessary to implement new instructional programs, to implement existing programs of study, and to participate at the school level in planning and executing local and district priorities.

The parties recognize that professional employees must continue to review curricular content, teaching methods and materials, educational philosophy and goals, social changes and topics related to education. The parties also support the principal of continuing training of professional employees and the improvement of instruction.

To work towards the ends stated above, the Board agrees to pay full cost of tuition and other reasonable expenses incurred in connection with any courses, workshops, seminars, conferences, in-service training sessions, or other sessions a professional employee is required to attend.

All in-service programs shall be conducted during the in-school workday if professional employee's attendance is mandatory. All such programs conducted after the professional employee's workday or during the summer shall be voluntary. Course credit shall be granted for in-service programs in the same manner as graduate credits.

(See Also: COURSES; DEPARTMENTAL MEETINGS; FACULTY MEETINGS; MEETINGS)

INSURANCE

insurance enrollment card...

PLEASE USE INK & PRINT

SCHOOL DISTRICT

Group Life, Accidental Death and Dismemberment and Dependent Life Insurance

Enrollment Card

Policy Number

Employee's Name____
Last First Middle Initial

Employee's Address____
Street City State Zip Code

Employee's Soc. Sec. No.____________________ Date of Birth____________________
Month Day Year

Employee's Date of Employment____________________
Month Day Year

Male ☐ Female ☐ Single ☐ Married ☐ Divorced/Sep. ☐ Widowed ☐

Beneficiary Designation____
Last First Middle Initial

Relationship to Employee____

Beneficiaries Address (if different from that of Employee)

____
Street City State Zip Code

If you wish to name a contingent beneficiary, see reverse side.

Dependent Life Coverage Desired ☐ Yes ☐ No Number of Eligible Children__________

I apply for enrollment in the coverages indicated on this form and authorize the required deductions, if any, from my pay.

____
Signature of Employee (Date Signed) Month Day Year

(front of card)

CONTINGENT BENEFICIARY DESIGNATION

____
Name Relationship

____
Name Relationship

CHANGE OF BENEFICIARY

Subject to the terms of the contract between the Life Insurance Company and the school district, I request that the following beneficiary(ies) be substituted under said contract as my designated beneficiary(ies), in lieu of any and all beneficiaries previously named by me:

____
Name of Beneficiary Relationship Address

____
Name of Beneficiary Relationship Address

Signature of Insured Person: ____

Date Signed: ____

(back of card)

insurance waiver form...

INSURANCE WAIVER FORM

Payroll

Name:__________________ __________________ _______ Hourly ☐
(Last) (First) (Initial)

Monthly ☐

Social Security Number: ___ ___ ___ – ___ ___ – ___ ___ ___ ___

Position: __________________ Building: __________________ Food Service ☐

SECTION 1–EMPLOYEE'S ELIGIBLE FOR FRINGE BENEFITS: Complete this section and sign below if you are eligible to participate in the following insurance plans but choose not to.

I certify that I have been given an opportunity to participate in the following District insurance plans for which I am eligible, however, I do not wish to participate in the plans checked below at this time:

PLEASE CHECK ONLY THE INSURANCE PLANS YOU DO NOT WANT

- ☐ Health Insurance–Blue Cross and Blue Shield
- ☐ Dental Insurance–Blue Cross and Blue Shield
- ☐ Other–Please specify____________________

I understand that I am giving up all District contributions for any plans declined to which I may otherwise be entitled. I understand that if I change my mind, it will be necessary for me to complete the proper forms by the proper date. I also understand that if I later decide to enroll in any of these plans, there may be restrictions and limitations in doing so as specified by the various plans, District policies and practices.

SECTION II–EMPLOYEE'S NOT ELIGIBLE FOR FRINGE BENEFITS: Read this section and sign below if you are not eligible to participate in the above District insurance plans.

I understand that under the terms of the District insurance policies I am not currently eligible to participate in the plans shown above because I am either a temporary employee or I am working less than half-time. I am aware that should I become eligible to participate in these plans, I must contact the Personnel or Payroll Office and complete the necessary forms by the proper date if I wish to participate. (Note: These forms normally must be completed within 30 days of the date you first become eligible.) I am aware that if the proper forms are not completed by the proper date there may be restrictions and limitations as specified by the various plans, District policies and practices if later I wish to participate.

Note: If you have any questions regarding any of these plans, check with your supervisor or the Personnel Office. Watch the District's weekly Information Bulletin for announcements of open enrollment periods and other information relating to these plans.

Employee's Signature ____________________ Date ____________

policy statement on...

Insurance

The insurance programs for the employee shall cease as of the last day of employment. Teachers who finish the contract year will be covered under health insurance through August 31.

The employee who is on a leave (except career exploration leave) is eligible to participate in insurance programs if permitted under the insurance policy provisions and the employee shall pay the entire premium for such program.

report form for insurance records...

REPORT OF PROPERTY LOSS OR DAMAGE

Name of Building	Location of Building	Report Date
Type of Incident ("X" appropriate type(s)) Vandalism ☐ Theft ☐ Burglary ☐ Illegal Entry ☐ Fire ☐ Other ☐		Estimate Amount $

ACTION	Yes	No	DATE	TIME AM	TIME PM
1. Time or estimated time of incident					
2. First noted by (name and position):					
3. Reported to:	Yes	No			
a. Police—State ☐ local☐					
b. Fire Department					
c. Operations Department					
d. Facilities Department					
4. Was alarm system "ON" at time of incident?			xxxxxxxxxxxxxxxxxxxx	xxxxxxxxxx	xxxxxxxxx
5. Other action taken:					

6 . List Damages/Loss

7. Describe Incident

8. Activity(ies) in Progress During Incident

9. APPREHENSION RESULTS—Complete this portion at the time of incident, if possible; or when the information becomes available, prepare a report of apprehension and reference the report date above.
   a. Was suspect(s) apprehended? Yes ☐ No ☐
   b. Disposition of case:

10. RESPONSIBILITY FOR COST–(Check one)
    a. Charge School Budget
    b. Charge responsible party

    Name ____________________

    Address ____________________

    ____

11. Enter Requisition No. ____________________ or

    Work Request No. ____________________ for repair/replacement.

    ____
    Principal's Signature

INSTRUCTIONS

1. Call Police/Fire Department, as required.
2. Call Operations or Facilities, if immediate attention is required.
3. Send Original and two copies of report to Deputy Executive for Business Management.

ADMINISTRATIVE USE

Received by Deputy Executive for Business Management	By (Initials)	Date

(See Also: ACCIDENT; AUTOMOBILES; BUS; DANCES; DRIVING; FIELD TRIPS; SICK LEAVE; TRAVEL)

INTERNSHIP

policy on...

A program of Internships shall be established at the Board's discretion under which members of the professional staff shall be eligible to act as temporary assistants to members of the administrative staff. Internships shall not exceed one year.

The purposes of the program shall be:

1. To provide specific services which have been clearly recognized as desirable for the improvement of the school system.
2. To promote among the staff a better understanding of the functions performed by the various departments of the school system.
3. To develop administrative ability among staff members who have administrative certification.

There will be no change in salary classification.

(See Also: COLLEGE; CONTRACT; DUTIES; STUDENT TEACHER)

INTERVIEW

interview recommendation form...

INTERVIEW RECOMMENDATION

ADVERTISEMENT NO.: ________ DATE: ________________
POSITION NO. ______

TO: ____________________ RE: ________________

FROM: __________________ ________________

____

CERTIFICATION: ________

This applicant is being referred to you for an interview and for your consideration as a possible candidate for the vacancy in your school advertisement number ______. This applicant has the following scores on the screening items:

Wesman ________

Omaha ________

Written Work ______ Errors

Once you have completed your interview, please complete the information below and return to me.

Sincerely,

____

Interview Notes ______________________________________

____

Summary and Recommendation:

Of the candidates you have interviewed for this position, what ranking (1, 2, 3, 4, 5, 6, 7, 8, 9, 10) do you give to this candidate? Please circle.

I recommend this person for employment at this time. ____________________
Principal's Signature

I recommend this person as a possible candidate but not for this position.

____
Principal's Signature

I do not recommend this person for employment. ____________________
Principal's Signature

(See Also: APPLICATION; CONTRACT; NEGOTIATIONS; QUESTIONS; RESOURCE TEAM)

INTRODUCTION

to handbook for parents...

Through the **Handbook for Parents**, we hope to directly communicate to you a better understanding of some of the policies, regulations, and services of our elementary schools in the School Disrtrict. Please read and keep this copy in your home throughout the year so that it is readily available. Should you have questions which are not covered in the **Handbook**, please call or see your principal for assistance.

Close cooperation between the home and the school is essential to promote the best interests of the child. Parents are encouraged to visit school and to attend scheduled meetings of parents and teachers. Mutual benefits accrue when there is a meaningful exchange of information between home and school.

It is our hope that this **Handbook** will be helpful to you and that it will promote that understanding.

A parent or guardian is asked to detach and sign the receipt at the bottom of this sheet and return it to the child's teacher.

to handbook for parents and students...

It is a profound pleasure for us to welcome you and your parents to Jones Middle School. I voice the sentiment of the faculty and staff in saying we are happy to have you as a part of the Jones Middle School family and we hope that this year will be a successful one for you.

This handbook will acquaint you with information about the general organization, operation and policies of your school.

We hope that you and your parents will read it together. Please feel free to ask your advisor, another student or any staff member for additional information or explanation of the material in this handbook.

The faculty and staff have worked hard to establish a spirit of cooperation and an atmosphere of friendliness here that makes it easy to become a member of the Jones family.

We hope that this spirit of cooperation, respect and concern for others at Jones can be a part of your character and make going to school here a happy and positive experience.

We are glad that you are here and we are depending on you to help keep our standards high.

Sincerely,

to public relations flyer...

I am pleased to present you with this view of the Rock Township Public Schools, which will acquaint you with general information about your schools.

The staff, administration and school board are dedicated to quality education for all children. Many types of special services coordinate with the teaching of knowledge and skills to provide all students with an opportunity to become informed, responsible and contributing members of society. A wide range of programs are offered to enhance physical, cultural and intellectual development along with leisure time skills and interests. We realize the importance of developing in each student an attitude of self-respect and self-worth and of providing opportunities for students to form meaningful and responsible relationships.

You and the school personnel are partners in the important endeavor of educating children. We welcome your suggestions and we encourage your active interest and participation.

(See Also: HANDBOOK; NEW POLICY OR PROGRAM; NEWSLETTER; NEWS RELEASES; PHILOSOPHY; WRITING)

INVENTORY

multi-purpose form for inventory...

PUBLIC SCHOOLS INVENTORY FORM

Sheet No.__________

Room No.__________

Dept.__________

Bldg.__________

DISTRIBUTION CODE

1. Agriculture
2. Dist. Ed.
3. Office Ed.
4. Trade, Industry, Health
5. Home Economics
6. Special Needs
7. Exemplary
8. Research
9. Guidance
10. ABE
11. Title I ESEA
12. Title II ESEA
13. Title III ESEA
14. Title VI-B
15. State Spec. Ed.
16. Hwy. Traffic Safety Act
17. NDEA
18. Surplus
19. Title IV B
20. Title IV C
21. Industrial Arts
22. Rental IMC
23. Badlands Multi-County
24. __________
25. __________

Dstrb. Code	Inventory Count	Item Description	Disposition	Serial Number	Cost 19	Cost 19	Cost 19	Cost 19	Cost 19
				SHEET TOTALS					
				Inventory by					
				Grand Total by (Room or Dept.)					

ORDER OF LISTING

1. Teacher & Office desks
2. Teacher & Office chairs
3. Student Desks
4. Tables
5. Typewriters (Electrical & Manual)
6. Adders & Calculators (Desk & Portable)
7. Copy & Thermo fax machines
8. Other office or education machines
9. Files or file cabinets
10. Folding chairs
11. Testbooks & Library books
12. Musical Equipment
13. Automotive Equipment
14. Home Ec. Equipment
15. Audio-Visual Equipment
16. Phy. Ed. Equipment
17. All other items

(See Also: BOOKS; BUDGET; EQUIPMENT; REQUISITIONS, REPAIRS, AND REPLACEMENTS; TEXTBOOKS; WORK)

JOB DESCRIPTION

two sample job descriptions...

A. SCHOOL-RELATED

ATHLETIC DIRECTOR'S DUTIES

1. Develop, maintain and foster an athletic program that is attractive to participants and spectators
   a. Work closely with all of the coaches in matters pertaining to budgeting, scheduling, transportation, arrangements, etc.
   b. Provide participating opportunities to as many boys and girls as possible.
   c. Provide the best equipment for the players to insure their safety and health.
      1.) Arrange coverage of all athletes in athletic insurance.
      2.) Arrange physical examinations for all athletes prior to participation in their respective program.
2. Assign and supervise coaching personnel
   a. Submit recommendations to principal for final selections.
   b. Promote good working relationships among coaches.
3. Supplies and equipment inventory
   a. Keep close track of supplies (medical and athletic).
   b. Keep accurate records of equipment, to be kept up to date by the coaches.
4. Transportation
   a. Arrange transportation (land and air) for all athletic contests
5. Publicity
   a. "Minor" releases to be made periodically.
   b. "Major" releases to be cleared with; and all made by principal.
6. Maintain good public relations
   a. Intra and inter-school
   b. With press & radio
   c. With community

7. Finances
   a. To be taken care of by Vice Principal in charge of finance.
   b. Budget
      1. To be submitted by each coach, approved or corrected, and then submitted to V.P.
      2. A close watch should be kept on the financial balances and overall picture at all times.

8. Purchasing
   a. The athletic director will have the final say in all matters pertaining to equipment and supplies purchases. Purchase Orders to be made by him or her.
   b. Suggestions and requests for equipment and supplies purchases to come from coaches. These will be submitted to the Athletic Director, who in turn will make the purchases after clearance for funds from V.P. in charge of Finances.

B. PUBLIC AND COMMUNITY-ORIENTED

HIGH SCHOOL PFA (PARENT FACULTY ASSOCIATION) JOB DESCRIPTIONS

President

- Preside over meetings of the Executive Board
- Represent the PFA at public functions and Presidents' Council meetings
- Coordinate PFA efforts with school administrators and faculty
- Direct the effort of the Budget Committee
- Coordinate the work of the officers and committees

Vice President

- Substitute for, and otherwise assist, the President when necessary

Recording Secretary

- Record and distribute minutes of all meetings
- Provide access to bylaws during meetings

Corresponding Secretary

- Conduct correspondence as necessary

Treasurer

- Keep custody of funds
- Keep records of receipts and expenditures
- Pay out funds in accordance with the budget
- Provide financial reports at Board Meetings

High School Representatives

- Represent the PFA and PAC meetings

Ways and Means

- Establish plans and budgets for fund-raisers
- Participate in the budgeting process
- Keep records of fund-raiser expenses and income

Volunteer Coordinator

- Provide and distribute (through homeroom teachers) interest sheets
- Collect and distribute interest sheet responses to committee heads
- Secure volunteer workers for fund-raisers and other special events

Newsletter (PFA Gazette)

- Publish a newsletter at least three times annually
- Solicit faculty, administration and PFA inputs for the letter

Art Alive

- Provide exhibits in the library and/or display cases
- Conduct after-school workshops
- Make posters for PFA and teachers for special occasions

Publicity

- Promote school and PFA functions through advertising
- Provide notices, posters, and newspaper coverage as appropriate

Safety

- Promote safety through student/parent awareness
- Coordinate with Site Safety Representative to identify and correct hazardous situations

(See Also: ASSIGNMENTS; DUTIES; PRINCIPAL; SECRETARY; TYPISTS; WORK)

job availability form...

PLEASE POST

ANNOUNCEMENT OF POSITION AVAILABLE

Date of This Announcement: ____________________

Date Position Available: ____________________

Applications Accepted Starting: ____________________

POSITION AVAILABLE:

JOB TITLE: ____

DESCRIPTION (DUTIES): ______________________________

____

____

QUALIFICATIONS: __________________________________

____

____

HOW, WHERE AND WHEN TO APPLY: ________________________

____

____

SALARY RANGE: ___________________________________

PLEASE POST

sample newspaper ad for available position...

TEACHER—Mathematics, Grades 10–12. Must have State Certification. M.A. preferred but not necessary. Experience useful. Salary per negotiated guide. Apply in person 9–5, Rock Township Bd. of Ed., 123 Crescent Dr., Rock Township.

(See Also: BABY-SITTING; CAREERS; COUNSELING; JOB DESCRIPTION; PRINCIPAL; SECRETARY; TYPISTS; WORK; WORKING PAPERS)

KEYS

examples of policies and procedures on...

Keys will be issued by the assistant principal to each teacher for the areas where they have direct assignments or responsibilities. **At NO TIME** should keys be loaned to students or other teachers. In the event of a lost key, notify the assistant principal immediately. **At NO TIME will students be permitted to be in the school building for activities unless supervised by a teacher.** This includes all athletics, school clubs, debate, drama, etc.

Keys

a. Keys are issued to teachers in the secretary's office. Teachers are responsible for these keys and should not pass them on to students. A charge of $1.00 will be made for each key lost.

b. Any teacher desiring to borrow duplicate keys from the office should do so in person or send in a written request. This will prevent any misuse of school keys by unauthorized persons.

Every teacher will be issued keys to their room and room lockers. Experience has shown that the BEST PRACTICE is to leave your keys in your mailbox in the Office each afternoon. This assures you of having your keys every day, as well as assuring keys for the substitute if you are absent. It prevents such common errors as forgetting them, leaving them in another purse, losing them, etc. The only requirement is that keys issued must be turned into the Office at the end of the school year.

key distribution form...

SCHOOL: ______________________________

ADMINISTRATOR IN CHARGE: ______________ SCHOOL YEAR: __________

Serial Number	KEY to: (What does it open?)	Issued to:	Date Issued	Date Returned

PAGE ________ OF ________

Person who compiled this list (please sign): ______________________

(**See Also:** BUILDING; CUSTODIAL SERVICES; HALLS AND HALL DUTY; LOCKERS)

KINDERGARTEN

definition of...

A good kindergarten is much more than a play class. Your child will learn to get along with other children, to share experiences, to work and play in group situations, to listen to and follow directions, and to enjoy activities involving art and music. The first steps in reading readiness will begin during this school year.

We shall attempt to make kindergarten experiences enjoyable as well as helpful in building attitudes which will be most important to a child's future growth.

kindergarten list form...

NAME OF KINDERGARTEN ______________________________

LIST PREPARED BY______________________________

Name of Child	Parent/Address	Phone #	Intended School of Attendance, Sept.

kindergarten "schedule" for child and parent...

MY KINDERGARTEN SCHEDULE

I will be in the ______________________________ class.

My first day will be ______________________________

Time: ______________________________

I will spend my first day getting acquainted with my teacher and school.

I should come to school *just before* the bell rings.

I will learn to be on time.

I will go directly home when I am dismissed.

My teacher's name is ______________________________.

message to parents on clothing for kindergarten...

Parents often ask about the kind of school clothes a child should wear. They realize that the kindergarten child particularly needs to feel comfortable and free in work and play activities. Here are some helpful hints:

- Choose simple washable play clothes for inside school, warm and serviceable clothes for outside.
- Buy clothes that your child can manage—big enough to get on easily, big buttons and buttonholes, big loops for hanging coats and sweaters, large rubbers, boots and overshoes, mittens fastened to coat or jacket, and simple, easy to manage underwear.

Label everything removable (snowsuit, rubbers, mittens, boots, coats, caps, sweaters). You may use name tapes or adhesive tape lettered with indelible ink. A special color, mark or sticker inside boots or rubbers will tell your child which one goes on which foot. Find a way to attach mittens firmly to the jacket or coat. Mitten clips are fine.

Kindergarteners are taught to take care of clothes and materials, but paint does spill and clay and paste do smear. When dressed for work, children don't worry. Your child's teacher may suggest that you send certain materials for use in class.

public information flyer for parents and community...

KINDERGARTEN ROUND-UP

WHAT: a registration for all children who will enter kindergarten in September, 19____.

WHEN: April ____, 19____(8:00 A.M.–10:30 A.M.)

WHERE: At the elementary building in which the child will attend.

WHO: Parents or any adult may register for the child.

It is recommended that the child not be present.

ENTRANCE REQUIREMENTS

Age

Children who will be five (5) years of age on or before September 30, 19____may register for kindergarten.

Early Entrance

Children eligible for consideration for early admission are those whose fifth birth dates are in October, 19____. An exception includes students who may be accepted into kindergarten by having had preschool experience (other than public kindergarten) with a properly licensed teacher. For additional information contact the principal of the elementary school or the Director of Elementary Education.

Birth Certificates

Birth Certificates issued from the *Bureau of Vital Statistics* are required and must be presented before registration is official. Hospital certificates will not be accepted.

Health Records

The State law requires that all children shall have the complete DPT and polio series, measles and rubella vaccine and the tuberculin test. A written record which states the month and year of a child's immunization must be presented before registration is official.

Registering Out of District

A child must register in the district in which he/she lives unless the parent is applying for a permit. Then the child registers at the school in which he/she wants to attend and makes application at the school for the permit. Consideration to the granting of permits is based upon the following:

1. Nursery school or Day Care Center enrollment in the district.
2. Location of the residence of the baby sitter in the district.
3. Recommendations of a medical doctor, school psychologist or other qualified school or medical personnel.
4. Evidence that parents or guardians are purchasing or building a home in the district.

IN KINDERGARTEN YOUR CHILD WILL LEARN

- to recognize full name, telephone number, address, birthday, and age
- to recognize colors
- to do handwork (cutting, pasting, coloring, painting)
- to express ideas through dramatic play and other creative activities
- to understand calendar concepts, i.e., days of the week
- to recognize numerals and small groups of objects by counting, and to count by rote
- to understand the meaning of one, two, three, four, five and of first, second, etc.
- to match circles, squares, triangles and other shapes
- to draw a given number of objects
- to tell a story suggested by a picture
- to retell a story, following a sequence of events
- to repeat fingerplays, nursery rhymes, and poems
- to enjoy books through looking at books and listening to stories
- to follow left-to-right progression required for reading
- to differentiate between likenesses and differences in pictures, letters, and words
- to recognize alphabet letters and words that begin with the same sound
- to recognize and print name and show interest in labels and signs
- to develop awareness of plants, animals, seasons, and the world around him/her

(See Also: CHILD STUDY TEAM; CONFERENCES; ELEMENTARY EDUCATION; PROGRESS REPORT; REGISTRATION; REPORTS; SUPERVISION; WRITING)

LAVATORIES

directive to teachers...

Lavatory check is the responsibility of all staff members. Many of you could help keep vandalism and obscene drawing at a minimum if you would walk in and check lavatories when you see people enter whose motives may not be the normal use of the lavatories. If you will check occasionally, you will help prevent some of these undesirable practices. If we don't get the supervision which is needed, we will have to initiate a mandatory supervision schedule.

memo to staff concerning...

TO: Faculty and Staff
FROM: J. Benson, Principal
RE: Use of Lavatories

Due to several instances of vandalism and graffiti in the student lavatories, we are asking that you institute a new procedure regarding student use of the lavatories. While no student may ever be denied the use of lavatory facilities, it would seem necessary to institute some control over the procedure.

We are asking, therefore, that every teacher keep a list of those students who are issued lavatory passes including the times out and back to the classroom. Please indicate your name and the room number for each period of the day. The list is to be turned into the office at the end of the teacher's day. People on hall duty will henceforth be required to check the lavatories at present times for damage. If such damage is discovered, we will then be able to determine the time it happened and, thanks to your recordkeeping, narrow down the field of possible perpetrators.

I will be letting the students know of this new procedure in the hope that it may act as a deterrent to a potential vandal.

I thank you in advance for your cooperation in this matter.

(See Also: BUILDING; CUSTODIAL SERVICES; HALLS AND HALL DUTY; HEALTH; MAP OF THE SCHOOL; SAFETY; VANDALISM)

LEAVE OF ABSENCE

application for sabbatical leave...

Applicant's Name ______________________________ Age ________

Educational Qualifications ______________________________

____

____

____

____

Employment Record and Principal Fields of Work ______________________________

____

____

____

Purpose of Sabbatical Leave ______________________________

____

____

Will work remuneration be performed while on leave?______________________________

And if any, amount of such remuneration ______________________________

SIGNATURE FOR APPROVAL: ______________________________

Chairperson, Board of Trustees
School District

ATTEST:

____

Clerk of School District

____

I, the undersigned applicant for sabbatical leave, agree to return to the employment of School District ________, ________________ County, State of ________________, at the expiration of the sabbatical leave, and to serve in my present teaching capacity at the salary scale provided by agreement between the School District ________ and the ________ Teachers' Union, for at least one year thereafter. In the event of any subsequent refusal to perform such service, I agree to refund to School District ________, not later than one year after the expiration of the sabbatical leave, the compensation so received for the sabbatical leave.

____

Signature of Applicant

Dated this ______________ day of ________________ 19________.

leave confirmation form...

LEAVE CONFIRMATION FOR DISTRICT EMPLOYEES

Check Position:
☐ *Certified*
☐ *Classified*

School Employed: ____________________ **Name:** ____________________

Reason for Leave:

Check Reason

☐ **53 54 PERSONAL ILLNESS**
☐ **53 54 PERSONAL DOCTOR OR DENTIST APPT.**
☐ **55 56 FAMILY ILLNESS**
☐ **55 56 FAMILY DOCTOR OR DENTIST APPT.**
☐ **55 56 DEATH WITHIN FAMILY**

☐ **51 52 ANNUAL LEAVE**
☐ **OTHER SCHOOL BUSINESS (specify)** ____________________

☐ **PERSONAL LEAVE DAY – First**
☐ **PERSONAL LEAVE DAY – Second**
☐ **PERSONAL LEAVE DAY – Third**
☐ **PERSONAL BUSINESS (DOCK)**

List Dates of Leave — *Time Missed* — *List each class period when more than one substitute is used.*

Month	Day	Year		Hours	Minutes		Substitute's Name
			Total Time Missed				

This form must be returned to the main office of your school immediately as it is needed for the processing of payroll.

____________________ Supervisor's Approval

____________________ Employee's Signature

personal leave record form...

DATE: ______________________

NAME: _____________________

SCHOOL PRINCIPAL: ___________________________

Our records show that you have used ________ days of personal leave this year. Please sign below and return this slip to me unless you disagree with our record, in which case you should discuss the discrepancy with me at the earliest possible time.

In the case of people who have not used all of their personal leave, please check one of the boxes below.

☐ Will use remaining day(s).

☐ Apply remaining days to my sick leave accumulation.

☐ Reimburse me for remaining days at the substitute teacher rate ($50.00 per day).

☐ Accumulate personal leave (19 –19)

SIGNED: _________________________________

request for annual leave/vacation time form...

REQUEST FOR ANNUAL LEAVE/VACATION TIME

I request ________ days vacation time beginning ________________________ and ending ______________________. I have ________ days leave time accumulated.

____
Employee Signature

I have examined ______________________________ leave credit and he/she has ________ days credit.

____
Payroll Department

APPROVED: ____________________

NOT APPROVED: ____________________

____
Immediate Supervisor Signature

RETURN THIS FORM TO CLERK'S OFFICE TEN (10) WORKING DAYS BEFORE LEAVE IS TO BEGIN

APPROVED: ____________________

NOT APPROVED: ____________________

____
District Clerk Signature

staff request for leave form...

STAFF REQUEST FOR LEAVE

(Make in Duplicate)

If a teacher desires or must be absent from scheduled school duties for any reason, personal, emergency, appointment, professional activity, or for other valid reasons, fill in the following. (When absence is covered by sick leave, proper deductions are to be calculated, or if personal deduction, so indicate.)

Check Reason for Absence

_______ Professional _______ Appointment _______ Personal

_______ Activity _______ Emergency _______ Other

PROFESSIONAL MEETING OR ACTIVITY:

____

____

Purpose or Reason for Attending _______________________________

____

____

Date(s) of Meeting ____________________19________. Place ________________

Total Time Absent from School Duties ________________ Days.

OTHER REASONS FOR ABSENCE:

____

____

____

____

Date(s) of Such Absence ____________________19________. Place ________________

Total Days of Planned Absence ____________________ Days.

PERSONNEL COSTS

	Paid by School District	Paid by Applicant	Other
Substitute	_______ Days	_______ Days	_______ Days
Sick Leave Allowance	_______ Days	_______ Days	_______ Days
Personal Deduction	_______ Days	_______ Days	_______ Days

Signed ____________________ Building ____________________ Date__________

Approved ____________________ Prin. Dated ____________________19________

Approved ____________________ Supt. Dated ____________________19________

weekly report of staff leave form...

School or Building ______________________ Week of ______________ through ______________
(Monday Date) (Friday Date)

CODE: DA – Doctor Appt.
DD – Days Deduct
DF – Death Family
J – Jury
SF – Sickness Family
SS – Sickness Self
V – Vacation (Personal Leave)
PL – Professional Leave
A – Activity Leave

FRACTION: Denotes portion of day missed. Personal, sick, doctor appointment, and emergency must be 1 or ½. Others may be entered by period or hour, such as 1/7, 1/6, etc.

	Monday		Tuesday		Wednesday		Thursday		Friday	
Staff Member	Code	Fraction	Code	Fraction	Code	Fraction	Code	Fraction	Code	Fraction

(See Also: BOARD OF EDUCATION; CONTRACT; DOCTORS; EMERGENCY; MEDIATION; NEGOTIATIONS; SICK LEAVE**)**

LESSON PLANS

policy on...

A. Every teacher shall plan lessons in reasonable written form within the curriculum guidelines. These should be sufficiently clear so that in a crisis another teacher could follow them. Each department has a lesson plan format which is to be followed in the preparation of plans.

All teachers are to hand in their lesson planbooks as indicated below on Monday before school starts:

Foreign Language Mathematics Physical Education	Mr. Henderson

Social Studies
Science — Mr. Connors
Industrial Arts

English
Activity Arts — Mrs. Kiley
All "Specials"

B. Emergency Lesson Plans for Department Coordinators: By the end of our first week, teachers will be expected to provide the Department coordinator and to keep in current supply at least one Emergency Lesson Plan to be used by substitute teachers in the event of unexpected absences. These plans should include the work to be done in each class, as well as seating charts, duty assignments (hall duty, bus duty, etc.), the entire daily schedule, location of supplies (extra textbooks, paper, etc.), any other information needed by a substitute to carry on in your absence, and the names of responsible students in each class.

Please place these plans in a manila folder, identify on the tab with your last name, and submit them to the Coordinator of your department.

C. If the Emergency Lesson Plan is used, a new plan should be prepared and given to the Department coordinator within two days of the teacher's return.

teacher handbook notices...

All teachers are required to prepare lesson plans one week in advance. Lesson plans for the following week should be prepared by Friday of the previous week. Leave your lesson plan book in the office by 3:50 p.m. on Friday. This is essential to facilitate a good program of teaching and to supply necessary information for substitute teachers. Lesson plans will be checked periodically by the Principal.

Class Record Books should be kept neatly and accurately. They will be turned in at the end of the year and filed in the office.

LESSON PLANS

In order to teach effectively, it is obvious that one should have plans that are adequate and flexible to meet varying needs of students. While we will not be asking for plans on a regular basis, there may be times when we would like to review your plans.

Plans may be requested for review by department head/administration with at least 48 hours advance notification.

(See Also: ACADEMIC FREEDOM; CLASS; CONTROVERSIAL TOPICS; CURRICULUM; GOALS; MINI-COURSES; OBJECTIVES; SUPERVISION; WARNING NOTICES)

LIBRARY

duties of librarian...

1. Select and prepare purchase orders for books for the central library circulating collection.
2. Check on the receipts of orders, bills, and books.
3. Keep a running balance of state library funds.
4. Process books
   a. classify
   b. catalog
   c. number
   d. varnish
5. Process and control other library materials
   a. magazines
   b. filmstrips
   c. phonograph records
   d. tapes
   e. slides
6. Instruct students in the use of the library.
7. Circulate all materials to students and teachers.
8. Train student helpers in library procedures.
9. Submit inventories of book stock and audio-visual aids to the principal.
10. Consult with the principal, finance committee, and department heads on the expenditure of funds.
11. Keep up the book collection by repairing and discarding.
12. Admit only students with a special form.

library policies...

1. The Library opens each morning at 7:45 and remains open throughout the day until 4:00 in the afternoon.
2. Students may use the Library before classes begin in the morning and after school in the afternoon.
3. Individuals or groups of students are permitted to use the Library throughout the school day with the written permission of teachers.
4. The Library can accommodate at least two full classes at the same time. If teachers wish to bring their classes to the Library, request must be made three days in advance of the Library visit. First requests will receive priority. Teachers are expected to accompany their classes to the Library.

5. Students are free to check out books from the Library for a period of two weeks. If the book is not returned on the date it is due, a fine will be imposed. The fine is two cents for the first day and five cents each day thereafter. Books may be renewed at the end of the two-week loan period.
6. Some teachers request the librarians to place books on reserve. These books are normally checked out only overnight. If they are not returned the next day, a fine of five cents per day is imposed.
7. Magazines and pamphlets are checked out for only overnight. They are to be returned the next day. Late magazines and pamphlets carry a fine of five cents a day.
8. If a student loses a book, he or she is expected to pay the cost of the book. If the book is later found and returned to the Library, all money paid in excess of the accumulated overdues will be returned to the student.
9. It is a privilege to use the Library. Each student is expected to exemplify good conduct and show evidence of study and learning.
10. The librarians' role is three-fold: they are available to teach library usage; assist in research; and to assemble a collection of a wide range of desirable reading and other materials.

LIBRARY POLICIES

1. All library materials are to be checked out from the circulation desk.
   a. Fiction and non-fiction for two weeks; special material for one week.
   b. Periodicals—past issues for one week.
   c. Filmstrips, records, tapes may be borrowed out by students and/or teachers.
   d. Reference and resource materials may be checked out only to the teachers on special request.
   e. Library materials placed on RESERVE are to be used in the library during the school day and may be checked out for overnight use from 1:55 p.m. to 8:00 a.m. the next morning.
2. Requests for the purchase of library books may be made to the librarian in writing. Orders must include author, title, publisher, copyright date, price, and number of copies. Get request cards for this purpose from the librarian. Teachers are also encouraged to assist in making book selections by reviewing centralized processing order lists available each month in the library. Textbooks are to be ordered through department heads.
3. Textbooks in sets stored in the library may be requested by teachers for classroom use on "Request for Textbooks" forms. The order will be prepared by the librarian; the teacher will be notified and sent blue and yellow cards to sign. The blue card remains with the teacher as his or her record, the yellow card is returned to the textbook charge file.
4. Teachers are responsible for having students sign for texts and collecting texts at the end of the school year. Special forms are available in the library. When collecting texts at the end of the school year, the teacher should check for books in need of repair and report to the librarian. Charges for lost books will be based on a depreciated value.
5. Inventory of all books must be turned in by the teachers to the librarian before the end of school. Texts may be kept in the classroom but an accurate accounting should be made by the teacher.

a. Teachers must have the librarian's signature on the final check out sheet. Early clearance avoids last-minute confusion.

6. Students may come to the library from classes. During regular class time all must have library passes. If a class of ten or more students come in for research work, the teacher should accompany the class. Students should return the passes to the teacher at the end of the period for verification.
7. Make-up tests are allowed in the library by prior arrangement.
8. The Library should be used as a study center or for recreational reading or research. Students should not be sent to the library as a disciplinary action. Students not properly utilizing the library will be sent back to the classroom or referred for disciplinary action.
9. Photocopy reproduction is available for 10 cents per sheet upon request through the librarians.
10. Students and teachers are encouraged to use the glass window display for class or individual projects.

library tips for teachers...

FACTS	RECOMMENDATIONS
1. It is impractical for the library to have enough copies of a single title for every child in a class.	1. Give students a choice on reading lists or advise them to select another title of equal value.
2. Mass assignments on a specific subject result in the first few students borrowing all the material available.	2. Notify your librarian in advance of this assignment so that she may locate and hold the material for equal distribution. School librarians should act as liaison with the public library. Use the RESERVE MATERIAL system.
3. Many times, reading lists of assignments are given for which the library cannot supply the required material.	3. As a teacher, please visit the library whenever possible to find out what material is available before making assignments.
4. Request for many references on a single item often require such extensive research that it would have to be done by the librarian rather than the student.	4. Accept fewer references if necessary. Try to arrange class visits for library instruction so that students can develop independent research techniques. Instruction on the use of libraries should be given in the school.
5. Entire books on a limited phase of a subject often do not exist or may already be loaned out.	5. Accept page or chapter references from books, magazines, and pamphlets.
6. Some subjects have only been treated on an adult reading level.	6. Encourage students to investigate subjects that have been presented on their own reading levels unless they are capable of handling the more difficult material.

7. Current topics often have not been published in book form.
8. Oral assignments are sometimes remembered inaccurately by students or garbled in transmittal.
9. Only brief information can be given on the telephone. Student reference work should not be done by telephone or mail.
10. *The illustrated student notebook* at times has the effect of providing an incentive to mutilate library materials.
11. The library's central collection should have an excellent selection of titles in every subject field.

7. Alert students to use magazines, pamphlets, and newspapers. Train them at school, or through a class visit to the library, to use periodical indexes.
8. Where library use is involved, it is suggested that pupils present written assignments verified by the teacher.
9. Please impress upon your students that they must visit the library in person for detailed information.
10. Stress the value of original illustrations and the use of personal newspapers and magazines. Teachers should remind students often to protect materials being used. Assignments can cause mutilation of materials. Copies can be made for a charge of 10 cents a page.
11. Teachers are encouraged to suggest titles for the central collection and to assist in weeding out obsolete titles.

(See Also: ACADEMIC FREEDOM; BOOKS; BUDGET; CONTROVERSIAL TOPICS; PASSES; PURCHASING; TEXTBOOKS)

LOCKERS

locker assignment list . . .

____________ HOMEROOM __________ ____________________
Locker # Series Teacher

LOCKER #	KEY SERIAL	ASSIGNED TO:
________	__________	____________________
________	__________	____________________
________	__________	____________________
________	__________	____________________
________	__________	____________________

PAGE ________ OF ________

locker search policy...

The Board acknowledges its respect for the privacy of the student attending the schools of this district, and provides each student with the use of a locker in which he may store clothing, school materials and other personal property. Although each student is responsible for locking the locker assigned to him against incursion by other students, all lockers are and shall remain the property of the Board.

The Board also recognizes that a locker may from time to time be improperly used as a depository for substances or objects which are illegal or which constitute a threat to the health, safety and welfare of the occupants of the school buildings. The Superintendent, therefore, shall develop regulations for the inspection of student lockers that protect the school community from harm, cooperate with municipal or state authorities and insure the rights of the student to whom the locker has been assigned.

Nothing in this policy or attendant regulations shall be construed to relieve school officials of their responsibility for the health, safety and educational welfare of the students in their care. Such officials shall retain the right to open and search school lockers with or without the knowledge or presence of the student or parent involved, but only when the circumstances are such that the protection of life and property demand such action.

Searches of a student's person, or his/her personal possessions, without a valid search warrant shall be prohibited unless the principal has a reasonable basis for believing that the student is concealing material the possession of which is prohibited by Federal, State, or Local law.

message in student handbook...

Student Lockers

All lockers made available for student use on the school premises, including lockers located in the hallways, physical education and athletic dressing rooms, industrial and agricultural education and the art classroom, are the property of the school corporation. These lockers are made available for student use in storing school supplies and personal items necessary for use at school but the lockers are not to be used to store items which cause, or can reasonably be foreseen to cause, an interference with school purposes or an educational function, or which are forbidden by state law or school rules.

The student's use of the locker does not diminish the school corporation's ownership or control of the locker. The school corporation retains the right to inspect the locker and its contents to insure that the locker is being used in accordance with its intended purpose, and to eliminate fire or other hazards, maintain sanitary conditions, attempt to locate lost or stolen material and to prevent use of the locker to store prohibited or dangerous materials such as weapons, illegal drugs or alcohol.

(See Also: ASSIGNMENTS; CLEANUP; HALLS AND HALL DUTY; KEYS; PASSES; RECORDS**)**

LUNCH AND LUNCH DUTY

directive in teacher handbook...

Classes should pass to the lunchroom at the time designated on the lunch schedule. It is very important to follow this schedule as closely as possible, as the lunchroom is set up to accommodate a specific number. Teachers will walk their classes to the lunchroom and then pick them up at the scheduled time.

lunchroom supervision form...

LUNCHROOM SUPERVISION

SCHOOL YEAR: ____________________ FOR LUNCH PERIOD: ____________________

DUTY	TEACHER ASSIGNED
LUNCH LINE SUPERVISION	______________________________
CASHIER SUPERVISION	______________________________
CLEAN-UP SUPERVISION	______________________________
TABLES 1–5	______________________________
TABLES 6–10	______________________________
TABLES 11–15	______________________________
TABLES 16–20	______________________________
SUPERVISION OF EXIT A	______________________________
SUPERVISION OF EXIT B	______________________________

TEACHER IN CHARGE: ______________________________

(See Also: CAFETERIA; DUTIES; FREE LUNCHES; TIME**)**

MAP OF THE SCHOOL

examples of school maps...

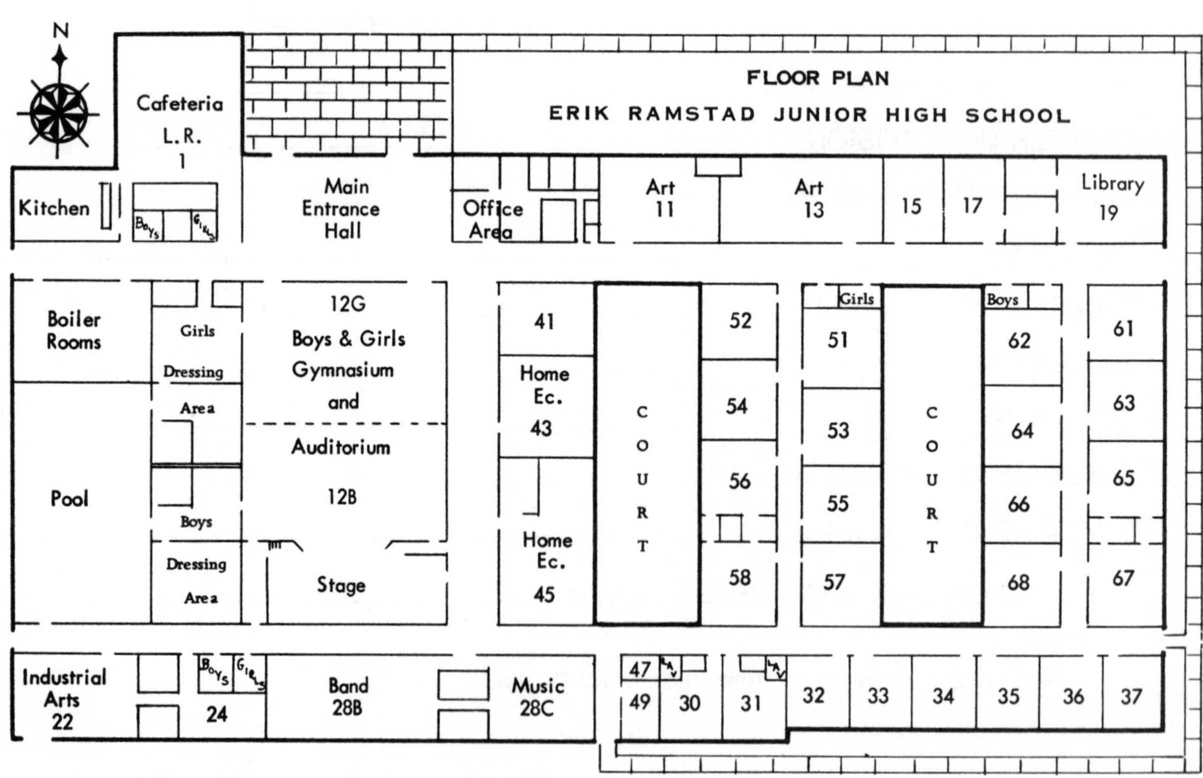

(See Also: BUILDING; HANDBOOK; NEWSLETTER; OPEN HOUSE; ZONES AND ZONING)

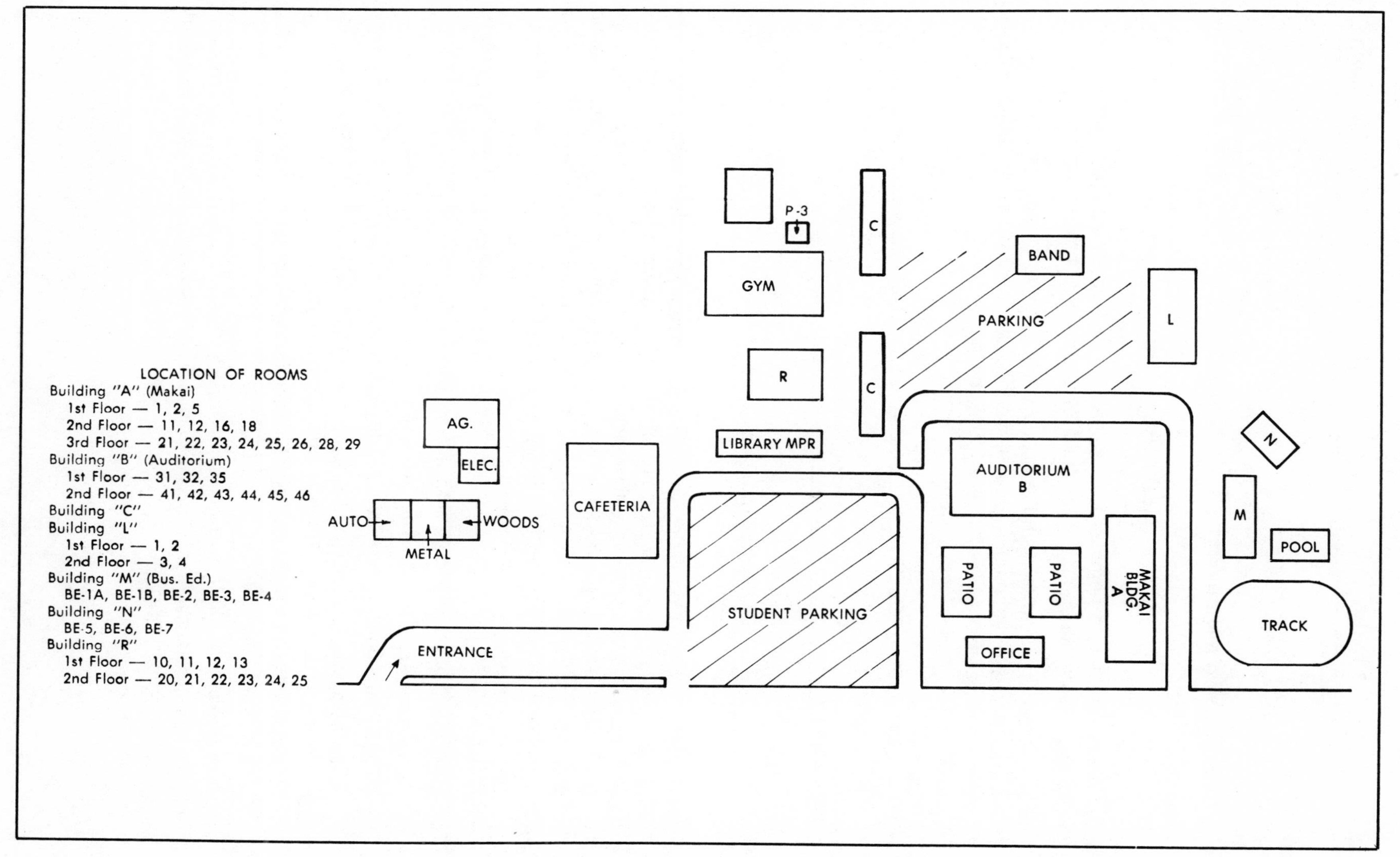

LOCATION OF ROOMS
Building "A" (Makai)
1st Floor — 1, 2, 5
2nd Floor — 11, 12, 16, 18
3rd Floor — 21, 22, 23, 24, 25, 26, 28, 29
Building "B" (Auditorium)
1st Floor — 31, 32, 35
2nd Floor — 41, 42, 43, 44, 45, 46
Building "C"
Building "L"
1st Floor — 1, 2
2nd Floor — 3, 4
Building "M" (Bus. Ed.)
BE-1A, BE-1B, BE-2, BE-3, BE-4
Building "N"
BE-5, BE-6, BE-7
Building "R"
1st Floor — 10, 11, 12, 13
2nd Floor — 20, 21, 22, 23, 24, 25
AG.
ELEC.
AUTO
WOODS
METAL
ENTRANCE
CAFETERIA
LIBRARY MPR
GYM
P-3
R
C
C
BAND
PARKING
L
STUDENT PARKING
AUDITORIUM
B
PATIO
PATIO
MAKAI
BLDG.
A
OFFICE
N
M
POOL
TRACK

MEDIA

media release form...

MEDIA RELEASE

I, the undersigned, give permission for release of various media (video tape, tape recordings, photographs, etc.) of my child for purposes of project support.

I will be notified in advance (with the exception of local newspaper releases) of any public release of the media and reserve the right to refuse such public release if I believe it is not in the best interests of my child.

Parent's Signature ______________________________ Date ____________________

Child's Name ______________________________

public information request form...

The Public Information Office is seeking information about students in our school district who have made an important contribution or achieved a noteworthy distinction, especially in the area of academic achievement.

If you have a student who fits this description, please complete this page and return to the Public Information Office. (Teachers or other school employees might also qualify if they have contributed "above and beyond" the call of duty in furthering academic achievement.)

We will use the information you provide to promote community recognition of our outstanding students. Examples of the type of student(s) we are looking for might include:

1. a student who has won an academic award
2. a student who has a straight "A" record for several successive years
3. a student who has overcome his or her handicaps to achieve a significant honor
4. a student who has completed a major achievement, such as winning a district-wide contest or completing an outstanding science project
5. a student or group of students who have made an important contribution to the school (or community)
6. a student with unusual artistic abilities, such as art or music
7. a student who has won a special citation from a federal, state or local agency or organization

Public Information Office

SCHOOL: ______________________________

NAME OF STUDENT (or employee): ______________________________

DESCRIPTION OF ACHIEVEMENT (please include date(s) if applicable and be as specific as possible):

____

____

____

____

NAME AND TELEPHONE NUMBER OF CONTACT (person who can provide additional information): ______________________________

PRINCIPAL: ______________________________

(See Also: BULLETIN, DEMONSTRATIONS; HANDBOOK; NEWSLETTER; NEWS RELEASES; VISITORS)

MEDIATION

section on mediation from master contract...

MEDIATION AND APPEAL

A. School Board

In the event that agreement is not reached, and members of the Board have not participated directly in the deliberations, the Association representatives and the Superintendent or representative may present separate reports stating their points of agreement and disagreement to the Board. The procedure outlined in III will then be followed in an effort to reach understanding and agreement, with the full Board or Board members selected by the Board participating in the deliberations.

B. Local Mediation

In the event that an agreement is not reached, a mutually agreed upon mediator, chosen from a previously established list of ten people, shall be appointed to review the subject of disagreement and shall make within ten days a written report to both parties. Any expense incurred shall be shared equally by the Board and the Association.

(See Also: BOARD OF EDUCATION; CONTRACT; DUE PROCESS; GRIEVANCES; JOB DESCRIPTION; NEGOTIATIONS; NONRENEWAL OF CONTRACT; TRANSFER)

MEDICAL FORMS

dental screening form...

DENTAL SCREENING REPORT

Grade ________ Room ________ School ____________ Date ____________________

Dear Parent of ____

During our dental health program, the following conditions were noted in your child's mouth:

________Cavities ________Stains (should be checked for decay) ________Gingivitis (bleeding or inflamed gums)

________Other abnormalities____

Oral hygiene appears: Good Fair Poor

(PLAQUE CAN BE 100% REMOVED
BY CORRECTLY BRUSHING AND FLOSSING DAILY)

Comments: ____

____

________An immediate examination by a dentist is urgently needed for your child.

________Not of an emergency nature but should be checked by a dentist very soon.

________Teeth need to be cleaned.

________No evidence of dental disease is apparent from a visual screening. However, if your child has not had a dental X-ray or examination within the last six months, you are advised to make an appointment with a dentist.

____
Screening Technician

____
School Health Nurse

(Form continued)

DENTIST'S REPORT TO THE SCHOOL

(To be filled out by the dentist and returned to the School Health Nurse)

Student's Name ____________________

Service rendered ____________________

____

Follow-up needed ____________________

Comments ____________________

____

Date ____________ ____________________

Dentist's Signature

(Form continued)

growth and development history...

GROWTH AND DEVELOPMENT HISTORY REGISTRATION ______________
Date

Child's Last Name First Middle D.O.B. School

Address (Number, Street, Town) Phone No.

Father's Name Mother's Name Last School Attended

Is your child subject to: (Please circle Yes or No)

Frequent Colds	Yes – No	Running Ears	Yes – No
Bronchitis	Yes – No	Chronic Cough	Yes – No
Frequent Sore Throats	Yes – No	Vision Loss	Yes – No
Speech Difficulties	Yes – No	Poor Posture	Yes – No
Earaches	Yes – No	Emotional Problems	Yes – No
		Weight Problem	Yes – No

Has your child had:

Poor Eating Habits	Yes – No	Difficulty Sleeping	Yes – No
Eye Disease	Yes – No	Eye Injury	Yes – No
Head Injury	Yes – No	Eyeglasses Prescribed	Yes – No
A Severe Fall	Yes – No	Hearing Loss	Yes – No

Development: Age Walked ______________ Age Talked ______________

Family History: (Please circle)

Tuberculosis	Kidney Conditions	Asthma	Deafness
Diabetes	Heart Disease	Epilepsy	Eyeglasses Worn
Cancer	Allergies	Blindness	

Has your Child Had a History of: (Please circle–give dates)

Allergy	High Fever	Tuberculosis
Asthma	Hospitalizations	Whooping Cough
Chicken Pox	German Measles (3 days)	Measles
Chorea (St. Vitus Dance)	Mononucleosis	Operations
Diphtheria	Mumps	Appendicitis ______________
Enuresis (bed wetting)	Pneumonia	Rupture (hernia) ______________
Epilepsy (convulsions)	Rheumatic Fever	Tonsils Removed ______________
Heart Disease	Poliomyelitis	Ear Operation ______________
Hepatitis	Scarlet Fever	Other ______________
Hernia	Tonsillitis	Medication Now ______________

Please list other childhood diseases, accidents or problems: ______________

Signature Grade Date

head lice report...

Dear Parent:

We have discovered several instances of head lice at our school. The children found with lice were excluded from school until corrective steps were taken. The school nurse has conducted an organized inspection of classmates and contacts of the affected children and will continue to monitor this throughout the year. We will disinfect any areas of the school which may have been involved with lice.

At the present time we believe the situation is under control. There is no reason to be alarmed. If you are concerned about your child, please call the school and the school nurse will inspect the hair and scalp. The nits (eggs) can be observed clinging to the hair near the scalp. Nits differ from dandruff in that they are regular and oval in shape and cannot be shaken easily from the hair as dandruff can.

Head lice are becoming increasingly common. They spread by direct contact and do not indicate lack of sanitation.

Please note the steps below for prevention and treatment. A concerted effort by all of us will quickly eliminate any problem that may still exist.

Sincerely,

____

Principal

STEPS TO ERADICATE HEAD LICE

TREATMENT:

1. Shampoo with Kwel R_x (1% lindane) shampoo for 4–5 minutes, rinse and dry.
2. Change bed linen and night clothes for the next day.
3. Launder infested linen and clothes in hot, soapy water—no special additives are necessary. Close attention is necessary to hoods, caps, etc., which are in direct contact with nits and lice.
4. Repeat steps 1–3 in 4 days.
5. Nits may be removed by combing the hair with a fine-toothed comb dipped in warm vinegar. The head may have to be immersed in vinegar. It is necessary to keep the hair moist with vinegar for the 15-minute period which is necessary for combing the nits out of the hair.
6. R & C Spray insecticide may be used on bedding, clothing and non-washables. (A solution of ammonia and water can also be used for cleansing purposes.)

PREVENTION

1. Keep hair a reasonable length.
2. Shampoo hair regularly with ordinary shampoo and water.
3. Change clothes and bed linen regularly.
4. Do not share combs, towels, caps, pillows, or clothing.
5. Repeat delousing with Kwel R_x shampoo if lice or nits reappear.
6. CHILDREN ARE TO BE EXCLUDED FROM SCHOOL IF LICE OR NITS ARE PRESENT UNTIL CHILD HAS BEEN TREATED TWO TIMES WITH KWEL R_x.

immunization record...

IMMUNIZATION RECORD

Pupil's Name ______________________ Date of Birth ____________

School ______________________ Grade ____________

Parent/Guardian ______________________ Telephone Number ____________

Address ______________________

____

		Primary Series			Boosters	
Vaccine Type	Disease	1st dose date mo./yr.	2nd dose date mo./yr.	3rd dose date mo./yr.	date mo./yr.	date mo./yr.
DPT						
TD (Adult)						
Oral Polio (Indicate type: I, II, III in box.)						
Rubeola						
Rubella						
Mumps						

I hereby certify that I have inspected the medical record and that this child has received the immunizations listed above.

______________________ Date

______________________ Date

______________________ Date

______________________ Date

scoliosis screening release...

Dear Parent:

Students in your child's school will have the opportunity to have general posture and scoliosis screening by the school health nurse. As this appraisal will consist of observation of your child's chest, back and legs, he/she may be viewed in underwear only. There will be separate screening of boys and girls. If in the opinion of the nurse the student has some postural deviation, you will be notified so that your child will be seen by your own physician or orthopedic doctor.

This program has been in effect in other school districts in the United States, and many boys and girls have benefited from the early recognition of a correctable deformity, thus preventing permanent disability.

Please sign below if you want your child to participate in the posture screening clinic.

____
School Health Nurse

I give my permission for my child ________________________ to participate in the postural screening clinic.

yes ______

no ______

______________________________ ____________________
Parent's Signature Date

(See Also: ACCIDENT; DOCTORS; DRUGS; EMERGENCY; HEALTH; ILLNESS; MEDICATION; NURSE; X-RAYS)

MEDICATION

medication use form...

Medication Use Form

This form is designed to assure parents and protect children in need of receiving medication during the school day or school activity appropriate handling of such needs. The general contents of the form have been reviewed by the Department of Public Instruction of the Department of Health. The School District does not in any way want to discourage parents from dispensing or supervising medication to their children at school if they are able to so, but is assisting only as an alternative.

Date: ______________________

Student's Name: ______________________ School: ______________________

I hereby give my permission to the staff at ______________________ school to dispense

medication prescribed by Dr. ______________________ for my child, beginning

______________________ ; ending ______________________.
DATE DATE

Name of medication or prescription number (including drug store): ______________________

____

Special instructions for dispensing: ______________________

____

If there are any side effects of this medication, please indicate: ______________________

____

______________________ ______________________
Physician's Signature Parent or Guardian

notice to parents...

Dear Parents:

Students needing occasional medications, such as penicillin, ampicillin, etc., for colds, earaches and sore throats, are to take those medications at home if possible. Medication that is prescribed three (3) times a day can be given before the student comes to school, after school, and again at bedtime.

Medications to be given at school must have a completed medication instruction form. Forms for your doctor to fill out may be obtained from the principal. ALL medication that comes into the school must be turned in to the principal or school nurse.

Any medication sent to school without proper identification will NOT be given.

We ask your cooperation as we are primarily concerned with the safety and health of your child.

Thank you.

____
School Nurse

(See Also: DOCTORS; DRUGS; HEALTH; ILLNESS; MEDICAL FORMS; NURSE; SICK LEAVE; X-RAYS)

MEETINGS

meeting notice form for daily bulletin...

MORNING BULLETIN – MEETING NOTICE

Announcement for: ____________________ ____________________
Day(s) Date(s)

ORGANIZATION ____________________________

EVENT ____________________________

PLACE ____________________________

TIME ________________ DATE ________________

ADVISOR/TEACHER'S SIGNATURE ____________________

NOTE: Request must be submitted before the end of the lunch period preceding the day the announcement is to be made. *PLEASE KEEP IT BRIEF.*

teacher handbook directives...

Meeting Agenda

The administration welcomes ideas for more productive and meaningful faculty meetings. These suggestions, however, should be channeled through your governance committee. The agenda will be strictly adhered to and *Robert's Rules of Order* will prevail in conducting the meeting.

Meetings will be called within contract provisions. However, keep the third Wednesday free for regular teachers' meetings; subsequent Wednesdays in the month will be set aside for Department meetings.

(See Also: BOARD OF EDUCATION; CHAIRPERSONS; DEPARTMENTAL MEETINGS; DUE PROCESS; FACULTY MEETINGS; NEW POLICY OR PROGRAM**)**

MINI-COURSES

examples of mini-course descriptions...

HELPERS IN EDUCATION

0700 "HIE" Student program—2 hrs/day/1 Semester/1 Credit

Open to Grade 12

This course is designed to be an opportunity for interested grade 12 students to become involved in the educational process by serving an internship program for credit in one of the classrooms of the school district. The program is an attempt to help students decide for themselves if teaching is the proper career for them.

The procedure followed is:

1. Each student will be interviewed by the Supervisor of Elementary or Secondary Education before being assigned to individual teachers. The students will be placed with a teacher on a semester basis. An additional semester may be approved upon review of the student's interests and achievement. Each student will be allowed to request the grade level or subject matter in which to become involved.
2. The HIE coordinator and the special guests will teach 6 to 12 hours of seminar sessions on general education and related fields at the beginning of each semester to help prepare the students for their experience. Monthly seminars will be held throughout the semester.
3. Students will spend two hours daily observing and assisting staff members at the grade level they choose.
4. Students will attend faculty metings, when possible, and do many other things that serve to acquaint them with teaching and to interest them in teaching as a profession.

5. Each student will keep a daily notebook based on his or her observations and will be required to submit a written research project at the end of the semester.
6. Students will be graded on a pass/fail basis. The decision of a grade will be made in cooperation by the teacher and the assistant principal. Upon a successful completion of the class, each student will receive an appropriate certificate indicating such completion.
7. When the students are in the cooperating schools, a button provided by the school district will be worn for identification purposes.
8. Transportation to the assigned school is the responsibility of the student.

1025 Humanities II: The Romantics & Realists—½ Credit—Phase 3

Open to Grades 11, 12

This course is designed to give the student a chance to continue to examine man's role in the community which began in Humanities I, although it is not a prerequisite for this course. Literary selections include the medieval morality play *Everyman*, and selections by Shakespeare and Archibald MacLeish. The major work of the course, an abridged translation of the novel *War and Peace* by Leo Tolstoy, shows man as a romantic realist. The course closes with a romantic look into the future through the novel *Childhood's End* by Arthur C. Clarke. The student should have a definite interest in drama, literature and the arts, and be willing to examine his or her own life in the light of these.

(See Also: CLASS; CURRICULUM; ELECTIVES; GRADES; LESSON PLANS; NEW POLICY OR PROGRAM; OBJECTIVES; SCHEDULE; TEXTBOOKS**)**

MONEY

daily school money record form...

DATE: ______________________

AMOUNT REC'D:	FROM WHOM:	REASON:	INITIAL:
	TOTAL FOR DAY		

memo on...

TO: Faculty and Staff
FROM: J. Benson, Principal
RE: Cash

I know we've all seen those signs in gas stations and groceries that state the attendants do not carry cash. Unfortunately, these are necessitated by the number of robberies to which these places are prey. From practical experience, they have come to realize that would-be thieves are after money, and where there is no chance of getting cash, there is a reduced risk of robbery.

While we at this school have made every effort to reduce crime and violence and produce an atmosphere conducive to learning, it only takes one anti-social act to prove how vulnerable we are to violence.

Therefore, let's make every effort to remove any motivation for such despicable acts.

Please advise your students that large amounts of money should not be brought to school at any time. Only sufficient cash required for a normal school day (that is, lunch money, etc.) should be brought. Moreover, money should not be left in lockers or classrooms at any time. In the event that a large sum of money is brought to school, remind students that the school safe will be available for the storage of that cash during the school day.

Personally, I think these suggestions should apply to ourselves as well. Please remember to leave no purses, pocketbooks, collection envelopes, etc., unguarded at any time. The facilities of the safe are, of course, available to the faculty at all times.

Let's make every effort to eliminate any incentive for crime.

policy on...

It shall be the policy of the Board of Education that the Board will not be responsible for sums of money carried by students or employees on school property. Students and Board employees are to be discouraged, at the individual school level, from carrying or bringing large amounts of money to school. Individuals who are carrying such amounts may be made aware that the school safe is available to them for the storage of the cash sum during regular school hours. Any cash collected during the school day for recognized, school-related activities or purposes such as trips, book clubs, etc., is to be tagged and identified by the individual in charge of collection and turned in to the individual school office by the end of each school day for storage in the school safe.

(See Also: AWARDS; BIDS; BUDGET; FEES, FINES, FUNDS, AND CHARGES; PAYROLL; PURCHASING; VENDORS; VOUCHER**)**

MOVIES

film order form...

DATE ____________________

TEACHER ______________________________________ ROOM ________

1. Fill out form in duplicate
2. Order well in advance—4–6 weeks ahead for District and State films.

source of film	film title	film number	date needed

(See Also: BUDGET; LIBRARY; MEDIA; REQUISITIONS, REPAIRS, AND REPLACEMENTS**)**

NATIONAL HONOR SOCIETY

letter to parents of inductee...

Dear Mr. and Mrs. Williams,

I have already spoken to your daughter, Judy, and offered her my congratulations upon her election to the National Honor Society. I would like to extend those congratulations to you as well. If ever the word "honor" could be extended to describe an individual, it would be proper and fitting in Judy's case. Her high academic record, as well as her record of care and concern for the good of others, mark her as an individual truly worthy of this distinction. I know you must be justly proud of her as we are at the school.

I look forward to meeting you at the induction ceremonies later this month. I just wanted you to know how highly we regard your daughter and how pleased we are that she is receiving recognition for her continuing expressions of excellence.

Sincerely,

principal's speech at ceremony...

Ladies and Gentlemen...

For better or for worse, an institution is often judged by the caliber of its members. Quite often, we hear groups of people derided and chastized because of the negative actions of some members of the group. Perhaps this is natural, since we tend to judge on that which is known to us, and the negative is often that which is splashed across newspaper front pages and made lead stories on the TV news.

But, let us not concentrate on the negative. Let us instead go searching for the positive. It isn't that difficult to find if we make up our minds to see the total picture. We will then see the fine young men and women present on this stage tonight. Then, we will see the record of their achievements, a bright and shining record of academic achievement and personal service to others. Then, we will see a positive future, filled with hope because they will be a part of it.

Therefore, as these fine young people gather here tonight to be inducted into the National Honor Society, let us all take pride in their accomplishments and, for a while at least, judge the future by our knowledge that these are the citizens of tomorrow and, because of that fact, tomorrow will be bright, indeed.

I extend my personal congratulations as well as that of the entire faculty and staff of our school to the inductees along with our sincere and fervent hope that this will be the beginning of continued success throughout their years as productive citizens of a better tomorrow.

NEGOTIATIONS

letter confirming representation at negotiations...

Dear Mr. Sarenen,

As the date approaches for the first negotiations session between the Rock Township Board of Education and the Rock Township Education Association, it is only fitting that we begin to detail certain procedural elements of those negotiations. We are in possession of your letter of October 10 in which you name the representatives of the Association who will constitute the negotiations committee for your side. The Board has no objections to anyone named on that list.

On behalf of the Board, the following individuals shall represent the Board during these negotiations:

Mrs. Estelle Waverley, Negotiations Committee Chairperson
Dr. George Bailey, Assistant Superintendent of Schools
Mr. Harold Daniels
Mrs. Mary Martinsen
Mr. James Oliver

If there is any objection on the part of the Association to any of these representatives, please let us know within ten (10) days of the receipt of this letter.

All else being equal, the Board looks forward to meeting with you at the agreed location of the Board of Education office on Thursday evening, November 4, at 7:30 p.m. for the first negotiations session.

On behalf of the entire Board of Education, may I extend our sincerest wishes that the negotiations into which we are about to enter may run smoothly and prove amicable for all concerned.

Yours sincerely,

(See Also: ACCEPTANCE; BOARD OF EDUCATION; CONTRACT; DUE PROCESS; GRIEVANCES; MEDIATION)

NEW POLICY OF PROGRAM

memo to faculty...

TO: Faculty
FROM: J. Benson, Principal
RE: New Testing Program

Of course there are going to be problems. We all know that from experience. No new program comes to us error-proof and problem-free. The new testing program which goes into effect next week will be no exception. I know, however, and you know it, too, that there is no problem which, working together as we have so many times in the past, we cannot solve.

You are a credit to our profession. As educators, we realize that education is an ongoing process; something developmental which tries and evaluates and sometimes fails and sometimes succeeds, but keeps striving for the best of which we are capable. I have seen you work on this new program and give your time and efforts to give it the chance it deserves. I am proud of that fact, and no one could ask for more.

As this new program beings, I want you to know that I support and applaud your efforts. Working together, there is nothing we cannot accomplish.

parental notification of the start of a new program...

Dear Parents,

Education is an ongoing process. Methods and techniques are constantly undergoing revision in order to insure the best possible education for your child. In today's society where there is just so much to learn, it is essential that your children be taught in the most efficient and effective manner possible.

Toward that goal, a new program of reading instruction is under consideration for use in our elementary school. It is a program that has been used with great success in many localities, and one which we hope will prove beneficial in our district.

Since the ability to read is so fundamental to success in all areas of education as well as life itself, this is not a step we have taken without a great deal of testing and evaluation. We sincerely believe that this program will be the best for your child and all the children of our district.

Since the program is far too long to explain in a letter, we will be holding a meeting of all concerned parents on Wednesday, October 1 at 8:00 p.m. in the school auditorium. At that time, the entire program will be explained and discussed, and any questions you may have will be answered.

You are most cordially invited to attend. We look forward to meeting you at that time and have the opportunity of explaining this program to you.

I hope to see you there.

Sincerely,

(See Also: ACADEMIC FREEDOM; BUDGET; CHANGE; COURSES; ELECTIVES; GUIDANCE; INQUIRIES; JOB DESCRIPTION; NEWS RELEASES; PHILOSOPHY; QUESTIONS)

NEWSLETTER

format for newsletter...

The following format has been established for our school newsletter. It is published here in order that there may be a consistency from issue to issue.

PAGE ONE — Logo; Volume and Number of Issue (NOTE: Each year is its separate VOLUME and each issue is its separate NUMBER. Hence, the 3rd issue of the 2nd year would be Volume II, Number 3.); Major News.

PAGE TWO — Major News Continues; Datebook of Events Occurring Between This and Next Issue.

PAGE THREE — Features; Happenings in Classrooms; Special Activities; Field Trips, etc.

PAGE FOUR — Personal and Personnel Items; Special Accomplishments, etc.

Presented consistently, our newsletter will be readable, enjoyable, and provide a real service for those who read it.

request for copy and deadline notification...

TO: All Teachers
FROM: PTA Newsletter Committee
RE: Deadline for Next Newsletter

If you have any items you feel could be used in the PTA newsletter, place them in the PTA mailbox prior to November 8. Please try to meet this deadline, as it will be difficult to get items into the November Newsletter after that date.

Items of interest would include department news; class events; students who have done something which should be spotlighted; sports, club or activity news; student work which would be appropriate for the Newsletter; and any other items you think would make a good addition to our Newsletter.

Thank you in advance for your cooperation. It is your contributions that help make the Newsletter a success.

(See Also: ADVERTISING; ALUMNI; HANDBOOK; INFORMATION; INTRODUCTION; MEDIA; NEWS RELEASES; REPORTS; TYPISTS; WRITING)

NEWS RELEASES

example of a news release...

PRESS RELEASE

KINDERGARTEN REGISTRATION SET FOR WEDNESDAY, April 14

Registration for all kindergarten students eligible for the kindergarten program in Rock Township Schools will be held from 8 to 4 p.m. Wednesday, April 14. This also includes handicapped students.

Students should register in the following primary school zones in which they reside. These schools are: Clover Elementary, East Elementary, George Elementary, Hines Elementary, Salem Street Elementary, and South Elementary.

Parents bring their child with them since a screening test will be given to each child registering for kindergarten.

Parents must also bring a valid birth certificate and a certificate of immunization.

Criteria for qualifying for the program are as follows:

Children reside in one of the school zones above.
Children must be five years old on or before October 2.
All kindergarten children will be given a screening test.

If you are not certain of the school zone for your child, call 555-6676 for correct information.

PLEASE REGISTER YOUR CHILD ON THE ABOVE DATE TO PROVIDE HIM/HER WITH THIS EDUCATIONAL OPPORTUNITY!

policy on...

The Superintendent and staff shall decide upon and follow a continuing program of information designed to acquaint the citizens of the community and the public generally with the achievements and the needs of the schools. The Superintendent shall be responsible for:

a. news releases and the publication of educational reports

b. the photographing of school activities for publication

c. information liaison between the school system and the community at large

News releases by the Board are to be considered official Board releases only if approved by a majority of the members prior to release, either in a meeting of the Board or verbally to the Secretary/Business Administrator. The Superintendent shall approve for release all staff-prepared statements for publication regarding districtwide concerns. Staff members submitting to any publication articles in which the public schools are mentioned are also requested to show these to the Superintendent for clearance.

(See Also: HANDBOOK; INFORMATION; MEDIA; NEWSLETTER; REPORTS; WRITING)

NON-RENEWAL OF CONTRACT

general policy for non-professional employees...

The contract with each non-professional and/or non-probationary employee not under tenure shall specify that two (2) weeks' notice shall be given by either party prior to unilateral termination of the contract.

Each full-time non-professional employee shall serve up to a 90-day probationary period, unless otherwise specified by the terms of a collectively negotiated contract, during which time he or she may be discharged without notice.

general policy for professional employees...

The contract for each full-time professional employee not under tenure shall specify that sixty (60) days' notice shall be given by either party prior to unilateral termination of the contract. In addition, the Superintendent shall submit to the Board of Education a written evaluative summary for all professional employees recommended for employment in their tenure year.

It shall be the policy of the Board that personnel covered by special contracts, for which special State certification is not required, are employed on an annual basis with the proviso that continuation of employment is a prerogative of the Board. Special contracts are listed in the current agreement. It is not the intent of the Board to provide tenure status to any employee in these categories.

grounds for non-renewal...

It is the duty of the Board to protect the pupils of this district from the classroom influence of inefficient staff members.

For a tenured staff member of this system to be charged by the Board with inefficiency, the following conditions must be demonstrated by the Superintendent:

1. The staff member was aware of the terms and conditions expected of him at the start of his assignment.
2. The staff member was found to be wanting by evaluators certificated to perform evaluations using generally endorsed professional methods.
3. The staff member was given written notice by the Superintendent upon order of the board of the alleged inefficiency, specifying the nature thereof with such particulars as to furnish him an opportunity to correct and overcome the same.
4. The staff member was found at least ninety (90) days after being given notice (but less than 135 days) still to be inefficient in the performance of his duties.

Upon the demonstration of the preceding conditions by the Superintendent and following the determination by the Board in accordance with statute that the charge and the evidence in support of the charge are sufficient, if true in fact, to warrant a dismissal or withholding an increment, the Board shall certify the charge of inefficiency to the Commissioner.

non-renewal of non-tenured employee contract...

In connection with the offering and non-offering of contracts to non-tenured employees, the Board of Education shall be bound by Article XXIX, Fair Dismissal Procedure, as contained in the existing collective bargaining agreement between the Board of Education and the Rock Township Education Association.

In the event a non-tenured teacher is not offered a contract of employment for the next succeeding year, he/she may, within thirty (30) days of the date of official notification, request in writing from the Assistant Superintendent (Personnel) a written statement of reasons. Such statement shall be supplied within fifteen (15) days of receipt of such request.

The employee may also, within five (5) days of receipt of such statement, request and receive an interview with the Superintendent and following such interview, may request, within five (5) days, an informal appearance before the Board of Education. The employee may be represented by counsel or one individual of his/her choosing. The employee shall also have the right to present persons to the board who will make statements on his or her behalf. Such persons shall be called into the meeting to address the Board one at a time and shall be excused from the meeting after making his or her statement.

Such informal appearance must be scheduled within thirty (30) calendar days of receipt of such request and the Board shall notify the teacher, in writing, of its final determination within five (5) days following the informal appearance.

(See Also: ABILITY; ACADEMIC FREEDOM; CONTRACT; CONTROVERSIAL TOPICS; DUE PROCESS; EVALUATION; GRIEVANCES; MEDIATION; NEGOTIATIONS; OBSERVATIONS; REDUCTION IN FORCE; TRANSFER**)**

NURSE

nurse's daily record form...

HEALTH DEPARTMENT – Nurse's Daily Record

Date ______________________

School ______________________

Time In	Name of Pupil	Grade	Complaint	Treatment	Return to Class	Taken Home	By Whom	Accident Report

report on communicable disease...

REPORT ON COMMUNICABLE DISEASE TO HEALTH OFFICER

School ______________ Month ________ Nurse ______________

Disease	Total	Disease	Total
Chickenpox	____	Strep Throat	____
Measles	____	Whooping Cough	____
Mumps	____	German Measles	____
Scarlet Fever	____	Hepatitis	____
Meningitis	____	Encephalitis	____

Name	Age	Address	Suspected Disease

(**See Also:** ACCIDENT; DOCTORS; DRUGS; EMERGENCY; HEALTH; ILLNESS; MEDICAL FORMS; MEDICATION; SAFETY; X-RAYS)

OBJECTIVES

example of specific course objectives...

1. The student will demonstrate his/her ability to classify literary selections by genre (novel, short story, drama, poetry, non-fiction).
2. The student will demonstrate his/her ability to identify main and supporting ideas in a given literary selection in either written or oral form.
3. The student will demonstrate his/her knowledge of cause and effect relationships in a given literary selection in either oral or written form.
4. The student will demonstrate his/her ability to identify character, setting, and plot development in a given literary selection.
5. The student will demonstrate his/her ability to make inferences based upon details in a given literary selection.
6. The student will demonstrate his/her ability to master and apply selected literary terms.
7. The student will demonstrate his/her ability to understand the intellectual and social implications in a literary selection.
8. The student will demonstrate his/her ability to write a paragraph containing a topic sentence, at least two sentences with supporting details, and a clincher sentence.
9. The student will demonstrate his/her ability to use the parts of speech, the basic sentence patterns, and correct punctuation in written and oral expression.

guidelines for writing behavioral objectives...

STATING BEHAVIORAL OBJECTIVES FOR CLASSROOM INSTRUCTION	**USING THE TAXONOMY OF EDUCATIONAL OBJECTIVES**	
Major Categories in the Cognitive Domain of the Taxonomy of Educational Objectives (Bloom, 1956)	Examples of General Instructional Objectives and Behavioral Terms for the Cognitive Domain of the Taxonomy	
Descriptions of the Major Categories in the Cognitive Domain	*Illustrative General Instructional Objectives*	*Illustrative Behavioral Terms for Stating Specific Learning Outcomes*
Knowledge. Knowledge is defined as the remembering of previously learned material. This may involve the recall of a wide range of material, from specific facts to complete theories, but all that is required is the bringing to mind of the appropriate information. Knowledge represents the lowest level of learning outcomes in the cognitive domain.	Knows common terms Knows specific facts Knows methods and procedures Knows basic concepts Knows principles	Defines, describes, identifies, labels, lists, matches, names, outlines, reproduces, selects, states
Comprehension. Comprehension is defined as the ability to grasp the meaning of material. This may be shown by translating material from one form to another (words to numbers), by interpreting material (explaining or summarizing), and by estimating future trends (predicting consequences or effects). These learning outcomes go one step beyond the simple remembering of material, and represent the lowest level of understanding.	Understands facts and principles Interprets verbal materials Interprets charts and graphs Translates verbal materials to mathematical formulas Estimates future consequences implied in data Justifies methods and procedures	Converts, defends, distinguishes, extimates, explains, extends, generalizes, gives examples, infers, paraphrases, predicts, rewrites, summarizes
Application. Application refers to the ability to use learned material in new and concrete situations. This may include the application of such things as rules, methods, concepts, principles, laws, and theories. Learning outcomes in this area require a higher level of understanding than those under comprehension.	Applies concepts and principles to new situations Applies laws and theories to practical situations Solves mathematical problems Constructs charts and graphs Demonstrates correct usage of a method or procedure	Changes, computes, demonstrates, discovers, manipulates, modifies, operates, predicts, prepares, produces, relates, shows, solves, uses

(Form continued)

Descriptions of the Major Categories in the Cognitive Domain	*Illustrative General Instructional Objectives*	*Illustrative Behavioral Terms for Stating Specific Learning Outcomes*
Analysis. Analysis refers to the ability to break down material into its component parts so that its organizational structure may be understood. This may include the identification of the parts, analysis of the relationships between parts, and recognition of the organizational principles involved. Learning outcomes here represent a higher intellectual level than comprehension and application because they require an understanding of both the content and structural form of the material.	Recognizes unstated asumptions Recognizes logical fallacies in reasoning Distinguishes between facts and inferences Evaluates the relevancy of data Analyzes the organizational structure of a work (art, music, writing)	Breaks down, diagrams, differentiates, discriminates, distinguishes, identifies, illustrates, infers, outlines, points out, relates, selects, separates, subdivides
Synthesis. Synthesis refers to the ability to put parts together to form a new whole. This may involve the production of a unique communication (theme or speech), a plan of operations (research proposal), or a set of abstract relations (scheme for classifying information). Learning outcomes in this area stress creative behaviors, with major emphasis on the formulation of new patterns or structures.	Writes a well-organized theme Gives a well-organized speech Writes a creative short story (or poem or music) Proposes a plan for an experiment Integrates learning from different areas into a plan for solving a problem Formulates a new scheme for classifying objects (or events, or ideas)	Categorizes, combines, compiles, composes, creates, devises, designs, explains, generates, modifies, organizes, plans, rearranges, reconstructs, relates, reorganizes, revises, rewrites, summarizes, tells, writes
Evaluation. Evaluation is concerned with the ability to judge the value of material (statement, novel, poem, research report) for a given purpose. The judgments are to be based on definite criteria. These may be internal criteria (organization) or external criteria (relevance to the purpose) and the student may determine the criteria or be given them. Learning outcomes in this area are highest in the cognitive hierarchy because they contain elements of all of the other categories, plus conscious value judgments based on clearly defined criteria.	Judges the logical consistency of written material Judges the adequacy with which conclusions are supported by data Judges the value of a work (art, music, writing) by use of internal criteria Judges the value of a work (art, music, writing) by use of external statements of excellence	Appraises, compares, concludes, contrasts, criticizes, describes, discriminates, explains, justifies, interprets, relates, summarizes, supports

(Form continued)

(See Also: CURRICULUM; EVALUATION; GOALS; LESSON PLANS; OBSERVATIONS; PHILOSOPHY)

OBSERVATIONS

observation form for targeted needs improvement...

TEACHER: ______________________________ DATE: ____________________

SUPERVISOR: ____

This is to certify that we have met and discussed needs improvement relative to classroom instruction. The following have been mutually agreed upon as targeted needs improvement for the 19____–19____ school year:

SIGNATURE OF TEACHER: ______________________________________

SIGNATURE OF SUPERVISOR: ____________________________________

OBSERVATION REPORT

TEACHER:____________________ DATE OF OBSERVATION: ____________

TIME OF OBSERVATION: ____

CLASS: ________________________ SUBJECT: ____________________

OBSERVER/SUPERVISOR:____

Targeted Needs Improvement Area Comment

____

____

____

____

____

I have conferred with ____________________ concerning the above observation.

TEACHER COMMENT:

SIGNATURE OF TEACHER: ______________________ DATE: ____________

SIGNATURE OF SUPERVISOR: __________________ DATE: ____________

(See Also: CHILD STUDY TEAM; CLASS; EVALUATION; INTERNSHIP; LESSON PLANS; PROFESSIONAL IMPROVEMENT PLAN; PROGRESS REPORT; REPORTS)

OPEN HOUSE

invitation to parents...

Dear Parents,

On Wednesday, November 16, from 8:30 a.m. until 3:00 p.m., we will be holding an open house at Rock Township High School.

On that day, parents and community members are invited to visit our school, tour our facilities, sit in on classes, and see for themselves the educational process at work in Rock Township. We can promise no special activities geared for one day only, but we can promise that you will see the day-to-day operations of the place that occupies such a vitally important part of your son's or daughter's life.

The only thing we need to make the day a success is YOU. You are most welcome, and we look forward to seeing you on that day.

Please stop by the main office that I may meet you personally and welcome you to our school.

Sincerely,

John Benson, Principal

memo to teachers...

TO: Faculty and Staff
FROM: J. Benson, Principal
RE: Open House

This coming Wednesday will be our annual open house at Rock Township High School. As in the past, parents and community members will be visiting our school from 8:30 a.m. until 3:00 p.m. I know that I can count on you to make them feel welcome.

We are proud of the quality of our instruction here at Rock Township, and I want to emphasize that we will continue with our normal educational process on that day. If you have visitors in your room, I know you will treat them with respect and try to involve them in the class being presented, but I want to emphasize that we must carry on business as usual.

We have a fine educational program—let's acquaint the public with the good and valuable things we are doing.

(See Also: ADVERTISING; AMERICAN EDUCATION WEEK; BACK-TO-SCHOOL NIGHT; BUILDING; MEDIA; NEWSLETTER; NEWS RELEASES; SCHEDULE VISITORS)

OPENING PROCEDURES

policy and procedures...

It will be the policy of the Rock Township Board of Education that the school day shall be opened with the following procedures in every school in the Township:

Shortly after the beginning of Homeroom Period or the First Period of the day, the students will be called to order via the public address system. They shall then be led in the recitation of the Pledge of Allegiance to the United States of America. Following this there will be the playing of the National Anthem or an equivalent patriotic song ("America the Beautiful," "My Country 'Tis of Thee," etc.).

If students do not want to participate in these opening procedures because of religious and/or philosophical reasons, they may not be required to do so, but they may be required to remain silent during them and in no way distract the others.

(See Also: AMERICAN EDUCATION WEEK; ASSEMBLIES BACK-TO-SCHOOL NIGHT; MEETINGS; OPEN HOUSE)

ORGANIZATIONAL CHART

example of box chart...

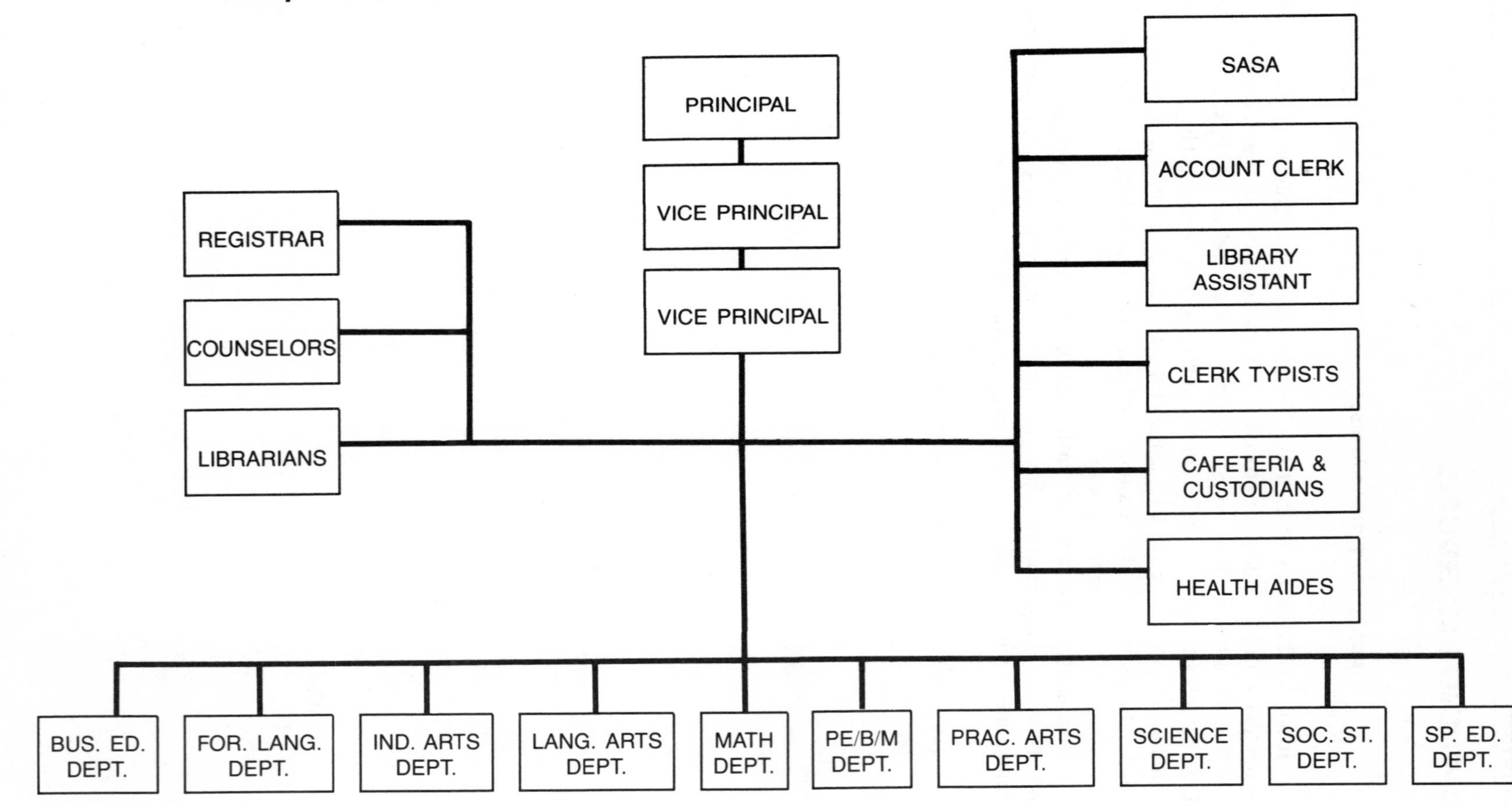

organizational chart by responsibilities...

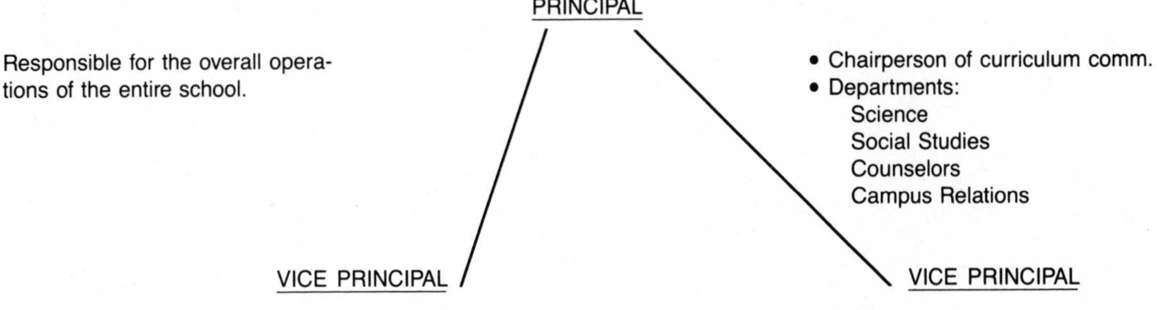

Departments:
- Business Ed.
- Math
- Special Ed.
- Foreign Lang.
- AV/ETV Coord.
- Registrar

Facilities and Maintenance:
- All matters pertaining to repairs and maintenance of buildings and equipment in the school

Budget and Finance:
- All matters in the school pertaining to the business operations (i.e., budget and finance)

Registration:
- All matters pertaining to the office of the registrar and attendance

(All matters pertaining to their assigned departments and the evaluation of teachers are to be included in their responsibilities.)

Departments:
- English
- PE/Band/Music
- Practical Arts
- Industrial Arts
- Librarians

Personnel:
- Teachers, classified staff and classroom cleaners

School-related Activities:
- i.e., advisors and chaperones

Note:
Matters pertaining to discipline and student activity concerns can be referred to any administrator. It should be understood that while there are some divisions of responsibilities, any teacher may refer any concerns or problems (personal or departmental) to any administrator.

(See Also: BOARD OF EDUCATION; BUSINESS; CHAIRPERSONS; CLUBS; JOB DESCRIPTION; PRINCIPAL; STUDENT COUNCIL (GOVERNMENT); VICE-PRINCIPAL)

PARKING REGULATIONS

policy on...

It is the policy of the Board that students not park motor vehicles on school property unless an official permit has been obtained. No student shall drive or occupy any motor vehicle during school hours without specific permission of the administration.

Minibikes are banned from Board property.

regulations for...

CARS IN HIGH SCHOOL

If you want to bring a car to school you must have written permission from your parents.

The note should include the license number, the model, and color of the car. The note should also state that no passengers will be transported in the car unless the high school office has given permission. This permission will be given only after the passenger's parents have requested so in writing.

Also, any vehicle operated on school property must have liability and property damage insurance. You must present proof of such coverage to the high school office in order to receive permission to operate a car on school property.

A $1 fee must accompany your request for a parking permit. This parking sticker should appear in the left rear window on the driver's side of the car. You must park in the student parking area, and are not to use the car during the school day. If any of the privileges of operating a car on school property are not adhered to, your privileges may be revoked.

(See Also: AUTOMOBILES; DISCIPLINE; FEES, FINES, FUNDS AND CHARGES; INSURANCE)

PASSES

all-purpose pass...

DATE: ______________________ TIME OUT: ______________________

STUDENT: ______________________ TIME IN: ______________________

DESTINATION:

TEACHER: ______________________________________ ROOM: ________

permit to leave campus (with policy)...

PERMIT TO LEAVE CAMPUS

PERIOD ________ TEACHER ________ HOMEROOM ________ GRADE ________

DATE ____/____/19____ TIME ____________ A.M. P.M.

PERMISSION
HAS BEEN GRANTED TO ______________________________________
TO LEAVE THE SCHOOL CAMPUS FOR THE PURPOSE OF

☐ MEDICAL: ______________________________________

☐ DENTAL: ______________________________________

☐ GENERAL: ______________________________________

____

THIS PERMIT IS TO BE SIGNED BY ☐ PARENT ☐ GUARDIAN ☐ DOCTOR ☐ DENTIST

X ______________________________

PUPIL MUST TURN IN THIS SLIP TO THE ATTENDANCE OFFICE IMMEDIATELY UPON RETURN TO SCHOOL

Any permit to release students from the campus should come as a request of the parent or guardian. Any teacher or counselor permitting students to leave are acting in place of the parent and will be held accountable and liable for any injuries incurred by the student or students.

When emergencies arise and it is necessary to permit students to leave, please call the parent and at least get verbal approval. In the event that a student is injured, only the school nurse and administrators are legally responsible in transporting him or her to the hospital.

(See Also: CUTTING; HALLS AND HALL DUTY; IDENTIFICATION; LAVATORIES; LIBRARY; LOCKERS; TARDINESS AND TRUANCY; TELEPHONE; VISITORS)

PAYROLL

general payroll information form...

1. Name ______________________ 2. Birth Date ______________________
   (No nicknames, please)

3. City Address ____
   (P.O. Box and Street)

4. Home Phone ______________________ 5. Position ______________________
   (include extracurricular, if any)

6. Building ______________________ 7. Payment: 10 mos. ______ 12 mos. ______

8. Health Insurance: Family ______ SPD ______ Single ______ None ______
   (Is this a new or changed policy? Yes ____ No ____)

9. Cancer Care: Yes ______ No ______
   (Is this a new or changed policy? Yes ______ No ______)

10. Term Life: $30,000 paid by District; Optional $30,000 paid by employee–Yes ______ No ______
    (approximately $43.20 per year)

11. Payroll Deduction for Dues: Yes ______ No ______

12. Payroll Deduction for State Income Tax: According to chart ______________
    Specified Amount ______________

Date of Employment ______________________

Attached:

Term Life Form: __________

State Certificate of Residence Form: __________
(For those who do not want state income tax withheld—this is an option only for those who paid State Income Tax last year.)

W-4 Form: __________

Date ______________________

payroll deduction form (1)...

Payroll

Hourly ☐
Monthly ☐

Food Service ☐

Name: ______________ ______________ ______
(Last) (First) (Initial)

Social Security Number: ___ ___ ___ ___ ___ ___ ___ ___ ___

Position: ______________ Building: ______________

(Please indicate only those deductions to be changed)

	Payroll Deduction
Credit Union and Savings Bonds:	
1. County Teachers Federal Credit Union	1. ______
2. United States Savings Bonds	2. ______
Health and Dental Insurance:	
3. Blue Cross/Blue Shield Health Insurance	3. ______
4. HMO Health Insurance	4. ______
5. Blue Cross/Blue Shield Dental Insurance	5. ______
Life Insurance:	
6. PERA Group Life Insurance–Prudential Life	6. ______
7. PERA Group Life Insurance–New York Life	7. ______
8. Northwestern EGO Life Insurance	8. ______
Organization Dues:	
9. Education Association Dues	9. ______
10. Union Dues	10. ______
11. C.A.S.E. Insurance and Dues	11. ______
TAX SHELTERED ANNUITIES:	
12. Franklin	12. ______
13. Metropolitan	13. ______
14. Lincoln	14. ______
15. Horace Mann	15. ______
16. Equitable	16. ______
17. Variable–VALIC	17. ______
18. Hartford Variable	18. ______
United Way and Other:	
19. United Way Contributions	19. ______
20. Other: (Please specify)______________	20. ______

See instructions on reverse side of last copy.

I authorize the School District to make the above monthly deductions. These deductions will remain in effect until changed on this form and submitted to the Payroll Office.

______________ ______________ Change to occur in ______ ______ paycheck.
(Employee's Signature) (Date) (Month) (Year)

payroll deduction form (2)...

SOCIAL SECURITY NUMBER	CD	NAME–Last First Middle

Check and sign all blocks where applicable. To stop a deduction write the word DELETE in the amount. PLEASE READ AND CHECK CAREFULLY.	CARD CODE	Administrative Use Only CODE	AMOUNT	LIMIT
1. TEACHER'S RETIREMENT REINSTATEMENT $________ per month	K	0203		
2. TEACHER RETIREMENT ARREARAGES $________ per month	K	0202		
3. PUBLIC EMPLOYMENT RETIREMENT REINSTATEMENT $________	K	0252		
4. SAVINGS BONDS $________ per pay period	K	0802		
5. UNITED WAY $________ per month $________ Annual Limit	K	0500		
6. TOTEM $________ per month	K	0465		
7. FOOD SERVICE ASSOCIATION DUES $________	K	0460		
8. PUPIL TRANSPORTATION TEAMSTER'S DUES $________ per month	K	0450		
9. TEAMSTER'S MAINTENANCE DUES $________ per month	K	0457		
10. LABORER'S LOCAL $________	K	0453		
11. LABORER'S LOCAL INITIATION FEE $________	K	0454		
12. PRINCIPAL ASSOCIATION $________ per month $________ Annual Limit	K	0410		
13. OTHER $________ ________ $________ ________				
14. CREDIT UNION $________ per month Account Number________	K	0700		
I understand that all new accounts or changes must be processed at the Credit Union. This amount will replace all other established deductions. Account number must be present.	J	Account Number ________		

CLERK

I hereby authorize the above deductions with the understanding that written notice is required FIFTEEN (15) days prior to payday to change a deduction.

Name ________________________

Location ________________________

Date ________________________

request for wage change form...

REQUEST FOR WAGE CHANGE FOR NON-CERTIFIED PERSONNEL

Employee Name: ______________________________

Position: ______________________________

Principal or Supervisor
Requesting Change: ______________________________

Present Wage: ______________ Proposed Wage: ______________

Effective Date: ______________________________

Reason for Change: ______________________________

____

____

____

Approved: ______________ Disapproved: ______________

Explanation (if any): ______________________________

____

____

______________________________, Superintendent

wage-hour payroll form...

TIME/EFFORT WAGE FORM

Pay Period Ending ______________________ 19____
(Month and Day)

Employee ______________________ Social Security Number ______________________
Fund Account Number ______________________
Home Address ______________________ Hourly Wage Rate $____ Overtime Wage Rate $____
Weekly Wage Rate $____ Monthly Wage Rate $____
Building Employed ______________________ Annual Wage Rate $____

In order that we may comply with the Wage Hour law, each employee is required to fill in the time worked each day and turn in this slip, signed, at the end of the month. If called away during working hours, notation of this time should be made on the back of the slip. Paychecks will be distributed on the 20th of the month.

Date	Day		No. of Hrs & Min	Daily Total Hrs & Min
		A.M.		
	Wednesday	P.M.		
		Even		
		A.M.		
	Thursday	P.M.		
		Even		
		A.M.		
	Friday	P.M.		
		Even		
		A.M.		
	Saturday	P.M.		
		Even		
		A.M.		
	Sunday	P.M.		
		Even		
		A.M.		
	Monday	P.M.		
		Even		
		A.M.		
	Tuesday	P.M.		
		Even		

Weekly Total ____________

Date	Day		No. of Hrs & Min	Daily Total Hrs & Min
		A.M.		
	Wednesday	P.M.		
		Even		
		A.M.		
	Thursday	P.M.		
		Even		
		A.M.		
	Friday	P.M.		
		Even		
		A.M.		
	Saturday	P.M.		
		Even		
		A.M.		
	Sunday	P.M.		
		Even		
		A.M.		
	Monday	P.M.		
		Even		
		A.M.		
	Tuesday	P.M.		
		Even		

Weekly Total ____________

(Form continued)

TIME/EFFORT WAGE FORM (continued)

Date	Day		No. of Hrs & Min	Daily Total Hrs & Min
	Wednesday	A.M.		
		P.M.		
		Even		
	Thursday	A.M.		
		P.M.		
		Even		
	Friday	A.M.		
		P.M.		
		Even		
	Saturday	A.M.		
		P.M.		
		Even		
	Sunday	A.M.		
		P.M.		
		Even		
	Monday	A.M.		
		P.M.		
		Even		
	Tuesday	A.M.		
		P.M.		
		Even		

Weekly Total ______

Date	Day		No. of Hrs & Min	Daily Total Hrs & Min
	Wednesday	A.M.		
		P.M.		
		Even		
	Thursday	A.M.		
		P.M.		
		Even		
	Friday	A.M.		
		P.M.		
		Even		
	Saturday	A.M.		
		P.M.		
		Even		
	Sunday	A.M.		
		P.M.		
		Even		
	Monday	A.M.		
		P.M.		
		Even		
	Tuesday	A.M.		
		P.M.		
		Even		

Weekly Total ______

Date	Day		No. of Hrs & Min	Daily Total Hrs & Min
	Wednesday	A.M.		
		P.M.		
		Even		
	Thursday	A.M.		
		P.M.		
		Even		
	Friday	A.M.		
		P.M.		
		Even		
	Saturday	A.M.		
		P.M.		
		Even		
	Sunday	A.M.		
		P.M.		
		Even		
	Monday	A.M.		
		P.M.		
		Even		
	Tuesday	A.M.		
		P.M.		
		Even		

Weekly Total ______

Wage Determination (Complete monthly unless based on uniform pay period.)

______ Hrs & Min × $______ = $______
(Regular Rate)

______ Hrs & Min × $______ = $______
(Overtime Rate)

Monthly Total $______

Remarks: I state the above is a true and accurate statement of hours and rates of employment.

______
Employee

______
Supervisor

(See Also: BUSINESS; CONTRACT; INSURANCE; MONEY; SALARY; TIME; VOUCHER; WORK)

PERMANENT RECORDS

sample permanent records...

Elementary School Record

NAME USED ______________________________ (Last / First / Middle) Sex [ ]

PHONE NO. ______________ (Make Pencil Entry)

LEGAL NAME ______________________________ (Last / First / Middle)

______________ Date of Admittance Withdrawal Date ______________

Date of Birth ______________________________ (Month / Day / Year / City & State or Country)

______________ Citizenship Transferred To ______________

BIRTH CERTIFICATE [ ] OTHER (Please Specify)

Circle Relationship		
Step Foster	FATHER	Last First Middle
Step Foster	MOTHER	Last First Middle
	GUARDIAN	Last First Middle

ADDRESS RECORD (List Changes in Consecutive Order)

1. ______________________________
2. ______________________________
3. ______________________________
4. ______________________________

OTHER RECORDS

Type	Location

Additional Data

____

School and Year	Grade	Names of Teacher	ATTENDANCE: Days School in Season	Days Enrolled	Days Absent	Days Tardy	SCHOLARSHIP: Arithmetic	Art	Language	Listening	Penmanship	Reading	Speaking	Spelling	Writing	Music	Physical Ed.	Science	Social Studies					
19___ 19___																								
19___ 19___																								
19___ 19___																								

19___ 19___

19___ 19___

19___ 19___

19___ 19___

19___ 19___

19___ 19___

RECORDS VIEWED BY			
NAME	DATE	RECORDS SEEN	REASON

RECORDS SENT TO			
NAME	DATE	RECORDS SENT	REASON

ANNUAL INSPECTION		
NAME	DATE	POSITION

Sex

NAME USED ______ Last First Middle

LEGAL NAME ______ Last First Middle

DATE OF BIRTH ______ Month Day Year City & State or Country

PHONE NO. ______

Date of Admittance ______

Withdrawal Date: ______

Transferred To: ______

Date Reentered: ______

Graduated ______ Date

Additional Data

Circle Relationship				
Step Foster	FATHER			
		Last	First	Middle
Step Foster	MOTHER			
		Last	First	Middle
	GUARDIAN			
		Last	First	Middle

ADDRESS RECORD (List Changes in Consecutive Order)

1. ______
2. ______
3. ______
4. ______

7 Date ______ 8 ______ 9 ______ 10

School ______

Counselor ______

11

12

request for permanent record transfer...

School ________________________________

Address ________________________________

____

TO: ________________________________
New School

____
Address

____

Dear ________________________________:

Re: ________________________________ Date of Birth ______________

Address ________________________________

____

Please forward all mandated records for the above-named student who has enrolled in the ________ grade of the Rock Township Public Schools.

In addition, we would appreciate receiving copies of all permitted records as per parent release below.

Thank you for your prompt attention to this matter.

____
Principal/Guidance Counselor

Please underline appropriate response:

I (do) (do not) authorize the release of all permitted records of the above-named student to the Rock Township Public Schools.

________________ ________________________________
Relationship Signature of Parent/Guardian or Adult Pupil

____
Address

________________ ________________________________
Date

(See Also: ENROLLMENT; GRADES; PROGRESS REPORT; RECORDS; REPORTS; STUDENT RECORDS)

PERMISSION SLIPS

excursion permission from other teachers...

EXCURSION PERMISSION FROM TEACHERS

Student's Name ______________________ Grade ______ Date ____________

Date(s) of Excursion ______________________ Time of Excursion–Depart ________

Return ________

Place of Excursion ____

Teacher in Charge ____________________ Signature ____________________

Periods to be missed: (circle)

	Subject	Teacher's Signature*	Comment or Disapproval
1			
2			
3			
4			
5			
6			

*Teacher's signature indicates approval to go on trip with the understanding that work missed will be made up. No signature indicates that the student is not permitted to go.

THIS FORM IS TO BE RETURNED TO THE TEACHER IN CHARGE THREE (3) DAYS PRIOR TO THE EXCURSION/TRIP.

extended participation permission for the school year...

My (son) (daughter) ____________________ H.R. ________ GR. ______ has my permission to participate in excursions planned by the school.

It is understood that my permission is to remain effective for the entire school year, September 19______–June 19______, provided I do not, in the meantime, notify you of any change.

Date: ________________ ____________________________

Parent's Signature

parental consent form (detailed)...

PARENT CONSENT FORM

1. I hereby give my permission for my child, my ward, ______________________
(child's name)

to go to ______________________________________.

2. I understand that my child or ward will leave on ______________________ and
(date) time)

will travel by __________________;
(type of transportation)

and is expected to return on ______________________________.
(date) (time)

3. (a) In granting this permission I hereby expressly waive any claim for liability against the Board of Education, including its employees and representatives, and release them from all liability in connection with this trip.

(b) Further, I assume full responsibility for any damage to persons or property caused by my child or ward. I further expressly agree that in the event the health of my child or ward, or disciplinary action may make it necessary, at the discretion of the sponsors, my child or ward may be forthwith returned home at my expense. I understand that I will be personally notified if it becomes necessary for my child or ward to be returned home and/or require health treatment.

(c) I further consent and will be responsible for any medical or dental treatment that may be advisable at the discretion of any physician or dentist.

(d) It is further warranted that if this CONSENT FORM is signed by one of two parents or guardians, it is with the authority of the other.

4. Student will be charged all costs, lodging and meals, insurance fees, entrance fees, and honorariums.
The sponsors and/or chaperones for this extracurricular field trip are:

______________________ ______________________
(Name) (Position) (Name) (Position)

______________________ ______________________
(Address) (Telephone) (Address) (Telephone)

______________________ ______________________
(Name) (Position) (Name) (Position)

______________________ ______________________
(Address) (Telephone) (Address) (Telephone)

5. ______________________ ______________________
(Signature of Parent or Guardian) (Date of Signature)

______________________ ______________________
(Telephone) (Address) (City)

permission form for a specific activity . . .

My son/daughter, ______________________________, has permission to participate in the following excursion function:

Purpose: ______________________________

____

____

Place: ______________________________

Date/dates: ______________ to ______________

Time:
Leaving ______________________________
Returning ______________________________

Teacher(s) in charge: ______________________ Phone __________

In case of an accident, please call:

______________________________ Phone __________
Name of Parent

______________________________ Phone __________
(neighbor, relative, employer)

______________________________ Phone __________
Name of Doctor

Other comments: (by parents or teachers)

1. Permit to stay beyond required period. Include name of authorized adult, address, relationship, telephone number, and inclusive period.

____

____

2. Extreme health problem, if any.

____

3. Others.

____

____

______________ ______________________________
Date Signature of Father or Guardian

______________ ______________________________
Date Signature of Mother or Guardian

permission for participation in extracurricular activities...

1. School: ______________________ Location: ______________________

____

____

2. I authorize my dependent child ______________________ to participate in

the following extracurricular school activity: ______________________

____

____

and to perform such travel associated with this activity.

____

3. Personal funds, in the amount of $__________, are provided to cover costs of:

____

____

4. Check One:

☐ There are no special requirements (medical, health, dietary, other) that would affect my child's full participation in the planned activity.

☐ My child requires special consideration for the following requirements:

____

____

____

☐ I hereby consent to and authorize any medical doctor or dentist to treat said student for any injury or illness, including in said treatment any surgical operation.

____

5. Authorization:

______________________ ______________________________

Date Parent/Guardian Signature

(See Also: BUS, CLUBS; FIELD TRIPS; SPORTS; TRAVEL; TRIPS; WORKING PAPERS)

PHILOSOPHY

of an individual school...

Rock Township High School is organized for the purpose of educating young people for a satisfying and productive life. The challenge of the school is to recognize each student as an individual and to help the student develop a feeling of self worth. Education should stimulate the student to develop those attitudes, skills, ideals, and appreciations which help him/her to become a useful and knowledgeable citizen. The school affirms high moral and ethical standards.

As part of a total community, the school should seek to cooperate with the community, recognizing that this relationship contributes to the development of its youth. The school encourages parents to play a significant role in this cooperative effort.

Because the development of man and society is an ongoing process which cannot be separated from the past, and because the preservation of man's past achievements and failures can make it possible for man to enhance his present and future condition, it is necessary to preserve and transmit the heritage of mankind.

The past does not provide all the answers, however, and today's world is characterized by change. Because change is inevitable, because it can be beneficial, and because it necessitates major adjustments for society, it is essential to provide our students with the learning tools with which to meet successfully the challenge of change.

As students respond to the educational experience provided for them, it is the expectation that they will recognize that school is a challenge, a privilege, a responsibility, a right, and an opportunity.

of a school system...

It is the educational philosophy of the Rock Township Public Schools to provide quality education that will give special emphasis to the basics and provide a comprehensive education to meet the demands of our complex society. It is important to recognize the sanctity of the home and hold in high regard the traditional family unit and to emphasize its importance as the basic unit of our American society. The educational program shall encourage loyalty to the United States and emphasize the teaching of our heritage and the responsibilities of good citizenship.

The general philosophy is to provide a broad and balanced curriculum, but the study of the basics of reading, writing and arithmetic shall be presented as worthwhile academic pursuits essential for communication and development of functional individuals in our society. Profanity, immorality, illegal use of drugs and alcohol and other such practices shall be represented as unacceptable modes of behavior.

It is the responsibility of the Rock Township Public School System to respect the rights of all individuals and to provide for every student regardless of race, creed or sex, the opportunity of a successful learning experience by giving the students the highest quality of professional instruction, the best materials and the greatest motivation we can provide.

(See Also: BOARD OF EDUCATION; EDUCATION; and all those topics that generally require a philosophy such as ACADEMIC FREEDOM, etc.)

POLICE

memo concerning police investigations...

TO: Assistant Superintendents, District Superintendents, Principals
FROM: Deputy Superintendent
RE: Release of Information of Incidents Under Investigation by the Police

Acting upon the advisement of the Attorney General, we ask that you refrain from releasing information to the news media about student(s) involved in incidents where such incidents are being investigated by the police.

Making statements or releasing information on such incidents may (1) hamper police investigation and/or prejudice a case and (2) could violate the federal law requirement that schools protect the confidentiality of the student's school records.

Your full cooperation in this regard is appreciated.

policy on police at school functions...

1. At least two police officers or security guards are to be hired for Rock Township High School evening activities. All officers and guards should report to the head advisor for information and direction.
2. Duties of officer outdoors:
    a. Patrol parking lot area.
    b. Direct traffic after activity.
    c. Remove from premises persons under the influence of liquor and/or other intoxicants.
    d. Remove loiterers after the doors of the activity are closed.
    e. Patrol area near all entrances to activity.
3. Duties of officers indoors:
    a. Help chaperones supervise the entrances. Do not admit any intoxicated people.
    b. Patrol areas of activity to help keep control.
    c. Remove from premises unruly persons.
    d. Patrol the bathrooms at least once every half hour.
    e. Remove loiterers in area after activity has ended.

4. Officers are to remain a half hour after the activity has ended.
5. Do other things as the advisor or chaperone of event may request as matters arise.
6. In the event there is only one security personnel, ask the Police Department to have one of their officers on duty patrol the campus as often as possible.
7. Officers are to check in with the advisor of the activity before and at the end of the activity.

(See Also: ACCIDENT; BOMB THREATS; BUILDING; DANCES; DEMONSTRATIONS; DRUGS; EMERGENCY; VANDALISM)

PRINCIPAL

detailed job description and duties of...

Duties Summary:

The principal operates under the general administrative directions of the District Superintendent, District Schools, Department of Education, and is responsible for the administration, management, and operations of his school, grades 10–12. He provides directions for the certified as well as the classified staff. He is responsible for evaluating and assisting personnel in the performance of their jobs. He organizes the instructional and co-curricula program to maximize learning opportunities that will help the students grow individually and as participating members of their school and community.

Duties and Responsibilities

Administers the overall personnel program of the school including administrative, teaching, clerical, custodial, cafeteria and other support personnel.

1. Provides the overall direction and leadership for the school.
2. Organizes the staff to maximize instructional as well as co-curricula opportunities.
3. Provides general leadership and assists in the orientation, evaluation and assessment of all personnel.
4. Assumes general responsibilities over faculty and curriculum meetings.
5. Helps in interviewing teachers and makes first decisions in the selection and assignments of teachers.
6. Assumes responsibility for any grievance and all disciplinary actions taken against teachers or other staff members.
7. Assumes responsibility of meeting with governance committee.
8. Assumes responsibility of overall concerns arising out of teachers, departmental, teacher-student and teacher-parent interactions.
9. Answers to all student, parental and public inquiry regarding the effectiveness or lack of effectiveness of all school personnel.
10. Provides for overall leadership in matters pertaining to accreditation.

Provides direction to pupil program:

1. Assesses students' needs in instructional as well as co-curricular areas so they may be incorporated in scheduling and in the organization of the school day.
2. Keeps in communication with student government leaders, class leaders, leaders in athletics, band, and those representing many diversified groups within the school.
3. Provides for the overall directions in guidance and counseling service extended students.
4. Confers with students arising out of hundreds of disciplinary and other referrals by teachers.
5. Provides for the health and safety of pupils.
6. Involves students in curriculum development in registration.

7. Provides plan for the registration of pupils.
8. Maintains effective communications with agencies that provide for extended services to students, which include OEO, LEAA, Department of Continuing Education, Police Department, Department of Social Services, Job Corps, Community Colleges, Universities and with other private and public businesses and governmental agencies that affect students in various ways.
9. Provides overall control over the total athletic program (8 separate sports) and attends as many athletic events as possible.
10. Attends satellite PTA meetings and other special meetings in seven (7) areas within the District.
11. Responds to numerous calls by teachers to aid in responding to campus disruptions.
12. Tends to matters dealing with District Exceptions.
13. Processes reports on students' accidents, transports students to hospital, writers recommendations for students entering college, etc.
14. Involves students in the accreditation process.

Provides leadership and assists teachers in developing the instructional program and in bringing about curricula changes:

1. Provides technical and other assistance necessary to help teachers implement curricular projects.
2. Conducts monthly curriculum meetings.
3. Encourages internal evaluation to determine effectiveness of program or teacher effectiveness.
4. Studies new trends and keeps up with current materials on curricular developments.

Administers to matters dealing with the general administration and the business affairs of the school.

1. Sets overall direction in all budgetary matters but delegates operational procedures to vice principal.
2. Provides overall direction in capital improvement programs.
3. Oversees the school facilities and maintenance program including matters pertaining to the health and safety of students.
4. Oversees matters pertaining to bus transportation.
5. Reviews all correspondence, surveys and questionnaires, and responds to them.
6. Responsible for a sound accounting system.
7. Signs leaves, suspensions, other routine reports and memoranda.
8. Oversees matters pertaining to all school inventories.
9. Meets with district personnel.
10. Attends principals' meetings and other meetings called by the District Superintendent.
11. Signs for all requests for the use of school facilities.
12. Writes letters of recommendation and other correspondence.
13. Banks monies on a rotation basis.

Administers the community and public relations program:

1. Assumes responsibility of communicating with all agencies connected with the school.
2. Meets with satellite PTA groups as well as any individual or groups of parents interested in the school.
3. Works with all booster clubs, alumni, and other groups connected with the school.
4. Participates in the articulation programs with the Community College and other colleges.
5. Speaks to business and other groups on such topics as school programs and innovations.
6. Cooperates and appears on radio stations or interviews.
7. Attends community functions on behalf of the school.
8. Acts as host to all visitors.

Supervision Received and Exercised

Receives general directions and supervision from the District Superintendent. However, the principal may seek advice or consult with district personnel at all times. The primary responsibility of operating the school is clearly with the principal.

(See Also: ASSIGNMENTS; DUTIES; INTERNSHIP; VICE-PRINCIPAL; and all items in which the principal of a school is involved)

PROFESSIONAL IMPROVEMENT PLAN

sample form (1)...

ANNUAL WRITTEN PERFORMANCE REPORT

TEACHER ____________ SCHOOL ____________ SUBJECT ____________ DATE ____________

1. STRENGTHS

2. NEEDS IMPROVEMENT

3. INDIVIDUAL PROFESSIONAL IMPROVEMENT PLAN
   (EVALUATION OF PAST CYCLE)

4. INDIVIDUAL PROFESSIONAL IMPROVEMENT PLAN
   (OBJECTIVES FOR NEW CYCLE)

   a. OBJECTIVES

   b. PROCEDURES

   c. RESOURCES

   d. EVALUATION

5. PUPIL PROGRESS

6. PROFESSIONAL ACTIVITIES (IN-SERVICE, CURRICULUM COMMITTEES, POSITIONS IN PROFESSIONAL ASSOCIATIONS, ETC., DURING LAST CYCLE)

I have read and conferred with ____________________ on the Annual Written Performance Report and acknowledge receipt of a copy.

Teacher's Signature ____________________ Evaluator's Signature ____________________

NOTE: Performance data that have not been included in this report may be entered into the record by the teacher within ten (10) working days after the signing of this report.

sample form (2)...

PROFESSIONAL GROWTH PLAN

This plan includes all you want to do as an individual in terms of professional growth. It must include systematic and building-level participation along with your individual growth objectives.

TASK/NEED	OBJECTIVE	ACTIVITY	HOURS OF PARTICIPATION	EVALUATION
(Identify the task or need upon which you are basing objectives)	(Write in behavioral terms)	(What and When)		(How will you evaluate the completion of this objective in recordable form to be given to your supervisor?)

(See Also: EVALUATION; GOALS; OBJECTIVES; OBSERVATIONS; REPORTS**)**

PROGRESS REPORT

in all subjects...

GRADE ______

In my opinion, ______________________ has been doing approximately as well as he/she is able to do and has been showing a proper attitude in his/her work for the week ending ____________________.

Period	Subject	Teacher's Signature	REMARKS: If teacher cannot conscientiously sign the above statement, please state the reason
1.	____________________	______________	______________________
2.	____________________	______________	______________________
3.	____________________	______________	______________________
4.	____________________	______________	______________________
5.	____________________	______________	______________________
6.	____________________	______________	______________________
7.	____________________	______________	______________________

Student should present these forms with name, date, and subject properly filled and ready for the teacher's signature each FRIDAY.

I have examined the above form the week ending Friday ____________________

______________________________.

Parent's Signature

I understand the student is fully responsible for:

1. Presenting these forms to the teachers Fridays during the class period.
2. Bringing these forms Friday nights to me, properly filled out.
3. Returning these forms to the Guidance Office Monday Morning.

in specific subjects...

Date: ____________________

Dear Parents,

The following is a summary of your child's progress for the ________ marking period, which ends on ____________________. Please sign this report below and return to the cluster.

	ENGLISH	MATH	SCIENCE	SOC. STUD.
YOUR CHILD'S PERFORMANCE:				
Is satisfactory	☐	☐	☐	☐
Needs improvement	☐	☐	☐	☐
YOUR CHILD NEEDS TO IMPROVE IN THE AREAS CHECKED BELOW:				
Class preparation	___	___	___	___
Completing homework	___	___	___	___
Quality of homework	___	___	___	___
More effort on classwork	___	___	___	___
Study more for quizzes and tests	___	___	___	___
Make-up work missed	___	___	___	___

OTHER COMMENTS:

ENGLISH: ____

____

MATH: ____

____

SCIENCE: ____

____

SOC. STUDIES: ____

____

☐ Please call the Guidance Office to arrange a conference.

____
(Parent's Signature)

(See Also: ACHIEVEMENT; CHILD STUDY TEAM; GRADES; PERMANENT RECORDS; RECORDS; REPORT CARDS; REPORTS; RESOURCE TEAM; STUDENT RECORDS; UNDERACHIEVERS)

PROMOTION

percentage of promotion form...

SCHOOL: ______________________ DATE: ______________

FOR THE SCHOOL YEAR 19____–19____:

GRADE/YEAR	TOTAL ENROLLED	TOTAL PASSED	TOTAL FAILED	% OF PROMOTION

FOR THE SCHOOL:

TOTAL ENROLLED	TOTAL PASSED	TOTAL FAILED	% OF PROMOTION

NOTE: Percentage of Promotion is determined by dividing the total number enrolled into the total number passed. For example: Total enrolled = 1000; Total Passed = 978; 978/1000 = .978 or 97.8% of Promotion.

summary of promotion sheet...

SUMMARY OF PROMOTIONS

FOR SESSION 19 –19

Summarize for the school in one report

SCHOOL ______________________ PRINCIPAL ______________________

DATE ______________________

TEACHER	TOTAL NO. PUPILS IN ROOM	NO. PROMOTED TO WHICH GRADE	NO. RETAINED TO WHICH GRADE

(See Also: ACHIEVEMENT; FAILURE; GRADES; PERMANENT RECORDS; REPORT CARDS; RETENTION; STUDENT RECORDS**)**

diagnostic services referral form...

DIAGNOSTIC SERVICES REFERRAL*

1. All referrals are to be submitted to the director of special education.
2. All referrals are to be approved by the building principal as recommended by the resource teams.
3. Please attach copies of Request for Resource Team Meeting form and Resource Team Meeting Minutes with this referral.

Name of Student ______________________ Building ______________

Date of Birth ______________________ Grade/Classroom ______________

Reason for further evaluation: ______________________________

____

____

____

Has the evaluation consent form been signed by the student's parents?__________

Check type of diagnostic evaluation requested:

____ Psychological
____ Vision

____ Social History
____ Hearing

____ Physical Therapy
____ Medical

____ Occupational Therapy
____ Complete diagnostic team evaluation (psychological, speech, language, academic, social, medically related consultation, etc.)

____ Other (please specify): ______________________________

____

____
Principal's Signature

*Place one copy in special services file and give one copy to director of special education.

record of special services form...

***RECORD OF SPECIAL SERVICES AND LOCATION OF FILES**

Name ______________________ Date of Birth ______________________

The intent of this record is to provide a sequential description of a student's special services and the location of files. Entries should be made whenever a child is placed in a special education program.

Service Area	Date Initialed	Date Terminated	Personnel	Location of File

*Place this form in the student's cumulative file.

(See Also: BEHAVIOR; CHILD STUDY TEAM; DOCTORS; DRUGS; HEALTH; MEDICATION; REFERRAL; SICK LEAVE)

P.T.A.

sample P.T.A. goals...

P.T.A. Goals for the current school year shall be:

1. Increase P.T.A. membership and expand the base of participation in P.T.A. activities.
2. Provide forums for the exchange and discussion of ideas on issues and topics of current interest.
3. Improve communications between faculty, parents, and students.
4. Enhance the image of our school throughout the community.
5. Provide support for the leadership at our school and throughout the district.
6. Establish incentives for excellence in performance by both faculty and students.

"volunteers needed" sheet...

P.T.A. VOLUNTEERS NEEDED

The P.T.A. of Rock Township High School once again needs the support of all parents. If you would like to help in any of the areas listed below, please indicate your choice and interests and return this form to your child's homeroom teacher. Please consider participating in some way. The P.T.A. needs your help!

1. DANCE CHAPERONES (Parents to chaperone one or more school dances) (   )
2. LIBRARY (One hour per week: 2:15-3:05 p.m.) (   )
3. PUBLICITY (Newspaper articles, posters, etc.) (   )
4. NURSE'S OFFICE (Two hours per week typing and/or clerical) (   )
5. TUTORING (As a helper or aide to a Department Head) (   )
   A. Math (   ) B. Reading (   )
6. REFRESHMENTS (Baking for school functions) (   )
7. P.T.A. NEWSLETTER (To help with typing, etc.) (   )
8. TELEPHONING (Occasional phoning if necessary) (   )
9. PEP CLUB (To help promote school spirit) (   )
10. OTHER (All time, talents and ideas welcome) (   )

NAME: ______________________________

TEL. #: ______________________________

GRADE OF CHILD IN SCHOOL: ______________________________

COMMENTS: ______________________________

____

(See Also: AIDES; BULLETIN; CHAPERONE; INFORMATION; NEWSLETTER; NEWS RELEASES; VOLUNTEERS**)**

PUBLIC ADDRESS SYSTEM

form requesting use of...

NAME: ____________________ DATE: ____________

I hereby request the use of the school's public address system on

(Date of Intended Use): ____________________

at (Specify Time): ____________________

Content of Message (Be specific; attach a separate sheet if necessary):

You will be notified as to the disposition of your request. You are reminded that overuse of the public address system leads to student and staff apathy concerning messages read over it. Therefore, only those messages that cannot be effectively delivered any other way will be broadcast.

request for portable public address system form...

Location Desired: Auditorium ____________________

Multi-Purpose ____________________

Swimming Pool Area ____________________

Other (Specify) ____________________

Dates Desired: ____________________

Month Day Day of Week

____

Month Day Day of Week

Times Desired: ____________________

____

____

Purpose of Program: ____________________

____

____

____

Equipment Desired: ____________________

____

____

____

DO NOT WRITE IN THIS SPACE ____________________

____

____

____

Notice: If you want a special set-up, please submit a sketch of location desired.

Approved: ____________________

Advisor

Date: ____________________

____________________ ____________________

PAS (Teacher) Coordinator PAS (Student) Coordinator

(See Also: ASSEMBLIES; BACK-TO-SCHOOL NIGHT; BULLETIN; REQUISITIONS, REPAIRS, AND REPLACEMENTS)

PURCHASING

policy on...

It is the policy of the board to insure that each item purchased represents the best possible value to the district. In order to do so, the purchasing procedures shall provide equal opportunity to each responsible vendor to furnish supplies and equipment and to keep the administration, board, and public informed on business matters. Records shall be kept in sufficient detail to show that this was done.

The budget adopted by the board represents the annual spending plan for the district. The purchasing agent designated by the board is authorized to issue purchase orders upon the receipt of a requisition, properly approved per district regulations, and without prior approval of the board; provided each purchase order is in accordance with the budget. Each building principal shall be given the opportunity to specify purchases for his school within his budgeted amount and in accordance with procedures of the district.

In the case of supply items involving an expenditure of less than $1000, the purchasing agent should request quotations from prospective suppliers when a significant savings to the district could result, and whenever feasible shall place an order to purchase with the lowest quotation. He shall maintain such quotations on file for a minimum of three years.

purchase order form...

INSTRUCTIONS, TERMS, AND CONDITIONS

1. Render separate invoices for each and every shipment.
2. Mail invoices to school system's Purchasing Department.
3. State or other taxes from which schools are exempt will not be shown on your invoice.
4. Packing lists must accompany all shipments and show purchase order number and contents.
5. Our count will be accepted as final and conclusive on all shipments not accompanied by packing ticket.
6. Show our purchase order number on packing and delivery tickets, on packages and invoices, and correspondence.
7. We reserve the right to reject any shipments not in accordance with our order.

PURCHASING DEPARTMENT

PURCHASE ORDER

THIS PURCHASE ORDER NUMBER MUST APPEAR ON ALL INVOICES, PACKAGES AND CORRESPONDENCE.

No. ______

TO:

FOR DEL'Y ______ DATE ______

SCHOOL QUOTE NO. ______ SHIP TO: ______

VENDORS QUOTATION NO. ______ F.O.B. ______

TERMS ______

ITEM	QUANTITY	UNIT	DESCRIPTION	UNIT PRICE	TOTAL PRICE	ACCOUNTABILITY
				TOTAL		

POSTED ______

______

REC'D BY ______

______

______ MANAGER, PURCHASING & MATERIALS

Ordered by:
Building Name ____________ No. ______

Orginator ____________

Supervisor ____________

Director Approval ____________

Transfer ____________

Required Delivered Date ______ ______ ______
Day Month Year

PRQ ______ ______ ______ ______ ______ ______
Unit No.
Purchase Order No. ____________

Date: ______ ______ ______
Day Month Year

Vendor ____________ No. ______

ITEM NO.	QNTY	UNIT/ ISSUE	DESCRIPTION *Include following: Item Name, Size, Color, Model, Type, Brand, Supply Source, Catalog No., Descriptive Information	FUND/SCH	TYPE	FUNCTION	OBJECT	AREA	ESTIMATED UNIT COST	ESTIMATED TOTAL COST
1										
2										
3										
4										
5										
6										
7										
8										
9										
10										
									PRQ Total	

Packed By ____________ Date ______

Delivered By ____________ Date ______

Received By ____________ Date ______
(sign full name)

(See Also: BIDS; BUDGET; BUSINESS; EQUIPMENT; REQUISITIONS, REPAIRS, AND REPLACEMENTS; VENDORS)

QUALIFICATIONS

teacher qualification record...

I Personal

Name ______________________*(______________________) ______________ ______________
Last First Middle

Birthdate: Year ________ Month __________ Day ________ Marital Status ______________________

Local Address**______________________________Telephone No.**__________

Home Address ______________________________Telephone No. __________

In emergency notify ______________ Address ______________ Tel. No. ________

Social Security No. ______________

II Education

Type of School	Name and Location of School	Years Attended	Yr. Grad.	Course	HOURS				Degree
					Under		Grad.		
					S.	Q.	S.	Q.	
Elementary		19 – 19							
Secondary		19 – 19							
College or U.		19 – 19							
College or U.		19 – 19							
College or U.		19 – 19							
Graduate		19 – 19							
Summer School or Workshops		19 – 19							
		19 – 19							
		19 – 19							
		19 – 19							
		19 – 19							
		19 – 19							

(Form continued)

teacher qualification record form (cont'd)

		HOURS					HOURS			
		Under		Grad.			Under		Grad.	
		S.	Q.	S.	Q.		S.	Q.	S.	Q.
Academic Training	Major ________					Major ________				
	Minor ________					Minor ________				
	Education ________									

Extracurricular ________________________________

____

III Certificate

Name of Certificate ________________________ No. ________

Date Issued ________________ Date of Expiration ________________
Year Month Day Year Month Day

Valid for grades or subject fields ________ ________ ________

* Married women are to record their maiden surname in parentheses.
**Use pencil.

IV Teaching Record

YEAR	SCHOOL	ASSIGNMENT

(See Also: APPLICATION; BOARD OF EDUCATION; CERTIFICATION; ELECTIVES; GRADUATION; JOBS; NATIONAL HONOR SOCIETY; PRINCIPAL; PROMOTION; VICE-PRINCIPAL; WORKING PAPERS**)**

QUESTIONS

approach to topic questionnaire...

NOTE: Since administrators must often conduct workshops, give speeches, and prepare all sorts of written materials, the following questionnaire is invaluable. Whatever the topic, applying these questions will allow you to formulate a new approach to even the oldest topics.

1. How was it in the past?
   How is it now?
   How may it be in the future?
2. How does it appear?
   What is it really like?
   Why is there a difference?
3. What does society think?
   What does a smaller group think?
   What do I think?
4. What is one type?
   What is another type?
   What is a third type?
5. What is its most obvious characteristic?
   What is its least obvious characteristic?
   Why is the most (or least) obvious characteristic so significant?
6. What is its best quality?
   What is its worst quality?
   What conclusion can be drawn?
7. When did it happen?
   Why then?
   Could it happen again?
8. How can it be done?
   Steps A, B, C.
   What is the result?
9. My first impression.
   My later view.
   My present evaluation.
10. A notable mistake.
    Efforts to adjust, correct.
    The outcome.
11. One way to get there.
    An alternate way.
    Why one is better.
12. The theoretical approach.
    The practical approach.
    The difference between them.
13. How is A like (unlike) B?
    Why is A like (unlike) B?
    So what?

(See Also: **ADVISORS AND ADVISORY COMMITTEES; BULLETIN; INFORMATION; NEWSLETTER; NEWS RELEASES)**

RECOMMENDATION

letter of, for an administrator...

Dear ,

I am in possession of your recent letter requesting a recommendation for Mr. Harold Wainsford whom you are considering for the post of principal in your district.

I take the greatest personal and professional pleasure in recommending Mr. Wainsford to you without qualification. For seven years he has served as vice-principal of our school, and I have found him to be a highly responsible and competent individual who has performed above and beyond the call of his duties. He accepts responsibility squarely and always goes that "extra inch" with the good of the students and the school in mind. If our school enjoys a reputation for academic excellence, an enthusiastic and cooperative faculty, and a student body filled with positive spirit, it would only be stating the truth that it is due, in large part, to the efforts of this man.

I sincerely believe that Mr. Wainsford would make an invaluable contribution to your school system, and I recommend him to your serious consideration. My only regret will be the effort I will have to put in trying to find someone to fill his shoes. It will not be an easy task.

Sincerely,

letter of, for a teacher...

Dear ,

I take great pleasure in responding to your request for a recommendation for Mr. Thomas Giger, who has applied for a teaching position in your district.

Mr. Giger has taught in my school for the past seven years. During that time, his record has been impeccable, his knowledge and expertise unquestioned, and his capabilities as a teacher and leader of youth have been an inspiration to us all. He is respected by his colleagues (teachers and administrators alike) and literally loved by his students. The school system that employs Mr. Giger will benefit beyond question.

While I deeply regret the loss of Mr. Giger from our school, I can only envy the administration and staff of the school to which he will go. Without qualification, I recommend him to your attention.

Sincerely,

(See Also: APPLICATION; BOARD OF EDUCATION; CHANGE; ELECTIVES; EVALUATION; HONOR ROLL; INTERVIEW; TRANSFER)

RECORDS

policy statement on public records...

The Board recognizes that as a public body of this State, certain of its records are open for public inspection. This shall include all records which are required by law, have been received by law, or have been received by an authority in connection with the transaction of public business; but shall not include pupil records or personnel records, nor may student or staff rosters be released.

Any person having an interest in the records of this Board and wishing to review any part thereof, except as noted above, shall submit a written request to the Secretary stating the specific records he or she wishes to review.

record of inspection form...

DATE: ____________________

*RECORD OF INSPECTION

Name of Student: ____________________ Date of Birth: ____________________

In accordance with Public Law 94-142, the following people have access to the information contained in this record without the written consent of this student's parents or legal guardian.

1. The student's parents or legal guardian until student is 18 years of age at which time the student has access to records.
2. Personnel from the public school involved in the educational programming of the student (that is, administrators, teachers, special services staff, etc.).
3. Personnel from the Department of Public Instruction.

Record Examined By	Date	Purpose

*Attach this form inside of student special services folder.

status report record...

Date ____________________

Signature ________________

A. CURRENT PROJECTS

1.
2.
3.
4.

B. COMPLETED PROJECTS

1.
2.
3.
4.

C. PLANNED PROJECTS

1.
2.
3.
4.
5.

D. PROBLEMS AND REQUESTS

1.
2.
3.
4.

(See Also: ENROLLMENT; GRADES; PERMANENT RECORDS; PROGRESS REPORT; RECORDS; REPORT CARDS; REPORTS; STUDENT RECORDS**)**

REDUCTION IN FORCE

policy statement on...

It shall be the policy of the board that the primary consideration for retention or non-renewal of staff due to inadequate enrollment or economic factors shall be the maintenance of a sound and balanced educational program that is consistent with the functions and responsibilities of the school district. Any reduction in staff will require consideration of the various needs of the district, such as, but not limited to, the best staff possible as determined by overall evaluation of teaching performance, academic preparation, professional growth, the staffing of specialized curriculum areas, and the staffing of extracurricular assignments. Seniority shall also be a consideration and will begin with the first reporting date of the most recent continuous service to this district, and not the date of the first contract. Board-approved leave, military service and other approved interruptions in service shall not reduce seniority achieved. Those teachers who have lost their position in the district due to a reduction in force are to be given first consideration for a period of up to 18 months from the issuance of their non-renewal notice for any teaching position available in the district for which they are qualified.

(See Also: **BOARD OF EDUCATION; BUDGET; CONTRACT; ENROLLMENT; NEGOTIATIONS; TRANSFER)**

REFERRAL

policy on student referral...

OFFICE REFERRALS

It is generally agreed that teachers should be responsible for discipline in their own classrooms. This is the case at North High School. Under certain conditions it may be necessary for the teacher to refer a student to the office. Examples of this would be:

1. When the teacher has lost control and cannot regain it without help.
2. When the disturbance, such as a mental disturbance, stems from a cause that requires special attention.
3. When the teacher feels that a student must be removed temporarily from the class. In this case he may prefer to deal with the case himself at a later time and will indicate this by note or telephone call to the office. In any case where a student is sent to the office, a message should follow immediately.
4. When a teacher has exhausted his resources and feels that a case must be turned over to the administration. In this event the teacher should feel that decisions as to punishment also be referred. The principal or his assistant will not assign

punishment in terms of the student's total school record and should not be expected to avenge the teacher's injured feelings. It is reasonable to expect that a recommendation from the teacher be considered, but with the referral of the problem should go the referral of the judgment. Otherwise, the principal's role would be merely that of executioner.

5. If a student is asked to leave class, the assistant principal's office will be notified immediately by a discipline referral and the student will be sent to the office at once.
6. The principal and/or his assistant principal will be available at any time to discuss any problem with you. We are most eager to help. If you see difficulties on the way, tell us about them. We may be able to help keep them from materializing.

LENGTH OF REFERRAL

Truancy: (An unexcused absence before or after reporting to school)
3 days

Smoking: (Outside designated area or at undesignated time)
3 days

Fighting: 3 days

Severe Cases of Fighting: (With use of weapon or when student's presence may cause further disruption in school) Up to 10 days

Other Offenses or an Accumulation of Offenses: Up to 5 days
Up to 10 days extrme situations

If after three referrals, cooperation with school personnel is not obtained, legal action will be taken against the student through the court. A conference with the parent, student, Alternative School Counselor, and the Secondary Supervisor is mandatory after these referrals before the student can be readmitted to the regular school.

sample referral form...

HIGH SCHOOL
REFERRAL FORM

PART I (To be completed by teacher making referral)

To ______________________________ Date ______________________________

From ______________________________ Period __________ Subject ______________

Student ____ Class ______________
(Last Name) (First Name) Soph, Jr., Sr.

Statement of Problem

PART II (To be completed by recipient of the referral) Disposition (By Principal and/or Counselor)

(See Also: ASP (Alternate School Program); BEHAVIOR; CHILD STUDY TEAM; DISCIPLINE; PSYCHOLOGICAL SERVICES; RESOURCE TEAM)

REGISTRATION

duties of a registrar...

1. Keep records of all students presently and formerly enrolled.
2. Keep daily count of enrollment, total and by grade.
3. Register new students
   a. Those not qualified for any one of the three grades are special students, counted separately, programs and information to be recorded on pink forms
4. Process dropouts and transfer students
   a. Written request from parent or guardian
   b. Check-Out form to be signed by student's teachers, librarians, school nurse attendance and finance offices, principal's office, and counselors
5. Prepare and send transcripts for former students, graduating seniors, and transfers to school (private or parochial) within the state or outside the state.

6. Prepare tracer cards for students who have transferred to public schools within the state and send forms to schools from which notification of enrollment has been received.
7. Update all students' program cards and schedules, make changes in all offices which keep a file of students' programs, including dropouts and transfers.
8. Send information to Data Processing re: program changes of students and teachers.
9. Check grade cards received from Data Processing and send to teachers for grading.
10. Check graded cards before returning to Data Processing.
11. Check report cards for distribution to students in homerooms.
12. Prepare alphabetical file, by grade, of all report cards each quarter, for the active file drawers (for teachers' reference).
13. Prepare pre-registration information sheets for all students including: all courses, credits, grades, standardized tests' percentiles, group recommendations by English and social studies teachers, beginning with grade 9.
14. Calculate and record identification number for homogeneous grouping.
15. Prepare forms to be sent to English and Social Studies teachers for group recommendations.
16. Prepare "Mechanics of Recording Grades" for teachers.
17. Send "Personality Rating Sheets" to teachers to be completed for each senior; prepare composite copies to be included with each transcript.
18. Obtain estimated enrollment for next school year in each of the three grades.
    a. Check with feeder school counselor for incoming 10th graders.
19. Prepare registration information:
    a. Refer to Policies re: fees, courses, requirements, titles, prerequisites.
    b. Refer to School Code.
    c. Confer with principal re: teaching schedules and assignments.
    d. Confer with teacher re: supplies and materials which students will need to purchase for a particular course.
20. Screen all registrations for prerequisites and graduation requirements; tally enrollment by courses and grades.
21. Schedule students in classes (bin IBM cards which have been sent by Data Processing, course information and scheduling of classes by teachers and periods provided by registrar as soon as available).
22. Record final grades in permanent records (permanent record labels provided by Data Processing for regular school term, summer school reports files in Forms).
23. Send binned cards to Data Processing for preparation of students' program cards after checking on necessary changes due to final grades or summer school courses.
24. Arrange for distribution of program cards to students before the opening of the new school term.

sample registration form...

School Year: 19______ Grade: ________ School: ______________________________

Date of Registration: __________________ Date of Admittance: __________________

Legal Name: ____
Last First Middle

Legal Address: ____________________________________ Telephone: ______________

____
City State Zip

Date of Birth: ____
Month Day Year City State County

Evidence: Birth Certificate (________-__________) Other (________________)

Citizenship: __________-- ____________________________

(Circle relationship)

Father ____
Last First Middle
Step
Foster

Mother ____
Last First Middle
Step
Foster

Guardian ____
Last First Middle

Number of Brothers: Younger __________ Older __________
Number of Sisters: Younger __________ Older __________

Languages spoken at home: ____________________ ____________________
Primary Secondary

Has child attended another school in Township? Yes ______ No ______

If "yes," where? ____ Grade? ________

Has child attended another school outside of Township? Yes ______ No ______

If "yes," give name and location of school: ______________________________

____

Notes: ____

____

____

sample registration sheet...

CARD CODE S M SCHOOL CODE STUDENT NUMBER DATE ______

NAME HOME ROOM

LAST FIRST MI

SEX ETHNIC GROUP (I/A/H/B/W) PRIORITY LEVEL KEY 1 KEY 2

CURRENT GRADE SCHEDULING GRADE COUNSELOR NUMBER

BIRTHDATE (MM) (DD) (YY) HOME PHONE

COURSES SELECTED

CARD CODE S R

SCHOOL CODE FIRST SEMESTER

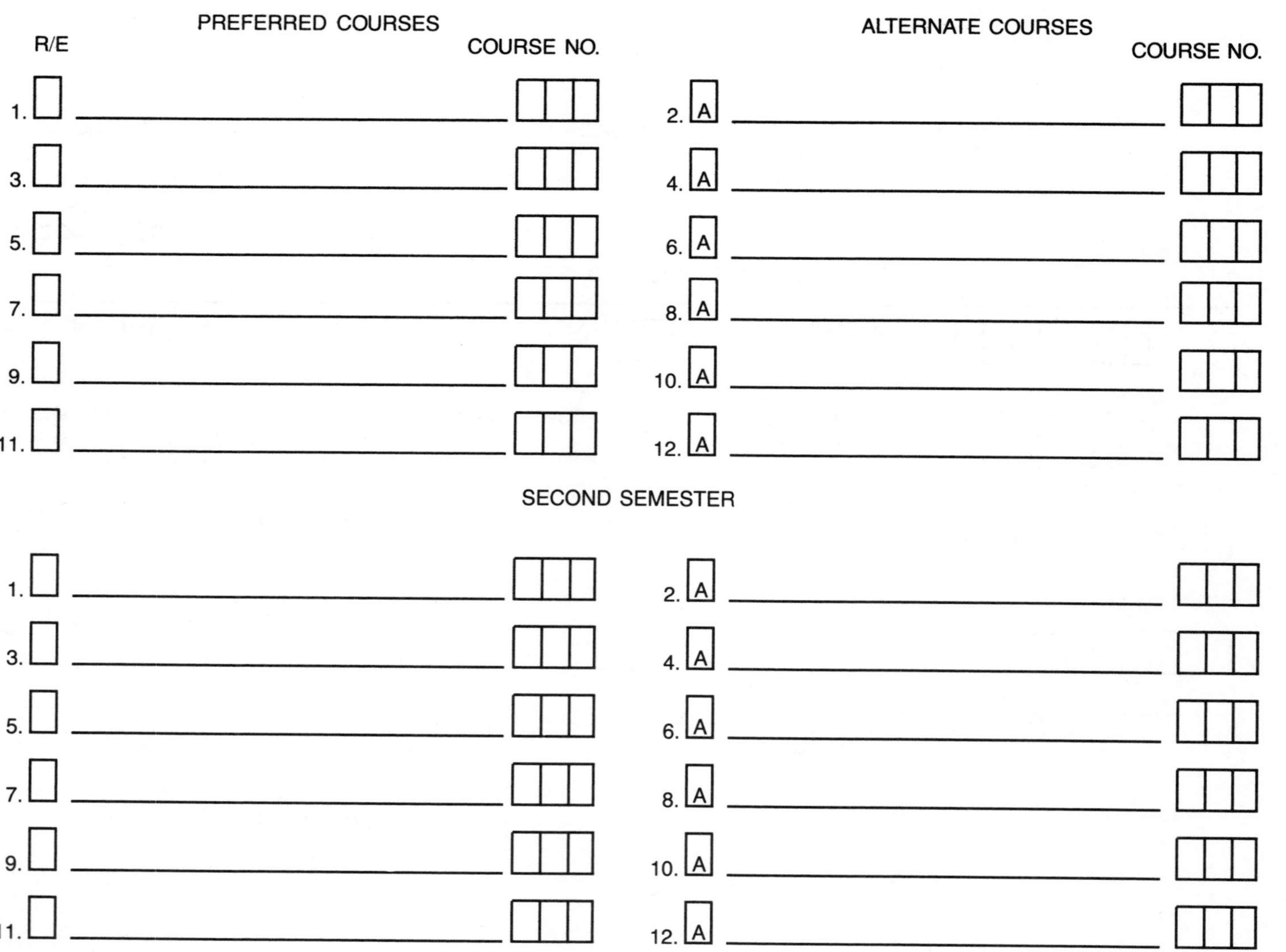

R/E	PREFERRED COURSES	COURSE NO.		ALTERNATE COURSES	COURSE NO.
1. ☐	________	☐☐☐	2. A	________	☐☐☐
3. ☐	________	☐☐☐	4. A	________	☐☐☐
5. ☐	________	☐☐☐	6. A	________	☐☐☐
7. ☐	________	☐☐☐	8. A	________	☐☐☐
9. ☐	________	☐☐☐	10. A	________	☐☐☐
11. ☐	________	☐☐☐	12. A	________	☐☐☐

SECOND SEMESTER

1. ☐	________	☐☐☐	2. A	________	☐☐☐
3. ☐	________	☐☐☐	4. A	________	☐☐☐
5. ☐	________	☐☐☐	6. A	________	☐☐☐
7. ☐	________	☐☐☐	8. A	________	☐☐☐
9. ☐	________	☐☐☐	10. A	________	☐☐☐
11. ☐	________	☐☐☐	12. A	________	☐☐☐

HOMEROOM INSTRUCTOR ______ LOCKER NUMBER ______ HOME PHONE ______

HEAD OF HOUSEHOLD ______

ZIP CODE

HOME ADDRESS ______ ______

BUS PHONE ______ EXT ______ NEIGHBOR PHONE ______ DOCTOR PHONE ______

ONLY CHANGES TO CORRECT CLERICAL OR COMPUTER ERRORS WILL BE MADE

STUDENT'S SIGNATURE ______ PARENT'S SIGNATURE ______

COUNSELOR'S SIGNATURE ______ DATE ______

(**See Also:** ATTENDANCE; CLASS; CONFIRMATION; ENROLLMENT; INFORMATION; PERMANENT RECORDS; STUDENT RECORDS; ZONES AND ZONING)

RELATIONSHIPS

policy and guidelines for...

STUDENT–TEACHER RELATIONSHIPS

In a student-teacher relationship, the teacher should make a study of the whole child, including his or her physical, social, intellectual, and emotional needs.

You will be a more effective teacher if your actions speak acceptance rather than mere tolerance. You don't have to accept the child's standards for yourself, but you should accept the child's standards as his or her own.

Your role is to teach *ALL* children, not merely those with clean shirts, quick minds, or good manners.

A good way for a teacher to win the loyalty of students is to show them he is truly concerned about them, individually and as groups. Demonstrate, for example, your interest in the athletic events, plays and dances. The important thing is not to *pretend* you are interested in these things. Actually get interested in them.

WHEN IT BECOMES NECESSARY TO REPRIMAND AN INDIVIDUAL, REMEMBER TO REPRIMAND IN PRIVATE, PRAISE IN PUBLIC.

PROFESSIONAL RELATIONSHIPS

In our professional relationship we should be:

1. Ever mindful of the requirements of our profession.
2. Operate by the Code of Ethics.
3. Belong to and participate in the activities of local, state, and national education groups.
4. Keep up an effective in-service program.

COMMUNITY RELATIONSHIPS

Each teacher should always remember that he or she is a member of the community and should participate in community activities.

1. Use cooperative school–community planning.
2. Utilize advertising media such as TV, radio, and newspaper.
3. Be a public relations agent to give information to the public about the functions and needs of the school.
4. Use resource specialists.

(See Also: ADULT EDUCATION; AMERICAN EDUCATION WEEK; BACK-TO-SCHOOL NIGHT; BILINGUAL EDUCATION; CLASS; DISCIPLINE; JOB DESCRIPTION; MEDIATION; NEGOTIATIONS)

RELIGION

exemption for religious belief form...

As parent(s) or legal guardian(s) of ____________________
I/we hereby affirm that a physical examination would conflict with the tenets or practices of the church or religious denomination of which the applicant is a member. We further request that said student be exempt from a physical examination due to my/our religious beliefs and convictions.

DATE ____________________ Signed ____________________

Address ____________________

____

As parent(s) or legal guardian(s) of ____________________
I/we hereby affirm that immunizations conflict with the tenets or practices of the church or religious denomination of which the applicant is a member. We further request that said student be exempt from immunizations due to my/our religious beliefs and convictions.

Date ____________________ Signed ____________________

Signed ____________________

Address ____________________

THIS IS TO CERTIFY that on this ______ day of ____________________, 19____ before me, the undersigned Notary Public in and for the state, personally appeared ____________________ known to me to be the persons named in the foregoing instrument, and acknowledged to me that they executed the same freely and voluntarily, for the uses and purposes therein contained.

IN WITNESS HEREOF, I have hereunto set my hand and seal the day and year first hereinabove written.

____
Notary Public of State
My commission expires ____________________

(See Also: **ACADEMIC FREEDOM; CITIZENSHIP; DOCTORS; EXAMINATIONS; HEALTH; MEDICATION; NURSE; RIGHTS AND RESPONSIBILITIES)**

REPORT CARDS

message to parents concerning...

Report cards are prepared for every child each nine weeks. Wednesdays will be the day for sending home notices, news and other forms of information with your children.

Parent-Teacher conferences will be scheduled twice during the school year near the end of the *1st* and *3rd* nine-week periods. However, you are invited and urged to contact the teacher, the principal or any other school official at any time to discuss your child's welfare.

Satisfaction in learning should be encouraged. The report card recognizes competition, but stresses self-improvement and self-achievement.

The grading scale is as follows:

Grades 1–3	Grades 4–6
+ Above Average	A – Excellent
√ Satisfactory	B – Very Good
N Needs Improvement	C – Average
	D – Below Average
	F – Unsatisfactory

We recommend that you make appointments for after-school visits with your child's teacher whenever you have a question about your child's progress.

sample statements on...

REPORT CARDS

Report cards will be issued to parents four times during the school year. If you or your parents have any questions regarding your achievement, an appointment to discuss your report card with your teacher or counselor can be arranged by calling the guidance office.

Interim reports, warning of unsatisfactory work, are mailed to parents halfway through each marking period.

REPORT CARDS

Report cards are issued every nine weeks. Two Parent–Teacher Conferences are held each year at the end of the 1st and 3rd nine-week periods. Scheduling for the conferences is done through the office.

The report card is reviewed by the Report Card Curriculum Committee. Changes may be suggested to the representatives on the committee—two from Rock Township Elementary School.

Two types of report cards are issued—one in the primary grades and a slightly different one in the intermediate grades. The system uses "S," "N," and "I" at the present time with letter grades given in the academic subjects of the intermediate grades.

Further information on the report cards is available in the Curriculum Guide and will be given out as the time approaches for the first report cards.

(See Also: ABILITY; ACHIEVEMENT; CLASS; GRADES; HONOR ROLL; NATIONAL HONOR SOCIETY; PERMANENT RECORDS; STUDENT RECORDS; WARNING NOTICES)

REPORTS

policy on fiscal reports...

The Board takes cognizance of the legal obligation on the part of the Secretary/Business Administrator and the Custodian of School Monies to report to this body at each regular monthly meeting on the financial condition of the school district in the manner and form prescribed by the State Department of Education.

It is the policy of the Board that the Secretary/Business Administrator furnish each member and the Superintendent at least two days prior to the regularly scheduled monthly meeting a summary statement of major line items and revenues received to date in the following form:

Account No.
Description
Encumbered This Year ($)
Expended This Year ($)
Appropriation ($)
Unencumbered Balance ($)

In the event the Secretary/Business Administrator's Report and the Custodian's Report differ with regard to cash receipts or expenditures, the Secretary/Business Administrator shall take all possible actions within his authority to resolve the difference. But if said difference cannot be rectified by the next regular Board meeting, the matter shall be referred to the district auditor.

The Secretary/Business Administrator shall report to the building principals at least three times each school year on the status of the funds allocated to their building.

LAST NAME________________ FIRST NAME________________ MIDDLE NAME________________

SEX_____ DATE OF BIRTH ____________ PLACE OF BIRTH ________________ SOURCE OF RECORD ____________ Previous School Attended ____________

Address	Phone	Address	Phone
Address	Phone	Address	Phone

Name of Parents or Guardian	CHILD RESIDES WITH Check appropriate space	Birth Place	Education
Father			
Stepfather			
Mother			
Stepmother			
Guardian			

MARKING KEY: + Above Average
✓ Satisfactory
N Needs Improvement in this area

"A" – Excellent
"B" – Very Good
"C" – Average
"D" – Below Average
"F" – Unsatisfactory

ATTENDANCE & SCHOLARSHIP

School Year	Date Entered	Grade	Age Yr. Mo.	School	Teacher	Reading	Arith.	Lang.	Spelling	Sci. Health	Soc. St'd.	Writing	Music	Orch.	Art	Phys. Ed.		Days Pres.	Days Ab.	Times Tardy	Promoted to

Date of Withdrawal Transcript sent to Date Sent

HEALTH RECORD

CODE: 1 - Satisfactory; 2 - Needs Attention; 3 - Treating; 4 - Corrected

Date of examination									REMARKS:
Vision	R L	R L	R L	R L	R L	R L	R L	R L	
Hearing	R L	R L	R L	R L	R L	R L	R L	R L	
Speech									

Special Health Problems (please specify):________________

sample pupil report (complete)...

PUPIL'S REPORT

Name ______________________________ Teacher ____________ Teacher ____________
(LAST) (FIRST) (MIDDLE)

School ____________ School ____________ Sex ______ Grade ______ 19 ______ 19 ______

Age ______ Birth Date ____________ 19 ______ Place of Birth ____________ Source ____________

Address ____________ Phone: (Home) ____________ (Bus.) ____________ (Emg.) ____________

2nd Address ____________ Phone: (Home) ____________ (Bus.) ____________ (Emg.) ____________

Father ____________ Occupation ____________ Employer ____________

Mother ____________ Occupation ____________ Employer ____________

Church ____________ Brothers: (Older) ____________ Sisters: (Older) ____________

Marital Status ____________ Brothers: (Younger) ____________ Sisters: (Younger) ____________

ATTENDANCE RECORD

Date Entered System: ____________ 19 ______

P	M	T	W	T	F	M	T	W	T	F	M	T	W	T	F	M	T	W	T	F	M	T	W	T	F	M	T	W	T	F	M	T	W	T	F	M	T	W	T	F	M	T	W	T	F	M	T	W	T	F	T	A	Pres.
1																																																					
2																																																					
3																																																					
4																																																					
TOTALS																																																					

Date Transfer ____________ 19 ______ To ____________

Date Withdrew ____________ 19 ______ To ____________

Retained in Grade ____________ Passed to Grade ____________

Remarks ____________

(See Also: ACHIEVEMENT; CHILD STUDY TEAM; GRADES; PERMANENT RECORDS; RESOURCE TEAM; STUDENT RECORDS; UNDERACHIEVERS)

REQUISITIONS, REPAIRS, AND REPLACEMENTS

sample stores requisition form...

STORES REQUISITION

Ordered By:
Building Name________ No.____
Originator________ ________
Supervisor________ ________
Signatures

Transferred To SRQ __ __ __ __ __ __
Transferred From SRQ __ __ __ __ __ __

55 58 60
SRQ __ __ *Unit No.* | __ __ __ __

Date: ____ *Day* ____ *Month* ____ *Year*

________ *Director Approval*

TRAN CODE 1	BATCH NO. 3	FUND/SCH 11	TYPE	FUNCTION	OBJECT	AREA	BLDG NO. 25	ITEM NO. 65	WAREHOUSE INVENTORY CONTROL NO. 70	QUANTITY ORDERED 76	UNIT OF ISSUE	$ UNIT PRICE ¢	DESCRIPTION
								01					
								02					
								03					
								04					
								05					
								06					
								07					
								08					
								09					
								10					
								11					
								12					

Form Route:
1. Originator
2. Supervisor Approval
3. Inventory
4. Director Approval
5. Warehouse

Posted By________ Date________
Packed By________ Date________
Received By________ Date________

repair and maintenance project information sheet...

SCHOOL ______

SCHOOL CODE ______

SCHOOL'S PROJECT PRIORITY	BUILDING I.D.	JOB CODE NUMBER*	TOTAL ESTIMATED COST (DAGS Only)	PROJECT DESCRIPTION (Including Scope and Magnitude of Job)	ESTIMATED DESIGN COST (DAGS Only)	ESTIMATED CONSTRUCTION COST (DAGS Only)

Deteriorated Condition Caused By: ______

Impact If Project is Deferred: ______

SCHOOL'S PROJECT PRIORITY	BUILDING I.D.	JOB CODE NUMBER*	TOTAL ESTIMATED COST (DAGS Only)	PROJECT DESCRIPTION (Including Scope and Magnitude of Job)	ESTIMATED DESIGN COST (DAGS Only)	ESTIMATED CONSTRUCTION COST (DAGS Only)

Deteriorated Condition Caused By: ______

Impact If Project Is Deferred: ______

SCHOOL'S PROJECT PRIORITY	BUILDING I.D.	JOB CODE NUMBER*	TOTAL ESTIMATED COST (DAGS Only)	PROJECT DESCRIPTION (Including Scope and Magnitude of Job)	ESTIMATED DESIGN COST (DAGS Only)	ESTIMATED CONSTRUCTION COST (DAGS Only)

Deteriorated Condition Caused By: ______

Impact If Project Is Deferred: ______

*JOB CODE NUMBER:
1 = Reroof
2 = Paint Exterior
3 = Paint Interior
4 = Recarpet
5 = Termite Treat, Ground
6 = Termite Treat, Tent
7 = Resurface
8 = AC Overhaul
9 = Miscellaneous

Sheet ______ Of ______

School: ______________________

Prepared By: ______________________

Date: ______________________

REPLACEMENTS

REQUEST FOR FURNITURE & EQUIPMENT
SECONDARY LEVEL (7–12)

FISCAL BIENNIUM 19 —19

Page ______ of ______
Department Accounting & General Services
Division Central Services
Program Physical Plant Operation & Maint.

LOCATION				STAFF					17″ STUDENT'S CHAIR						STOOL		CLASSROOM TABLES					BENCH		MISC.		
Bldg.	Rm.	Subject Area	Grade	Teacher Desk Single Pedestal	Teacher Chair	File, 4-Drawer, Legal w/lock	High Swivel Metal Stool 24-33″ w/back	Metal Leg Table 30 × 60 w/ctr. drawer	Chair Desk (17″)	Student w/o rack	Posture w/rack	Chair, Draftsman w/backseat, swivel (Drafting cls. only)	Folding	Folding–Dropleaf Tablet Arm	Metal–18-27″ Ht. Adjustable	High Swivel Chair 24-33″ Adjustable	Multi-Purpose 36 × 72 × 29″ Ht.-Adj.	Business Machines	Typing-Metal-Adj.	2-Pupil or Single Pupil–Open Front	Drawing–Steel 10 Dr. Unit w/2 Wings	Wooden Top w/Vise & Cabinet Below	Work Bench w/Stainless Steel Top			

School: ______________________

Prepared By: ______________________

Date: ______________________

REPLACEMENTS

REQUEST FOR FURNITURE & EQUIPMENT
ELEMENTARY CLASSROOM

FISCAL BIENNIUM 19 —19

Page ________ of ________
Department Accounting & General Services
Division Central Services
Program Physical Plant Operation & Maint.

LOCATION				STAFF				CLASSROOM TABLES					CLASSROOM CHAIRS								
BLDG.	RM.	USE	GRADE	Teacher Desk Single Pedestal, 30 × 45	Teacher's Chair	File, 4-Drawer, Legal with lock	Study Carrel/Full Winged Dry-Adjustable	Trapezoidal Table 30 × 30 × 60 Adj.	2-Pupil Desk Adjustable	Single Pupil Desk Diameter–Adj.	Round Table 48″ Diameter–Adj.	Multi-Purpose Table 30 × 60 Adj.	11/12	13/14	15/16	17/18	TOTAL				

School: ______________________

Prepared By: ______________________

Date: ______________________

REPLACEMENTS

GENERAL OFFICE, LIBRARY, CAFETERIA & OTHERS

FISCAL BIENNIUM 19 –19

LOCATION			GENERAL OFFICE																
			DESK			CHAIRS								TABLE					
BLDG.	USE	GRADE	Executive–6" Overhang	Secretarial–L-Shape (Left or right return)	Teacher's–Single Pedestal	Executive, Swivel	Secretarial	Side Chair w/Arms	Side Chair w/o Arms	11/12 Chair, Student	13/14 Chair, Student	15/16 Chair, Student	17/18 Chair, Student	Credenza, 2 sliding drs. w/ adjustable shelves	Metal Leg Table w/Center Drawer	48" round reading-adj.	30 × 60, Multi-Pupil, adj.	36 × 72, Multi-Pupil, adj.	Conference Tbl. (96 × 44)

(Form continued)

Page ________ of ________
Department Accounting & General Services
Division Central Services
Program Physical Plant Operation & Maint.

(Form continued)

LOUNGE		CAFE			LIBRARY															MISC.			
					TABLES			RACKS/STANDS				CHARGING DESK					TRUCK					
												Accessories										
Individual Chair w/o Arms (5 each)	Coffee Table (1 each)	36 × 36 Dining Table	15″/17″ Table Top Bench	15″/17″ Mobile Convertible	Study Carrel Full-Dry Adj.	Sloping Top Table	Bench (For Sloping Top)	Book Display Rack w/Bulletin Board	Book Display Rack, Port.	Dictionary Stand-Revolv.	Dictionary Stand w/one Adjustable Shelf	15-Drawer Card Catalog Unit	Cornice or Top Unit	Reference Shelf Unit	16″ Low Leg Base	26″ High Leg Base	Book-w/Depress. Top	Book-w/Rubber Bumper	Kick Step Stool	Chair, Draftsman w/backrest Swivel Seat (Circ. area)	File, 4-Drawer, Legal w/lock	File, 3-Drawer w/lock

(See Also: BUDGET; BUILDING; CUSTODIAL SERVICES; EQUIPMENT; PURCHASING; VANDALISM**)**

RESOURCE TEAM

request for resource team meeting form...

Date: ____________

*REQUEST FOR RESOURCE TEAM MEETING

Child's Name ______________________________ Age: ________

School: ______________________________ Grade: ________

Classroom Teacher: ______________________________

Parent's Name: ______________________________

Parent's Address: ______________________________

Home Phone: ______________ Business Phone: ______________

Statement of Problems: ______________________________

____

____

____

*Place in special services file only if student receives special education services; if student is not placed in a program, place form in the student's cumulative file.

resource team meeting minutes form...

*RESOURCE TEAM MEETING MINUTES

STUDENT: ______________________ TEACHER: ______________________

TEAM PARTICIPANTS: ____

____

DISCUSSION: ____

____

____

____

____

____

____

____

____

____

RESULTS: ____

____

____

____

____

____

*Place in special services file only if student receives special education services; if student is not placed in a special education program, place form in the student's cumulative file.

(See Also: **COUNSELING; OBSERVATIONS; PERMANENT RECORDS; REFERRAL; REPORTS; SPECIAL EDUCATION; SUPPLEMENTAL INSTRUCTION)**

RETENTION

policies and procedures for...

Non-Promotion of Students to Next Grade Level

The teacher has primary responsibility to evaluate student efforts and achievements. Furthermore, the teacher is accountable for the accuracy and recording of the grades on the student's permanent record.

Non-promotion of a student to the next grade or failure of a specific subject is the responsibility of the teacher with the concurrence of the principal.

Notification of the parents/guardian of non-promotion or failure is the responsibility of the teacher and principal.

Parents and students will be given due process by the teacher, principal, superintendent and Board of Trustees if the non-promotion or failure is challenged.

The teacher in consultation with the counselor will take into consideration, in addition to academic attainment, such factors as the student's chronological age, mental age, social growth, attendance pattern, physical development, emotional status, effort, and purpose, in determination of non-promotion or failure of a student.

Individual conferences are scheduled during the month of November following the first-quarter report card. These conferences provide an opportunity for parents and teachers to discuss a child—his or her problems, weaknesses and his or her particular strengths. Suggestions for helping the child at home and at school can be mutually shared and a course of action can be planned. Individual conferences are scheduled for about fifteen minutes. The school staff will contact parents regarding a time and date which is convenient.

Children are dismissed during the time that the conferences are held. Other written communications and Parent-Teacher Conferences may be used to inform parents about pressing problems which arise through the year.

When a teacher has determined that a student will not be promoted, the teacher will discuss the situation with the counselor. The counselor will then schedule a session with the student.

Any inquiries from parent or student challenging a grade or non-promotion will be referred to the teacher involved.

Names of any students failing a course for the semester must be referred to the principal.

Prior to the end of the third quarter, the principal will notify, in writing, the parent that the student is not expected to be promoted to the next grade level. At this time a meeting will be scheduled with the principal, teacher and parent to discuss the situation. This meeting will be documented in writing. A meeting may be held during the fourth quarter if necessary or if requested by the parents.

sample policies on...

If you, as a junior high school student, fail the equivalent of two full-year subjects, you will be transferred, rather than promoted to high school, or you can be retained by your principal.

If you fail the equivalent of three, four-year subjects and/or both math and English, you will be retained.

If you fail 9th grade English and are transferred into 10th grade, you must take both basic skills and regular English classes. However, if you fail 9th grade math you must take basic skills math in 10th grade, and may opt to take an additional math course. If you choose another math elective, you will still be required to take basic skills math.

Your parents will be notified if you are doing unsatisfactory work and may not be promoted to senior high.

PROMOTION–RETENTION

1. Any student who fails the equivalent of two full-year subjects is to be transferred rather than promoted, and may possibly be retained at the discretion of the principal in conference with guidance.
2. Any student who fails the equivalent of three full-year subjects is to be retained.
3. Any student who fails both mathematics and English is to be retained.

These regulations apply to seventh, eighth, and ninth grades.

(See Also: ABILITY; ACHIEVEMENT; CHILD STUDY TEAM; EVALUATION; FAILURE; GRADES; PROMOTION; RESOURCE TEAM; STUDENT RECORDS; UNDERACHIEVERS; WARNING NOTICES**)**

RIGHTS AND RESPONSIBILITIES

guide to parental rights and responsibilities...

PARENTAL RIGHTS AND RESPONSIBILITIES AND THOSE OF YOUR CHILD UNDER DUE PROCESS OF LAW PROCEDURES

You have a right to:

1. Written notification before individual evaluation. This includes the right to an interpreter/translator if primary language of home is not English and right to participate in the evaluation.
2. Written notification before change in educational placement and child's educational status be unchanged during due process procedure.

3. Periodic review of educational placement and participation in same.
4. Opportunity for an impartial hearing, should you disagree with the evaluation and recommended placement of the Child Study Team, including the right to:
   a. Receive timely and specific notice of such hearing.
   b. Review all records.
   c. Obtain an independent evaluation:
      1. at your own cost, or
      2. at the cost of the state if evaluator selected by state is accepted by you
      3. be represented by counsel
      4. cross examine
      5. bring witnesses
      6. present evidence
      7. receive a complete and accurate record of proceedings
      8. appeal the decision
5. Assignment of surrogate parent for children when:
   a. The child's parent or guardian is not known.
   b. The child's parents are unavailable.
   c. The child is a ward of the state.
6. Acess to educational records.
   a. To challenge validity or content of materials in records and request removal.
   b. Written consent must be given by parent or individual (if 18 yrs. of age or older) before records may be released. Such release shall state:
      (1) records to be released; (2) reasons for release; and (3) agency, person or persons to whom records are to be released. Parents or individuals are entitled to copy of any or all records at cost of reproducing.
7. To refuse permission for the evaluation with the understanding that the District can then request a hearing to present its reasons and try to obtain approval to conduct the evaluation.
8. To receive a full statement and/or explanation of the evaluation in addition to the written summary.
9. To review and have explained the entire procedure of an impartial hearing.
10. To call, consult, or have a conference with any staff member concerned with the educational program/placement of your child at a time and place mutually agreed upon.
11. A copy of the State Rules and Regulations is available at Board of Education Offices at no cost upon request.

guide to students' rights and responsibilities (complete)...

GUIDE TO STUDENTS' RIGHTS & RESPONSIBILITIES

Students have a fundamental right to a free public education. You have a corresponding responsibility to join with other members of your school community in respecting the rights and responsibilities of others in that community and in establishing a climate for learning within the school.

This Guide summarizes your basic rights and responsibilities as a secondary school student, according to the laws of the land as expressed in the United States and State Constitutions, State school law, federal and state court decisions and decision of the Commissioner of Education and the State Board of Education as of August, 1972.

This law is a dynamic process: it is constantly being revised, amended, challenged, appealed and interpreted. These rights and responsibilities are complex issues; the laws and regulations are described here as they are written—not as some may feel they should be, nor are they consistently applied throughout our State. It is the responsibility of all members of the school community—students, parents, staff amdinistrators—to see that these rights are protected. You are also cautioned that "A Guide to Students' Rights and Responsibilities in the State" is only a guide; it should not be used by you as a definitive statement of your legal rights in any particular situation. The rule or rules of law which govern a case will depend on the facts in each case.

The guide is designed to help all members of the school community recognize your legal position as a student in our schools and avoid the confrontation caused by misunderstandings in this area. A school community facing a threat to its citizens caused by the anarchy of disturbances might be forced to suspend certain provisions for the brief period required to restore order. With the exception of this extreme circumstance, it is hoped that all schools might be guided by the following statement.

You may feel that you need additional advice concerning your rights. Your student council, principal, superintendent and board of education are all sources of information. You may want to discuss situations involving your rights and responsibilities with your parents or counselor. If you are under 18, you cannot initiate legal action on your own behalf; you must have the support of an adult. You may also want to seek help from legal counsel or from the people listed as resources at the end of this guide.

FREE EDUCATION

You have a right to a free and full education through secondary school between ages 5 and 20 unless you graduate before that age. You are required by law to regularly attend an approved educational institution until you are 16. You may not ask to leave school merely because you have reached 16 years of age if you are, in fact, fulfilling your responsibilities as a student. Those responsibilities also require you to follow and attempt to complete the course of study prescribed by your board of education. If it is determined that you are not fulfilling your responsibilities as a student, you may be subject to punishment (see section on suspension and expulsion). Married students share these responsibilities and rights, including the opportunity to participate in the full range of activities offered by the school. Local school district may determine policies for providing pregnant students with the elements of an education program designed to meet their specific needs.

SCHOOL RULES AND REGULATIONS

You have the right and a responsibility to live by the rule of law and to equal protection under that law, in school as the larger society. It is your responsibility to obey school regulations and the school authorities who enforce them. This responsibility extends to your conduct to and from school as well as in the building itself. Public information such as state school law, decisions by the Commissioner of Education, rulings by the State Board, and county and district bylaws and directives are available to you as students at your local board of education office.

HAIR AND DRESS

You may wear your hair however you wish as long as it does not endanger your health or safety or the health and safety of other students, or create classroom disorder. This applies to all school activities; you may not be barred from participation in any school program such as athletic teams, musical groups or other clubs sponsored by your school because of your hair.

You have a responsibility to dress according to the approved and reasonable regulations of your board of education.

BUTTONS AND ARMBANDS

You may wear or display buttons, armbands, flags, decals, or other badges of symbolic expression, unless the manner of expression "materially and substantially interferes with" the orderly process of the school or the rights of others.

FLAG SALUTE AND PLEDGE OF ALLEGIANCE

State law requires you to show respect for the flag of the United States of America. If you are conscientiously opposed to the pledge or salute, you may abstain from these ceremonies but you are required by law to stand respectfully.

DISTRIBUTION OF LITERATURE

The preparation, publication and distribution of newspapers, magazines and other literature is an exercise of freedom of the press. The freedom to express one's opinion goes hand in hand with the responsibility for the published statement. Literature that you want to distribute on school property is not only your responsibility, but that of your school authorities. State policy calls for reasonable guidelines setting forth the times and places for distribution of materials in school, and for defining fair standards for their content, to be jointly determined by representatives of all groups in the school community, with ultimate responsibility for determining the suitability of material resting with the local board of education. "Suitability" may not be defined as approval or agreement with the literature in question, but refers to a reasonable judgment intended to protect you and the entire school community from irresponsible publications such as those aimed at creating hositility or violence, "hardcore" pornography or material of libelous nature. Once your school has established such guidelines, you may distribute publications that meet the conditions of those guidelines on school property. You may also distribute publications next to school property subject to the same rules governing other citizens' rights to distribute literature on public property (you may not block pedestrian traffic or entrances to buildings). State school law is quite specific on one other point; distribution of partisan political literature supporting or opposing candidates or public questions in any general, municipal or school election is prohibited on school property.

ASSEMBLY AND PETITION

Your right to assemble and to circulate petitions carries with it the equal responsibility to respect the orderly operation of the school. School authorities have a right to restrict the times and places of such activities, and may require advance notice when necessary to avoid conflicts and to insure proper protection of the school community.

SCHOOL RECORDS

Your parents are entitled to inspect the official or permanent school records (those which are retained after you leave school) relating to you. This means that they themselves have a right to inspect the actual record, and not merely have items selected from the record by school officials. However, school officials may withhold items of information which, in their judgment, are of a confidential nature or in which the applicant for such information has no legitimate interest. School authorities may determine the time and manner of presentation of this information; for example, they may suggest a counselor, qualified to interpret data in the records, be present.

POLICE IN THE SCHOOLS

In our society, police have the responsibility to protect all citizens by enforcing the laws of the community. For example, police can enter schools if they are invited on the premises by school officials, if they suspect a crime has been committed, or if they have a warrant for arrest or search. It is the duty of the police, school authorities, teachers and students to cooperate with each other in order to insure that the rights of each individual are respected. If a student is to be questioned by the police, it is the responsibility of the school administration to see that interrogations take place privately in the office of a school official and in the presence of the principal or his representative and that every effort be made to give a parent the opportunity to be present. You need not answer any question which requires you to provide any more than your name, age, address and your business at the school until your parent and/or lawyer are present. You have the same rights in relation to the police in school as you have out of school: you have a right to be informed of your legal rights, to be protected (by school officials, if necessary) from coercion and illegal constraint, and to remain silent.

LOCKER SEARCHES

Under the Constitution all citizens are protected from unreasonable searches and seizures; however, this does not mean that you are legally protected from search or seizure of any material in your locker, which is school property.

SUSPENSION AND EXPULSION

Suspension, which is a function of the school administrator, and expulsion, which is a function of the local board of education, are serious disciplinary sanctions which may be imposed against you when it can be proved that you have "materially and substantially interfered with" the maintenance of good order in the school, and when, under procedures conforming with due process of law. Expulsion is permanent removal from school rolls. Continued and willful disobedience, the habitual use of profanity or obscene language or injuring of individuals or school property are causes for punishment and suspension from school. You can be suspended for something you have done off as well as on school property if school authorities can prove that such action is reasonably necessary for your physical or emotional safety and well being, or for the safety of other members of the school community. Certain rules governing suspension are designed for your protections:

1. The principal must report your suspension immediately to the superintendent.
2. The superintendent must report it to the school board at its next regular meeting.
3. Either the board or the superintendent may reinstate you before the board's second regular meeting after your suspension.
4. After that board of education meeting, only the board may continue your suspension or expel you.

In case of either suspension or expulsion you have the right to the following elements of due process:

1. A written statement of the charges against you and the grounds justifying the sanction to be imposed.
2. A hearing.
3. A means of effective appeal.

The following are your rights regarding hearings:

Informal hearing

Under ordinary curciumstances you are entitled to the opportunity to demonstrate to the authorities that there is a case of mistaken identity or some compelling reason why you should not be suspended pending a full hearing; where school officials believe that you may be dangerous to yourself or others, you may be suspended for a short period. If the suspension is to be extended, you are entitled to a full hearing.

Formal Full Hearing

Court and school law decisions have held that any situation where a fundamental right may be denied, students must be afforded all appropriate elements of due process. This may apply in cases involving expulsion, a long-term suspension which exceeds 21 days, a short-term suspension in which the timing of the punishment is crucial for that particular student, prohibition against certain student activities, or other instances of a serious nature.

1. The hearing must be held within 21 days after the informal hearing.

2. You may be represented by a lawyer.

3. The hearing may be held by the board of education or by a hearing examiner appointed to them.

4. You are entitled to a translator where necessary.

5. You are entitled to the rudiments of an adversary proceeding. Courts have held that these rudiments may include the right to be presented with the names of witnesses against you and copies of the statements and affidavits of those witnesses, the right to demand that any such witness appear in person to answer questions, and the right to testify and produce witnesses on your own behalf. The precise nature of the hearing depends upon the circumstances of the particular case, such as the sanctions to be imposed or at what level the hearing is held.

6. A record must be kept of the hearing procedures. You are entitled, at your own expense, to a copy of that transcript.

7. The proceeding must be held with all reasonable speed.

If you are found innocent, you may request that any written entry referring to the incident may be expunged from your school records.

APPEALS

You may appeal a decision made by your school officials to the superintendent and the local board of education. If this is unsuccessful you have two more appeals within the school system—first, to the Commissioner of Education, and (within 30 days after the Commissioner has made his decision) to the State Board of Education. You may appeal your case in court without going through the administrative procedures outlined above, but the court may require you to first exhaust those channels within the local and state school systems. Your local board of education also has the right of appeal.

The following are additional resources for legal aid or advice:

The State Office of Legal Services provides legal assistance to those persons, charged with civil offenses, who cannot afford to retain their own attorney.

The office of the public defender and Juvenile Administration Office provide legal assistance to those persons, charged with criminal offenses, who cannot afford to retain their own attorney.

RESOURCES: WHERE TO GO FOR INFORMATION

Your local Principal or Superintendent
State School officials

Department of Education

Commissioner of Education

Assistant Commissioner, Division of Controversies and Disputes

State Student Council Office

State Association of High School Councils

(See Also: ACADEMIC FREEDOM; BEHAVIOR; BUILDING; CITIZENSHIP; DUE PROCESS; EXPULSION; PHILOSOPHY; RELIGION; STUDENT COUNCIL (GOVERNMENT); SUSPENSION; USE OF FACILITIES)

SAFETY

message to parents...

SAFETY TO AND FROM SCHOOLS

Safety is important. Children should be encouraged to practice good safety habits. Safety instruction is given at school and safety measures are practiced in the building and on the playground. You can help your child develop good safety habits by providing safety instruction at home.

If your child is new at school,

1. Assist him/her in learning the safest route to and from school.
2. Encourage him/her to use intersections when crossing a street rather than the middle of the block. Where crosswalks are provided, he/she should stay between the lines. It is the child's responsibility to make certain that traffic from both directions has stopped.
3. If there are no sidewalks, the child should walk on the left side of the street facing oncoming traffic.
4. Encourage him/her to come home immediately after school is dismissed for protection and safety.
5. He/she should obey traffic lights and look both ways before crossing a street.
6. Remind your child to:
   a. Never accept rides or gifts from strangers.
   b. Report to his/her teacher, a police officer, his/her bus driver, or to you any strangers seen loitering on foot or in a car near schools, playgrounds, etc.
   c. Always try to secure the license number of the car and write it down.
   d. Always try to remember what the stranger looked like and how he/she was dressed.
   e. Contact a police officer any time he/she needs help.
7. **Kindergarten:** For those kindergarten children riding the buses at least for the first 3 days of school it is important that a name tag be attached to the child's clothing.
8. When a child is to go home with another child or to be left at another stop there should be a notice from home.

unit safety report form...

Unit ________________________________ Month of ______________

COMMITTEE MEETING Date of Meeting ______________

Persons in Attendance

1. ______________ 4. ______________ 7. ______________

2. ______________ 5. ______________ 8. ______________

3. ______________ 6. ______________ 9. ______________

Topics and problems discussed, action or resolutions recommended:

INSPECTION REPORT:	Adequate	Inadequate
1. Fire Prevention: Housekeeping, flammable storage	______	______
2. Fire Protection: Clear access to fire extinguishers and pull boxes, alarm systems working	______	______
3. Exit Ways: Clear and unobstructed, doors operable and clear at all times when bldg. is in operation	______	______
4. Electrical: Clear access to circuit panels, grounded extention cords (temporary use only)	______	______
5. Playground Equipment: Date checked ______________	______	______
6. Laboratory/Shop Equipment	______	______
7. Grounds and Walkways: Tripping hazards, ice	______	______
8. Emergency lighting and/or emergency generator condition	______	______

Inadequacies noted, temporary or permanent solution suggested:

Inspections by outside agencies, for example, Fire Dept., Dept. of Labor, etc.

Date of Inspection ______________ Agency ______________

FIRE DRILLS HELD DURING THE MONTH: Two required in Sept., Oct., April and May

Dates ________________________________

Fire Dept. official requested the drill or was in attendance?

Date of Report ______________ Report Prepared by (signature & title)

Principal's Signature

Distribution–Org. to Ins./Safety Office
Copy to Secon. or Elem. School Mgmt.
Copy for file

unsafe condition report form...

STANDARD UNSAFE CONDITION REPORT

SEND TO: Safety Council–Administration Building

____

SCHOOL/UNIT______________________________ Date ______________

Report Prepared by: ______________________________________

Unsafe Condition: ____

____

____

____

____

____

Corrective Action Recommended: ____________________________

____

____

____

____

____

What temporary action has been taken until a permanent solution has been initiated?: ____________

____

____

____

____

____

(See Also: ACCIDENT; ASSEMBLIES; BUS; DANCES; DOCTORS; FIELD TRIPS; FIRE DRILLS; MEDICATION; NURSE)

application for salary schedule adjustment...

SUBMIT TO: Building Administrator

FROM: ____________________

Teaching Assignment ____________________ Building ____________________

Extracurricular Assign. ____________________

Undergraduate Major(s) ____________________

Minor(s) ____________________

Graduate Major ____________________

	Step	Qt. Hrs.
Current:		
Educational—Horizontal		
Experience—Vertical		
Expected on Course Completion:		
Educational—Horizontal		
Experience—Vertical		

Course Name	(List in Qt. Hrs.) Under-Grad. #	Grad. #	College	Check areas of request: Experience Vertical 100%	Educational Horizontal 50%	100%

Teacher comments where justification of request may be questionable by course title:

____

____

I hereby submit the above information in order to assist in an evaluation of my application for additional or continuing credit on the salary schedule.

____________________ ____________________

Applicant Signature Date of Application

____________________ ____________________

Verification: Building Adm. Signature Date–Submit to Board Representative

Administrator Comments (Optional): ____________________

SCHOOL BOARD REPRESENTATIVE REPLY

____ Request Approved ____ Request Approved in Part ____ Request Rejected

Comments (optional except when rejected in whole or part): ____________________

____

____________________ ____________________

Assist. Supt., Instructional Services Signature Date–Return Copies to Building Administrator & Applying Teacher

(See Also: BUSINESS; CONTRACT; INSURANCE; MONEY; PAYROLL; TIME; VOUCHER; WORK)

SCHEDULE

change of schedule form...

SCHEDULE CHANGE

Name: ______________________ Grade: __________ Date: ______________

OLD SCHEDULE

Period	Subject	Room	Teacher	Initial
1				
2				
3				
4				
5				
6				
7				

NEW SCHEDULE

Period	Subject	Room	Teacher	Initial
1				
2				
3				
4				
5				
6				
7				

HOME ROOM #: __________

NOTE:

Recorded by: Nurse: ______________________ Attendance: ______________________

sample daily class schedule...

7:55	First Bell
8:00	Tardy Bell
	Orchestra–Grades 7 & 8
	Boys Chorus and Girls Chorus
8:30	Teachers report to duty stations
8:50	End of Period
8:55	Tardy to Homeroom
9:00	Pass to First Hour Class
9:05	Tardy to First Hour Class
10:00	Pass to Second Hour Class
10:05	Tardy to Second Hour Class
11:00	Pass to Third Hour Class
11:05	Tardy to Third Hour Class
12:00	Pass to Fourth Hour Class, Grade 7 or 8
12:05	Tardy to Fourth Hour Class, Grade 7 or 8
12:20	Pass to Fourth Hour Class, Grade 7 or 8
12:25	Tardy to Fourth Hour Class, Grade 7 or 8
1:20	Pass to Fifth Hour Class, All Grades
1:25	Tardy to Fifth Hour Classes, All Grades
2:20	Pass to Sixth Hour Class
2:25	Tardy to Sixth Hour Class
3:20	Dismissal of Students
3:50	Teacher's Day Officially Ends

The daily class schedule will rotate one period every six weeks. For example, the class you have first hour would be second hour during the second six weeks, third hour during the third six weeks, etc. Each rotation will move the sixth hour class to first hour. Our lunch schedule will change every six weeks.

SAMPLE ROTATION

FIRST SIX WEEKS
1. Social Studies
2. Math
3. Physical Education
4. Block or Band
5. English
6. Science

SECOND SIX WEEKS
1. Science
2. Social Studies
3. Math
4. Physical Education
5. Block or Band
6. English

THIRD SIX WEEKS
1. English
2. Science
3. Social Studies
4. Math
5. Physical Education
6. Block or Band

FOURTH SIX WEEKS
1. Block or Band
2. English
3. Science
4. Social Studies
5. Math
6. Physical Education

FIFTH SIX WEEKS
1. Physical Education
2. Block or Band
3. English
4. Science
5. Social Studies
6. Math

SIXTH SIX WEEKS
1. Math
2. Physical Education
3. Block or Band
4. English
5. Science
6. Social Studies

(See Also: ADULT EDUCATION; AMERICAN EDUCATION WEEK; BACK-TO-SCHOOL NIGHT; COURSES; MEETINGS; OPEN HOUSE; TIME**)**

SCHOLARSHIPS

parent's confidential statement...

PARENT'S CONFIDENTIAL STATEMENT

The following information is necessary to enable us to determine financial need.

Parent(s) Name(s): Father ______________________ Father's Age __________

Mother ______________________ Mother's Age __________

______________________ Yearly Salary or Income $__________
Principal Wage Earner's Occupation

____
Where Employed Address

How long have you been employed by this firm? ______________________

Circle how many years of employment you have before retirement: 1 2 3 4 5 More

Is your spouse employed? ______ If yes, occupation ______________________

____
Where Employed Address

Length of employment ______________ Yearly Salary or Income $__________

Have you filed a Financial Aid Form (FAF) for educational assistance? Yes ______ No ______

INCOME AND EXPENSES

1. Please copy from your current income tax returns:	FATHER	MOTHER
Adjusted Gross Income:	______	______
Federal Income Tax paid:	______	______
State Income Taxes paid:	______	______

Individual Return ☐ Joint Return ☐

(Form Continued)

PARENT'S CONFIDENTIAL STATEMENT (continued)

2. Please list all dependents, student applicant first.

	Age	Name of School or College	Current Year School Expenses	Amount of Scholarship (if any)
a. ______				
b. ______				
c. ______				
d. ______				
e. ______				

3. Do you own your home? Yes ______ No ______

   Monthly mortgage payment: Principal and Interest $______ Taxes $______

   Unpaid mortgage $______ Assessed Value by Tax Office $______

   If No, please complete: Amount of monthly rent $______

4. Do you own other property? Yes ______ No ______

   Location: ______

   Monthly mortgage payment: Principal and Interest $______ Taxes $______

   Unpaid mortgage $______

5. Do you own or partially own any business? If yes, please complete the following:

   Total Capital Value of your ownership/partial ownership in business $______

6. Please list holdings in other investments:

   Savings Account $______ Other Investments $______

7. Have you incurred any heavy debt due to serious illness, disability, or accident?

   ______ If yes, please explain briefly. ______

   ______

   ______

No further consideration will be given to this scholarship application and/or any scholarship awarded will be withdrawn, if any of the above statements prove to be willfully false.

I hereby certify that the foregoing statements are true to the best of my knowledge, information and belief, and agree to furnish proof if required.

Date ______ Parent's Signature ______

policy statement on...

It shall be the policy of the Board to consider acceptance of scholarships for the benefit of Rock Township students subject to the following:

1. The type of scholarship to be offered and criteria for award shall be submitted to the Superintendent a year in advance for Board approval.
2. The Board reserves the right to determine and/or approve the criteria for the selection of any scholarship award.

student's confidential statement...

STUDENT'S CONFIDENTIAL STATEMENT

(All applications must be submitted to the Guidance Office by April 15.)
College students must submit a transcript of work done.

Name ______________________________

Living with: ☐ Parents ☐ Father
☐ Mother ☐ Other ______________________________
(Please explain.)

Are parents: ☐ Divorced? ☐ Separated?

Check if living: ☐ Father ☐ Stepfather
☐ Mother ☐ Stepmother

College or school you expect to attend:

Name ______________________________ Check year ☐ Fr. ☐ Soph. ☐ Jr.

Tuition $__________ Room and Board $__________ Incidental Expenses $__________

Have you applied for any other scholarship award? ________ If yes, please state name and amount. ______________________________

Do you contribute any part of your earnings to help defray household expenses? ________ If yes, please state amount. $______________

Describe briefly your proposed major field of study and the reason for selecting this major.______________________________

____

____

____

____

____

____

Date ____________________ Student's Signature ____________________

(See Also: ACHIEVEMENT; APPLICATION; AWARDS; EVALUATION; INFORMATION; NEWS RELEASES; STUDENT RECORDS**)**

SECRETARY

outline of duties...

1. Office management
   a. Plans and coordinates clerical operation of the school office.
   b. Instructs, reviews and grades work of office training students.
2. Responsible for the routine of the principal's office
   a. Schedules appointments for the principal and vice principals.
   b. Handles principal's correspondence and maintains files of correspondence, reports, and records.
3. Payroll
   a. Keeps attendance record of total staff and submits payroll.
   b. Maintains sign-in sheets for all personnel.
   c. Secures leave of absence forms from personnel.
   d. Submits payroll for special programs (Driver Training, Lay Reader, Athletics, Classroom Cleaners, Overtime, Language Drillmaster, etc.).
4. Maintains personnel records for total staff
   a. Yellow Jackets (certificated)
   b. Blue Jackets (classified)
   c. Classification records
   d. X-ray certificates
   e. Other personnel records as required
5. Substitute teachers
   a. Calls substitute teachers when necessary.
   b. Submits payroll.
6. Workman's Compensation—prepares claims in case of injury for staff and students. Keeps updated log of injuries and submits quarterly and annual OSHA reports.
7. Responsible for bell schedule of school
8. Responsible for Daily Bulletin
9. Responsible for the message center facilities
   a. Receives and distributes mail with student help.
   b. Reviews incoming correspondence, reports and other material for dissemination and administrator's attention.

c. Teachers' mail boxes.

d. Serves as "general information" to the public.

e. In charge of switchboard and instructs students in operating it.

10. Has charge of official duplicating and mimeographing work
11. Serves as custodian of keys
12. Responsible for checking out teachers at the close of the school year
13. Coordinates school calendar
14. Screens Free Lunch application
15. Assists typist in screening School Bus Transportation applications
16. Issues parking stalls to faculty, staff and students
17. Performs other duties as required

secretarial time card...

POSITION ____________

EMPLOYEE NAME ______________________ (Last) ______ (First) ______ (Initial) SCHOOL ____________

SOCIAL SECURITY NO. ___ ___ ___-___ ___-___ ___ ___ ___ SCHEDULED HOURS PER DAY______

Instructions: Fill out completely. All hours, except hours actually worked at the straight time rate, must be coded with the appropriate pay time code.

Important: Use the OT (overtime) line for only those hours to be paid at time and one-half your regular rate. Check with your supervisor or union agreement to see when you are entitled to overtime pay.

	Mon	Tues	Wed	Thur	Fri	Sat	Sun	Total Weekly	Hours
									Reg.
									O T
									Sick
									Unpaid
Daily Totals									

	Mon	Tues	Wed	Thur	Fri	Sat	Sun	Total Weekly	Hours
									Reg.
									O T
									Sick
									Unpaid
Daily Totals									

	Mon	Tues	Wed	Thur	Fri	Sat	Sun	Total Weekly	Hours
									Reg.
									O T
									Sick
									Unpaid
Daily Totals									

	Mon	Tues	Wed	Thur	Fri	Sat	Sun	Total Weekly	Hours
									Reg.
									O T
									Sick
									Unpaid
Daily Totals									

PAID TIME CODES:

Reg. – Hours paid at Reg. Time
- H – Paid Holiday (12 mo. only)
- B – Bereavement
- A – Administrative Leave
- J – Jury Duty
- W – Subpoenaed Witness

O T – Hours paid at overtime (1½)

Sick – Paid sick leave hours
- S – Employee Sick
- F – Family Sick
- P – Approved Personal Leave

V – Paid vacation hours (12 month only)

UNPAID TIME CODES:
- X – Full Deduction

PAYROLL USE ONLY

Total Reg. Hours ____________

Total O T Hours ____________

Total Sick Hours ____________

Total Vac. Hours ____________

Total Paid Hours ____________

Mileage $____________

I certify that the hours recorded above are a true and correct record of this pay period and that all leaves have been taken in accordance with policy.

EMPLOYEE:

____

SUPERVISOR:

____

(See Also: ATTENDANCE; BULLETIN; CLERICAL SERVICES; DISTRIBUTION OF MATERIALS; RECORDS; TYPISTS; XEROXING**)**

SECRET SOCIETIES

memorandum on...

State law mandates and the Board affirms the prohibition of any secret society of public school pupils as inimical to the democratic ideals of public education. Accordingly, the following policy has been adopted:

A. Every organization of students formed within the school shall present to the principal of the school a constitution which shall set forth its purposes and qualifications for membership. It shall guarantee that membership is not invitational, but is open to all students of the school who qualify, and such qualifications are not based on considerations of race, creed, or political beliefs.

B. The Board reserves the right to require that any student attest that he is or is not a member of a secret organization within the school system.

C. No student who is a member of such a secret organization may receive any honor or award, hold any office within the school, be a member of any team or activity representing the school, or attend or participate in any school-sponsored function or event.

D. If it becomes known that a student is a member of such a secret organization and he persists in that membership after appropriate warnings, he shall be liable to suspension.

(See Also: BEHAVIOR; CLUBS; DUE PROCESS; PHILOSOPHY; SUSPENSION**)**

SICK LEAVE

policy statement on...

Sick leave is defined as a situation in which the employee is physically unable to be on the job. Ten (10) full days of personal sick leave for each year, cumulative to one hundred eighty (180) days shall be allowed every full-time employee of the Public School System without deduction in pay for the sick leave period to which the employee is entitled.

After the above amount of sick leave has been used, the School Board will cease payment to the employee until the employee has returned to his job. Deductions shall be based on the exact daily earnings of the employee in accordance with the contract.

An employee is advanced ten (10) days sick leave annually upon which to draw. If an employee does not complete the school year, and has used more than the proportionate number of sick leave days at the time of leaving the school's employ, one day's salary shall be deducted from the remaining pay for each sick leave day used over the number to which the employee is entitled. For example, if a teacher leaves at the end of the first semester and has used ten days sick leave, five full days shall be deducted from the final check.

A doctor's certificate may be required after ten (10) working days of continuous illness in order to continue the use of sick leave.

Deliberate misuse of the sick leave may constitute cause for dismissal proceedings.

(See Also: ABSENCE; ABSENTEEISM, ACCIDENT; ATTENDANCE; DOCTORS; HEALTH; ILLNESS; MEDICAL FORMS; NURSE; PAYROLL; SUBSTITUTE TEACHER; WORK**)**

SMOKING

message to faculty and staff concerning...

Please confine smoking to the teacher's lounge. Do not smoke in the classrooms or the halls.

There should be no smoking in the kitchen. This is following health department regulations.

There is a fan in the lounge. Please turn this on when smoking to try as much as possible to clear the smoke. The room is small and used by many.

procedures for enforcing smoking rules...

The following procedures will be applied in enforcing the smoking rule.

1. All school personnel shall report to the administrator all students observed smoking on school premises.
2. First Offense—a parent-student-administrator conference shall be held. The number of days suspended will be determined by:
   a. student attitude and behavior at the time of apprehension (insubordination, etc.)
   b. the extent of student and parental understandings and commitments reached
3. Second Offense—A parent-student-administrator conference shall be held and the penalty imposed will not be less than the one imposed on the previous offense. Serious discipline may be administered. A student may be directed to attend a stop smoking clinic if it is available in the district.
4. Third Offense—Serious discipline shall be administered. A contractual agreement between student-parent-administrators will be signed by all parties agreeing to the student's dismissal from school on the next offense.

If you have any reactions to the above penalties, please feel free to call one of the administrators at the school.

(See Also: DRUGS; HEALTH; ILLNESS; LAVATORIES; NURSE; SAFETY; SUSPENSION**)**

SPECIAL EDUCATION

explanation of certain special services...

SPEECH THERAPY PROGRAM

A speech therapist is assigned to Rock Township on a scheduled basis each week.

Referrals for speech therapy are made to her and those children in need of help are scheduled for classes. These children will need to leave the classroom for this help period, usually from about 20 minutes to half an hour.

The speech room is located in the new room in the basement. Please refer questions about students to the therapist. The most serious needs get first priority and others are placed on the waiting list. These students are then included as soon as possible.

SPECIAL LEARNING DISABILITY PROGRAM

A special learning disabilities teacher is available to give the classroom teacher help with students who have special problems.

His main duties include the testing, evaluation, and remediation procedures necessary to help correct student problem areas and promote progress. The work with the student will take on different dimensions depending on the problem and the need. In some cases it may involve work in the room; other cases may necessitate taking the child from the room for special help.

After testing and evaluation, conferences will be held with the teacher and with the parent.

policy statement on...

It is the desire of the Board to make available the best possible services for the identification, evaluation, and educational placement and programming for all students between the ages of five and twenty who are residents of the district and are not attending non-public schools, who need special help or placement. Toward this end, the Board directs that basic child study teams consisting of a psychologist, a learning disability teacher-consultant, and a school social worker be employed as an integral part of the progessional staff.

Children so identified by district personnel, medical and health professionals, parents, or agencies concerned with child welfare shall, after approval by the respective school principal, be referred to the child study team for examination in accordance with the Rules and Regulations of the State Board of Education. This examination shall be completed within 60 days of the referral.

Classifications and educational placements and programming shall be approved by the Director of Special Services and discussed with the parent or guardian of the child prior to their implementation and, whenever possible, shall be implemented within the facilities of the district. When the needs of a child require special educational facilities not available in the district, recommendation for outside placement shall be made to the Board by the Superintendent.

All records and reports relating to special education, identification, evaluation, classification, and placement shall be regarded as confidential, and access shall be limited to those personnel and approved agencies directly concerned with determining the classification or the making of recommendations for placement, and those directly involved in the educational program of the child. No records, except in the case of a court subpoena, will be sent to any outside source without the written authority of the parent or guardian.

Handicapped children less than five years of age will be considered for a program of special education at district expense only upon the recommendation of the Superintendent that such a program would benefit both the child and the district.

Names of children involved will be reported to the Board in executive session and will be recorded in the official minutes.

request for special services policy...

REQUEST FOR CHILD STUDY TEAM SERVICES

Requests for assistance from the Child Study Team, or an individual member of the team, are typically initiated by the classroom teachers who have identified academic, emotional, or social problems that interfere with a student's ability to learn. Requests may also be initiated by parents, guardians, outside agencies concerned with the welfare of the student, and by the student.

1. Request for Consultation

Consultative services will consist of a request to the Child Study Team, or an individual member of the team, to discuss a student's problems and to utilize their fields of expertise in exploring possibilities of handling the problem within the school situation. Prior to requesting consultative services, school personnel should have tried to remediate the problem using resource personnel available to them in the general education setting. Permission of the parent, guardian, or adult student shall be obtained in writing.

"Request for Consultation" should be completed by school personnel and two copies forwarded to the Unit Child Study Team Administrator, who will assign the case to the appropriate Team member.

2. Referral for Possible Classification

Based on observations and information obtained during the consultation period, the Child Study Team may, after discussion of the case with school personnel and as a team, recommend that a comprehensive evaluation is necessary as the student:

a. is potentially handicapped under the criteria established by law, and
b. if classifiable the student needs special education and/or related services that cannot be provided to the general school population

"Referral for Possible Classification" should be completed by school personnel upon the decision of the Child Study Team that a comprehensive evaluation is necessary. A parent conference must be held by the principal at which time the "Parental Permission for Formal Referral" must be completed. A copy must be attached to the referral form.

NOTE: TIME IS OF THE ESSENCE.

a. THIS MUST BE FORWARDED TO, AND RECEIVED BY THE UNIT CHILD STUDY TEAM ADMINISTRATOR WITHIN SEVEN CALENDAR DAYS OF THE DATE THE PARENT AGREED TO THE EVALUATION.

b. THE EVALUATION HAS TO BE COMPLETED WITHIN SIXTY CALENDAR DAYS OF THE DATE OF REFERRAL.

(See Also: CHILD STUDY TEAM; DOCTORS; DRUGS; MEDICATION; REFERRAL; RESOURCE TEAM; STUDENT RECORDS)

SPORTS

game report form...

GAME REPORT

__________________vs__________________ Date ________________________

Score We __________They __________ Sport ________________________

Officials: ________________________

____

____

____

Transportation: (Briefly describe any problems, if OK please mark so.)

Rating of Officials: (Brief)

Injuries:

Game Problems:

To be turned in to Athletic Director via interoffice mail after each and every game (all levels). Please include vouchers for Home Games.

permission to engage in sports form...

PERMISSION TO ENGAGE IN (Name Sport) ____________________

Name ____________________ Grade __________ Birth Date __________

Address ____________________ Telephone __________

MEDICAL HISTORY (Please give dates of following:)
Any serious accidents and/or injuries (type) ____________________

Surgical Operations (type) ____________________

Allergies ____________________

Hernia ____________________

Serious Medical Diseases (type) ____________________

Chest Diseases ____________________

Diabetes ____________________

Convulsive Seizures ____________________

Eyes (vision) ____________________

Ear, Nose, and Throat ____________________

Cardiac (heart defects) ____________________

Hypertension (High Blood Pressure) ____________________

Orthopedic ____________________

Present Medication ____________________ REASON ____________________

ANY PREVIOUS REJECTION FROM COMPETITIVE SPORTS (Date & Reason)

Girls: Menstrual Difficulties ____________________

PARENT'S FORM

The answers to the above are correct. I understand that any misrepresentation of any of the information contained herein will result in the student being denied the opportunity to participate. I hereby give my consent to the participation of

____________________ IN ____________________
(Full Name) (Sport)

conducted by the school against other schools and within the school. I shall assume all responsibility and expense for any injury received in practice or participation. I give my permission for my son/daughter to be diagnosed and treated by the team physician should such services be necessary.

__________ ____________________
Date Parent's or Guardian's Signature.

PHYSICIAN'S SIGNATURE

__________ ____________________
Date Medical Inspector's Signature

Height __________ Weight __________ Blood Pressure __________

This form must be turned into the School Nurse one week before Physical Examination. Parents will be notified if rejected and a statement from the student physician certifying his/her physical ability to participate will be necessary. Final decision, however, will be made by the School Medical Department.

sample team rules...

All players are required to follow the team rules outlined below. The breaking of these rules will be dealt with seriously. All players must know these rules. Ignorance is no excuse. Failure to follow them will result in a suspension from the team. If the infraction is considered serious enough, the suspension will become permanent. Above all, each player must understand that playing soccer for Rock Township High School is a privilege and not a right. All soccer participants are subject to S.I.A.A. rules and regulations.

SQUAD MAKE-UP

a. Making the team is based on 3 A's: ABILITY, ATTITUDE, and AGGRESSIVENESS.
b. Cuts from the squad are at the discretion of the coaching staff.
c. Players may be removed from the squad by the coach for disciplinary reasons.
d. If a player quits the team, it is his responsibility to notify the coaches that he is doing so.

PRACTICE

a. Practice is essential for success. You are expected to attend *every* practice, do what is asked of you, and give your best.
b. Practice begins at the time scheduled by the coach and you are expected to be on time.
c. The only excuse for missing practice is absence from school. If you work, schedule your hours around soccer practice. If you can't, you must make a decision as to whether to work or play soccer. Special circumstances require prior approval by coaches.
d. If you are absent from school, you cannot practice or play in a game on that date.
e. Practice is held rain or shine, unless otherwise noted by the coach. Do not go home "thinking" practice has been cancelled unless you know for sure.

INJURIES

a. All injuries of *any nature* must be reported to the coach at the TIME THEY OCCUR.
b. After the coach has been notified, you *must* report the injury to the nurse's office at the beginning of the next school day.
c. If a player sees a physician for treatment of an injury, he will not be permitted to return to the team to practice or play until he presents to the coach a note signed by the doctor, stating that he is physically able to play soccer.

PERSONAL CONDUCT

a. Do your school work and stay out of trouble in school. We cannot bail you out of detention, special classes, or A.S.P. Let the faculty and administration know that soccer players are gentlemen and good students.

b. If you are assigned to A.S.P. for any reason, or suspended from school, you may not practice or play until you return to school. Then you will have the coaching staff review the reasons for your transgressions. Don't get into a bad situation to begin with.

c. On the day of a game, you will dress for gym class, but DO NOT PARTICIPATE. If you encounter difficulty with your gym teacher, notify a coach and let him take care of the problem.

d. You are responsible for all equipment issued to you.

e. Smoking, drinking, or the abuse of drugs are totally inconsistent with your participation in the sport of soccer and you will refrain from their use. Failure to do so will result in the most serious consequences.

f. Coaches and fellow players are to be treated with respect at all times.

g. Hustle all the time. Be serious about exercises, drills, and practices. They will be used as the basis by which the coaches will judge your suitability to participate in games.

h. Shin guards will be worn for all practices and games.

i. Team members are expected to conduct themselves in a gentlemanly manner on all bus trips and at away contests.

If you have any questions concerning these rules consult your coach.

I have read the attached rules and regulations and agree to comply with them during the current season.

I understand the consequences of failure to comply with these rules and regulations.

____________________________ ____________________________

Student's Signature Date

____________________________ ____________________________

Parent's Signature Date

(See Also: ABILITY; ACHIEVEMENT; ADVERTISING; ALUMNI; AWARDS; BUDGET; CLUBS; EQUIPMENT; FEES; FINES, FUNDS, AND CHARGES; NEWS RELEASES; TRAVEL; VOUCHER)

STRIKES

policy on strikes and demonstrations...

The Board of Education is fully cognizant of the constitutional right of Peaceable Assembly and fully respects this guaranteed right of students.

But this right does not permit students to disrupt the orderly operation of the school program. The Board of Education, in discharge of its statutory obligation, must prevent any interference with the orderly operation of the school. Therefore, the following steps shall be taken in the event of any disruption of the normal operation of schools.

1. The disruption shall be immediately brought to the attention of the Superintendent or his representative by the administrative head of the school. The Superintendent shall have the authority at his discretion to alert the police authorities.
2. Students participating in a disruptive demonstration shall be directed by the building principal or his representative to go to their regular classroom assignment. At the same time, the principal or his representative will arrange for a meeting with the administration and the individuals, leaders of a group, or the group, if feasible, to discuss in a rational, orderly manner, the problem which has caused the disorder.
3. Non-student demonstrators and other unauthorized persons will be directed by the building principal or his representative to remove themselves from school property forthwith.
4. In the event Steps 2 and/or 3 fail to stop the demonstration, the Superintendent or his representative will ask the police to remove the demonstrators and any individuals failing to comply under Step 3.
5. When necessary for their safety, students and staff may be directed to leave the building and school property.
6. At no time, while any demonstration is in progress, is the Superintendent, or any School Board personnel, to enter into negotiations on the issues with the protestors, either orally or in written form.
7. As soon as the normal educational and business processes can be resumed, the Superintendent shall be charged with establishing communications with the leaders of the protesting group in order to resolve their requests or to refer them to the Board of Education in an orderly manner.
8. Students and/or employees participating in the demonstration on school grounds will be subject to suspension.

(See Also: ACADEMIC FREEDOM; CONTRACT; CONTROVERSIAL TOPICS; NEGOTIATIONS; VANDALISM)

STUDENT COUNCIL (GOVERNMENT)

message in student handbook...

STUDENT COUNCIL

Both the junior and senior high schools have student councils, each with its own constitution. Participation in student council activities provides each student with an opportunity to offer valuable service to the school and to develop those characteristics of leadership so vital to the American way of life.

policy statement on...

STUDENT GOVERNMENT

It is important in the maintenance and improvement of democratic institutions that students have the opportunity to participate effectively in the decision-making process necessary for developing responsible and productive citizens. Towards the attainment of this end, students shall have the right to organize and conduct student council or government association activities which contribute to the understanding and functioning of the objectives of the school system.

The objectives of the student government organization shall be to improve the quality of the educational program, to provide to the administration suggestions in that respect, and to assist students in processing grievances.

It shall be the policy of the Board that one student representative to the Board be elected annually from the sophomore and junior classes to serve the following terms of office:

Sophomore Class – 1 year
Junior Class – 2 years

The Board will officially accept these representatives at the annual organization meeting.

The organization, operation and scope of each student government organization shall be defined in a written constitution developed through effective student participation with the school administrators and approved by the Board.

(See Also: ADVISORS AND ADVISORY COMMITTEES; CITIZENSHIP; CLUBS; DANCES; NEWS RELEASES)

STUDENT RECORDS

policy statement on...

The educational interests of the student and of society require the collection, retention and use of information about individual students and groups of students. The welfare and progress of students is inextricably related to the maintenance of a thorough and efficient system of public schools; the latter cannot be achieved or assessed in the absence of appropriate information about the former.

It is no less the interest of society to protect the right of each of its members against an unwarranted invasion of privacy. Society's need to know, then, must be balanced by the individual's right to privacy and self-determination. The primary justification, therefore, of pupil recordkeeping shall be the educational welfare and advancement of the pupil.

The Board of Education has primary responsibility in this district for the compilation, maintenance, access to, and security of pupil records. Only records mandated by the State or Federal Government or the following may be compiled by the staff:

1. Observations and ratings of individual pupils by professional staff members acting within their sphere of competency.
2. Samples of pupil work.
3. Information obtained from professionally acceptable standard instruments of measurement, such as interest inventories, aptitude tests, vocational preference inventories, achievement tests, standardized intelligence tests.
4. Authenticated information provided by a parent or adult pupil concerning achievements and other school activities which the pupil wants to make a part of the record.
5. Verified reports of serious or recurrent behavior patterns.
6. Extracurricular activities and achievements.
7. Rank in class and academic honors earned.
8. Sibling order.
9. Language spoken.
10. Student Description Summary (Secondary Schools).
11. Photographs of individual students.

In addition to the foregoing, the administration is authorized to compile such districtwide information on ethnic groupings as required for State and Federal Reporting, such ethnic grouping to designate Black, Caucasian, Oriental, Spanish, American Indian, Other. No other records may be accumulated unless the collection of such facts has been authorized by the Board. Permitted records shall be preserved for a period of three years after graduation or after the student has left the district.

The Superintendent shall prepare an administrative guide for the implementation of this policy in which he shall define a record, indicate the manner of maintenance, describe the form of the record, identify those who shall be granted access to the records and under what conditions, and provide a procedure for challenging the contents of a pupil's records.

(See Also: ACHIEVEMENT; CHILD STUDY TEAM; ENROLLMENT; GRADES; PERMANENT RECORDS; PROGRESS REPORT; RECORDS; REPORT CARDS; REPORTS; RESOURCE TEAM; UNDERACHIEVERS)

STUDENT TEACHER

policy statement on...

The student teaching experience serves as the culmination of the future teacher's college preparatory program. The goal of the school district is to provide an environment that will encourage the maximum growth of the teacher candidate. Any activities of the school relative to student teaching may be implemented only after a thorough consideration of the effect on its primary objective, that of guaranteeing the best possible education for the children of the district. Additionally, the responsibilities and rights of the cooperating teacher should be considered in the organization of the student teaching program.

Student teachers shall be selected and assigned by the administrative staff with the consent of the principal and supervisor and the cooperating teacher. In the case of candidates with unusual qualification, that is, from unaccredited institutions or programs, from foreign institutions, from special programs of an exceptional or sectarian nature, etc., special approval from the Board is required prior to selection. Student teachers selected to practice in this district shall comply with the Board's policy for employee physical examination.

While serving in the schools, student teachers shall be responsible to the principal through the professional to whom they are assigned for their conduct, and to their college supervisor for their classroom performance. Student teachers shall be allowed to participate in school activities where their contributions would be appropriate to the educational program of the school.

It is not the intent of the school district to dictate the teacher education program of the preparatory institutions. Rather, the district is attempting to work with the college in the fulfilling of the responsibility for teacher preparation.

(See Also: COLLEGE; CONTRACT; DUTIES; EVALUATION; INTERNSHIP; OBSERVATIONS)

STUDY HALL

study hall guidelines...

Needless to say, a study hall is a place where students go to study. This may include doing one's homework, reading, doing research in the library. The teacher's responsibility is three-fold:

1. To develop a climate for learning.
2. To help students *learn* to use their time effectively.
3. If students are to be released, the following guidelines should be followed:
   a. The reason for release should be specific, such as, to do research in the library, to do reading under the oak tree and, on occasion, for a personal reason a teacher feels justifiable. Note: Reasons such as "I am bored and tired" on a repetitive basis (2 days or 3 days out of a week) should not be acceptable.
   b. The *time of release* should be clear. Students should return to the study hall class before going to the next class or to lunch.
   c. *Penalty*. The major effort should be directed at building positive study habits. It should be noted, however, that "permissiveness" should not be equated with a positive approach. In short, failure to comply with agreements reached should result in loss of privilege. The teacher is encouraged to use his or her judgment. In the event that he or she is not able to cope with the situation, he or she should

refer the student for counseling help or for disciplinary action by the administration.

HONORS STUDY HALL

Students recommended for Honors Study Hall should be referred to the vice principal before final commitment is made. The library/resource centers will be directly responsible for the supervision of these students throughout the day. Student eligibility is based on the following criteria:

1. Records and teacher recommendations indicate that the student is responsible.
2. Student fully understands that he is personally held accountable for his action and that this privilege may be removed for just cause.
3. That the student abides by rules and regulations of the school.
4. For off-campus privilege the student must secure permission from his parent and the vice principal, counselor or another administrator.

(See Also: ASSIGNMENTS; CLASS; DUTIES; HOMEWORK; PASSES; SUPERVISION)

SUBSTITUTE TEACHER

list of substitute's responsibilities...

To enable each child to pursue his/her education as smoothly and completely as possible in the absence of the regular teacher, the substitute's responsibility is to:

- ☐ Notify the office **immediately** should a student become ill or an accident occur
- ☐ Notify the office **immediately** if disciplinary assistance is needed
- ☐ Consult the secretary for supplies not available in the room
- ☐ Become familiar with audio-visual materials and machines
- ☐ Report damage of equipment or materials to the office

At the end of the teaching day, the substitute should:

- ☐ Leave the teacher's desk and room in order
- ☐ Return equipment to the proper place(s)
- ☐ Turn off lights, close windows or doors
- ☐ Leave keys and materials in the office
- ☐ Check with the secretary to see if services will be needed the next day
- ☐ Make certain time sheet has been signed
- ☐ If possible, leave comments and record of day's progress and assignments completed

A substitute teacher whose services will extend more than ten (10) days should attend faculty meetings.

A substitute teacher should recognize that he or she will benefit by:

- ☐ Considering all records confidential
- ☐ Avoiding discussion and comparison of situations in one school while serving in another
- ☐ Avoiding comment on the progress of pupils or the work of the teacher
- ☐ Making all observations, suggestions or criticisms to the principal of the school involved
- ☐ Using discretion in expressing personal reactions and opinions about what is seen and heard in a classroom

policy statement on...

1. A substitute must hold a valid state teaching certificate.
2. Substitute teachers will be paid $45.00 per day effective November 2, 1984.
3. A substitute teacher who has held the same position for a period of thirty (30) continuous contracted days will be placed on full pay. The pay shall be retroactive to the first day of substitute teaching in the position.

substitute teacher's record form...

Submission: Month ______ Day ______ 19____

Submit to School District Business Manager according to time sheet schedule for certified staff.

Name of substitute teacher: ______

Address: ______

Phone number: ______

Social Security number: ______

	Day	Teacher(s) for Whom Substituting Was Done	Day	Reason for Absence or Comments	Days or Periods	Daily Earnings	
	15		15			$	
MONTH	16		16				
	17		17				
	18		18				
	19		19				
	20		20				
	21		21				
	22		22				
	23		23				
	24		24				
	25		25				
	26		26				
	27		27				
	28		28				
	29		29				
	30		30				
	31		31				
	1		1				
MONTH	2		2				
	3		3				
	4		4				
	5		5				
	6		6				
	7		7				
	8		8				
	9		9				
	10		10				
	11		11				
	12		12				
	13		13				
	14		14				
				Pay Period Total			

Signed: ______
Substitute Teacher (sign exactly as on social security card)

Signed: ______
Bldg. Principal Authorization

(See Also: APPLICATION; CERTIFICATION; DUTIES; EVALUATION; ILLNESS; INFORMATION; SUPERVISION**)**

SUPERVISION

policy statement on...

It must be understood that students are expected to be under supervision at all times. A teacher's absence from his or her area of supervision does not relieve the teacher of responsibility. Absence may be proven as neglect and the liability then falls on the teacher. The teacher should NOT leave the area in which he or she is supervising students. Remain in your class at ALL times.

All student activities must be authorized and supervised by personnel of the school.

Teachers will be asked to supervise at least one party or other school activity each year—plus help out when needed by the administration.

(See Also: AIDES; ASSIGNMENTS; BUILDING; CAFETERIA; CHAPERONE; CLASS; DANCES; DISCIPLINE; DUTIES; FIELD TRIPS; HALLS and HALL DUTY; LAVATORIES; LUNCH and LUNCH DUTY; POLICE; SAFETY; SPECIAL EDUCATION; SPORTS; STUDENT COUNCIL (GOVERNMENT); SUBSTITUTE TEACHER; VISITORS**)**

SUPPLEMENTAL INSTRUCTION

progress report...

SUPPLEMENTAL INSTRUCTION–PROGRESS REPORT

This report is to be completed in duplicate by both classroom teacher and supplemental instructor in February and June. Both teachers are asked to report on the present academic, emotional and social progress of the student. Return one copy to the Office of Pupil Services. Retain one copy for the student's cumulative folder.

STUDENT_______________________________________ DATE _______________

School ______________________ Grade ________ Subject Area _______________

Classroom Teacher ____

Supplemental Instructor ____

Pretest ____________________ Score ________ Date Administered _____________

Posttest ____________________ Score ________ Date Administered _____________

Supplemental Instructor's Observations of Student's Progress. ________________

____

____

____

Signed ______________________________

Classroom Teacher's Observations of Student's Progress. ____________________

____

____

____

Signed ______________________________

Principal ______________________________

Date ______________________________

student record...

SUPPLEMENTAL INSTRUCTION

STUDENT RECORD

To be kept by Supplemental Instructor and sent to Office of Pupil Personnel Services:

a. When student is removed from program.
b. At the completion of program for the school year.

NAME ______________ ADDRESS ______________

PHONE ________ CLASSIFICATION ______________ D.O.B. ________

NAME OF PARENT ______________ ETHNIC ________

GRADE ____ SCHOOL ________ CLASSROOM TEACHER AND/OR GUIDANCE COUNSELOR ________

SUBJECT	DATE STARTED	SUPPLEMENTAL INSTRUCTOR	HOURS WK.	DATE ENDED	REASON

TOTAL HOURS OF INSTRUCTION RECEIVED (CUMULATIVE) ________

(See Also: ABILITY; CHILD STUDY TEAM; EVALUATION; FAILURE; GRADES; REFERRAL; RESOURCE TEAM; SPECIAL EDUCATION; STUDENT RECORDS; UNDERACHIEVERS; WARNING NOTICES)

SURVEYS

guidelines for...

Surveys can be useful and a great learning device if done properly. Without careful thought, it is not only a useless exercise but may be detrimental because it draws conclusions without adequate data.

The following guidelines should be observed:

1. Surveys within a specific class and/or department should receive the approval of the teachers and the department head.
2. Any survey that includes more than one department within a school should receive administrative approval.
3. Any survey outside of the school must receive, in addition to the above, the approval of the district superintendent.

Some suggestions in evaluating whether a survey is worth conducting are:

1. Is there a stated hypothesis?
2. Do questions relate to the hypothesis?
3. Are questions concise and to the point?
4. Is the format arranged and worded in such a way that it can be easily understood and responded to?
5. Will the instrument benefit the student and/or the school or schools being surveyed?
6. Is the student receiving help in composing, interpreting, summarizing and drawing conclusions of the survey?
7. Will copies of the result be presented to those surveyed?

(See Also: ACADEMIC FREEDOM; BOARD OF EDUCATION; COUNSELING; DISTRIBUTION OF MATERIALS; EVALUATION; QUESTIONS)

SUSPENSION

policy statement on...

The Public School Board, through formal action, has adopted a Student Suspensions and Expulsions Policy. This policy provides a code prohibiting student misconduct in the following areas:

1. disruption of school
2. damage or destruction of school property and stealing or attempting to steal school property

3. damage or destruction of private property and stealing or attempting to steal private property
4. assault on a school employee
5. physical abuse of a student or other person not employed by the school
6. weapons and dangerous instruments
7. narcotics, alcoholic beverages, tobacco and stimulant drugs
8. repeated school violations (failing to comply with directions of teachers, student teachers, substitute teachers, teacher aides, principals, or other authorized school personnel)

A procedural code for dealing with alleged violations is also adopted. The school district has a short-term suspension (suspends students up to ten school days) and a long-term suspension or expulsion (decision to seek suspension over ten days or expulsion).

Any chronic offender who has been suspended for a total of ten school days during a semester by the principal shall appear for a hearing as soon as possible.

procedures for...

SUSPENSION POLICY

1. Students will be advised that they are in jeopardy of being suspended, and parents may be notified by phone or mail. The counseling department, principal, and dean of students or vice-principal will make efforts to counsel the students for the purpose of adjusting the problem before a suspension will be imposed.

2. Flagrant defiance of and disrespect for school regulations, such as fighting or smoking in or around the building, may result in an immediate suspension of up to 10 days with only an informal hearing. A letter stating the offense, the results of the hearing, and the disciplinary action taken will be mailed within 24 hours to the parents.

3. The form below will be completed in the presence of parents, students and administration before suspensions will be imposed.

JUNIOR HIGH SCHOOL

Record of hearing on. . . . .

Date ______________________ Student ______________________

A hearing is used at the Junior High School when a student's repeated violations of school rules indicate that his parents may be asked to withdraw him from school.

On the above named date, the parents and student were called in for a hearing with school personnel. This was done with a sincere desire on the part of the school to keep the student in school if possible and to make sure that all the pertinent facts concerning the problems were carefully reviewed and discussed by all parties before making a decision on future attendance.

The decision reached by school officials as a result of this hearing is as follows:

( ) Student suspended from school for a period of

____

( ) Student allowed to remain in school on a probationary status with the following agreement signed and agreed to by the parties involved.

AGREEMENT

Due to repeated violations of the rules and regulations of the Junior High School by

____

this agreement will make it understood between student, parent(s), and school authorities that any further infractions of rules and regulations will be cause for suspension from attendance at the Junior High for ten school days.

Other Parties present at hearing:

______________________________ Student ______________

______________________________ Parent ______________

______________________________ School Official ______________

4. Upon parental request, assignments will be provided for any student on suspension out of school.

PURPOSE OF SUSPENSION

When a pupil is suspended, the school seeks the aid of the parents to help adjust the problem. The school and the parents can then work together cooperatively to adjust the problem.

All students are given informal hearings for any suspensions up to ten days' duration. Longer suspensions require and are given formal hearings.

FORMAL HEARINGS

Parent is requested to bring lawyer and/or anyone he/she wishes to a meeting in the principal's office. The results of the formal hearing places students on probationary status (one chance) or on suspension out of school.

(See Also: BEHAVIOR; BOARD OF EDUCATION; CHILD STUDY TEAM; DISCIPLINE; DUE PROCESS; EXPULSION; REFERRAL; RIGHTS AND RESPONSIBILITIES)

TARDINESS AND TRUANCY

message to students concerning...

When you are tardy, it will be necessary to secure an admit slip from the Dean of Girls or the Vice Principal. Tardies should be covered by a written excuse on the day you are tardy or on the following day. The parents of a pupil who is frequently tardy without apparent excuse will be notified that if the unexcused tardies persist, the pupil will be placed on special detention.

Students who get up too late or who miss the school bus or their ride are to report to school late. Late students are not penalized if they bring an excuse the following day.

Students who stay home for the above reasons will be counted as truant. Students who are late for class during the day are placed on detention. One night of detention is given each time you are late. If you are a bus student, you must report to the vice principal or dean of girls for a report topic instead of taking detention.

message to teachers concerning...

The student is to be admitted by the teacher in charge. The student will remain at school after regular dismissal to make up the time lost in the classroom; minimum time is 30 minutes. Each staff member will be responsible for his or her assigned evening. Please report the tardies by 4:00 on the day they occur. Sign and use the provided form.

(See Also: ABSENCE; ABSENTEEISM; CLASS; CUTTING; DISCIPLINE; STUDENT RECORDS; UNDERACHIEVERS)

TELEPHONE

samples of message concerning use of...

TELEPHONES

Public telephones are located on the first floor. The telephone in the office is to be used only in case of an emergency. No pupil or teacher will be called from a classroom to answer a telephone call.

There are two pay telephones for your use after school; one in the main hall and one near the door to the office. In the morning and before school and during the day, students who have urgent reasons for using the telephone are to have a written pass from their teachers and be excused from class in the regular manner.

Unless an emergency exists, students are requested to avoid asking permission to use the office phone.

TELEPHONES

There are five telephones in the building.

The phone in the hall is a call-out phone only. Students should be discouraged from using the telephone unless necessary. You should discuss this with the class so they get in the habit of checking with you ahead of time. It seems that the same students are often lined up using the phone day after day. Phone calls to go home with someone else to play, etc., are not really that necessary and should be discouraged so the lines are kept open for the child who really needs to call home. Children need to go directly home after school as parents expect them. Dial "7" first to get an outside line when using the hall phone.

There is also a phone in room #17. If you use this phone when classes are being held in either of those two rooms, please hold the volume down. There is a phone in the counselor's room and one in the fall-out shelter.

Please do not use school time to make personal phone calls. Try to limit the time on calls so as not to tie up the phone for too long.

All long distance phone calls should be cleared with the principal ahead of time. Long distance calls are to be logged at the time the call is made on the record available from the secretary.

You can take calls that come into the office on the phones in the hall or in room #17. We try to take messages and encourage people to call back if calls come during classes—if we contact you in regard to a phone call, let us know if you are busy at that time. Try to avoid taking phone calls or making them during instructional sessions.

(See Also: **HALLS AND HALL DUTY; HANDBOOK; MAP OF THE SCHOOL; PASSES)**

TEXTBOOKS

budget preparation guide and form...

TO: Principals
FROM: District Superintendent
RE: TEXTBOOK AND EQUIPMENT—MULTI-YEAR PLANS

The new law requires us to accurately and periodically determine textbook and equipment requirements.

A six-year Textbook and Equipment—Multi-Year Plan was initiated in 1980, which reflects the school's need for textbooks and equipment for each of six fiscal years.

A. UPDATING MULTI-YEAR PLAN
   1. Please revise your plan to reflect 1982 through 1988.
   2. Involve your instructional and support staff and the school community council.

B. PROCEDURES FOR UPDATING MULTI-YEAR PLAN
   1. Update your multi-year plan starting with the 1982–1983 school year.
   2. Copies of your initial multi-year plans, submitted in 1980, are provided for your guidance.
   3. Use *Multi-Year Plan to Meet Textbook Needs* form to prepare your updated plan.
      a. Form used for both elementary and secondary schools.
      b. Space provided to identify grade level (elementary) and department (secondary).
      c. Principal signs each plan.
      d. List titles which are to be purchased during the six-year period identified on the multi-year plan.
      e. Type in the year in which the *original set was purchased.* (Date may not necessarily coincide with copyright or year of printing.)
      f. Replacement Category—Check appropriate replacement category for each item:
         (1) "Obs."—Obsolete—no longer useful because of outmoded/outdated content or technology.
         (2) Lost—self-explanatory.
         (3) BER—Beyond Economical Repair.
      g. Additional Needs Category
         (1) List additional needs to existing program.
         (2) List additional needs due to new programs.

h. Unit Cost:

(1) Use the unit cost figures listed on Exhibit "A" for 1982–1983 and for all subsequent fiscal years up to 1987–1988. DO NOT INCLUDE inflation index. The State Budget Office will adjust the totals for all fiscal years for inflation.

(2) For books not listed on Exhibit "A," use current cost, which includes charges for shipping and handling.

(3) Total at bottom and at right—six-year requirement.

(4) Round off all figures to nearest dollar.

4. Form Format

a. Type all information.

b. Prepare in triplicate.

c. Use only forms provided. Request if you need more.

C. SUBMITTALS

1. Staple textbook plans.
2. Return the 1981–1987 multi-year plan.
3. Submit original and first copies of plans.
4. DUE DATE: Submit multi-year plans, together with School Level B & C Budget, to District Business Office by March 15.

MULTI-YEAR PLAN TO MEET TEXTBOOK NEEDS

School ______________
Principal ______________
Date ______________

DISTRICT ______________ Subject ______________

Grade (Elem.) ______________
Dept. (Sec.) ______________

SUBJECT	Yr. Orig. Set Acq.	Number of Units Needed					Unit Cost	AMOUNTS REQUIRED (To Nearest Dollar)						Total 6-Yr. Requirement
		Replacement			Additions									
		Lost	Obs.	B.E.R.	Add to Prog.	New Prog.		19 –	19 –	19 –	19 –	19 –	19 –	
TOTALS														

Page ______ of ______

messages to students concerning the use of...

TEXTBOOKS

Textbooks are lent to you by the school districts so you can receive an education. These books are often used from year to year so the utmost care should be taken to preserve them. Your teacher will assess the condition of the books in September when they are given to you and in June when they are collected. If there is any damage done to the book during ownership, you will be asked to pay for the damage.

Children are granted permission to take textbooks home for completing unfinished daily work. Parents are encouraged to show an interest in all work and material brought home by the child. Textbooks that have been lost or damaged due to negligence must be replaced by the pupil.

TEXTBOOKS AND LIBRARY BOOKS

All students are supplied with books at the opening of school. Deposits are not required, but students are responsible for keeping them covered at all times and seeing that they are returned in good condtion. Textbooks are the property of the school district and lost or damaged books must be paid for by the student at the cost of replacement. Library books must also be replaced.

(See Also: ASSIGNMENTS; BOARD OF EDUCATION; BOOKS; BUDGET; ELECTIVES; FEES, FINES, FUNDS, AND CHARGES; HANDBOOK; HOMEWORK; LIBRARY; OBJECTIVES; REQUISITIONS, REPAIRS, AND REPLACEMENTS)

TIME

employee time distribution sheet . . .

EMPLOYEE TIME DISTRIBUTION SHEET
Personal Services
Quarter ________ 19 ___

Date ______________________________

Name ____
(Last) (First) (Initial)

____
(Employee Signature)

Title ____

____
(Approved by)

		DAY OF MONTH																														TOTAL		
MONTH	JOB OR TASK	1	2	3	4	5	6	7	8	9	10	11	12	13	14	15	16	17	18	19	20	21	22	23	24	25	26	27	28	29	30	31	TIME	RATE	AMOUNT
																																	QUARTER'S TOTALS			

"An Equal Opportunity Employer"

sample schedule of class periods...

Teachers:	Regular Schedule	7:42–2:27
	Late Schedule	8:52–3:27
Students:	7 Period Day	8:15–2:12
	6 Period Day	9:04–2:12
Teacher Administrative		7:42–8:12

		Outside Warning Bells	
		8:12	
Period 1	8:15–9:01	8:51	P.E.
Period 2	9:04–9:51	9:41	P.E.
Period 3	9:54–10:38	10:28	P.E.
Period 4	10:41–11:26	10:59	Lunch
4a	10-41–11:02	11:16	P.E.
4b	11:05–11:26	11:23	Lunch
Period 5	11:29–12:38		
5a	11:29–11:50	11:47	Lunch
5b	11:53–12:14	12:11	Lunch
5c	12:17–12:38	12:28	P.E.
		12:35	Lunch
Period 6	12:41– 1:25	1:15	P.E.
Period 7	1:28– 2:12	2:02	P.E.
		2:50	P.E.

Buses Arrive/Activity Period begins	2:16
Buses Depart	2:20
Teachers Leave	2:27
End of Activity Period/ Late Buses Arrive	3:00
Late Buses Depart	3:05
Late Schedule Teachers Leave	3:27

time report (for food service)...

FOOD SERVICE - TIME REPORTS

MONTH ________ YEAR ________ Scheduled Hours ____

EMPLOYEE NAME ____________________

SCHOOL ____________________ SCHOOL NO. ____________

Social Security No. ____________

WEEK	SUN.	MON.	TUES.	WED.	THUR.	FRI.	SAT.	TOTAL	
1									
	BLDG. RENTALS OR OVERTIME							TOTAL O. T. HOURS	TOTAL HOURS
	Date	Reason					Hours		

WEEK	SUN.	MON.	TUES.	WED.	THUR.	FRI.	SAT.	TOTAL	
2									
	BLDG. RENTALS OR OVERTIME							TOTAL O. T. HOURS	TOTAL HOURS
	Date	Reason					Hours		

WEEK	SUN.	MON.	TUES.	WED.	THUR.	FRI.	SAT.	TOTAL	
3									
	BLDG. RENTALS OR OVERTIME							TOTAL O. T. HOURS	TOTAL HOURS
	Date	Reason					Hours		

WEEK	SUN.	MON.	TUES.	WED.	THUR.	FRI.	SAT.	TOTAL	
4									
	BLDG. RENTALS OR OVERTIME							TOTAL O. T. HOURS	TOTAL HOURS
	Date	Reason					Hours		

WEEK	SUN.	MON.	TUES.	WED.	THUR.	FRI.	SAT.	TOTAL	
5									
	BLDG. RENTALS OR OVERTIME							TOTAL O. T. HOURS	TOTAL HOURS
	Date	Reason					Hours		

LEAVE CODES

S - Sick Leave
F - Family Sick
X - Deduction
P - Personal Leave
D - Death Family
A - School Business

(For Office Use Only)

Reg. ________

Sick ________

Fam. ________

Pers. ________

Death ________

Sc. Bus. ________

O. Time ________

TOTAL HOURS ________

BLDG. CONTRACT: $________

MILEAGE ________

Employee Signature ____________________

Supervisor Signature ____________________

(See Also: BUSINESS; CONTRACT; MONEY; PAYROLL; SALARY; VOUCHER; WORK)

TORNADO

safety drill instructions...

The area in which we live is subject to turbulent weather. Because of the possibility of a tornado occurring during school hours, we have developed plans and will be conducting drills.

Tornado drills require different actions than fire drills. NO alarm will be sounded in the school—the command to take cover will be given verbally. When a tornado threatens, your immediate action can save your life! When the verbal command is given, begin immediately to act in accordance with the tornado safety rules below:

1. Students in classrooms are to move to the nearest north-south hallways in an orderly manner.
2. Students in the gym (Phy. Ed., Swimming, Outside Activities) and Industrial Arts report to their respective locker rooms.
3. Students in the lunchroom take cover under the tables.
4. Students shall face the wall in the hallway, and when the following command is given, all students shall assume the protective postures. "Everybody down! Crouch on elbows and knees! Hands over back of head!"
5. Remain in this position until the ALL CLEAR signal is given verbally.
6. At all times, follow the directions of the staff.
7. STAY AWAY FROM WINDOWS, DOORS AND OUTSIDE WALLS! PROTECT YOUR HEAD.

(See Also: BOMB THREATS; CLOSE OF SCHOOL; EARTHQUAKE; EMERGENCY; SAFETY**)**

TRANSFER

of classified personnel...

CLASSIFIED TRANSFER REQUEST
Food Service, Secretarial, Teacher Aide

TO: Classified Personnel Specialist

FROM: ______________________________ ______________
(Name) (Date)

______________________________ ______________
(Current Building Assignment) (Position)

My preference(s) for reassignment is: (Please list no more than four.)

	School	Position
1.		
2.		
3.		
4.		

____
(Signature)

—For Personnel Office Use—

Interview Schedule

School	Position	Date	Interviewer

Disposition: ______________________________

of professional personnel...

TRANSFER NOTIFICATION

Date ____________________

Name of Teacher ____

Current School ____

This is official notification of your transfer to:

____

(New Assignment School)

effective ____________________

(Date)

It might be well for you to arrange to meet with your new principal as soon as possible. We have made every effort to meet teacher requests in accordance with the need of the school district. Best wishes for the new school year.

Director of Personnel

cc: ____________________ Principal
Current School

____________________ Principal
New Assignment School

of students...

Any student who withdraws from Rock Township to attend another school must do the following:

1. **PARENT APPROVAL**—Have your parent or guardian call the school or write a brief note indicating **when** and **where** your family is moving.
2. **WITHDRAWAL SLIP**—Stop at the office before homeroom on the morning of your last day at Rock Township. The office will give you a **withdrawal slip** which you will take to each class to get your grades and a check-out signature from each teacher. Be sure you turn in all books, locks and equipment to your teachers so that you will not have to pay unnecessary charges. Your school records cannot be forwarded to your next school until all fees and lost or damaged books are paid for.
3. **FINAL CHECK-OUT**—Return the **withdrawal slip** to the office at 3:20 before you leave. At this time you will be given a copy of your subjects and grades to take to your next school. Any fee refunds due will be returned to you at this time.

Students transferring two weeks prior to the final day of school will be issued final grades and credit at the discretion of the building principal. Requests for a transfer prior to that time (assuming the student will not re-enter school the balance of this year) will result in students getting grades to date of withdrawal only. No promotions or credits will be issued.

TRANSFERRING TO ANOTHER COURSE

If you need to change a course within a department, for example, Algebra to General Math or English IA to English 1B, then no withdrawal designation will become part of your record. Rather, the grades of both courses will be used in determining a final grade.

Remember that you cannot transfer after the end of the 1st marking period.

(See Also: ASSIGNMENTS; CONTRACT; DUE PROCESS; GRIEVANCES; LEAVE OF ABSENCE; RECORDS)

TRAVEL

claim form for travel expense reimbursement...

Name ______________________ Month of ______________ 198____

School ______________________ Official Position ______________

School Address ______________________

Daily Expenses For Which Reimbursement Is Claimed (See Instructions On Reverse Side.)

Day	POINTS COVERED BY TRAVEL	Personal Vehicle Miles	Miscellaneous Expense	OUT-OF-STATE		IN-STATE	TOT MLS. & LODG.	
				Meals	Lodging	Qtrs. Day Claimed		
(1)	(2)	(3)	(4)	(5)	(6)	(7)	(8)	
1								
2								
3								
4								
5								
6								
7								
8								
9								
10								
11								
12								
13								
14								
15								
16								
17								
18								
19								
20								
21								
22								
23								
24								
25								
26								
27								
28								
29								
30								
31								

Purpose of Travel and Explanation of Expenses

Total Miles			
	Total Meals & Lodging		
	Total Misc. Expense		
	Miles @18¢ Per mile		
	Miles @25¢ Per mile		
	Miles @30¢ Per mile		
	Comm. Transport Expense		
	Total		

BUDGET CODING				
Acct. No.	Dept.	School	Check No.	Amount

request for travel form...

Please check one

1. Request for Travel Advance ☐
2. Claim for Reimbursement ☐

Receipts Attached ☐

FOR OFFICE USE ONLY Amount
_____@ $3.00 _____
_____@ 4.00 _____
_____@ 9.00 _____
_____@ 0.20 _____
Additional Lodging _____
Total Advance _____

Names: 1. _____

2. _____

3. _____

4. _____

5. _____

6. _____

7. _____

8. _____

Place _____

Dates _____ to _____

Time of Departure: (Date and Hour) _____

Time of Return: (Date and Hour) _____

Purpose of Trip: _____

_____

_____

(use additional sheets if necessary)

(Form continued)

request for travel form (cont'd)

APPROVALS:

1. ______________________
Unit Supervisor

2. ______________________
Superintendent

FOR OFFICE USE ONLY

APPROVED FOR PAYMENT

____

Director of Administrative Services

CHARGE TO: Department ______ Account Number ______ Amount ______

(See Also: BUS; FIELD TRIPS; PERMISSION SLIPS; SPORTS; TRIPS; VOUCHER)

TRIPS

request to arrange trip forms...

School ______________________

Class or Group Going ______________________ Date of Trip ______________

TIME OF LEAVING SCHOOL: __________ TIME OF RETURN: ______________
(ARRIVAL AT SCHOOL)

Destination (Address/Location) & Scheduled Itinerary: (Specify times of appointments and/or reservations or routing, if necessary) ______________________

____

____

No. Pupils to Go ________ Mode of Transportation: School Bus ______________

No. Adults to Go ________ Coach ______________

Personal Vehicle ______________

Other ______________

TRANSPORTATION ARRANGEMENTS:

If Board of Education is paying any part of transportation costs, arrangements MUST be made by the Transportation Office.

If contractor is preferred: ______________________

WILL BE ARRANGED BY TEACHER ____ TRANSPORTATION OFFICE TO ARRANGE ____

(If by teacher, complete following) CARRIER ______________________

Teacher or Teachers in Charge: ______________________

How many substitutes needed? ____________ For which teachers? ____________

____

DO YOU HAVE, OR WILL YOU HAVE BY THE TIME OF THE TRIP, A RELEASE FROM RESPONSIBILITY SLIP FROM THE PARENTS OF EACH PUPIL WHO TAKES THIS TRIP?

____

(Note: No pupil is to be permitted to go unless such a release is presented.)

TEACHER MAKING THIS REQUEST ______________ Date ______________

Approval of Principal ______________________ Date ______________

Approval of Superintendent ____________________ Date ______________

Board of Education Pays ________ Group Pays ________

PLEASE COMPLETE ALL OF THIS FORM SO THAT APPROVAL AND ARRANGEMENTS CAN BE EXPEDITED.

NAME ______________________ DEPARTMENT ______________________

DATE(S) ______________________

NUMBER OF STUDENTS EACH DATE: __________

DESTINATION: ____

____

DEPARTURE TIME: ______________________

RETURN TIME: ______________________

METHOD OF FINANCING

☐ STUDENT

☐ FUND RAISING*

*EXPLAIN ____

____

____

TOTAL COST PER PUPIL ______________________

HOW DO YOU PLAN TO PROVIDE ADEQUATE SUPERVISION? __________

____

____

APPROVAL OF DEPARTMENT COORDINATOR ______________________

trip impact report form...

FIELD TRIPS: OPERATIONAL IMPACT REPORT

Each Application for Field Trip utilizing the school day must now be accompanied by a report on how the principal plans to compensate for the impact of a field trip on the day's operation of the school. Impact is exemplified by a teacher or aide having a free period(s), other teachers not knowing the class was going on a trip, quality substitute not being booked in advance, how students will make up the classwork they will miss, etc.

Impact on School	Plan(s) to Compensate for the Impact

Date of Trip: ________________

School: ________________

Grade/Class Involved: ________________

Destination of Trip: ________________

(See Also: ACCIDENT; FEES; FINES, FUNDS, AND CHARGES; INSURANCE; PERMISSION SLIPS; SUPERVISION; TRAVEL; VOUCHER**)**

TYPISTS

outline of typist's duties...

1. Inventory
   a. Keep inventory up-to-date
   b. Prepare and type State and County inventories
2. Keys
   a. Custodian of keys
3. Typing
   a. Type letters, memos, reports, etc., for administration
   b. Duplicate and mimeograph materials
4. Student Bus Transportation
5. Daily Bulletin
6. Responsible for notifying parking violations and tagging vehicles; obtaining registration information from County Treasurer's office if not available.
7. Miscellaneous
   a. Process request for use of facilities by outside organization; bill organization when necessary
   b. Do routine office work—sorting mail, answering telephone, being receptionist, etc.
   c. Assist in supervision of student monitors assigned to the main office
   d. Perform other duties as assigned by secretary or administrators

(See Also: ADDRESS; ATTENDANCE; BULLETIN; CLERICAL SERVICES; DISTRIBUTION OF MATERIALS; SECRETARY; XEROXING)

UNDERACHIEVERS

form to parents of...

STUDENT: ________________ GRADE __________ MARKING PERIOD ENDS ____________

SUBJECT ____________________ TEACHER ____________________ DATE ____________

Dear Parents,

As your child's teacher, I am becoming concerned about a situation which is beginning to develop and which could have serious affects upon your child's school career if not handled soon. Therefore, I am sending you this in the hope that, acting as a team, we may help your child in his/her academic progress.

______________________________ appears to be working well UNDER the level at which he/she could be. He/she could be doing much better work than he/she is currently producing. I am certain that you are aware that should this trend continue, it could lead to poor grades, possible failure, and a lack of valuable skills on the part of your child.

I have checked below some of the things your son/daughter might do to help improve this situation. If you have any questions or if you believe that a conference would be helpful, please call the guidance department at ____________________.

(Form continued)

(Form continued)

Working together, I know we can help your child do the work he/she is capable of doing.

_______ be more attentive in class

_______ be more cooperative in class

_______ come prepared for class (bring books, pencils, etc.)

_______ listen to and follow directions carefully

_______ participate more actively in class

_______ learn to take notes in class

_______ learn to accept criticism and evaluation

_______ do the assigned work regularly (homework, classwork, etc.)

_______ find out about and make up assignments after absence

_______ try to improve the quality of assignments

_______ study more diligently for tests and quizzes

_______ respect the rights of others

_______ come for extra help when needed

_______ OTHER ____

____

____

____

Please sign this report and return it to me via your child. If you have any comments, please use the back of this report. Thank you.

PARENT'S SIGNATURE: ______________________ DATE: ________________

(See Also: ABILITY; ACHIEVEMENT; CHILD STUDY TEAM; COUNSELING; EVALUATION; GRADES; OBSERVATIONS; REFERRAL; RESOURCE TEAM; SUPPLEMENTAL INSTRUCTION; WARNING NOTICES**)**

USE OF FACILITIES

complete rules for use of facilities...

1. An application for a permit to use public school buildings by persons not officially connected with the schools must be filed with the Secretary at least two weeks prior to the date for which the building is to be used.
2. An application for a permit to use public school buildings by persons or organizations officially connected with the schools, when the school will be used after 5 p.m., must be approved by the Principal and Superintendent of Schools, and filed with the Secretary at least ten days prior to the date for which the building is to be used.
3. All permits shall be revocable and shall not be considered a lease, and the Board or its authorized agent may reject any application or cancel any permit. The charges will not be considered as rental charges, but will be limited to operating expenses with a reasonable allowance for wear and tear.
4. It is understood that in all cases the regular school activities of organizations of the school shall have first preference when requesting the use of any part of the building.
5. All entertainments are to be of high moral standard, and only as stated on application.
6. A permit is not transferrable.
7. An approved permit will be returned to the applicant.
8. The Secretary/Business Administrator will send a copy of any permit issued to the Principal or head of each school.
9. It is understood and agreed that the applicant assumes responsibility for the preservation of order in said building, and liability for any damage to or loss of school property, and for the strict observance of all regulations of the Board of Education with regard to the buildings.
10. Organizations, clubs, and individuals must furnish a certificate of liability insurance.
11. The holder of a permit to use any part of the school building or grounds must provide sufficient fire and police protection at each performance to uphold law and order, when recommended by the Secretary of the Board.
12. Only that part of the school building specifically mentioned in the permit is to be used.
13. As a general rule, there shall be no smoking in school buildings. Under approved conditions, smoking may be permitted in certain areas.
14. All national and state laws, local ordinances and rules of the Police and Fire Departments regarding public assemblies must be strictly complied with.

15. No pianos, projectors, scenery or other apparatus are to be moved into the building unless special permission is granted.
16. It is understood that school auditoriums are not adapted to receive professional entertainment equipment, and that special equipment of any kind, including spotlights, floodlights, Klieg lights, stage scenery, phonographs, band instruments, moving picture apparatus, signs, etc., will not be furnished by the Board, and permission must be granted by the Board to use any of the above equipment.
17. The services of Custodians do not include the erecting or dismantling of scenery or equipment unless such scenery or equipment is the property of the Board of Education.
18. Scenery, foliage, and other equipment provided by the holder of a permit must be removed from the building promptly after the performance so as not to interfere with school activities.
19. All meetings, entertainments, dances, etc., must cease as soon after midnight as feasible, but in any event no later than 1 a.m., and Custodians must see that the building is closed promptly.
20. The number of tickets sold must not exceed the seating capacity of the auditorium or gymnasium for which the permit is granted.
21. When a permit is granted, the schools must be in charge of the regular employees of the Board of Education, the number of whom, in each case, will be subject to the discretion of the Secretary/Business Administrator.
22. The auditorium, gymnasium, and other school rooms are for school uses, and a permit for other purposes will be issued only when no interference with school activities arises therefrom.
23. Whenever materials, equipment, furnishings, or rubbish are left after the use of a school building by persons not officially connected with the schools, the party to whom the permit is issued will be required to pay for the cost of removal of same, which will not be delayed for the convenience of the party who used the building.
24. The use of the gymnasium will require sneakers or basketball shoes, with the exception of Junior Proms and other special activities as approved by the Board.
25. No Custodians shall have the right to open any school building outside of school hours (including Saturdays and Sundays) for any person or persons unless they first have authority to open said building from the Board of Education Business Office.
26. Should the holder of a permit wish to cancel a reserved date, the Board of Education Business Office must be notified at least by 12 noon on the day of the meeting or performance. If no notice is received by the Board, and the holder of the permit fails to appear within one hour after the meeting or performance is scheduled to start, the holder of the permit must pay the regular charge for the extra services of each Custodian employed, and also the operating costs (if any) for the time the building is kept open.

27. The Board, or its representative, shall at all times have free access to all parts of the school building, and the Board of Education, or its representative, reserves the right to revoke any permit should action be deemed necessary or desirable and in the best interests of the school system and the public, generally.
28. The holder of a permit must pay *promptly* the charges stated on said permit.
29. If a course is offered by a university at the request of the administration, the building will be available at no cost; but if a university requests to use the building to offer a course or courses, then the usual fees will be charged.

policy statement on...

The purpose of this policy is to establish one central clearing house for the reservation of outside use dates at all schools in the district. The Secretary/Business Administrator shall be responsible on behalf of the Board for the rental of school facilities in accordance with established procedures. In the discharge of these responsibilities, he may receive applications and fees for the use of Board facilities and issue all necessary permits for the Board, provided the intended use is for educational, philanthropic or civic purposes. However, if the Secretary/Business Administrator deems it wise to hold an application for the Board's action, he may present such application at the next Board meeting. In the event any emergency situation arises, the Secretary/Business Administrator shall obtain approval of the President and Vice-President and report on their joint action at the next regular Board meeting.

The Secretary/Business Administrator shall not permit the use of schools if the purpose or result of such use is personal gain to any individual(s), or the use is of a political nature or the use is sectarian in character, unless special permission is given by the Board.

reservation form for the use of school facilities...

RESERVATIONS FOR USE OF SCHOOL BUILDINGS

TO: ______________________ ______________________
DATE PHONE #

FROM: ______________________ ______________________
ADVISOR/SIGNATURE ADDRESS

MAY I RESERVE THE:

_____ Auditorium _____ Cafeteria _____ MPR

_____ Gym _____ Pool Area _____ Other

ON: ______________________ ______________________
DATE PERIOD/TIME

____
TYPE OF FUNCTION

RESERVATION: __________ Approved ______________________
ADMINISTRATIVE APPROVAL
(for activity periods only)

__________ Not Approved

REASON: ____

(See Also: BUILDING; CUSTODIAL SERVICES; MEETINGS; OPEN HOUSE; REQUISITIONS, REPAIRS, AND REPLACEMENTS)

VANDALISM

sample statements concerning vandalism...

VANDALISM

If any student commits an act of vandalism on school property, the appropriate action will be taken by the school and parents will be held financially responsible for all damages.

VANDALISM

The Rock Township Board of Education has adopted stringent measures for dealing with school vandalism. The school administration is responsible for working with the Police Department in the investigation, apprehension, and prosecution of juveniles caught in the act of breaking, entering or commiting acts of vandalism on school property. After school punishment has taken place, parents of students who commit acts of vandalism will be held financially responsible for all damages.

(See Also: BEHAVIOR; BUDGET; CITIZENSHIP; DEMONSTRATIONS; EQUIPMENT; LAVATORIES; POLICE; REFERRAL**)**

VENDORS

vendor record form...

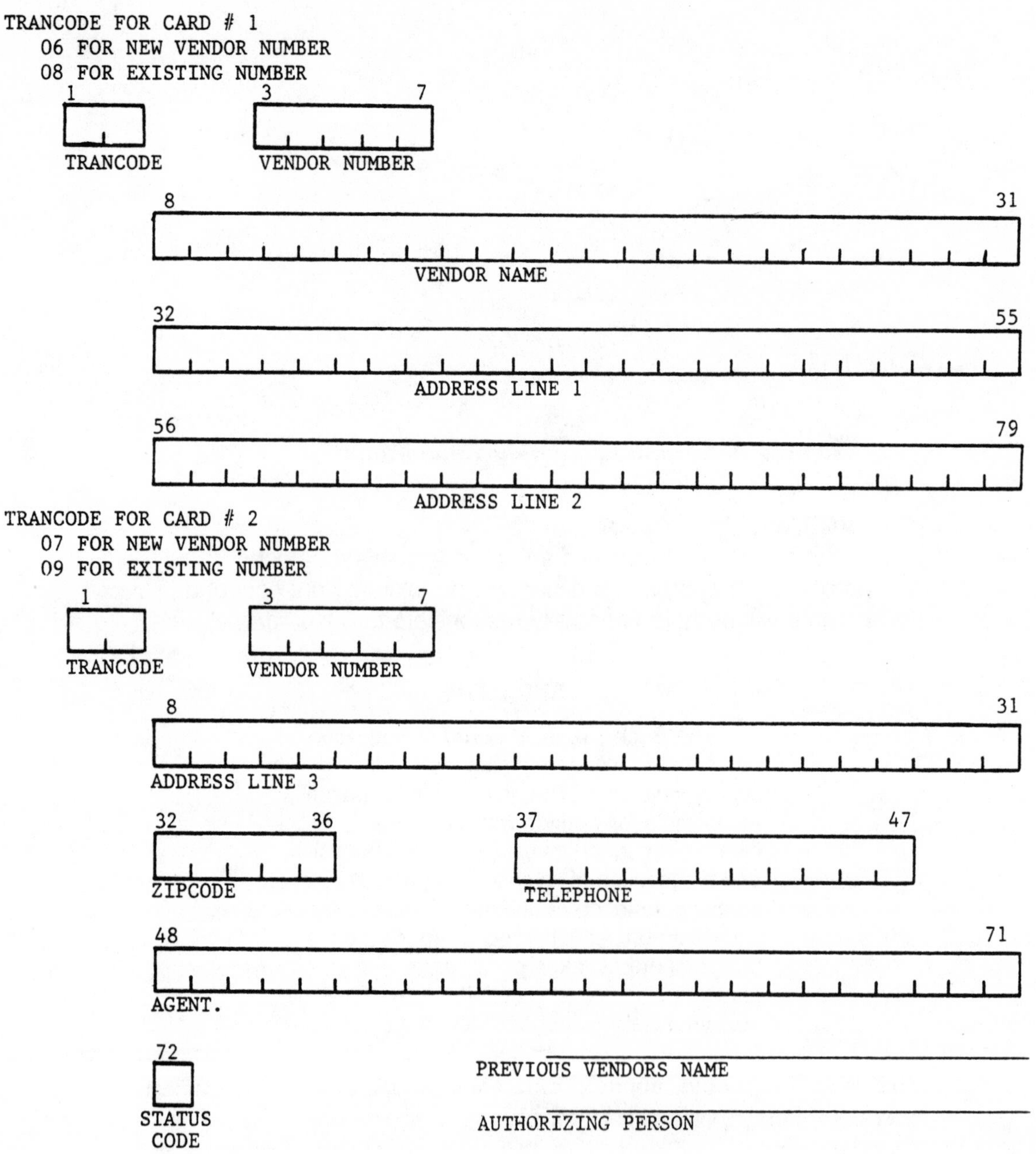

TRANCODE FOR CARD # 1
06 FOR NEW VENDOR NUMBER
08 FOR EXISTING NUMBER

1 TRANCODE
3–7 VENDOR NUMBER
8–31 VENDOR NAME
32–55 ADDRESS LINE 1
56–79 ADDRESS LINE 2

TRANCODE FOR CARD # 2
07 FOR NEW VENDOR NUMBER
09 FOR EXISTING NUMBER

1 TRANCODE
3–7 VENDOR NUMBER
8–31 ADDRESS LINE 3
32–36 ZIPCODE
37–47 TELEPHONE
48–71 AGENT.
72 STATUS CODE

PREVIOUS VENDORS NAME ____________________

AUTHORIZING PERSON ____________________

TRANSACTION CODE AND VENDOR NUMBER ARE <u>REQUIRED</u> ENTRIES. ALL OTHER ENTRIES ARE OPTIONAL, DEPENDING ON TRANCODE.

(See Also: BOARD OF EDUCATION; BIDS; BUDGETS; BUSINESS; EQUIPMENT; MONEY; PURCHASING; REQUISITIONS, REPAIRS, AND REPLACEMENTS)

VICE-PRINCIPAL

sample outline of duties of...

Duties Summary

Under the general administrative direction of the principal of Rock Township High School, Rock District School, Department of Education, the incumbent assists the principal in administering all aspects of the school program including personnel management, curriculum development, student discipline and guidance, student activities, business management, building and ground maintenance, school-community relations, and other related duties as may be required or directed. He, generally, shares the administrative responsibility for planning, implementing and evaluating all facets that lead to a better educational program for all students in the school.

Duties and Responsibilities

Assists the principal in the overall personnel program of the school which includes faculty, clerical, custodial, cafeteria, and other support personnel.

1. Interviews and helps to select and assign personnel to allocated or vacant positions based upon candidates' competencies and qualifications.
2. Establishes and implements a means by which teachers may volunteer or be assigned to school-related activities on a fair and equitable basis and thereby achieve the most effective overall program with due regard and respect for contractural provisions and faculty morale.
3. Supervises and evaluates the classroom cleaners and follows up on classroom teachers' complaints and/or criticisms.
4. Interviews all substitute teacher candidates; works with department heads in compiling subject field substitute lists; and supervises the substitute teacher program.
5. Communicates immediately and/or works with the Personnel Specialists, Rock District Schools, on matters pertaining to faculty and staff personnel concerns and problems and follows through to ensure a most hasty resolution.
6. Receives and acknowledges all correspondence pertaining to job inquiries.
7. Assists in the orientation, supervision and evaluation of all faculty and staff personnel.
8. Assists in the handling of grievance and/or complaints submitted by faculty and staff personnel.

9. Mediates or helps to resolve problems or concerns between and among faculty and/ or staff personnel.
10. Has direct supervision of the campus worker, hired under the Comprehensive Employment and Training Act of the Federal Government, to work with alienated students in the school.
11. Assists in the formalizing of personnel practices consistent with DOE policies and regulations, collective bargaining agreements and school policies, regulations and philosophies.
12. Assists in establishing the master schedule and program scheduling for teachers.
13. Assists in the preparation and planning for faculty and Curriculum Committee meetings.
14. Extends administrative assistance, guidance and participation in the accreditation program.
15. Sits in on meetings with the Governance Committee.
16. Works with department heads and faculty in the implementation of the Department of Education's reduction in force policy.
17. Determines position vacancies and communicates this through memos directed to the Personnel Specialists, Rock District Schools.
18. Assists in the supervision of the teachers' campus duty.
19. Writes letters of commendation or recommendation on behalf of teachers.
20. Assists in nomination of teachers for outstanding teacher honors or titles and writes up recommendations to send to sponsoring organizations.
21. Acknowledges and expedites requests by college faculty to place teacher training students in the school for classroom training experience. Coordinates these on-going requests with the department heads.

Assists the principal in providing direction to pupil personnel program.

1. Processes teacher referrals of student disciplinary cases and follows through to resolution of the problem.
2. Assists in the exercise of maximum use of counseling in having students select their courses.
3. Assists in providing for student health and safety programs.
4. Attends extracurricular program activities, such as band and choir concerts, and interscholastic contests.
5. Assists in the planning and organizing of student registration.
6. Advises student leaders or chairpersons through the asking of pertinent questions regarding their activity.
7. Assists in the encouraging and maintaining of supervision of all student activities, such as dance affairs, homecoming events, elections, and variety shows.

8. Assists in the supervision of the campus worker's coordination of the lunch-hour student activities program.
9. Works closely with class level and student body advisors in providing administrative support and reinforcement for student activity programs.
10. Handles student assistant applications and helps in the selection of students for these period-by-period assignments.
11. Attends satellite PTA meetings whenever these are programmed.
12. Renders decision on matters relating to new student enrolling, re-registering or requesting district exception.
13. Reviews Student Accident Report forms to ensure proper follow-through for corrective measures.
14. Writes letters of recommendation for student.

Assists the principal in providing leadership and assistance to teachers in developing the instructional program and in bringing about curricula changes.

1. Supervises and gives curricula advise, assistance and direction to the following departments/individuals:

   a. English . . . . 18 teachers
   b. Phys. Ed./Band/Music . . . . 6 teachers
   c. Practical Arts . . . . 5 teachers
   d. Industrial Arts . . . . 6 teachers
   Total . . . . 35 teachers

   Note: The principal and the other vice-principal supervise the remaining two-thirds of the departments.
2. Attends monthly curriculum meetings to meet with department heads and discuss curriculum concerns and needs.

Assists the principal in administering to matters dealing with the general administration and business affairs of the school.

1. Helps to review all correspondence, surveys and questionnaires, and responds to them.
2. Assists in the signing of form letters, routine reports and purchase orders.
3. Takes monies to the bank for deposit on a rotation basis with principal and the other vice-principal.
4. Assists in the repairs and maintenances of school facilities.

Assists the principal in administering the community and public relations program.

1. Works closely and cooperatively with all agencies or individuals that relate with the school, such as the County Government, legislators, Dept. of Health, Police Dept., the OEO, Job Corps, Community College, etc.

2. Responds accurately and factually to questions from the press and radio personnel.
3. Attends significant public or civic functions that may affect the school.
4. Meets with satellite PTA groups.
5. Attends all alumni association meetings and functions; works with booster clubs projects.

Supervision Received and Exercised

Under the general administrative direction of the principal of Rock Township School, Rock District Schools, Department of Education. Working directions to assigned certificated and classified personnel.

(See Also: ASSIGNMENTS; DUTIES; INTERNSHIP; PRINCIPAL; and all items in which the vice-principal of a school is involved)

VISITORS

general statements on...

VISITORS

If you wish to have a guest for the day, you should bring a note to the office signed by your parents, one day before the visit. Graduates who wish to visit teachers in the school must sign in at the main office and plan to see teachers when they are not involved with school duties.

VISITORS

To ensure your comfort and safety while school is in regular session, students from neighboring schools will not be permitted to visit. This rule also applies to school dances held throughout the school year.

All visitors must report to the office for approval to visit the school.

policy statement concerning...

Visits to our schools by parents, other adult residents of this community, and interested educators are welcomed and encouraged. In order to protect the educational programs from undue disturbance, the Board requires that persons wishing to visit on days other than those designated as visiting days, make arrangements in advance through the school office.

All visitors must register at the school office where they will receive identificaton and instructions. If a visitor desires, a student guide will be assigned to conduct him/her on a tour of the building.

At no time should a staff member transact business with a person in the school who does not possess a visitor's pass. No visitor may confer with a student in school unless it is with the specific approval of the principal. Should an emergency situation require a student to be called to the office to meet a visitor, the principal must be present during the conference. A minor student is never to be permitted to leave the school with anyone who is not clearly identified as his/her parent or person authorized to act on behalf of his/her parent.

The Superintendent or, in his/her absence, the building principal, is authorized to prohibit the entry of any person whose presence in the school is not required by reasons of enrollment or employment or to expel any such person when he/she has reason to believe that the presence of such person is or will become inimical to the good order of the school. If a person so identified and instructed refuses to leave the school premises or creates a further disturbance, the Superintendent or principal is authorized to request assistance from the local law enforcement agency.

(See Also: AMERICAN EDUCATION WEEK; BACK-TO-SCHOOL NIGHT; OPEN HOUSE; P.T.A.)

VOLUNTEERS

general statement concerning...

VOLUNTEER PROGRAM

The purpose of the Volunteer Program is to provide an opportunity for parents and other interested adults to assist school personnel in the operation of the schools. Such services are valuable in library work, hot lunch programs, aiding teachers within the classrooms, and assisting in the administrative offices. Contact the school principal to volunteer.

volunteer solicitation form (sample)...

P.T.A. VOLUNTEERS NEEDED

The Parent-Teacher Association of Rock Township High School needs the support of all parents. If you can help in any of the areas listed below, please indicate your interests. Please consider participating in some way. The P.T.A. needs your help.

1. Dance Chaperones (Parents to chaperone one or more school dance)
2. Library (One afternoon every other week)
3. Nurse's Office (Two hrs. per week typing and/or clerical)
4. Refreshments (Baking for school functions)
5. Telephoning
6. Committees and Fund Raisers
7. Dinner Dance Committees (June)
8. P.T.A. Executive Board (Positions still open to anyone wanting to get involved)

NAME ______________________________

TELEPHONE ______________________________

GRADE OF CHILD IN SCHOOL ______________________________

Comments ______________________________

____

(See Also: AIDES; CHAPERONE; INFORMATION; NEWSLETTER; NEWS RELEASES; P.T.A.**)**

VOUCHER

sample voucher form

VOUCHER FOR ATHLETIC EVENTS

Date ______________________

Please print full name and mailing address:

________________ vs ________________

____

Faculty Rep. or Coach ________________

____

Director of Ath. ____________________

____

I do solemnly declare and certify under the penalities of the law that the within bill is correct in all its particulars; that the articles have been furnished or services rendered as stated herein; that no bonus has been given or received by any person or persons within the knowledge of this claimant in connection with the above claim; that the amount stated is justly due and owing; and that the amount charged is a reasonable one.

Sign Here .... Date ....

Cross Country	____	Varsity	____	Official	____
Football	____	Jr. Varsity	____	Entry Fee	____
Soccer	____	Freshman	____	Tickets	____
Field Hockey	____	Girls	____	Dues	____
Gymnastics	____	Boys	____	Timer	____
Basketball	____	7 + 8 Official	____	Clinic	____
Wrestling	____	North	____	Crowd Control	____
Baseball	____	South	____	Banquet	____
Tennis	____	Others	____	Police	____
Track	____			Custodian	____
Softball	____			Ticket Mgr.	____
Bowling	____			Others	____
Swimming	____				
Others	____				

Fee ______________________

(See Also: BUSINESS; CONTRACT; MONEY; PAYROLL; SALARY; SPORTS; TRAVEL; WORK)

WARNING NOTICES

sample warning notice...

Date ____________________

Dear Parent:

This notice is to call your attention to the fact that your child, ____________________

____, is doing unsatisfactory work in the following subjects.

____________________________ ____________________________

This notice is being used to inform you of this situation at the present time, which is mid-way through the nine-week report card reporting period. The reason for the unsatisfactory work seems to be due to ____

____

____

____

Please fill out the bottom portion of this and return it to me. I will be available for a conference so we can discuss this situation if you would desire one.

Sincerely,

____

Teacher

Parent's Reply: ____

____

____

____

I would like a conference. ______

____

Parent

sample statements in student handbooks...

WARNING NOTICES

If you are in danger of failing a subject and are not working up to your potential, a warning notice will be mailed home prior to the end of the marking period to alert both you and your parents.

WARNING NOTICES

The purpose of the warning notice is to effect student behavioral change in order to prevent failure and to make parents aware of students who are not working up to their potential. It is hoped this will be accomplished through teacher, guidance and parental involvement which will lead to greater student awareness or responsibility. If any student is going to fail for a marking period, the parent or guardian of that child will receive notification of this fact in the form of a warning notice.

(See Also: ABILITY; ACHIEVEMENT; FAILURE; GRADES; REPORT CARDS RETENTION; SUPPLEMENTAL INSTRUCTION)

WEATHER ALERTS

general notice to parents...

School Closing

The schools in the Rock County School Corporation will be open on all regularly scheduled days unless closed by the Superintendent of Schools because of an emergency. When the school/s is/are confronted with an emergency, such as **extreme conditions** of snow or ice or mechanical failure, which necessitates the closing of the school/s for an entire day, an announcement will be given to radio and television stations at the earliest possible hour, but usually not later than 6:00 a.m. Emergency closings or early dismissals during the day will be announced via radio and television as soon as possible. Students will **not** be dismissed without attention to their safety in getting home.

(See Also: CLOSE OF SCHOOL; DISMISSAL PROCEDURES; EMERGENCY; SAFETY)

WORK

return-to-work form . . .

RETURN–TO–WORK NOTICE

THE SCHOOL DISTRICT REQUIRES THE FOLLOWING INFORMATION FROM THE ATTENDING PHYSICIAN TO AN ON-THE-JOB INJURED EMPLOYEE BEFORE HE OR SHE MAY RESUME WORK:

INSURED EMPLOYEE ____________________

JOB DESCRIPTION ____________________

ACCIDENT DATE ____________________

RETURN-TO-WORK DATE ____________________

THIS EMPLOYEE HAS BEEN UNDER MY MEDICAL CARE FROM ________TO ________ AND MAY RETURN TO WORK WITH NO RESTRICTIONS □, OR WITH THE FOLLOWING RESTRICTIONS:

____

____

____

____
PHYSICIAN'S SIGNATURE

____
DATE

DISTRIBUTION:
1. Employee: give to your Supervisor
2. Supervisor: forward to Insurance Office—original and copy
3. Retain one copy

statement on workman's compensation...

The clarification of our policy concerning Workman's Compensation was made at the regular meeting of the School Board on September 8. It is the purpose and intent of the Board that our sick leave policy provide economic, physical, and psychological relief at a time when an employee must be absent due to illness. Full salary is paid for the period to which the employee is entitled. It is not the intent or purpose of our sick leave policy that our employee make a "profit" on an illness absence.

State law requires that the Public School District carry Workman's Compensation liability insurance for all employees. This insurance provides certain payments for injuries that occur while on the job. For example, an employee may be absent for illness due to an injury. During the absence the employee may be on full pay from the school district, may be receiving hospital and surgical benefits from an insurance company, and in addition may receive payment from Workman's Compensation Insurance. The clarification of the policy provides:

> PAYMENTS MADE TO AN EMPLOYEE OF THE DISTRICT PROVIDED BY THE SICK LEAVE POLICY WILL BE REDUCED BY THE AMOUNT RECEIVED FROM WORKMAN'S COMPENSATION INSURANCE FOR THE SAME ABSENCE.

If the employee would prefer that no deduction be made, equal to the amount paid by Workman's Compensation, then the Workman's Compensation check shall be endorsed to the Clerk of the School District.

Payment from Workman's Compensation is retained by the employer for those days an employee is absent over the number of sick leave days accrued.

work order request...

Date Work ___/___/___ ___/___/___
Desired *Required*

Ordered By:
School______________________No.___

Teacher__________________________

Principal________________________

Date_____________________________

Work Order No. __ __ | __ __ __ __

Account Code_____________________

Budget Control No.________________

Cost Limit_______________________
(Cost limit must be stated for budgeted items)

Budget Control
Approved By______________________

Location In School:____

Description of Job:____

Requisitions Necessary
To Complete Work Order:

To Be Completed By Maintenance:

Job Assigned to_____________________Date________

Job Completed By____________________Date________
(print name)

work request form...

FACILITIES DEPARTMENT **WORK REQUEST NO.**

ACCOUNTING CODE	SCHOOL OR DEPARTMENT	REQUEST DATE
SIGNATURE PRIN. OR DEPT. HEAD	CAPITAL IMPROVEMENTS AMOUNT $ FUNDS AVAILABLE ☐ YES ☐ NO ACCT. DEPT., INITIAL	BUDGET YEAR

CHECK SERVICE REQUIRED	DESCRIPTION OF WORK–LIMIT ONE SERVICE PER WORK REQUEST
MAINTENANCE ☐ VANDALISM ☐ BUILDING REPAIR ☐ INSTALLATION ☐ ESTIMATE COSTS ☐ SET UP RELOCATABLES ☐ OPERATIONS EQUIPMENT ☐ FOOD SERVICE EQUIPMENT ☐ SWIMMING POOL MAINT. CAPITAL IMPROVEMENTS ☐ REMODELING ☐ MAJOR REPAIR ☐ NEW CONSTRUCTION	LOCATION WITHIN SCHOOL UNIT OR SITE

DO NOT WRITE BELOW THIS LINE

PRIORITY	DEPARTMENT	AUTHORIZED–DIRECTOR
1–EMERGENCY 2–URGENT 3–ROUTINE 4–DEFERRED	☐ 1–BUILDING ☐ 2–HEAT AND VENT ☐ 3–ELECTRICAL ☐ 4–GROUNDS	COMPLETED–FOREMAN

COSTS		ESTIMATE	ACTUAL
DIRECT LABOR (HRS.	)	$______	$______
EMPLOYEE BENEFITS (	%)	______	______
DIRECT MATERIALS		______	______
OVERHEAD	(%)	______	______
OTHER (SPECIFY BELOW)		______	______
TOTAL		$	$

CRAFT	TIME	MAT'L	OTHER
CARPENTER			
PAINT			
GLASS LOCKSMITH			
ROOFING			
WELDING			
HEATING			
PLUMBING			
SHEET METAL			
BOILER			
INDUS. ELEC.			
COM. ELEC.			
ELECTRONICS			
GROUNDS			

CONTRACTED SERVICES PURCHASE ORDER NO. AMOUNT $ VENDOR NAME AND ADDRESS	DATE STARTED	DATE COMPLETED
	INSPECTED AND APPROVED	FINAL PAYMENT AUTHORIZED

REMARKS:

(See Also: BIDS; BUDGET; CUSTODIAL SERVICES; EQUIPMENT; REQUISITIONS, REPAIRS, AND REPLACEMENT; TIME; VOUCHER; WORKING PAPERS**)**

WORKING PAPERS

statements in student handbooks...

WORKING PAPERS

Working papers are issued in the main office to students of Rock Township Schools. Further information and forms can be obtained in the main office.

WORKING PAPERS

Students desiring working papers may obtain applications in the school guidance office. Students having questions concerning eligibility for work may check with their counselors.

(See Also: APPLICATION; CAREERS; GUIDANCE; JOBS; MEDICAL FORMS; PERMISSION SLIPS**)**

WRITING

general statement on handwriting...

The Curriculum Guide for the school district provides that instruction for cursive writing will start in grade three.

To promote and also develop good manuscript (printing) as well as cursive writing, teachers are encouraged to provide a good sample for students and also put emphasis on good writing at all grade levels. Special materials are provided to help in this instruction.

(See Also: ASSIGNEMENTS; HOMEWORK; NEWSLETTER; NEWS RELEASES**)**

WRITTEN EXCUSES

policy on written excuses...

FAILURE TO BRING A WRITTEN EXCUSE

If you return to school after an absence without a written excuse, you will be instructed by the Dean of Girls or Vice-Principal to bring a written excuse for the absence upon the next school day. Failure to return a written excuse to the school on the second day following your absence will automatically place you on special detention after school.

Note to Parents: This rule was designed as a way to prevent truancy. It is the only way in which some parents can find out that their child was truant.

If a student comes to school without an excuse for two consecutive days following an absence, his or her parents will be informed via the telephone, the school case worker, or by mail.

(See Also: ABSENCE; ABSENTEEISM; ATTENDANCE; HEALTH; NURSE; TARDINESS AND TRUANCY**)**

XEROX

xerox copier request...

XEROX COPIER REQUEST

Instructional Media Center

Date/Time Received:
For IMC Use Only

______________________ ______________________ ____________

Name of Requester | School | Date Needed

______________________ ______________________ ____________

Title of Printing Request | Deliver to (name building) | Telephone

________ Number of originals to be copied from.

________ Number of copies to be made from each original.

YES NO Do you want to have your copies shot on both sides?
(circle one)

YES NO Do you wish want to have your copies reduced from the size of the original?
(circle one)

If so, what percentage of reduction?

________ 15%

________ 23%

________ 35%

________ 38½%

________ other

SPECIAL INSTRUCTIONS:

(See Also: CLERICAL SERVICES; BULLETIN; DISTRIBUTION OF MATERIALS; SECRETARY; TYPISTS**)**

X-RAYS

X-ray report form...

NAME Last, First, Middle Initial	SOCIAL SECURITY NUMBER (Student-Parent/Guardian)	BIRTH DATE	SEX	GRADE

RESIDENCE (Mailing Address)

Number	Street	Municipality	Zip

EVALUATION Retest Results PPD DATE Mo., Day, Year	Mantoux SIZE MM	X-ray Positive Negative Not Done	PREVENTIVE THERAPY INH-Daily Dosage Yes ____________ MG No	PHYSICIAN

(See Also: ACCIDENT; DOCTORS; EMERGENCY; HEALTH; ILLNESS; MEDICAL FORMS; NURSE**)**

YEARBOOK

administrator's message in...

A Yearbook is more than printed pages, clever sayings, and photographs. It is, in a very real sense, a record of memories—your memories—the memories you hold both individually and in common as students of Rock Township High School. It is my sincere hope as well as the hope of the faculty and administration that those memories are pleasant ones; ones which you will cherish throughout your life. It is our hope that your days here at Rock Township High have been enjoyable as well as filled with learning and growth. You have received an education that will serve you well throughout your lives, and the memories within these pages will serve you in those quiet moments when you turn your thoughts back to your days spent with us.

On behalf of the faculty and administration, I wish you health, happiness, and success throughout your lives.

(See Also: CLUBS; FEES, FINES, FUNDS, AND CHARGES; MEDIA; PRINCIPAL; P.T.A.; WRITING)

ZONES AND ZONING

resolution on attendance zones...

WHEREAS the City Board of Education is operating under an order from the United States Federal Court for the Middle District.

AND WHEREAS this order sets forth attendance zones for the said schools, which the City School Board is responsible for the enforcement thereof,

THEREFORE, NOW BE IT RESOLVED that if a student is attending a school other than the school he or she is assigned to by such zone lines, that student will not be allowed to continue in that school and will not be allowed to participate in extracurricular activities or represent the school to which he or she is zoned for the remainder of that school year.

BE IT FURTHER RESOLVED that this resolution become a part of the official City School Board Policy Manual and that it be included in each school's student handbook henceforth.

BE IT FURTHER RESOLVED that parents, teachers and students assist in the enforcement of this policy so that no student will attend an overcrowded school and efficient use can be made of existing buildings and facilities. The enforcement of this policy will help ensure that no student will suffer because of another person's violation of this policy.

This will not conflict with the present policy which states: "Students whose parents move to another attendance zone will be permitted to remain in the school of original enrollment until the end of that school year, if they have been enrolled for 90 school days or more. Students who have not been enrolled for 90 school days or more must transfer to the school in which their parents or legal guardians reside."

Done this day, Monday, April 9 by vote.

policy on attendance areas...

A child attending the City Schools must attend the school serving the attendance zone in which his or her parents or legal guardian reside.

If a child is residing with someone other than his parents or legal guardian and the place of residence is located in an attendance zone other than the zone in which the parents or legal guardian reside, proof must be submitted to the Superintendent of Schools that said place of residence is the permanent residence of the child.

Such proof must be submitted in the form of a statement, under oath, to the Superintendent of Schools to be presented to and acted upon by the City Board of Education. No transfer shall be made or become effective until approved by the City Board of Education. Said approval can be given only when verification by the Superintendent of Schools and board attorney established that the proposed action is not violative of federal court order provisions which presently apply to the City School System.

Administrators of the City School System shall assure that students' admittance to respective schools is done through procedures that are in accord with policies adopted by this board and with the Federal Court Order exempt, "Attendance Outside System of Residence."

Adopted: September 11.

(See Also: ABSENCE; ABSENTEEISM; ATTENDANCE; ENROLLMENT; RECORDS)